19 Urban Questions

Studies in the
Postmodern Theory of Education

Joe L. Kincheloe and Shirley R. Steinberg
General Editors

Vol. 215

PETER LANG
New York • Washington, D.C./Baltimore • Bern
Frankfurt am Main • Berlin • Brussels • Vienna • Oxford

19 Urban Questions

Teaching in the City

EDITED BY Shirley R. Steinberg
Joe L. Kincheloe

FOREWORD BY Deborah A. Shanley

PETER LANG
New York • Washington, D.C./Baltimore • Bern
Frankfurt am Main • Berlin • Brussels • Vienna • Oxford

Library of Congress Cataloging-in-Publication Data

Kincheloe, Joe L.
Nineteen urban questions: teaching in the city /
edited by Shirley R. Steinberg, Joe L. Kincheloe.
p. cm. — (Counterpoints; vol. 215
Includes bibliographical references and index.
1. Education, Urban—United States. 2. Critical pedagogy—United States.
I. Kincheloe, Joe L. II. Steinberg, Shirley R.
III. Series: Counterpoints (New York, N.Y.); v. 215.
LC5131.N56 2004   370'.9173'2—dc22   2003026733
ISBN 0-8204-5772-8
ISSN 1058-1634

Bibliographic information published by **Die Deutsche Bibliothek**.
Die Deutsche Bibliothek lists this publication in the "Deutsche
Nationalbibliografie"; detailed bibliographic data is available
on the Internet at http://dnb.ddb.de/.

Cover design by Lisa Barfield

The paper in this book meets the guidelines for permanence and durability
of the Committee on Production Guidelines for Book Longevity
of the Council of Library Resources.

to Maci Loree & Luna Miri

Table of Contents

Deborah A. Shanley

Foreword

The challenge of writing the foreword to a text that asks multiple questions in a complex world has impacted my ability to sleep at night. Every night before my bedside light is turned off, I find myself more emerged in the question "what did I accomplish today, and how did it make a difference in the lives of the children, teachers, and other members of the urban community that I am committed to serve?"

There is no hiding from the fact that as I read each chapter and reflected on the questions, I became more uncomfortable with the fact that our conversations are not all-inclusive—and that maybe we are misaligned with the daily conversations in schools, on college campuses, at dinner tables, and at school board meetings. Perhaps a dialogue might provide a unique opportunity to open this conversation with those that usually find themselves on the margins.

Can a book that is designed around the idea of questions which are developed around an ideological framework open the door to partnerships with others that were never considered? We are all hoping for the same results: opportunities for students presently not achieving within the urban school context—for them to gain access to what is currently denied to them. It goes far beyond a black/white agenda. It goes to the heart of what is right and just. Students deserve the best of what we can deliver in a safe, socially supported, and intellectually rich learning environment. Are we integrating into our discussions on urban education the rich research that has documented best practices? Are we inviting room for new research? Do we extend the conversations in our classrooms beyond our personal beliefs? Do we create forums for everyone to be heard and embraced?

Why do we continue to allow standards to stifle both teachers and students. Do we continue to talk to ourselves but not to those that are most affected by decisions and standards? We must take our words to the community.

We must ask these questions. We must ask if they extend beyond the urban environment. Do we focus too much on dropouts rather than pushouts? As we focus on a test-driven educational environment, whom do we lose? In this book, Flo Rubinson challenges some of our present beliefs on dropouts, as David Forbes speaks to a public system that too narrowly defines spirituality. We must listen to the voices of children entering young adultood and take the information, as Haroon Kharem speaks about—we must turn it into a positive direction. One cannot watch *Boyz N the Hood* and not know that Doughboy possessed superior leadership skills—skills that just needed redirection by both adults and peers.

Reading *19 Urban Questions: Teaching in the City* gave me the edgy feeling that there continues to be a disconnect—but with a reexamination that we must look again at each way in which we approach our work.

Joe L. Kincheloe

CHAPTER ONE

Why a Book on Urban Education?

Why a book on urban education? Because in the early twenty-first century one of the most compelling concerns involves the question of what to do about our neglected urban schools. Thirty-one percent of U.S. elementary and secondary students go to school in 226 large urban districts. There are nearly 16,000 school districts in the United States, and almost one-third of all students attend 1.5 percent of them (Fuhrman, 2002). As Philip Anderson and Judith Summerfield write in their chapter in this volume, another important reason for focusing attention on urban education involves the fact that in the urban context one finds "the emergent American culture." Indeed, they conclude, the ways in which urban educators shape the urban pedagogy in the coming years are central to the way Americans reinvent the nation. With this in mind, the United States faces an uncertain future because in these 226 urban districts, observers have found a wide diversity of problems and successes. Because of the scale of this diversity, this book or this chapter could be entitled "Urban Education: A Dialectic of Challenges and Opportunities." We'll keep the title *19 Urban Questions: Teaching in the City*, but we know that within every chapter this interaction between challenge and opportunity will manifest itself.

The Perpetual Crisis of Urban Education

Urban education is always in crisis—yesterday, today, and certainly in the near future. Teacher shortages force many urban school administrators to scramble madly during the first weeks of school to fill classroom vacancies. Inadequate funds cause cutbacks in essential services in the middle of the school year. In contemporary U.S. society, the use of the term *urban* itself has become in many quarters a signifier for poverty, nonwhite violence, narcotics, bad neighborhoods, an absence of family values, crumbling housing, and failing schools. Over the past several decades educational researchers have been producing data confirming the deficits of urban youth, while sensationalizing media produce images of urban youth running wild and out of control. In this context many urban school leaders attempt to hide the problems undermining education at their particular schools (Kozleski, 2002; Ciani, 2002; NWREL, 1999). As Florence Rubinson explains in her chapter in this book, many schools, under the flag of public relations, mask their dropout rates. The critical problems besiege many of us who work in urban systems, and we have come to realize that without significant structural changes, even increased funding will only prop up pathological systems and provide little help for students and teachers.

In the middle of the eye of the perpetual crisis, teachers keep on teaching and many students keep on learning. Indeed, there are urban teachers who perform good work in a context in which impediments are many and resources few. Even if resources were provided, if equal funding of urban school systems were mandated, there would still be inadequate monies. Poor urban schools are so in need of financial help that equal funding would have to be supplemented by additional infusions of resources just to get to where they might be able to visualize the equality of resources on the distant horizon. Overwhelmed by these disparities and the crisis atmosphere surrounding them, urban policymakers have sought to replace huge, bureaucratic systems overseen by boards of education with new smaller, locally operated organizations.

Chicago experimented with such a plan in the late 1980s, establishing local school councils that attempted to put communities in contact with their schools. Results have been mixed and their successes open to diverse interpretations (Halford, 1996). In New York City in 2002–2003, political and educational leaders debated the role of boards of education as Mayor Michael Bloomberg sought an alternative framework for governing the city's schools. The crisis atmosphere and the uncertainty of the continuity of urban educational governance structures make it difficult for urban school administrators and teachers to focus on long-term projects. Teachers learn quickly that numerous classroom interruptions are the norm and that they have precious little time for lesson planning and pedagogical reflection on their practice (Lewis & Smith, 1996). Crisis management and survival until the end of the school day too often become the modi operandi of urban education.

Gangsta Paradise: Representations of Urban Education

It has become obvious to many scholars and educators that something has changed in the contemporary era. Over the last several decades, new structures of cultural space and time generated by the bombardment of electronic images have colonized our consciousness, shaping the way we see ourselves and the world. Electronic transmissions from radio, TV, popular music, movies, video, e-mail, and the Internet have saturated us with information about the world around us. Some refer to this new world as *hyperreality*—a place with so much input that we have difficulty processing all the data we encounter. In hyperreality the information that is electronically produced often takes on a realism that trumps our everyday lived experiences. The world we view on TV often shapes our perspectives more profoundly than what we directly observe in the society around us (Kincheloe, 2001; Kincheloe, 2002). In this context, consider media representations of urban education. Portrayed in film and TV as a danger zone, inner-city schools are seen as homogeneous locales of peril where no one should ever venture.

In the 90s, Hollywood films about urban education moved from the feminine missionary of Michelle Pfeiffer's Lou Anne Johnson in *Dangerous Minds* to Tom Berenger's macho special forces operative Shale in *The Substitute*. Whereas *Dangerous Minds* promotes Pfeiffer as a white savior of the uncivilized African American and Latino students of the 'hood, Berenger's Shale represents the end of hope. Shale's final solution is to kill them all as he "terminates" the cocaine ringleading black principal (Ernie Hudson) and many of his students of color in full gangsta regalia, representing public education's Battle of Armageddon. The audience knows that tax-supported city schooling is a failure and that society must find a new way—prison—to deal with these "urban animals." *The Substitute* resonated with so many viewers that it spawned two appropriately named sequels—*The Substitute 2: School's Out* and *The Substitute 3: Winner Takes All*.

While there are many other films in this genre, such as *187*, suffice it to say that these films, combined with literally millions of TV news images of inner cities, city youth of color, and urban schools in poor neighborhoods, help inscribe particular affective and cognitive impressions with political/ideological consequences. Indeed, many Americans from suburban and rural areas know more about urban youth and city-dwelling African Americans, Latinos, Asian Americans, and Arab Americans from media images than from face-to-face contact. Thus, a sociocultural chasm has been produced between middle-class teacher education students and the students they will teach if they do their student teaching or obtain positions in urban schools in poor communities. Also, these representations, as they filter into the racial common sense and the folk psychologies of the larger society, present real obstacles to urban students attempting to succeed in schools. In this context such students have to deal with negative stereotyping in relation to their scholastic aptitude and their character.

Such representations even affect scholarly fields. In adolescent psychology, for example, it is interesting that so little research has been produced about factors of race and socioeconomic class as they relate to the identity development of young people. In many educational circles, inquiry into the representations of urban schools and students in media productions is still viewed as a frivolous form of research, with little to contribute to the study of teaching and learning (Henke, 2000). It is amazing that in the first decade of the twenty-first century, so little research has been produced in relation to urban education and urban students (Fuhrman, 2002). Indeed, most research on child and adolescent development involves middle-class whites. The lack of information on low-socioeconomic-class nonwhite urban youth is in itself a form of institutional racism (IUYL, 1996). A critical urban education that understands the complexity of the intersection of race, class, gender, sexual, religious, and ability-related dynamics as they relate to education seeks to address these racism-produced deficiencies.

The Blurred Boundaries of Urban Education: Addressing Complexity

There is nothing simple about urban education. Just when we think that we've made a definitive statement about the uniqueness of the category, up pops a contradiction that subverts our confident pronouncement. What passes as urban education involves a wide range of circumstances (Willard-Holt, 2000). Sometimes the boundaries between suburban, rural, and urban schooling are more blurred than we initially realized. As Anderson and Summerfield point out in their chapter here, analysts need to be very careful when they proclaim, for example, that urban schools are more dangerous than suburban schools. Violent crime statistics indicate that the difference in violence between urban and suburban schools is minimal. As Judith Hill puts it in her chapter, "What Is Urban Education in an Age of Standardization and Scripted Learning?"

> Urban environments are some of the most contradictory areas of our world, where the extremes of our civilization coexist—the richest of the rich and the poorest of the poor, the most privileged and the most disenfranchised, live and work here in large concentrations.

Researchers confirm that nowhere are the obstacles to success and the existential needs of students as great as in urban areas. Yet at the same time it has to be said that urban locales also contain some of the most helpful resources for young people and their families. We return to our dialectic of challenges and opportunities. Educators, researchers, and school leaders must view every school as a self-contained entity that might be similar to or different from the urban schools around it. Thus, we must rid ourselves of assumptions and study each school on its own merit. This means that we must focus attention on the sociocultural context of each urban school, examine student backgrounds, the positions of empowerment and disempowerment from which they operate, the knowledges they bring to the classroom, the languages they speak, and the ways in which all of these dynamics shape learning and teaching (Wang & Kovach, 1996; Willard-Holt, 2000). In his chapter, "What Is the Role of Counseling in Urban Schools?" David Forbes reflects this complexity when he contends that school counselors who are worth their salt must understand and act on the recognition of these diverse and complex dimensions of urban schooling, from the psychological domain to the ideological.

What Are the Unique Features of Urban Education?

Keeping in mind the complexity and contradictions of the category, it is important to ask whether there are features of urban education that are unique. After careful study of the question, I believe that the following characteristics apply.

Urban schools operate in areas with high population density. Technical definitions of urban areas typically maintain that they are characterized by plots of land on which population density is at least 1,000 individuals per square mile. In addition, many urban scholars contend that such areas average at least one building per two acres of land.

Urban schools are bigger, and urban school districts serve more students. Simply put, urban schools and their districts have larger enrollments than rural or suburban ones. These large urban educational institutions are more likely than their suburban and rural counterparts to serve large numbers of students of low socioeconomic class. In these densely populated urban areas and large schools, students are more likely to be ignored or overlooked in the crowds. In such a context it is difficult for urban students to experience a sense of community, and this alienation all too often leads to low academic performance and high dropout rates.

Urban schools function in areas marked by profound economic disparity. Even though numerous poor people can be found in rural areas, urban venues are characterized by high concentrations of poverty existing in close proximity to affluence. Over 80 percent of high-density poverty areas in the United States are located in the nation's 100 largest cities. A disproportionate percentage of minority students and their families are plagued by this concentrated urban poverty, which hampers their quest for academic success on many levels. In urban schools located in these areas, it is not uncommon to find an appalling lack of resources. Financial inequalities mar these schools and school districts, undermining efforts to repair dilapidated buildings, supply textbooks for all students, and provide teachers with instructional materials and equipment. Even when such schools get equipment such as computers, they may sit unused for months or even years because schools have no money for the wiring and phone lines necessary for their use. It is not surprising, therefore, that urban students in poor areas have less access to computers and the Internet than their rural and suburban counterparts. All teachers, no matter in what area they pursue their practice, face the challenges of teaching students from low socioeconomic backgrounds. There is a compelling difference in teaching a class in which 2 students out of 20 are poor and teaching one in which 36 out of 37 come from a low socioeconomic background.

Urban areas and urban schools have a higher rate of ethnic, racial, and religious diversity. In densely populated urban locales, people coming from different ethnic, racial, and religious backgrounds, to say nothing of different economic, social, and linguistic arenas, live in close proximity to one another. Nearly two-thirds of urban students do not fit the categories of white or middle class, and within these populations high percentages of students receive free or reduced-price lunches. Achievement rates for poor minority students consistently fall below those of white and higher-socioeconomic-class students. Surveys of teachers and staff in these highly diverse and poor urban schools consistently indicate that they often feel overwhelmed by the problems that undermine lower-socioeconomic-class minority students' quest to succeed in schools. The frustration of such teachers and staff members is exacerbated by the perception that few care about the well-being and the success of these students.

Urban schools experience factionalized infighting on school boards over issues concerning resources and influence. In almost all urban contexts, school boards have fought over salaries for particular school employees, personnel hiring and firing, school assignments for particular students, and the microdynamics of school construction. In densely populated, diverse, and poor areas, such disputes have erupted as local school boards find themselves as the major dispensers of jobs in the area. Because of the important role they play in areas with few resources and opportunities for employment, urban school boards have focused more and more on day-to-day school operations and less and less on policy-level deliberations concerned with improving student success.

Urban school systems are undermined by ineffective business operations. Urban schools in poor areas have more trouble obtaining the basic resources needed to operate schools than do their rural and suburban counterparts. School buildings are often run-down and in dangerous states of disrepair; substitutes are frequently used to cover classes for months at a time, and business staff at the district level often have obtained their jobs through political patronage and longevity rather than expertise. Promotions in the central offices, contracts for school services and supplies, and even curricular decisions with accompanying contracts for purchasing instructional materials are often made on the basis of political favors and influence, much to the detriment of educational quality.

Poor urban students are more likely to experience health problems. In many urban schools, the effort to construct a high-quality learning environment is, in the immediacy of everyday needs, less important than addressing issues of student health and safety. For example, school administrators are often more concerned with providing a warm building on a cold day or fixing unsanitary and disease-producing bathrooms than with more long-term academic concerns. When compared with rural and suburban students, urban students are less likely to have access to regular medical care. Concurrently, such urban students are more likely to develop cases of measles and tuberculosis and suffer the effects of lead poisoning. As Leah Henry-Beauchamp and Tina Siedler report in their chapter in this volume, the number of urban students with asthma has reached epidemic proportions and is growing. Far too many of these urban children with asthmatic conditions do not receive medical attention.

Urban schools experience higher student, teacher, and administrator mobility. In poor urban schools, researchers find that frequent moving between schools undermines student achievement. Some analysts have noted that the poorer the student, the more moves he or she is likely to make. The same schools experience higher teacher turnover—one out of every two teachers in urban schools leaves in five years. Poor inner-city schools find it difficult to retain teachers when school systems in surrounding suburban areas can offer teachers more lucrative salaries, better-maintained schools, a higher-achieving student body, and less demanding work conditions. In addition, studies illustrate that urban teachers are treated with less respect and participate less in decision making that affects their working lives. Thus, students in poor urban schools who are most in need of caring, experienced teachers often are taught by the least experienced teachers. In addition to high student and teacher turnover, urban administrators do not serve in their positions as long as their suburban and rural counterparts. Superintendents in urban systems stay for an average of three years—an insufficient period for their policy changes to have an effect.

Urban schools serve higher immigrant populations. In the twenty-first century, not unlike the nineteenth and twentieth centuries, urban schools educate a large number of students who are immigrants or whose parents are immigrants. Many of these families came to the United States to escape political harassment and/or financial despair. Along with these voluntary immigrants, urban schools serve students whose ancestors were involuntary immigrants (African Americans, for example) who share a history of discrimination and injustice. Each of these groups experiences problems unique to its background, and urban educators need to understand and know how to address these concerns.

Urban schools are characterized by linguistic diversity. Because of their large immigrant populations, urban schools have more students speaking different languages than their suburban and rural counterparts. In New York City, for example, more than 200 languages and dialects are spoken in the school system. Because our teachers and educational leaders are generally white and middle class, they usually do not have the heritage or educational background to make positive use of such linguistic diversity, which tends to be seen as a problem rather than a unique opportunity.

Urban schools experience unique transportation problems. When urban students are asked why they are late to school, one reason that particularly stands out involves their dependence on public transportation—subways and buses in particular. Such public transportation is not designed for school schedules and can often be unreliable. Subways sometimes are too crowded to get on in order to get to school on time. Schedules are sometimes changed abruptly and the subway train may skip stations. I have engaged in numerous conversations with urban students who pick up a subway or bus at one station and have to transfer two or three times in order to get to school. Each transfer, of course, increases the chance that they will experience a delay or cancellation. Urban teachers who do not understand these dynamics will often punish students for tardiness. Such teachers assume that the students made no effort to get to school on time.

Teachers working in poor urban schools are less likely to live in the communities surrounding the schools than teachers in suburban and rural systems. In this context teachers become socially, culturally, and economically isolated from their students and the parents. In their isolation, teachers do not understand their students' ways of seeing school as an institution and the world around them. Teachers who find themselves in such a situation are cut off from the helpful information that parents can give about their children and the communities in which they live. Without such valuable knowledge, teachers often make judgments about particular students without having more than one perspective to explain why these students perform as they do (Bamburg, 1994; Lewis & Smith, 1996; Halford, 1996; NWREL, 1999; Weiner, 1999; Kozleski, 2002; Fuhrman, 2002; Westview Partnership, 2002; Ng, 2003; Mezzacappa, 2003).

Keeping Hope Alive: Possibility, Change, and Resilience

Often in the literature of urban education, wide-angle views of the field project a depressing picture of inner-city schools. More specific studies and analysis often uncover success stories that play out daily among dedicated and knowledgeable teachers, visionary administrators, and brilliant students. It is very important that as we paint a macroportrait of the problems of urban education, we do not forget the heroic efforts of these individuals. This is the case especially in relation to the children and young people who attend poor urban schools. Despite the poverty, racial and class discrimination, intelligence and achievement tests that distort their abilities (Kincheloe, Steinberg, & Hinchey, 1999; Kincheloe, Steinberg, & Villaverde, 1999), the linguistic differences, and the many other problems of inner-city life, many students still succeed. No educator should ever forget this. The editors and authors of *19 Urban Questions* keep this knowledge in mind every day that we walk into urban schools and work with students and teachers. In this context we fervently believe that positive change is possible. Indeed, it is this hope that animates Derrick Griffith, Kecia Hayes, and John Pascarella in their chapter, "Why Teach in Urban Settings?" Buoyed by hope and empowered by their knowledge of the complexity of urban education, Griffith, Hayes, and Pascarella's conversation illustrates the wide body of knowledges and insights needed to succeed as an urban educator.

Thus, while refusing to ignore the problems, we continue to struggle to help more urban students succeed in their academic pursuits and their quest for socioeconomic mobility. In this context we walk a tightrope between pointing out the problems (while avoiding cynicism) and calling attention to the successes (while avoiding rose-colored perspectives). We advocate a curriculum that draws on the strengths of urban students, rather than relying on indicators that point out only their weaknesses. In the domain of linguistic diversity, for example, instead of framing this reality as a problem, we might view it as a dynamic asset in planning one's vocational life. In a globalized world, Americans in a variety of occupations need bi- or multilingual skills, and employers will pay to find such individuals (Halford, 1996; IUYL, 1996; NWREL, 1999).

This critical reframing of urban education in terms of possibility is no easy task in the first decade of the twenty-first century—but it is necessary. Jonathan Kozol (2000) is helpful in this reframing effort in his book *Ordinary Resurrections*, which examines urban life and education through the eyes of children in a poor neighborhood in the South Bronx. Documenting the difference between teaching in 1960s Boston, in the hopeful atmosphere that racism and poverty would soon be eliminated, and teaching in the more cynical South Bronx of the 1990s, Kozol uses the phrase "ordinary resurrections" to signify that in the worst of times educational victories can be won. In a sociopolitical atmosphere in which the public and even the educational conversation about promoting racial justice is not commonly overheard and when precious few political leaders speak of making urban schools less separate and more equal, some urban teachers and educators become very discouraged. Other teachers and even educational leaders, so caught up in the right-wing discourse of urban minority-student incompetence, lose faith in their students' abilities and the possibility of teaching them rigorous academic material (Bamburg, 1994).

In such an atmosphere, diatribes against urban teachers and their "criminal students" become the order of the day (Willard-Holt, 2000). As a teacher-educator in New York City during the Rudolph Giuliani administration, I was amazed at the mayor's verbal attacks on the alleged across-the-board incompetence of the city's teachers. On numerous occasions Giuliani attempted to humiliate teachers to punish them for their "failures." In his chapter in this volume, Joe Valentine speaks as a special educator in the New York City public schools. In a climate in which urban teachers as failures have been the order of the day, Valentine confides that he often forgets how much good pedagogical work takes place in special education. He remembers why he and many other teachers entered the field and how hard he and they work to help special education students and their parents negotiate the complex terrain of urban schooling and succeed in it. Students going into urban education need to understand the harsh and unfair representations of urban teachers that circulate in the twenty-first century pedagogical zeitgeist.

In this hostile context, many urban educational researchers and scholars are using the term *resilience* to describe the amazing perseverance of poor urban students. Never ignoring for a second the problems that exist, this emphasis on resilience focuses our attention for a while on the ways that savvy students make use of urban resources. Haroon Kharem's chapter here on why urban youth join gangs can be read on one level as a celebration of ingenuity in dire circumstances. Rebecca Goldstein's chapter also speaks of this strength and resilience of poor urban students. The popular stereotype of minority-group urban students is that they don't try in school and have no inclination to succeed in academic affairs. In an interview with *Education World* (2001), Jonathan Kozol maintained:

> No matter how we treat them, no matter how many times we knock them down, no matter how we shortchange them, no matter how we isolate them, no matter how we try to hide them from the rest of society, they keep getting up again, and they refuse to die.

In this context of hope, it is probably time to move from a rhetoric of "at risk" to one of resilience. Instead of constructing services to overcome their deficits, it might be better to formulate programs that cultivate the strengths of urban students. Even in the worst situations, brilliant teachers can change students' lives. Setting high expectations for students deemed to have low academic ability by positivistic assessments can pay high educational dividends for such individuals. Engaging marginalized students in everyday classroom decisions, bringing their interests into lessons, and granting them the right to express their opinions can contribute to miraculous transformations. In addition to these relatively simple steps, urban teachers can work to connect students to unique urban resources such as museums, the arts, urban architecture, and developments in science and industry that are found in cities. Taking advantage of such learning resources can change the lives of poor urban students (NWREL, 1999; Wang & Kovach, 1996; FAUSSR, 1998). In her chapter in this volume, Koshi Dhingra reflects these ideas as she delineates urban resources for science teachers.

It is essential that urban educators keep hope alive by working to reframe the ways that many people view urban schooling and urban students. A critical urban education views education as an effort not merely to prepare students for jobs but to develop new forms of consciousness that help urban students conceptualize ways of inventing *new* jobs that change the status quo. Such a vision of urban education addresses marginalized students' social and personal needs, recognizes their too often overlooked cognitive abilities, and taps into the forces that motivate them. Such a pedagogy helps urban teachers succeed with students, and it is important to note that urban teachers in low-income schools need to see students succeed. Just as physicians need to see their patients return to health, teachers need to see students learn (Lewis & Smith, 1996). It is not surprising that teachers who don't see their students learning are less likely to stay in the profession. Teachers need to keep hope alive, not only for their students but for themselves as well.

Teacher Education in the Urban Context

Another answer to the question of why write a book on urban education involves the fact that there is simply not enough compelling information about the subject for teachers and other professionals. The information that exists often fails to develop a deep understanding of educational purpose vis-à-vis the complexity of "teachin' in the city" and the nature and needs of urban students. Although I am a critic of colleges and schools of education in their urban and other forms, I am also critical of the arts-and-sciences dimensions of higher education that are just as much responsible for the failings of teacher education as are colleges and schools of education. With that caveat, it is important to improve urban teacher education and to produce literature that helps us understand the larger purposes and contexts of urban education as well as scholarly work which grants insight into working in the everyday world of urban schools and other educational locales.

Producing literature and research on urban education in the contemporary sociopolitical climate is difficult in that it has to address the dominant representations of the urban poor and poor urban students as "the undeserving poor." Such individuals are often seen as the sole makers of their own fate. They are poor because they are lazy, dumb, immoral, and/or incompetent. Producers of literature on urban education must help teacher education students, teachers, and other professionals understand the politics of the construction of such fabrications while concurrently facilitating their efforts to gain a more trustworthy perspective on the urban poor (Henke, 2000). Such fallacious but widely accepted images of urban students from lower socioeconomic classes keep tens of thousands of talented students from entering the field of urban education.

Unfortunately, such representations sometimes negatively influence urban teachers and school leaders in their perceptions of students. I have heard educational leaders at the highest levels echo these prejudices as they express the belief that such students "can't learn even if they try." This is why it's so important to get teacher education students into poor urban schools and communities. Such experiences grant them a far more balanced viewpoint, and studies indicate that when this is combined with teaching experience in professional development schools, teachers come to know far more about the unique needs of urban students and how to deal with them. Moreover, such teachers are more likely to spend more years teaching in urban schools. They tend to feel better both about themselves as professionals and about the quality of their pedagogical work (Kozleski, 2002).

Teacher educators must understand and confront the notion that urban schools are thorny and complicated places for teachers because of the unique characteristics previously listed. Many new teachers experience culture shock during the first few weeks and months in their new positions. Too often these teachers leave the profession without ever learning diverse ways of working with and motivating urban students. As we know, many times these young urban teachers come from socioeconomic levels very different from those of their lower-socioeconomic-class students. These are the teachers who are sometimes the most vulnerable to the social representations of urban poverty and poor urban students. Living lives so culturally distant from their students, these teachers and teacher education students need to understand both the communities in which poor urban students live and the nature of their daily lives. They need to have field experiences during their teacher education in urban schools so they won't experience culture shock when they assume teaching positions. These are also teachers and teacher education students who—moving to the other end of the spectrum—sometimes develop an unhealthy desire to "save" or "rescue" poor Latino or African American students. In this mode such teachers see the cultural capital of white middle-class lifestyles as the antidote to "urbanness." These rescuers are missionaries who bring salvation through "proper ways of being."

Urban teacher education must work to help teachers avoid the prejudiced view of poor urban students as dangerous criminals incapable of learning or, at the other extreme, as communicants who may be reformed by the gospel of white culture as pedagogy. This is one of many reasons that teachers must develop a strong notion both of self and of the forces that have shaped them. In other works, I have referred to this knowledge as the ontological dimension of teacher knowledge, i.e., the philosophy of *being* itself—what it means to *be* human, to *be* an urban teacher. Too infrequently are teachers in university, student teaching, or in-service professional education encouraged to confront why they think as they do about themselves as teachers, especially in relation to the social, cultural, political, economic, and historical world around them. Mainstream teacher education provides little insight into the forces that shape identity and consciousness. Becoming educated as a critical practitioner necessitates personal transformation.

With such dynamics in mind, a critical urban education asks teachers to confront their relationship with some long-term historical trends rarely discussed in the contemporary public conversation and in urban teacher education. Critical teacher educators maintain that these trends hold profound implications for both the cultivation of professional awareness and the development of a teacher persona vitally needed in urban education. Indeed, everyone in the contemporary United States is shaped by this knowledge in some way, whether or not we are conscious of it. We cannot erase the fact that European colonialism dominated the world from the late fifteenth century until the twentieth century, when it mutated into a neocolonialism grounded in economic and cultural dynamics led primarily by the United States. By the middle of the twentieth century, anticolonial activity had developed in India, Indochina, Africa, Latin America, and other places around the world seeking self-determination for colonized peoples. It was this movement that provided the spark for the Civil Rights movement, the anti-Vietnam War movement, the women's movement, gay rights, and other liberation movements in the United States.

While anticolonial activity continues into the twenty-first century, such discontent achieved its apex in the United States in the 1960s and early 1970s. By the mid-1970s a conservative counterreaction was taking shape with the goals of "recovering" what was perceived to be lost in these movements. Thus, the politics, cultural wars, and educational debates, policies, and practices of the last three decades cannot be understood outside of these efforts to "recover" white supremacy, patriarchy, class privilege, heterosexual "normality," Christian dominance, and the European intellectual canon. We all must decide where we stand in relation to such profound yet blurred historical processes. We cannot conceptualize our teacher persona outside of them. They are the defining macroconcerns of our time, as every topic is refracted through their lenses. Any view of the purpose of urban education, any curriculum development, any professional education conceived outside of their framework ends up becoming a form of ideological mystification.

In this ideological context, urban teacher education students from white backgrounds must understand the power of whiteness in shaping their perspectives toward urban schools and urban students. How does their racial identity position them in relation to educational purpose and the lives of their poor and nonwhite students? How does their relation to whiteness shape their sense of privilege and their understanding of the forces shaping urban students' lives? These are questions that a critical urban teacher education must raise with its students. While such questions elicit difficult and often contentious responses, they are necessary in twenty-first-century urban education. Numerous curricular experiences can help students gain more insight into the race, class, gender, and sexual dimensions of their identities and the impact of these dynamics on their teaching.

As urban teachers, we are invested in the ontological knowledge of teacher selfhood, the knowledge of what it means to be a teacher in the culturally different settings that many white upper-middle-class urban teacher education students must confront before they enter the profession. Contemporary studies show that about 59 percent of beginning urban teachers feel unprepared to work with students who are having academic trouble (Kozleski, 2002). Also many new urban teachers feel estranged from both schools as social units and the urban communities in which the schools are located. Knowing the context in which students live, gaining experience in urban communities from preservice field placements, and developing a strong sense of the construction of one's consciousness along race, class, gender, and religious lines are all profoundly important aspects of urban teacher education.

The knowledges of teacher education coming from both colleges of education and colleges of liberal arts and sciences are too often based on an acceptance of the status quo in urban education. As Florence Rubinson contends in her chapter in this volume, urban schools often provide "a single and dominant worldview that is incompatible with the values students receive in their homes." When teacher education and schools fall into this monological trap, they are telling urban students from diverse backgrounds that their knowledges, values, and ways of living are not important. Schools are here to provide them with the correct ways of being, the proper ways of seeing that come from dominant white upper-middle-class culture. Such insights force us to rethink knowledge production, curriculum development, and the core of urban educational practice. In this context we begin to see urban education not as a means of socially controlling the poor and nonwhite but as a means of liberating and cultivating the intellect while providing the tools for socioeconomic mobility.

Understanding the Importance of the Context in Which Urban Education Takes Place

Urban education teachers and educators need a rigorous, inter/multidisciplinary understanding of urban education. They need to draw on a number of disciplines and transdisciplines such as history, cognitive studies, sociology, anthropology, cultural studies, philosophy, political science, economics, geography, and others to help them understand the complex context in which urban education takes place. In this way teachers and educators gain unique and powerful insights into research on educational policy, pedagogy, and the lives of children living in densely populated urban settings. Understanding this wide range of disciplinary and interdisciplinary knowledges about the urban context, teachers are much better equipped to understand the interrelationships that shape their professional practice. Too often in university arts and sciences and professional education courses, professors fail to help students make connections between the issues confronting urban schools and the historical and sociological contexts in which both cities and educational systems have developed. Schools mirror and refract these historical and sociological dynamics. Teachers operate at a distinct disadvantage if they don't recognize these interrelationships (Slaughter-Defoe, 2002; FAUSSR, 1998).

Indeed, the role of context in understanding and engaging in good work in urban education cannot be exaggerated. When teachers understand the historical, cultural, and political context of urban education, they develop a frame of reference, a big picture that not only helps them appreciate why some things work as they do but facilitates their construction of a sense of purpose. Such contextual understandings help them answer the questions about *why* they do what they do. It helps them develop a vision of what they want to accomplish in their professional activities. In contemporary education, this sense of purpose is too often lacking. Educational leaders and teachers must appreciate the ecological embeddedness of teaching and learning. While a school is a local institution, it is inscribed by the macro- and microstructures that surround it. While individual schools and individual teachers can succeed despite the problems of the contexts in which they are embedded, long-lasting educational reform must include changing the inequitable and problematic social and cultural dynamics surrounding schools. Schools are part of a larger public democratic space. When the public democratic space is unhealthy, the schools are negatively affected. Given that the world is becoming more and more urban, educators around the world will have to deal with similar contextual factors as they begin their efforts to improve urban education in the twenty-first century.

When teachers in urban schools discern that students are not ready for learning, they often can connect such problems to the context in which students operate. What is often referred to as the "achievement gap" in urban schools simply cannot be understood as a problem of individual students in particular urban schools. When such a problem is reduced to an individual issue, researchers and educators often mistake an ecologically contextualized problem for a failure of particular individuals. The field of psychometrics often makes this very mistake by insisting that the so-called achievement gap is a manifestation of the intellectual inferiority of poor and nonwhite urban students. In a politicoeconomic context, the decline of urban schools and student achievement has paralleled the decline of the manufacturing and tax base of U.S. cities.

The poorer and more hopeless the residents in the inner cities of the country become, the more likely their children are to have trouble in school. In the 1950s urban schools in the United States tended to be largely white and middle class and boasted some of the wealthiest tax bases in the country. With the white, middle-class flight to the suburbs and the migration of industry to other regions and nations, urban schools now draw for financial support upon an area of continuously shrinking economic production. Knowing these contextual problems, educational leaders must promote a metropolitan outlook that views the economic problems of urban schools as more than a local issue. City residents in higher socioeconomic neighborhoods and suburbanites must help support poor urban schools. Without such help, the crisis of urban education will be exacerbated.

Urban teachers have no choice—they must work with what they have. Until more well-to-do citizens assume their civic responsibility to help the fiscal condition of inner cities, urban teachers in poor schools will have to operate in a hostile socioeconomic environment. The popularity of massive tax cuts in the political climate of the first decade of the twenty-first century does not bode well for the future of urban schooling. Observing the shift from an industrial to a service-based economy (Kincheloe, 1999) over the last few decades, urban economists maintain that most of the newly created jobs in cities either are highly specialized or fail to pay subsistence wages. Economically isolated, poor urban residents also find themselves politically marginalized by the electoral power of their more economically solvent suburban counterparts (USSR, 1998; Wang & Kovach, 1996; Halford, 1996; Ng, 2003).

Urban teachers, of course, need to be students of the microcontexts in which their schools operate, namely, the communities surrounding them and the network of families with children in the school. Knowledge of these communities, families, and parents can change the lives of urban educators, as they are able to make connections that lead to indispensable modes of educational involvement of these groups and individuals in the emotional, social, and intellectual life of the school. Some of the urban teachers with whom I work in New York City have developed interactive bonds with local communities and families that have not only helped students from lower socioeconomic backgrounds negotiate the minefield of school but have helped their parents as well. As they interacted with the teachers and the local school their children attended, such parents came to understand the educational landscape in a way that empowered them to go back to school to get their general equivalency diplomas and even begin college. Thus, they not only gained the ability to better help their children academically but changed their own lives in the process.

Connectedness is a central dimension of a critical vision of urban educational and social change. There is no limit to what can happen when urban teachers possess the intellectual and interpersonal savvy to forge relationships based on a vision of educational purpose, dignity, respect, political solidarity, and cooperation with the local community. Once again, Florence Rubinson in her chapter on dropout prevention illustrates an important theme in this book. To lower the urban dropout rate, she maintains, teachers must address contextual issues within communities and families. Rubinson asserts that one way to establish connections between school and community is to employ schools as "centers of community activity." Schools should not be locked up when school is not in session but should be used as recreational, academic tutoring, health, mental health, and social support centers for the residents of the communities surrounding them. In this way, she concludes, students and families gain the ability to forge unique connections with schools toward which they presently harbor a debilitating sense of alienation.

Understanding context, thus, is essential, but a caveat concerning the application of such an understanding in urban pedagogy is important at this juncture. Much of my work in education has involved researching the context in which education takes place and theorizing the effects of contextual forces on the pedagogical process (Kincheloe, 1993, 1999, 2002; Kincheloe & Steinberg, 1993, 1997). Understanding the effects of such forces, however, must not lapse into a deterministic view of how such contextual forces inexorably shape the schooling process and student performance. Understanding the impact of the political and economic factors and the cultural mismatches between home and school culture referenced in this chapter does not mean that students, teachers, and parents *cannot* overcome these contextual impediments.

Indeed, the better we understand these factors, the more empowered we are to mitigate their influence—a position that undermines any lingering determinism in the act of contextualization. A critical urban pedagogy studies the context of education for the purpose of enhancing human agency—the capacity to act in transformative ways—not to minimize it. Such a pedagogy fervently believes that brilliant and committed urban teachers can make a positive difference in the lives of students and communities, no matter how bad the situation may be. Honestly, I would love to witness a sociopolitical revolution based on equity and social justice before I leave this earth—but I don't think it's going to happen at least in the next few months. Until the revolution comes, I will continue to work to make good things happen in individual school systems, schools, classrooms, and nontraditional educational venues.

Luis Mirón picks up on these themes in his chapter, "How Do We Locate Resistance in Urban Schools?" Public schools, he asserts, are profoundly connected to their communities, but one would never know this by observing the everyday practice of some educational leaders and building administrators. These functionaries too often operate, Mirón writes, as if "schools had no connections to the broader community and political economy." Interestingly, many of the urban high school students he interviewed clearly recognized the contextual connections and wanted them made explicit in their curriculum in order to help them overcome their socioeconomic class location. What brilliant students, eh? If urban students can recognize the importance of context and its pedagogical implications, one would think that national, state, and local educational leaders could as well. Since so many of these leaders don't get these connections, I believe that the students are operating at a higher cognitive level than many of these functionaries.

In my postformal cognitive theory (Kincheloe & Steinberg, 1993, Kincheloe, 1995), the ability to contextualize is viewed as a central dimension of higher-order thinking. Contrary to the pronouncements of the types of cognitive theory taught in mainstream psychology courses, lower-socioeconomic-class minority-group urban students are as capable of learning as students from higher socioeconomic and majority-group backgrounds. Our rigorous understanding of the context in which urban schooling takes place informs our cognitive assertion. As Mirón's research informs us, there is no reason that urban students themselves can't understand such contextual insights. I have argued in numerous works (Kincheloe, 1995; Kincheloe, Steinberg, & Villaverde, 1999) that a central aspect of a curriculum for marginalized students involves analysis of the social, cultural, political, economic, epistemological, and historical forces and contexts that limit their chances for success. Such analysis becomes a central feature of a critical urban pedagogy.

Cognition and Urban Education

A key dimension of urban education that is too often left unexamined is the role of cognition and cognitive theory. One of the most important problems plaguing urban education involves prevalent beliefs about the nature of intelligence and how human beings learn. Intelligence in the mainstream psychometric formulation is defined simply as how one scores on an IQ test. It doesn't matter where we come from, the educational attainment of our parents, the valuing of education in our peer group, our expectations for translating hard academic work into vocational reward, or the language we speak in our homes. None of these factors matters in the psychometrics used in most urban schools. Test scores are all the evidence needed to determine students' intelligence and academic ability. Humans are culturally embedded entities wracked by the unpredictability of both rationality and irrationality and operating spontaneously in response to the complex machinations of everyday life. Psychometrics and the pedagogies it spawns do not view urban students, or anybody else for that matter, in those contexts in which they exhibit profoundly intricate forms of thinking. Their intelligence is measured by their performance on one decontextualized activity—taking a written test.

With these ideas in mind, urban education can no longer afford to organize curriculum and instruction around cognitive assessments that are used to undermine the success of children who come from lower-socioeconomic-class and nonwhite backgrounds. Such theories and practices have harmed such children in irreparable ways. These ways of assessing intelligence and academic ability have provided "scientific" validation to those inclined to believe that poor urban students can't perform as the academic equals of more privileged students. This allows urban educators, as Judith Hill points out in her chapter, to exclude these marginalized students from specific curricular experiences, particular forms of knowledge, and the benefits of great expectations. This exclusion is grounded by a sorting system based on standardized test scores. Critical urban educators throw a monkey wrench into the sorting machine as they expose the ways that such technologies operate to reproduce racial and class-based power relations (Bamburg, 1994; USSR, 1998; Halford, 1996; FAUSSR, 1998). In this context, Roymieco Carter's chapter "Can Aesthetics Be Taught in Urban Education?" can be read as a pedagogical monkey wrench, as he describes a rigorous aesthetics curriculum for urban education classrooms.

Many poor and/or minority-group students clearly understand that they are not viewed as intelligent in urban schools that assume the validity of psychometric data. Why stay, many of these students understandably ask, when they think we're stupid? Why be subjected to the classifying and sorting that goes on in the name of helping us? It is said that once a child has been labeled as a weak student, there's little that can be done to change the perception. These savvy students realize that the psychometric paradigm creates sorting systems and special-needs categories requiring that students be removed from regular classrooms and assigned to specialist teachers. Eleanor Armour-Thomas provides a powerful analysis of these issues of evaluation and assessment as they relate to urban students in her chapter in this book. While good things may happen when highly proficient and dedicated teachers work with students in these contexts, student performance is undermined by the low expectations that accompany the categorization of special needs. A multitude of studies over the last three decades have reported that expectations play a profound role in shaping the quality of a student's school experience (Bamburg, 1994). As long as norm-referenced tests are misused as reliable measures of a student's academic ability, these low expectations will continue to subvert the efforts of poor and nonwhite students to make positive use of schools.

Many urban school leaders in the United States continue to believe—especially with the influence of the psychometrically driven No Child Left Behind legislation of the G. W. Bush administration—that the key factor in shaping student performance is *ability*. One would think that after Vygotsky's delineation of the importance of the context in which a learner operates that the centrality of ability might be questioned. Indeed, numerous cognitive and sociocognitive theorists in the contemporary academy question the idea that we can even isolate an individual's intellectual ability as a discrete entity. Such an emphasis on ability assumes an acceptance of a mechanistic worldview that is caught in a socially decontextualized cause-and-effect, hypothetical/deductive system of reasoning.

Such a way of viewing intelligence is unconcerned with questions of social-cultural-linguistic context and power relations and the way they structure human identity and the nature of our interactions with institutions such as school. Coming from a family that valued education as a child, I had a very different relationship to school and learning than did some of my peers from very poor and often illiterate families in the mountains of eastern Tennessee. I walked into school with a body of knowledges and dispositions that allowed me to succeed academically. They walked into school not knowing what to expect and not sure that anything going on there was relevant to their lives. These orientations at the very least had as much to do with school success as the abstract notion of ability. When they were deemed to have low IQs—a.k.a. low abilities—they were *predestined* by the existing cognitive paradigm to do poorly in their studies.

In other works, I have delineated a cognitive theory, postformalism, that asserts that most students who don't suffer from brain disorders or severe emotional problems can (and do) engage in higher-order thinking. Such students engage in sophisticated forms of cognition outside of school in everyday life but are sometimes perplexed by the unfamiliar tasks and ways of thinking demanded of them in school. Their inability to successfully negotiate such assignments has less to do with ability and more to do with their lack of familiarity with the culturally and class-inscribed ways of communicating (discursive practices) of school. Poor urban students of color are often baffled by the culture of school. It is unlike anything they have previously experienced. Middle- and upper-middle-class children from white backgrounds typically see little that is unusual in the cultural dimensions of schooling. They know what teachers are talking about and see their requests of them as logical and reasonable. It is important that teachers and school leaders appreciate these dynamics and understand the harm caused by the myth that poor urban students have low ability.

To overcome these designations of low ability, every teacher must know every student in order to develop curricula specifically designed for their interests and needs. Only with this type of individualized pedagogical work can the stigma of inability be exposed and countered in urban schools. Children's cognitive abilities often exhibit themselves in situations in which teachers can't see them. The cognitive theory embraced here contends that teachers identify these abilities and use them as a framework on which to build a variety of academic skills. Again, these students are capable of higher-order thinking; teachers need to understand how to tap into such cognitive abilities. Using these postformal perspectives, Elizabeth Quintero writes in this volume about her studies of urban students whom she labels "at promise," not "at risk." In this context Quintero analyzes the strengths of the linguistic, cultural, and lifestyle diversity that characterizes many of these students' lives. It is through efforts such as Quintero's that we begin the nuts-and-bolts process of making sure that urban students' cognitive/academic potentials are recognized and rewarded.

Developing a Powerful Urban Pedagogy

What other reasons move us to write a book on urban education? One of the most important answers to such a question involves delineating and discussing the construction of a rigorous and just urban pedagogy. Such a discussion is extremely important in the first decade of the twenty-first century because of the prevalence of test-driven, standardized curricula in urban school systems. The teaching that results from these standardized curricula, proponents claim, is rigorous, fair, and equitable. These advocates do not take into account the unique situations and needs of particular urban students. When a curriculum is standardized, the students suffering from the effects of poverty, racial discrimination, and other problems are less likely to receive the specific pedagogical help they need to overcome the effects of such impediments. Please do not confuse the argument being made here—I am not asserting that these students are not able to deal with the academic requirements. The point is that they have very special orientations, which teachers must have the curricular freedom to address. For example, the decision to introduce reading instruction to students from socioeconomically, ethnically, and linguistically diverse backgrounds may involve factors that differ profoundly from normalized criteria. Different pedagogical actions and interventions are needed in diverse circumstances.

The paradigmatic basis on which technical standards and their standardized curricula are grounded assumes a positivistic notion that learning takes place in a linear way and the context in which the learner operates is irrelevant. First one teaches certain basic skills, and then once these are mastered through repetition, more advanced skills can be taught. With particular learners, especially those who fall outside the category of white/upper middle class/English speaking, such a "logical" pedagogy may not work at all. Indeed, the first lesson such students might need to set them on a rigorous learning path could involve the valuing of the type of knowledge and skills one confronts in school or learning to feel comfortable in the culture of the school. Also, when the decontextualized linear basic skills curriculum is taught to many poor nonwhite urban students, researchers uncover particular problems. Emphasis on drill and repetition of the so-called basics tends to exclude experiences involving higher-order academic skills such as higher-order reasoning, reading grounded in the making of meaning, and particular forms of writing exercises (FAUSSR, 1998; Bamburg, 1994).

In the positivistic linear model promoted by technical standards, what often ends up happening is that drilling for the standardized tests consumes the entire school day. No real learning takes place, and students who learn the fragmented content of the drills soon forget it. It has no meaning in their lives beyond its use on the tests. Watching this mindless drill for standardized evaluations, many brilliant teachers refuse to seek positions in the schools. As Judith Hill puts it in her chapter in this book:

> So am I interested in urban public schools? Profoundly. Do I want to work under the authority that governs them? Never…. There is no standardized test for my students at the end of their experiences. But there is highly exacting rigor. I work for an institution in a cultural organization where artists and teachers come together to talk about skills of perception, interpretation, and imagination. We hold workshops on inquiry?on asking ever-deeper layers of provocative, penetrating questions?instead of "staff development" on how to perform scripted lessons.

Luis Mirón in his chapter here picks up on these themes as he describes Chicago's ambitious urban education reform agenda grounded in high-stakes testing, where nearly two months of the academic high school year were wasted in preparation for the standards tests. Urban students often, I think understandably, resist such low-level, pedagogically deformed curricula. This pedagogy of low expectations fragments curricular knowledge, in the process removing learning from the lived worlds of students. It relegates motivation to the trash heap of education, as it avoids thinking about learning activities designed to get students interested in becoming scholars. A critical complex urban pedagogy uses students' fervent desires to make their communities better places as a motivational basis for learning. It is important to prepare lessons in which students can easily discern the ways such learning can be applied to the world around them. A pedagogy of low expectations treats urban students as if they were produced by a cookie cutter. It assumes that all humans learn in the same way; thus, one pedagogy fits all of their needs. Such a deficit pedagogy refuses to question the knowledge taught to these "inferior" learners. The curriculum is presented simply as "the truth," as it is assumed that such students do not have the ability to evaluate the information they are provided.

Grappling with many of the same issues raised by concerns over a rigorous and just urban education vis-à-vis a pedagogy of low expectations, Alma Rubal-Lopez in her chapter in this book answers questions about bilingual education. In this context she argues that a rigorous and just urban pedagogy promotes a bilingual education that is interdisciplinary and multidisciplinary and that engages urban students in the linguistic, sociolinguistic, and psycholinguistic dimensions of knowing two languages. Represented as a deficit pedagogy that keeps students who speak other languages from speaking English, bilingual programs that have existed over the last couple of decades have been undermined by right-wing policymakers (Lamb, 2002). As Anderson and Summerfield frame it in their chapter here: "Bilingualism is treated as a problem to be eradicated in U.S. schools." Following Rubal-Lopez's logic, bilingual education escapes its deficit status as a remedial program to become a program that holds compelling benefits for all students, even those from mainstream backgrounds. Research indicates, she reports, that bilingual students possess "greater communicative sensitivity than monolingual speakers . . . an increased sensitivity to the social nature and communicative functions of language." Bilingual education doesn't undermine the learning of English, as it takes advantage of the cognitive abilities many urban students bring to school, and contributes to the rigor of their education.

As we pursue a rigorous and just urban pedagogy, we are informed by the insights of Vanessa Domine in her chapter, "How Important Is Technology in Urban Education?" Operating in the same ideological frame as Rubal-Lopez, Domine argues that unless those who would integrate technology into urban education are aware of larger educational purposes and the scourge of the fragmented education of low expectations, technology can be virtually irrelevant in the urban school. Of course, she argues, students should be proficient in the use of various technologies, but unless these abilities are integrated into an understanding of the larger context in which urban education takes place, they are of minimal value. Technology provides no educational panacea and can be harmful when it diverts attention from the political, economic, and social forces that shape urban education. Domine is specific in delineating her disgust with many of the government officials who promote technology as a cure for urban educational ills. Those political leaders who passed the No Child Left Behind Act in 2002, for example, required that all pupils be technologically literate by the time they reach the eighth grade, while they themselves concurrently cut funds to programs designed to teach technological literacy. Such showmanship and cynicism about truly facilitating the work of urban educators can be psychologically distressing for those of us committed to the well-being of urban students.

As we stress throughout *19 Urban Questions*, urban educators face numerous obstacles in the first decade of the twenty-first century and must work extra hard to develop educational and political strategies to counter the landmines placed in our path. In the name of social justice and racial and class equity, urban educators must devise and teach a rigorous curriculum that takes into account the needs of different learners with diverse backgrounds. If we want to talk about standards, then we must move beyond defining high standards in terms of students' memorizing fragmented information represented as final truths. We must engage the profession, political leaders, and the public in a conversation about what constitutes a rigorous education. In addition, we must make one of the most important standards the realization of high academic achievement by students from diverse socioeconomic, racial, and linguistic backgrounds. A large failure rate, contrary to the pronouncements of some, is not a manifestation of high standards.

One of the most important dimensions of developing a rigorous and just urban education is expecting even more from our teachers and our teacher educators. Obviously, so many urban teachers are dedicated professionals who give so much to their students, their schools, and their communities. At the same time, some of the most brilliant scholars I have ever observed in higher education have been teacher education scholars. We need more, however. Teachers must become researchers and curriculum developers who take the lead in shaping the scholarly atmosphere of urban schools. Teacher educators, especially those in the arts and sciences, must help preservice and in-service teachers become researchers and more adept knowledge workers, as well as psychologists and sociologists who understand the contextual forces that shape student learning. There is absolutely no reason to believe that teachers are not capable of such work. I wince when I hear colleagues in teacher education or in the arts and sciences argue that teacher education students are inferior to the "other students." Such biases must be confronted directly.

The teacher-scholars emerging from these invigorated and rigorous teacher education programs will help transform urban schools into learning organizations, "postformal workplaces," as I refer to them in *Toil and Trouble* (Kincheloe, 1995). In such schools, educational purpose is discussed in relation to the social context in which schools exist. Questions that address the needs of the community and the special needs of particular students help teachers develop curricula that embrace the challenges of their classrooms. Teachers who are effective in these schools approach subject matter as a historical artifact, analyzing the discursive practices that shaped it, the epistemologies assumed within it, the knowledges that compete with it, and what is important for their particular urban students to know about it. In other work, I refer to this rigorous pedagogy in an era of standards as "standards of complexity" (Horn & Kincheloe, 2001; Kincheloe and Weil, 2001). In this book, Winthrop Holder in his chapter, "How Can Urban Students Become Writers?" describes the rigorous pedagogy he pursues at Walton High School in the Bronx.

At Walton, students with Holder's guidance publish a literary journal of their work (*Crossing Swords*) that is widely read and touted. It is a treat to watch Holder work his pedagogical magic with these accomplished students. We can help produce thousands of Winthrop Holders who can capture the imagination of urban students from all backgrounds.

Developing a Vision of a Rigorous Urban Education

A key purpose of writing a book on urban education at this period of history involves helping to develop a sense of purpose for urban educators. We can discuss collaborative school cultures and reflective practice all we want, but such concepts mean very little outside of a rigorous, informed discussion of the purpose of education in general and urban education in a specific setting in particular. Many urban educational leaders and school boards are crippled by the absence of informed discussion about educational purpose. Without this grounding, their conversations about urban schooling go around in circles, with little direction and less imagination. As Susan Fuhrman (2002) argues, in the contemporary era there are endless attempts at urban school reform with little improvement to show for the efforts. She is correct, and one of the most important reasons for these failures at reform involves the lack of a sense of educational purpose. Without this key ingredient, most educational reforms amount to little more benefit than taking an aspirin to ease the pain of a kidney stone. The urban education promoted here demands a fundamental rethinking, a deep reconceptualization of what human beings are capable of achieving; the role of the social, cultural, and political in shaping human identity; the relationship between community and schooling, and ways that power operates to create purposes for schooling that are not necessarily in the best interests of the children who attend them.

A complex vision of urban education, grounded as it is in social, cultural, cognitive, economic, and political contexts, understands schooling as part of a larger set of human services and community development. Any viable vision of urban education has to be grounded in larger social and cognitive visions. In this context urban educators deal with questions not only of schooling, curriculum, and educational policy, but also of social justice and human possibility. Understanding these dynamics, critical urban educators devise new modes of making connections between school and its context as well as catalyzing community resources to help facilitate quality education. With this larger vision in mind and knowledge of these different contexts, urban educators are empowered to identify the insidious forces that subvert the success of particular urban students. This ability is not typically found in urban educational practice. Without it, educators and school leaders experience great difficulty in determining what is important knowledge in the field of urban education. Such individuals cannot determine why some policies and pedagogies work to accomplish certain goals, while others do not (Peterson, 1994; Bamburg, 1994; Wang & Kovach, 1996; MDRC, 2002).

An educational reform promoted by many—eespecially in New York City—is the "small-schools movement." I agree with the basic principles of the movement as they are generally articulated. But when small schools are promoted without a complex view of educational purpose, they are simply another wasted aspirin. We can build 500 new small schools in New York City, but without the type of vision promoted here, we may find 500 principals and thousands of teachers asking, "Now what?" Reform proposals are a dime a dozen; an informed, contextualized, rigorous vision of what urban schools can become is priceless. When we examine the history of urban education, we find that too often urban schools served as impediments for students of color and those from lower socioeconomic classes. A critical vision of urban education takes this historical knowledge seriously and works to avoid the same mistakes. As Deborah Meier (as quoted in NWREL, 1999) asks: "How could the children at the bottom of America's social ladder use their schools to develop rather than stunt their intellectual potential?"

This stunting of potential takes place in the pedagogy of low expectations, where concern with disciplining the incompetent poor to create a more ordered and efficient society takes the place of a democratic social vision. Historical accounts of urban schools designed for these purposes alert us to the dangers of such educational structures. Such schools in the past and unfortunately in the present have served to categorize, punish, restrict, and restrain those students who failed to fit the proper demographic. Our critical, complex, democratic vision of urban education enables us to see education in a systemic context, in which we gain an appreciation of the importance of the relationship between education and other social dynamics (FAUSSR, 1998). These interactions are complex, as all social, political, economic, cultural, and educational decisions are interrelated. With such an understanding, we can begin to reshape these relationships and the decisions we make in relation to them in new and previously unexplored ways.

What this means in concrete terms is that teachers can begin to develop distinct practices to help particular students flourish in urban schools located in specific communities. Teachers draw upon their larger vision to help them determine what types of human beings they want to graduate from urban schools. Do we want socially regulated workers with the *proper* attitudes for their respective rungs on the workplace ladder? Or do we want empowered, learned, highly skilled democratic citizens who have the confidence and the savvy to improve their own lives and to make their communities more vibrant places to live, work, and play? Such students will confront and change the encoded use of "urban" as menacing alterity—a dangerous place for "good people" to be. If such meanings in the public consciousness are not modified, then the job of urban schooling will continue to involve taming, controlling, and/or rescuing the progeny of the urban jungle. We write a book on urban education to avoid such a dystopian pedagogy.

References

(Websites acccessed November 14, 2003)

Bamburg, Jerry D. (1994). *Raising expectations to improve student learning.* http://www.ncrel.org/sdrs/ areas/issues/educatrs/leadrshp/le0bam.htm

Ciani, Alfred (2002). *Teacher education issues for urban middle schools.* http://www.nmsa.org/ about/urban_ teachered.pdf

FAUSSR [First Annual Urban Schools Symposium Report] (1998). *Relationship, community, and positive reframing: Addressing the needs of urban schools.* http://www.inclusiveschools.org/ proc_sho.htm

Ferguson, Dianne L. (2000). *On reconceptualizing continuing professional development: A framework for planning.* http://www.edc.org/urban/op_rec.htm

Fuhrman, Susan (2002). *Urban educational challenges: Is reform the answer?* http://www.urbanedjournal.org/ archive/Issue%201/FeatureArticles/article0004.html

Halford, Joan M. (1996). Policies of promise. *Urban Education,* Summer. http://www.ascd.org/ publications/infobrief/issue5.html

Henke, Suellyn M. (2000). *Representations of secondary urban education: Infusing cultural studies into teacher education.* Dissertation, Miami University http://www.units.muohio.edu/ eduleadership/ DISSERTATIONS/ Henke_dis/ Henke_0_Preliminaries.pdf

Horn, Raymond A., & Kincheloe, Joe L. (Eds.). (2001). *American standards: Quality education in a complex world: The Texas case.* New York: Peter Lang.

Irvine, Jacqueline J. (1999). The education of children whose nightmares come both day and night. *Journal of Negro Education,* 68, 244-253.

IUYL (1996). *Institute for Urban Youth Leadership—summer 1996.* http://www.siena.edu/uyli/ manual1996.htm

Kincheloe, Joe L. (1993). *Toward a critical politics of teacher thinking: Mapping the postmodern.* Westport, CT: Bergin and Garvey.

——(1995). *Toil and trouble: Good work, smart workers, and the integration of academic and vocational education.* New York: Peter Lang.

—— (1999). *How do we tell the workers? The socioeconomic foundations of work and vocational education.* Boulder, CO: Westview.

—— (2001). *Getting Beyond the Facts: Teaching Social Studies/Social Sciences in the Twenty-First Century.* New York: Peter Lang.

—— (2002). *The sign of the burger: McDonald's and the culture of power.* Philadelphia: Temple University Press.

Kincheloe, Joe L., & Steinberg, Shirley (1993). A tentative description of post-formal thinking: The critical confrontation with cognitive theory. *Harvard Educational Review,* 63, 296-320.

—— (1997). *Changing multiculturalism.* Philadelphia: Open University Press.

Kincheloe, Joe L., & Weil, Danny (2001). *Standards and schooling in the United States: An encyclopedia.* Santa Barbara, CA: ABC-CLIO.

Kincheloe, Joe L., Slattery, Patrick, & Steinberg, Shirley (2000). *Contextualizing teaching.* New York: Addison Wesley Longman.

Kincheloe, Joe L., Steinberg, Shirley, & Hinchey, Patricia H. (Eds.) (1999). *The post-formal reader: Cognition and education.* New York: Falmer.

Kincheloe, Joe L., Steinberg, Shirley, & Villaverde, Leila E. (1999). *Rethinking intelligence: Confronting psychological assumptions about teaching and learning.* New York: Routledge.

Kozleski, Elizabeth (2002). Educating special education teachers for urban schools. *Urban Perspectives Newsletter,* Summer/Fall. http://www.edc.org/collaborative/summer02.txt

Kozol, Jonathan (2000). *Ordinary resurrections: Children in the years of hope.* New York: Crown.

———. Edication World (2001) "Ordinary resurrections: an e-interview with Jonathan Kozol. http://www.education-world.com/a_issues/issues164.shtml

Lamb, Terry (2002). *Language policy for education in multilingual settings.* http://tntee.umu.se/lisboa/papers/abstract-g.html [Abstract]. http://tntee.fceduc.umu.se/0001256b-80000008/g4terrylamb.rtf [authorization required].

Lewis, Karen S., & Smith, BetsAnn (1996). Teacher engagement and real reform in urban schools. In B. Williams (Ed.), *Closing the achievement gap: A vision for changing beliefs and practices.* Alexandria, VA: Association for Supervision and Curriculum Development.

MDRC [Manpower Demonstration Research Corporation] for the Council of the Great City Schools (2002). *Foundations for success: Case studies of how urban school systems improve student achievement.* http://www.cgcs.org/reports/foundations.html

Mezzacappa, Dale (2003). Turmoil in teaching: Teacher attrition sapping urban schools. http://www.philly.com/mld/inquirer/living/education/5369853.htm

Ng, Jennifer (2003). Multicultural education in teacher training programs and its implications on preparedness for effective work in urban settings. In G. Lopez & L. Parker (Eds.), *Interrogating racism in qualitative research methodology.* New York: Peter Lang.

NWREL [North West Regional Educational Laboratory] (1999). *Lessons from the cities, part two: The strengths of city kids.* http://www.nwrel.org/nwedu/winter99/lessons2.html

Peterson, Kent (1994). *Building collaborative cultures: Seeking ways to reshape urban schools.* http://www.ncrel.org/sdrs/areas/issues/educatrs/leadrshp/le0pet.htm

Slaughter-Defoe, Diana (2002). Introduction: The Clayton lectures. http://www.urbanedjournal.org/ archive/Issue%201/HomePage/guest.html

USSR [Urban Schools Symposium Report] (1998). Relationship, community, and positive reframing: Addressing the needs of urban schools. Available at: http://www.inclusiveschools.org/proc_sho.htm. Accessed November 15, 2003.

Wang, Margaret C., & Kovach, John A. (1996). Bridging the achievement gap in urban schools: Reducing educational segregation and advancing resilience-promoting strategies. In B. Williams (Ed.), *Closing the achievement gap: A vision for changing beliefs and practices.* Alexandria, VA: Association for Supervision and Curriculum Development.

Weiner, Lois (1999). *Urban teaching: The essentials.* New York: Teachers College Press.

Welcome to Urban Education Module (2003). http://jewel.morgan.edu/~seus/module.html

Westview Partnership (2002). http://www.edu.yorku.ca/~westview_web/info.html

Willard-Holt, Colleen (2000). Preparing teachers for urban settings: changing teacher education by changing ourselves. *The Qualitative Report,* 4. http://www.nova.edu/ ssss/QR/QR4-3/willard.html

Philip M. Anderson and Judith P. Summerfield

CHAPTER TWO

Why Is Urban Education Different from Suburban and Rural Education?

The question posed as the title of this chapter suggests certain assumptions about urban education—first, that urban education is *different* from other forms of education. Second, urban schools are not the "norm" and are to be contrasted with, or measured against, suburban and rural schools rather than the other way around. Furthermore, given generally held notions about urban schools, the implication is that urban is deficient in relation to the other categories, or that urban has problems the other two categories do not.

Historically, the urbanization of schooling took place after the Civil War. By 1880, the number of city high schools had surpassed that of the old rural academies, and by the turn of the century, they were the dominant institution in American education (Sizer, 1964, p. 40). The urban institution of learning *replaces* the rural: Ideologically, the rural, i.e., the normative or "natural," is replaced by the urban, the "artificial." As we will discuss below, the distinction is important for understanding both the perceptions about urban schools and many of the proposals for reforming urban education.

The suburban school not become a force until the vast suburban development in the years following World War II. Since then, suburban high school systems have replaced both the rural and urban institutions as the "successful" model of education in the United States. Suburban schools are typically perceived to be academically sound, physically safe, and the best routes to the best colleges, which provide the best career and life opportunities. At the same time, the "burbs" and suburban schools are often vilified as white-flight, middle-class enclaves, the epitome of artificiality in Western culture. Whichever view one takes, the original ideals of suburbia represent the pervasive rural bias in American life. The suburbs signify fresh air, trees, and grass, the *natural* environment, and, more significantly, the persistent attempt to construct the urban present and future out of remnants of the rural past.

However, like any other marker in the American semiotic, whether it be Wyatt Earp or Helen Keller, the Horatio Alger hero or the American commonsense individualist, the *rural*, the *suburban*, and the *urban* aspects of our culture need to be unpacked. Fact must be separated from perception and deliberate fictions. If we are not comfortable with the fact that the Earp brothers and associates were a gang controlling gambling interests in Tombstone, Arizona, or that Helen Keller was a Socialist, we turn to the "heroic" elements of the story. If the Horatio Alger kid was always a lost member of the nobility in the first place (or married into it) and if large overseas corporate mining, trapping, and logging trusts or government land giveaways sponsored our frontierspeople, we ignore the subtext and dream of our ability to "be anything we can be."

Looking at the urban, suburban, and rural school question provides a similar set of problems for us as a culture: Narratives prefigure each of these categories of schooling. Images in our minds are called up by the myths of rural, suburban, and urban schooling, reinforced by our information and entertainment culture. In popular iconography, urban schools are coated with graffiti and are dangerous. Urban schools are successful when ex-Marines enforce "tough love" on "minority" students. Rural schools are set in meadows and are white (inside and out, place and people). Rural teachers are sad-eyed country philosophers (everyone from Ichabod Crane to Conrack) or caring, unmarried young women. Suburban schools are surrounded by cars; student problems are about relationships and getting into college (all suburban students are "college bound"), and social events crucial to the lives of the students provide the plot development. Differences in the literary form of popular books and films about schools are as distinct as the content: Urban school stories are almost always drama or tragedy, and suburban school stories are almost always comedies with happy endings. Rural school stories are usually fairy tales.

Fact and Fiction in American Education

First, we will look at the facts of the matter, based primarily on research by the National Center for Education Statistics (NCES, 1997; DeVoe et al., 2002). In the classifications and data defining urban and rural education, one finds that the myths do not hold. Is the west more rural than the east? The NCES figures for 2000 show, for example, that Nevada schools (11.5 percent rural) were more urbanized than New York State's schools (16.7 percent rural). That translates into Nevada supporting only 39,062 rural students, while New York manages 477,997 rural students. While Delaware's schools are 25 percent rural, only 14.2 percent of Arizona's students attend rural schools. In the south, interestingly, both Texas' and Tennessee's school populations are 79 percent urban/suburban. The numbers make us question our preconceptions.

And the questions about rural *versus* suburban *versus* urban suggest that the categories, constructed as dichotomies, as one or the other, are part of a larger discussion about often competing cultural values. The categories of data collected by the NCES presuppose questions about values or systems of belief of particular constituencies. In other words, the questions are asked in the first place because they represent important interests and positionings of power, privilege, and resources. Embedded within the NCES demographic constructs are cultural tensions among urban, suburban, and rural values.

The NCES categories reflect established national trends, issues, and priorities. Within the demographic categories are implicit questions about the organization and funding of schooling. The categories, in effect, represent vested interests and deeply rooted belief systems that define the educational "problems" of American schooling. We begin with the most controversial data concerning rural, suburban, and urban schooling: crime statistics.

The latest are from 1999, measuring what are defined in the table titles as the "number of nonfatal crimes against students ages twelve through eighteen at school or on the way to or from school." The crimes are differentiated as *theft*, *violent*, and *serious violent* (this parameter is included as well in the violent crime column in the NCES report). *Serious violent* equates with rape, sexual assault, robbery, and aggravated assault; *violent* is simple assault added to the *serious violent* category. According to the NCES 1999 data, the largest total number of crimes in these categories was in the suburbs, with a significant increase from 1998 to 1999 in violent crime and a commensurate drop in the urban violent crime numbers. Suburban students were victims of crime 1,340,700 times in 1999, while 681,600 urban students were victims. During the same period, 467,300 rural students were victims of a crime. More interesting is the number of *serious violent* crimes as a percentage of total crime. Both urban and suburban *serious violent* crimes tally as approximately the same percentage of total crime: 63,700 out of 681,600 and 110,400 out of 1,340,700, respectively. The long-held beliefs about urban school violence and the suburban school environment would appear to be challenged by the national crime figures. And yet, who of us has not known someone who moved to the suburbs so that their child(ren) could attend safe schools?

Interested in moving to the suburbs to lower the student/teacher (S/T) ratio for your child's education? According to the NCES, the average student/teacher ratio for all schools is approximately the same. In the central city of a large metropolitan statistical area (MSA), the S/T ratio average is 17.0:1. For the urban fringe of a large MSA (i.e., the suburbs, where, by the by, 31.5 percent of U.S. students attend school), the S/T ratio is 17.2:1, higher than that of the central city. With one exception, all other categories listed—small town, urban fringe of midsize town, etcetera—have an S/T ratio of 16:<1. For rural areas outside an MSA, it is slightly lower, at 15:1. Class size, on average, cannot be meaningfully addressed by location or type of geography and demographics.

Okay, how about school size? Here the myth appears to be fact: NCES statistics for 1993 show that there were more schools in rural areas in relation to the percentage of the student population; if one looks at only the number of public schools enrolling twelfth graders, rural schools outnumbered central urban and suburban schools 11,091 to 2,949 and 3,798, respectively. While rural students outside an MSA and within an MSA equal the number of urban fringe students in an MSA nationally, the individual school populations are, on average, half the size. This, of course, is logical, based on population density. Here, at last, is a number that supports the rural expectation: the small(er) school.

The numbers reported by the NCES on small schools then become interesting. Most current reform focuses on the "small-schools movement." Smaller schools are less expensive and better, we hear, because more money is spent on instruction than administration. Yet, NCES numbers show that the percentage of expenditure on instruction is virtually identical regardless of the geography and demography of the school. Every NCES demographic category of school averages around 62 percent of expenditures on instruction.

Citizens in the MSA urban fringe, on the other hand, pay more than three times the total property tax of central city inhabitants ($39,044,000,000 vs. $12,936,000,000 in 1998–99), four times that of midsize central city citizens ($10,568,000,000) and more than five times what rural citizens pay on average to support the schools ($7,278,000,000). The suburban schools are spending the most real dollars on something other than instruction, a surprising finding to some who believe that it is urban schools that are overburdened with administrative costs. Equally surprisingly, rural schools, which generally demand the lowest property taxes, also have the highest percentage of state tax support. The schools are less expensive to the locals, more expensive to the rest of the citizens of the state, and provide the same S/T ratios.

All right. If small schools are not more efficient financially and do not provide smaller classes, they should still be a place of stability, where teachers come to stay and teach multiple generations of each family. The NCES statistics on teacher mobility provide some interesting facts, specifically from 1987–88 to 1988–89 and 1993–94 to 1994-95 (NCES, 1997). During those two periods, teachers in schools of 750 or more pupils were more likely to stay in the same school than teachers in smaller schools though the differences appear insignificant. But, in the 1993–94 to 1994-95 school year report, while 87.7 percent of the teachers in schools of 750 or more students stayed in the same schools, only 78.6 percent of those teaching in schools of under 150 students stayed. The percentage staying in other small-sized schools remained just slightly less than those in the 750-or-more-students category. In that same time period, the percentage of teachers who stayed in the same school was essentially the same for central city, urban fringe/small town, and rural/small town demographics (86 percent).

One also expects that students in rural schools would be receiving more vocational training, especially given rural economies and the lack of career opportunities in general. According to the NCES, vocational education is much more likely to be found in urban and suburban schools than in rural schools. The NCES's Survey of Vocational Programs in Secondary Schools finds that urban and suburban schools offer similar types and equal numbers of programs. Rural schools offer much less to students in vocational training, especially in areas that "were projected to be fast-growing" (NCES, 1997).

The U.S. government is not the only one interested in the distinctions between urban, suburban, and rural schools. The United States' largest teachers' union, the National Education Association (NEA), sees rural education as a major problem for teachers, according to the NEA website. After first paying homage to the necessary rural myths ("the success of rural education is linked with what makes rural and small town America unique"), the NEA cites significant problems for rural teachers, including low pay, lack of professional resources and development for teachers, and significant extracurricular work.

According to the NEA, 40 percent of America's students attend rural schools but receive only 22 percent of federal funding for education. The NEA calculated the 40 percent figure by adding small-town schools (NCES = 12.9 percent) to the two rural categories. But, remember, although there are more rural *schools* per student population, small-town and rural *students* make up only 28 percent or so of the total student population according to the NCES. But the idea that a high percentage of students in the United States attend rural schools is important to America's sense of itself, as we will discuss later.

There is something at the NEA website that is relevant to our discussion of the small-schools movement below. The NEA credits small-town and rural schools with "pioneer[ing] many successful education reform tools in widespread use today:

- Peer assistance
- Multi-grade classrooms
- Block scheduling
- Mentoring
- Site-based management
- Cooperative learning" (www.nea.org/rural/)

We do not have time to critique the NEA's attribution of all of these "pioneering" (that myth-making word in the American lexicon) changes to progressive rural education. However, the point here is that the NEA is engaging in its own myth making: The idealized, small rural school is the source of all democratic, egalitarian, humanistic, romantic, and progressive ideals in American school administration and teaching.

The picture of the rural school as the source of good pedagogy, wise administration, and community integration is a necessary fiction to balance the reality of rural schooling. What are the *interests*, and *whose* interests are they, represented in the rural myths? We need first to explore the rural myth as a part of American culture, as the essential American myth.

The Myth of Rural America

Thomas Jefferson once famously wrote that he envisioned the future of America as a nation of yeoman farmers (*yeoman*: "a person who owns and cultivates a small farm; *specifically*: one belonging to a class of English freeholders," according to *Merriam-Webster's Dictionary*). Part of Jefferson's agrarian ideal, which represents a central anachronism of our neoconservative times, includes the role and notion of the rural school, the romanticized one-room schoolhouse, or better yet, in keeping with Jefferson's notion of the self-contained farm, the home-schooled child.

The recent neoconservative movement in the United States holds many of these Jeffersonian values quite dear. Part of the neoconservative reading of the Constitution made evident in the hearings to confirm Judge Robert Bork to the U.S. Supreme Court in 1987 was Bork's argument that the Constitution should hold to the intentions of the original framers. This view symbolizes a longing for a simpler agrarian past, when "we" all lived in the country in our extended families, self-sufficient and God-fearing. At its extreme, it is an idealized world like Jefferson's Monticello. But slave labor built that idealized rural world, and the slaves, regardless of progenitor, lived out of sight so as not to spoil the views (though Jefferson's household was certainly "mixed race," i.e., multiethnic).

The other mythic view is that of the simple farmer getting his book-larnin' from the Holy Bible and the *New-England Primer*, living in the natural goodness of the New World like Daniel Boone and Davy Crockett.

Attempts to return the United States to its rural past was a hallmark of various educational reforms in the twentieth century. Henry Ford made the earliest serious attempt in the 1920s when he sponsored the republication of *McGuffey's Eclectic Readers*, those ubiquitous nineteenth-century (1836–1895) reading texts promoting morality and mental discipline, for distribution to America's classrooms. He also sponsored the development of Greenfield Village near Detroit, an open-air museum to America's past that predated Disney's idealization of that past in California.

Ford's interest in the rural ideals of America's farming and small-town past may have been piqued by conscience stemming from his own contributions to industrialization and mass production. More likely, he saw salvation from America's increasingly urban, immigrant-saturated society in its rural idealized past. After all, it was in the 1920 census that the United States was first discovered to have a larger urban than rural population, to have become an urban society. The rural was the ideal of a lost America—the industrial, urban, and immigrant present was a "problem" to be mitigated by educational ideals defined by a romanticized rural past.

"Orphans" from urban centers, frequently taken from their biological parents, were shipped to the country to be adopted by farmers and were thus "saved" from the corrupting influence of the urban centers (the Fresh Air Fund, which sends minority youth to rural centers during the summer, is a modern version). In the notorious Five Points section of lower Manhattan before and after the Civil War, the Five Points Mission sent Irish Catholic children to live with Protestant farmers out west (Anbinder, 2001). The adoption was to save them from urban influence—and from Catholicism. We make this observation to introduce the other underlying ideology of anachronistic-past pursuit in the United States: The rural ideal is *American*, i.e., Anglo-Saxon/Germanic Protestant, while the urban represents the foreign and different (the rest of the world).

The orphans and their rural neighbors were also schooled through the patriotism in the *McGuffey's Readers* and Noah Webster's *Blue-Backed Speller*. And, of course, there were Bible lessons and morality tales in American rural schools. The *New-England Primer*, the eighteenth-century antecedent to the *McGuffey's Readers* as the central reading text of American education, begins with Adam and Eve (or, according to new school publishing guidelines these days: Eve and Adam) in the Garden of Eden. Who can avoid the obvious symbolic connection between the rural and the Garden of Eden? The last great effort at romanticized schooling and social reform took place in the late 1960s. Joni Mitchell's generation-defining song "Woodstock" speaks about getting back to the *garden*. In the late 1960s we were all trying to "get back to the Garden, man." Our schools became "open," and our culture became obsessed with returning to "innocence." Where was that innocence? In the country.

The personifying movie of the time, *Easy Rider* (1969), provides a pretentious example of that hippie natural ideal when our antiheroes spend some time with the flower people at a rural commune. The "innocence" of the rural space is central to the scenes, and we see children being "free" as key to the mise-en-scène. The commune is actually a parallel with an earlier scene in which our antiheroes enjoy a simple meal with a farm family ("Not every man can make a living from the land," says one antihero in admiration). The farmer in the movie is the contemporary analog to the Jeffersonian yeoman farmer, as are the hippie commune members who are planting their own food for self-sufficiency. In the end, the moral, "We blew it," is about rejecting the natural and communal in favor of drugs, money, motorcycles, and Mardi Gras.

We are spending time on the idealization of the rural in American culture because it is important to an understanding of educational discourse around the subject of school organization and curriculum. One needs to recognize that the rural ideal is central to both neoconservative and neoliberal thinking. Both value community, common sense, self-reliance, and "the simple life." Both stances are antiestablishment; both reject the larger bureaucratic views of human society. This is not a new trend in thought: Voltaire's Candide responds to the indignities of eighteenth-century civilization by moving to a small farm in Switzerland and tending his garden.

School Reform in the United States

In the United States, one can trace the full democratic development of urban schools from the progressive reforms of the early twentieth century that resulted in the establishment of the *comprehensive* high school, i.e., with the vocational track added for the laboring classes, culminating in the Smith-Hughes Vocational Education Act of 1917. Urban schools would develop new tracks for the formerly excluded working-class students, and the cities would develop new "vocational" high schools to supplement the "academic" high schools. The next two decades saw various attempts to develop a comprehensive system of education practice for urban centers that promoted progressive views of a modern industrial society while maintaining democratic ideals. The famous Eight-Year Study of the 1930s was focused on researching the effectiveness of democratic education practices as opposed to foreign models of schooling from modernized, i.e., urbanized, Europe, which was promoting Fascism, Communism, and National Socialism to replace the monarchies recently deposed in the new European nation-states. World War II then made most of that discussion irrelevant until the 1950s.

The Second World War marked the end of a half century of war, the only respite being during the 1920s, which was followed by a decade of worldwide economic depression (what historian Robert Graves called "the long weekend"). The only way to undo the psychological and social damage of those years was to reinvent society. Besides, the world had changed. There was no going back to the farm for the returning servicemen and the displaced working women. We needed an equivalent space, a way to recapture the rural ideals of America.

In the postwar search for meaning, the attempt to reinvent the world, the United States invented the *suburb*. The suburb was the perfect compromise between the urban and the rural. The men could work in the city while the children were raised and schooled in the country. The suburb was the ideal of living in the industrial world. As for schooling, the suburban had the advantages of the urban, providing sophisticated academic high schools for the elite, while it avoided the corrupting influences of the urban school system. *Corrupting influences* is a euphemism for nonwhite, for foreigners, and worse, their ideas and morals, religions, and genetics.

Suburban high schools have remained the ideal of American education, the standard against which urban schools, constructed *ideologically* as failing, are measured. Suburban schools have the test scores; they have the football teams, and they have the Ivy League acceptances. Despite the intellectual contempt with which suburban life is held in some sophisticated urban circles, many urbanites give up the city for the "children's education."

The rural school, and rural life, has been disappearing in the twentieth century. Recent newspaper articles have contrasted the 1940 census with the 2000 census and marveled at how far America has come, with universal electricity, indoor plumbing, and telephones in American homes, in contrast to 60 years ago. But the real assault on rural life, that is, the transformation of the rural into the modern, i.e., the civilized, was the invention of the comprehensive, consolidated rural school system spurred by the reports of James Bryant Conant in the late 1950s and the development of the state university systems in the 1960s.

In Conant's case, there was a simple argument that the small rural high schools, and rural areas, could not provide adequate scientific laboratory space (to accommodate post-*Sputnik* National Defense Education Act spending), gymnasiums (sports were considered patriotic and healthy), or properly educated and supervised teachers (many rural teachers had two-year degrees) for education in the modern era. America rushed to build new, modern schools on a suburban model, bringing together children from any number of communities, and many small schools were closed.

Times have changed once again. The urban is "good," in certain neighborhoods at least, and the urban "pioneers" and "homesteaders" (always the romanticized rural imagery!) have rediscovered urban life. Most of the criticism of urban schools recently is over their *size*. Now it is Conant's vision of the comprehensive school that has become the "problem." The old leftist criticism that schools were artifacts of an industrial society in a postmodern information age was picked up in the 1980s by the neoconservatives. Large schools have been deemed artifacts of a bygone industrial era. Add to that criticism the critiques of neoliberals who see the large high school as a "shopping mall," with its implication of fragmentation and, of all things unholy, suburban values. The movement toward small schools is all the rage these days for both neoconservatives and neoliberals.

Prominent among the neoliberal thinkers is Theodore Sizer, father of the "essential school" movement. The important issue for our purposes is the ideology of the curriculum associated with the essential school: the essential or core curriculum. In all of his writings, Sizer calls for schools to strip away the nonacademic to get back to the essentials, the essentials being the academic curriculum. The pedagogy of the essential school is driven by the imperatives of the Paideia curriculum, as reinvented by Mortimer Adler, which is an attempt to go back to the roots of Western civilization in the ancient Greek ideal. Back to the symposium, back to the garden. Sizer's model is a direct reaction against the comprehensive school and the consolidation movement spearheaded by Conant.

What is most interesting about the essential school movement is its historical antecedent: the New England academy of the nineteenth century, which Sizer

(1964) documented. The academies, like essential or core curriculum schools, did not have vocational education. Essential schools tend toward the size and organization of the academy model; they tend to be community based, i.e., homogeneous. The administration is minimal, the bureaucracy limited, and one finds the teacher facing his multiaged homogeneous community and teaching the essential knowledge of the world to the future small farmers that Jefferson so revered. And, in an 1885 NEA document, "The Place and the Function of the Academy," we are reminded that the original Academy was a "garden or grove near Athens" that numbered Plato among its members. This was the *original* rural school.

Except the future isn't in the rural past. How well does the rural ideal fit the needs of modern society? Sizer himself says, "The academy failed because it was primarily a rural institution" (p. 40). And the world has changed. The modern urban world is diverse, complex, and large in scale. The small-school movement appears to focus on single, simple, and small-scale answers to large issues. The solution, rural anachronism, may not fit the problem, urban futurism. The solution, a simple, basic education for all, may not fit the problems, the complex intellectual demands of the urban global world. The solution, small communities of like-minded people, may not meet the challenges of cross-cultural understanding. In any case, a longing for a simpler past is not likely to be an answer to the complex future we face in the twenty-first century.

But certainly there is something different about urban schools that distinguishes them from suburban and rural schools. Based on funding figures from the NCES, there are three areas in which the federal government puts more money into schools in central city MSAs than schools elsewhere: bilingual education, vocational education, and Title I (supplemental services for economically disadvantaged children). Children-with-disabilities funding is a significant item, but as much federal money goes to the suburbs. Nonetheless, resources are necessary for a higher proportion of nonnative speakers, children of poverty, and students with job training needs in urban schools as well as for the number of children with disabilities.

One could argue that a simple core academic approach serves none of the needs of the students who bring these preconditions to the classroom. One can see why neoconservatives are obsessed with a core curriculum of cultural literacy and immersion programs for learning English. The melting-pot myth is at work here, but one wonders how the melting pot works in a transnational world. One also wonders why bilingualism, so common in other western nations, is treated as a problem to be eradicated in U.S. schools. Looking back to a preindustrial, romanticized rural America for answers may be a form of wishful thinking or a reactionary political stance. One wonders if something more than school reform is at stake.

The schools are, inevitably, a battleground for defining the nation. Do we envision an old United States or a new United States? The proponents of the new see the United States as a complex, urban, global, multiple entity—multiethnic, multiracial, multireligious, multiclass, multigendered, multinational, multidimensional. The plurality of all constituencies needs to be accounted for in the new vision. The students in the schools, public and private, cannot just "become Americans": They live in and represent multiple cultures. Urban education *is* different because it is the emergent American culture, a complex, urban, multidimensional culture. The "problems" of urban education represent opportunities to transform the culture. How we invent the next phases of American urban schooling is how we invent the nation.

References

Anbinder, Tyler (2001). *Five Points: The 19th-century New York City neighborhood that invented tap dance, stole elections, and became the world's most notorious slum*. New York: Free Press.

DeVoe, Jill F.; Peter, Katharin; Kaufman, Phillip; Ruddy, Sally A.; Miller, Amanda K.; Planty, Mike; et al. (2002). *Indicators of school crime and safety: 2002*. Washington, DC: U.S. Departments of Education and Justice. NCES 2003(009/NCJ 196753. http://nces.ed.gov/pubs2003/2003009.pdf. Accessed November 14, 2003.

Sizer, Theodore R. (Ed.) (1964). *The age of the academies*. New York: Teachers College Press.

NCES (1997). *Characteristics of stayers, movers, and leavers: Results from the teacher followup survey: 1994–95*. Washington, DC: U.S. Department of Education. http://nces.ed.gov/pubsearch/pubsinfo.sp?pubid=97450. Accessed November 26, 2003.

Rebecca A. Goldstein

CHAPTER THREE

Who Are Our Urban Students and What Makes Them So "Different"?

A simple question, yet answering it can prove to be anything but easy. It requires delving into aspects of American society that few people are truly comfortable confronting, because exploring such questions requires us to consider other, linked, and equally important questions: With whom are we comparing our urban students? Who are our urban students *not*? What makes these questions so difficult for many students of teaching—indeed, what makes them difficult for teachers—is the fact that answering such questions requires us to come face to face with our assumptions about "American" society, teachers, students, families, and communities, particularly those that are urban. We must push beyond our initial understandings, to tease apart what we know, or think we know, about what it means to be urban. We must question the very definition of *urban* itself.

The purpose of the following discussion is to consider what we know versus what we think we know about our urban students, using the above questions as a general frame of reference. These questions are ones that I love to answer, because I take pleasure in letting people know that what they assume about urban schools and students is not always reality. When I first began to teach in Rochester, New York, I was very excited. I finally had the chance to put into practice all of the things that we had been talking about in my doctoral program at the University of Rochester. Teaching was an entirely new world to me. To watch students learn and to see how powerful they could be in their classrooms and in their immediate communities was a truly incredible experience. I craved the energy of teaching, especially the dynamic of working in an urban school with students from the communities in which such schools are located.

When friends of the family were told of my "latest" interest, reactions were mixed. Some were surprised and disappointed that I chose to expand my world beyond the immediate range of the doctoral program in which I was enrolled. Others thought that it was great that I was teaching, because "they need good people" like me. I had to ask who "they" were, and what made me a good person, let alone what being a good person ever had to do with being a good teacher. A favorite response was, "Is she safe? Can she teach them anything? It's not like their parents care." Friends and family assumed that my talents were being lost on the students simply because they were kids from the inner city.

My abilities as a teacher were inconsequential to many because of their own definitions of *urban* and *inner city*. It is important to think about these definitions. Understandings of them usually include: crime, poverty, minorities, gangs, drugs, crisis, failure, welfare. Most descriptors are negative. And unfortunately, these words are applied to the families and students who live within the bounds of the inner city. And while it's true that urban areas have particular needs that must be addressed, we first make *assumptions* about urban areas and often fail to look beyond our assumptions to explore the realities of *being* urban.

As a result, any story or personal experiences that challenge these assumptions frequently cause extreme discomfort, if not disbelief, for those who are unfamiliar with urban students and communities. Here is a typical conversation I would have with people who knew nothing about working with urban students:

PERSON: So what are you doing with yourself now?

REB: I just started an internship in Rochester, New York. It's a lot of hard work, but I love it.

PERSON: Really? Isn't Rochester dangerous? Aren't you afraid of getting hurt?

REB: Why would I be afraid of getting hurt? I love my students. They are great kids.

PERSON: Yeah, but all those gangs. And they're violent, the drugs…

REB: Okay, sure there are kids who are in gangs, but it's not like a student is going to jump me because she or he is in a gang. And it's not about the gangs.

PERSON: But the crime! And the parents, they don't care, and they aren't involved. And they are all so poor. It's such a noble thing you do.

REB: I haven't been mugged. And the parents, they do care. Whenever I have called home, the parents have been able to help me out. Only once did a parent not respond. And that wasn't because the parent didn't care; it was because she didn't know what to do. And you know what? Not all the kids are poor. And if they are, that doesn't make them bad people, and it certainly doesn't mean that they can't learn and be as successful as folks who are not from the city.

PERSON: Well, you should be careful. You never know what's going to happen with those people.

Danger, gangs, drugs, poverty, crime, *those people*. These terms are all code words that some people use to talk about and blame urban families, communities, and students for having to live where they live, regardless of the veracity of the situation. In addition, anyone who chooses to work with students from urban communities must be more than human.

Whenever the topic of urban education came up, friends and family cast me in the role of savior: one who saved students in need of saving from themselves. The urban students weren't the ones who needed saving; it was I who needed to be saved from the myths, the stereotypes to which I had been socialized. The thought of the students, the parents, the community, and the schools was a nightmare for respectable people. It was always students' and parents' faults (to say nothing of those horrible urban teachers). The communities were bankrupt, and the teachers and schools were incompetent. The really scary thing was that this deficit model of urban education (pointing to a lack or weakness in the individual, group, or culture, thus placing the blame on the individual, group, or culture for failing to fit in) penetrated my psyche at one point in time or another, so that sometimes I too found myself saying, "What is wrong with these kids?"

The truth is, there is nothing "wrong" with urban students. They are strong, powerful, beautiful young people who are searching for their individual and collective futures. What makes teaching in urban communities such a challenge has less to do with the students, parents, and communities than it does with the limited resources, bureaucracy, lack of support, and constant change that occurs within the schools themselves. It is not the fault of students that a school is staffed for 1,600, and 2,100 students show up the first day of the new school year. It's not the students' fault that a district cannot hire enough teachers because there is no more money in the budget, or worse, waits until the end of August to complete new hiring searches. And yet, when students aren't academically successful (that is, they don't or can't pass the latest standardized test), we first blame students and their families, then teachers, and then all things urban.

It's been years since I've taught at the secondary level. I now work with undergraduate and graduate students of education. I still find myself defending my love of urban education. At the beginning of each semester, I survey my students regarding what they think they know about urban schools, teachers, students, parents, and communities. We then unpack the messages we have received about urban students and communities. Here are some of the responses:

All urban kids are in gangs.

The students can't control themselves.

The students don't know how to behave because the parents don't care.

The students don't have good family values because they are all from single-parent homes.

The children would have better role models if the parents got off welfare and got jobs.

Students have no role models.

Students don't know right from wrong.

All girls from urban communities do is get pregnant and drop out of school.

The only aspiration that urban students have is to "go pro" or become a famous rap star.

Urban students don't care about school.

The teachers are undertrained, so they don't know how to handle the students.

Urban children are mostly from poor, dysfunctional homes, homeless shelters, or foster homes and come to school "just to grow up" and then drop out.

The list goes on.

Most of the folks who make these statements have never talked to a young person from the inner city or from an urban center, nor have they spent any time in an urban school. And yet, they feel qualified to make judgments about urban communities, students, and their teachers and firmly believe that what they think they know must be true, because they heard it or saw it in the media or heard it from their parents and friends. Let's be honest. Many of us have been exposed to or have believed these statements at one time or another. And challenging the assumptions behind these statements does not mean that we ignore the realities of urban students' lives. Some *are* poor, *are* homeless, *are* in gangs, *don't* care about school, and some don't speak English and some are in need. But you will also find students in nonurban communities for whom the same can be said. So what makes urban students and being urban different?

When you talk to students from urban communities, they frequently tell a very different story from the ones portrayed in the media. They will freely admit that there are people from urban centers who personify all of the negative myths that I have listed above. At the same time, think of what it means for you as a human being when people automatically judge you without knowing you, simply because of the way you dress, the music you listen to, the color of your skin, your gender, your sexuality, and where you are from. True, many young people grapple with these issues as they try to figure out who they want to be. In fact, such grappling is really expected as a sort of rite of passage that is culturally constructed (it's part of our culture and we expect it to happen—some people are actually concerned when it doesn't).

Frequently for urban kids, the assumptions are different, and those assumptions are not always good ones for anyone, let alone urban students. One young woman with whom I worked, we'll call her Gina, said the following about life as an urban student:

There are a lot of stereotypes out there right now [about urban students]. And when you are a stereotype, you're really not given a chance for people to find out who you are just because they look at your skin color. And a lot of opportunities, you don't get to have because people look at your skin color.

It makes [us] [black students] feel like there is nothing better to do. If they [whites and people outside of urban centers] are saying that about us, we might as well live up to that stereotype, which is like the most stupidest thing to think. You should never prove somebody right when you know they are wrong. If you prove them right, that means you have no self-esteem for yourself or for anyone else…. It's bad enough that the media is exaggerating the facts. Then you gotta come and live up to them. That makes it even more ridiculous, and makes you look bad.

The stereotypes that Gina refers to are the same ones that I spoke of earlier, only instead of these stereotypes and assumptions being about people we've never met, they are about a young woman with feelings, hopes, and dreams for the future. For Gina, such stereotypes are not only dehumanizing, they are also hard to fight against because they have become the image that comes to people's minds the moment they think about all people, things, and places urban. While Gina knows that, being stereotypes, such assumptions aren't true, she also knows that it is a constant, long, and hard battle for her and other youth from the inner city to be seen for who they are. Sometimes the battle becomes so hard that they give up and give in. This can mean drugs, gangs, succumbing to the pull of a certain hopelessness and a sense of futility; in other words, some learn to accept what others have predetermined is inevitable. For some urban students, the stereotypes become their reality.

So, when we talk about what urban students are like, we have to remember that they are far different from who we think they are. Students like Gina know that people have particular assumptions about who urban youth are, without having ever met them. This does not mean that these youth want to live up to the stereotypes. In fact, many of them come up with very complex ways to fight against the stereotypes and assumptions to make their own way. Thus, in order to be a successful urban teacher, you can't simply say you believe in your students or that caring for them will pave the way to their success. Paulo Freire has noted that simply caring is not enough, unless it moves one to action. As a teacher of urban students, you have to know what the stereotypes are, and you also need to think about how those stereotypes affect the students they describe. Most important, you must actively explore all the myths you have about urban students, teachers, families, and communities; question where these myths came from; and separate truth from fiction. That is also true if you are from an urban community because you too are bound by the myths you've seen on television, heard on the radio, and experienced in your daily interactions with others. Finally, you must engage your students in the same process of exploring the myths that bind us to our current ways of understanding.

Recently a teacher, Karen, said to me:

Until I came here (to the university), I never knew I was from the ghetto. Well, I knew I was from the ghetto, but I never thought that was a bad thing. I never thought there was something wrong with me because I was from the inner city. I thought I was a good student who worked hard, whose parents love me and have helped me the best they can. It wasn't until I left the city that I learned that people think there might be something wrong with me because I am from the inner city.

Karen too has experienced that cruel and pervasive assumption that she was "less than" because she was from the inner city. At the same time, she has used this experience to her advantage in her student teaching. She views her personal experiences as a source of strength when working with her students. Rather than believe her students can't do, she firmly believes that they can and tells them so whenever they waver. She also demands from them their very best effort and will send them back to work on an assignment until they know that they have gotten it. What sets Karen apart from other student teachers is also the fact that she both values her students' strengths—community and cultural knowledge—and uses those strengths and knowledges to develop new knowledge that enables students to challenge assumptions that others have about them. Most important, she believes in them and works hard to connect the subject matter to authentic and challenging learning.

Granted, believing in students does not automatically mean that urban students will miraculously become "A" students and score well on all standardized tests. That takes hard work and an intricate understanding of other aspects of students' lives as well as teachers, students, and communities having access to quality educational programs that acknowledge student and community strengths and needs. To be honest, school is not, and sometimes cannot be, the first priority of poor urban students. Some have to help raise younger siblings. One young woman with whom I worked was chronically late. Her first-period teacher gave her detention and sent her to the disciplinarian's office. When she came to see me, I asked her why she was late so often. It turned out that she walked her seven-year-old sister to school every morning and was uncomfortable leaving her outside the school without a supervising adult there because of its close proximity to a highway entrance ramp (to say nothing of the fear of child molesters, etc.). So, this young woman would wait until she could send her sister into the school building itself. She would then walk the half-mile to the high school and, more often than not, arrive after the first bell. I asked her if she had talked to a teacher or anyone in the office about whether there was a before-school program at her sister's school. If there was, she might be able to enroll her sister. It turns out that there was. The young woman enrolled her sister in the program and was rarely late again. In this case, chronic lateness was not a result of a student not caring about school, being lazy, or being a bad kid. On the contrary, this young woman was being incredibly responsible and mature. She simply needed someone to walk her through her options while respecting and recognizing her other equally important responsibilities. She also needed to know that she had the right to explore options and seek out the help she needed.

It's not just about understanding students' needs and their other priorities, though. We also have to keep in mind that we have been raised on a particular set of images about the inner city and urban communities, teachers, students, and families. These images themselves create an incredible amount of fear, if not terror, in people who are unfamiliar with the situation. Let's be clear on this: It is healthy to be apprehensive about something with which you are unfamiliar. But too often the fear we have about urban places is irrational and can make people do and say really inappropriate things that are damaging to all, but in particular to urban students. For instance, Karen shared another story that illustrates just how irrational people unfamiliar with urban communities and schools can be:

> When I was in high school, we had the chance to host a group of students from the suburbs. They came here for a day, and we also went there for a day. So, this girl comes with her friends, and they pair us up. Later on I find out that they [the students from the suburbs] were told not to wear any jewelry or nice clothes or bring any money with them so they wouldn't get robbed. And here we were dressed nicely like we always do. She wanted to know if we were scared of being robbed. I just laughed. She never thought that we could or would dress nice to come to school. When I went to visit her school, what I noticed were all the things the school had: the books in the classrooms, the library. They had all of these computers and new books, and everything shined like it was new. That was what I saw. All they saw when they visited us were people who might rob them.

Students from urban communities are different not because they are going to commit acts of crime, do drugs, are poor, etc. They are different because of the politics (e.g., the division of social goods that people, groups, and communities have) that play out as a part of their daily lives. It is true that there is a lack of resources in many communities, but that doesn't mean that they have nothing. It does mean that they value what they have and protect it from outsiders. In fact, a colleague and former gang member shared with me that gangs were very protective of their local communities and did what they could to make sure that community members were protected from outsiders who might do them harm.

Another frequent myth about urban students is that they are all bad students and simply want to become rappers or professional ballplayers. Not so. Yes, there are students who dream of making it big. I don't know many communities where that dream doesn't exist. It's a modern (or postmodern) version of the American Dream, only instead of the wife (or husband) with the cute Cape Cod, yard with picket fence, and the 2.3 kids and the dog, it's playing ball, becoming a rap star, or making it big in the dot.com world and getting the mansion, cars, and enough money so you can take care of your family, friends, and dependents. Same myth, different incarnation. Many urban students don't see academic and athletic success as mutually exclusive. In fact, they benefit from each other. Jen, a ninth grader with whom I worked, relayed the following personal experience that illustrates the assumptions about urban students, academics, and sports:

So they ask me where I'm from and I tell them [from an urban high school]. And they're like, "Oh you from [that school]? You can't be playing on this team [a region-wide youth league team], you don't have the grades." And when I tell them I get good grades and that I'm not a bad student, they don't believe me.... They think that because I'm black and from [the city], all I can do is play ball. But that's not true. I'm smart. I get the grades. But they think that all I can do is play ball.

It is important to note that Jen's ability to play basketball was never questioned. She had made the youth league team and was a competent player. Rather, Jen's teammates questioned her academic abilities. For her, the experience was particularly distinct because her teammates, the students with whom she was supposed to work, questioned her legitimacy, her right to play on the team. Even after she told them that she was eligible to play on the team, they still doubted her and hinted that the league made an exception (e.g., she needed the "enrichment experience") and allowed her to play even though she might not have been a good enough student. Students like Jen from urban schools are automatically constructed as deviant or deficient within the normative discourses that function to define them regardless of their real academic and athletic ability. So what if Jen played ball because it kept her "out of trouble" (her words)? She saw it as a means to get a scholarship to go to school so she could ultimately become a lawyer. Unfortunately, her suburban teammates refused to believe her because of the many assumptions they had about urban kids and urban schools before they even met her.

It might seem that students from urban communities aren't that different. They are but not in the ways that people might focus on. Yes, many students from urban communities are students of color, and they attend schools that frequently fail to meet their needs academically, socially, culturally, and economically. But many of the challenges these young people encounter have less to do with who they are than where they are from, where they attend school, and the historical and structural discrimination that continues to plague many urban communities, particularly those of color. While I was teaching in Rochester, one young woman was suspended for a month for carrying a box cutter to school. Before she was allowed back into school, members of the administrative review board asked if she had learned her lesson. She explained that she left her house at 6:00 A.M. (in the dark) to get to school on time and worked until 10:00 P.M., at which point she had to get back home safely. The commute to school and from work back home was not safe, so she carried the box cutter. She further noted that she would continue to carry the box cutter because no one could protect her or guarantee her safety to and from school. Until they could, she would protect herself. The administrative review board responded by telling her that if school security caught her again with the box cutter, she would be suspended again, according to the school district's zero-tolerance policy. Was this young woman a bad person? No, but she wanted to feel safe and believed the only way to do so was by carrying a box cutter (which, incidentally, she also needed at her job, where she worked stocking shelves).

Chapter Three

When we forget that our students sometimes have to go to great lengths to be safe, we overlook the things that shape their learning experiences.

When I first started working in New York City, I was shocked by the number of elementary-aged children who rode the subway by themselves to and from school. Many parents take their children to and from school when they can, but many can't, so these young people go by themselves. Think about that. As adults, many of us don't deal well with the jostling, pushing, and lack of room on the subway during rush-hour traffic. Many of these young people will get on a subway car, sit down (when a seat is available), maybe talk with a friend, and read a book or listen to music. These students know which transfers they need to take and at what stop to exit. In some cases, New York City public school students are commuting an hour and a half each way to and from school every day. Not many of us were that self-reliant at that age. These long commutes also affect parent's abilities to interact with school personnel. It's important to remember that many families from urban communities don't drive and therefore rely on public transportation just as urban students do. Combine the hour-and-a-half commute with the cost of babysitting, and it very quickly becomes clear that saying that students or urban parents don't care is a terrible misperception. Sometimes it's an enormous feat of will to make it to school. Learning may be secondary.

Finally, there are cultural experiences and identities that make urban students different. Many of them have a great deal of knowledge about different cultural groups that many people seem to forget or trivialize. When some people talk about how urban students are different, they do it in a way that implies that urban students are at fault, that there is something wrong with them, because of their rich cultural heritages. This conviction is so deeply embedded in some that they refuse to consider any alternative. Other students of education are so sure that there is no difference between urban students and students from the suburbs or rural areas that when asked to talk about what teachers need in urban settings, they manage to talk about everything but what specifically bears on urban students.

Educators like Lisa Delpit and Gloria Ladson-Billings have addressed the concepts of race, ethnicity, and culture and how these notions relate to teaching students from urban centers. Most of us who are not from urban centers, indeed most of us who are white and/or of European descent, have been raised not to talk about race, ethnicity, or skin color, because to do so is wrong. We are told, from a very young age, to treat all people the same, regardless of their race, class, or gender. Somehow, that gets translated in our heads so that we begin to believe and say things like, "I don't see skin color. I just see children. They are all the same." This "political correctness" is dangerous because it masks the fact that we are in fact different. Instead of viewing difference as strength, we see it as a weakness. We also begin to believe that pretending not to see race, gender, ethnicity, class, or culture is the correct response, because to acknowledge these attributes would be racist and discriminatory. The irony of this is that the first thing most of us notice is the race/ethnicity of people. So, imagine that you are a teacher in an urban school and you hold that belief. How might this affect your students? Think about that for a moment. You are choosing to ignore a major defining factor of *who they are*. In doing so, you also fail to recognize part of who you are and what shapes your identity as a teacher. Acknowledging who students are, acknowledging race or ethnicity, does not mean that you are racist — in fact, quite the opposite. When you truly begin to see children — their strengths, their richness of culture, and the societal baggage that plagues them — you come to a better understanding of the forces that shape their experiences, and this will help you to be a better teacher.

Urban students, particularly those of minority status, have lived all of their lives being acutely aware of who they are *not*. That makes them very different from suburban students. Who urban kids are is talked about in terms of who they are not. For instance, when some people talk about multicultural education and culturally sensitive teaching, they seem to frame it as if only black kids, Latino kids, Asian kids, etc., are multicultural, as if they are the only ones who have cultural highlights. In addition, when some people talk about culturally sensitive teaching, they seem to frame it as if it were only for urban students, implying that these students can't handle the same standards, expectations, or rigor with which students in the suburbs are taught. Wrong. They are as capable as the latter when provided with adequate resources (which make it into the classroom) and taught in ways that build upon their strengths and values that they bring to the classroom. Students from the suburbs are taught in culturally sensitive ways that work for the predominantly middle-class white kids from the suburbs, and for the most part these ways are effective (at least for the elites). So, because it works there, people assume it will work everywhere. Wrong again. It works in suburban communities because, for the most part, suburban communities reflect the cultural norms *expected* in the United States.

People simply don't think of the way that white middle-class students are taught as being "culturally sensitive," because the way they are taught is the norm; it's what most of us think of as being normal, at least for suburban, middle-class students. Schools have functioned to make sure that middle-class, Eurocentric values are the norm — the folkways and notions that are most valued and have the most weight in American society (United States society, anyway). If you fit this American norm and buy into it, you benefit, on some level, from the power that comes with it. Students of color are more aware of this than are their "white" counterparts, because relative to the dominant cultural and economic majority, students of color tend to have the least power. As a result, they tend to be more aware of the effects of such power relations in society. Such a perception is reflected in their ambivalent views of the value of education as well as in the music, television, and other social practices featured in their local culture. So, yes, urban students are different and perhaps they learn differently and come from and to different understandings because of their varied experiences, realities, and identities.

It's not that students' cultural experiences are a weakness (unless you think of them as such). Yes, there is crime in the city; yes, there tends to be more poverty in the inner city. There are drugs, single parents, underserved schools. But this does not necessarily mean that all urban kids are criminals or victims of crime, are poor or on drugs, come from single-parent homes, or receive substandard educational experiences. They have more exposure to these issues, and such exposure does affect their learning. One urban teacher named Sara told me the other day that she has found that many of her students seem to doubt that they can be academically successful; that is, they are unsure of themselves as students, and they aren't sure that they know what they know. As a result of this "low academic self-esteem" (Sara's words), many students second-guess themselves about what they think they know and can do and often think they can't do something before they try. As a result, they get frustrated and give up, not because they can't do it, but because many of them have been told for a long time that they can't.

Sara also notes that she isn't preparing her urban students for life; they are already living their lives in very intense and fierce ways. She feels there is nothing she can teach them about living; rather, they teach her a great deal. She can teach them academic subjects and believes strongly that her job is to convince them that they can be academically successful and to help them to not give up on their futures. In doing so, she believes that they will be able to change the things they want to change. That is perhaps the most important thing that we, as urban teachers, must understand about our students: They, too, have dreams.

Let's return to the questions that first framed our discussion: Who are our urban students? In what ways are urban students different? With whom are we comparing our urban students? Who are our urban students *not*? Clearly, what we've attempted to cover in this chapter and this text as a whole can barely scratch the surface of what it takes and what it means to teach in an urban school. What I hope I've accomplished here is to push you, the reader, to think about what you *know* versus what you *think* you know about the urban students with whom you might someday work. I encourage you to look beyond what you think you know about urban students and communities to find their strengths and to use those strengths to engage your students in the learning process. More importantly, I hope that you remember to question everything: It's important to engage your students as well as yourself in questioning the things both you and they have been taught to believe about yourselves and the world. Most important, it is crucial to remember that the world in which we live, indeed the world in which urban students live, is far more complex than we frequently consider it to be. If we are to truly understand the ways in which urban students are different, if we are to truly understand who we are as their teachers, we must embrace this complexity, struggle with it, and use it in our teaching.

Florence Rubinson

CHAPTER FOUR

Urban Dropouts: Why So Many and What Can Be Done?

Ricardo's story is distressing but similar to the experience of many urban adolescents for whom leaving school represents the culmination of a long process of disengagement. For these students, disengagement is the result of a combination of their marginalized status in society and institutional neglect on the part of the schools they attend.

Ricardo began kindergarten enthusiastic and eager to learn. His first-grade teacher became concerned when Ricardo was not learning to read at the expected pace. In third grade, Ricardo was evaluated for special education but did not receive services. Instead, the school retained him that same year. Throughout his remaining elementary and middle school years, Ricardo struggled with academics, and he had acquired only six credits over the past four years of high school. Because he remained a poor reader, he spent a good deal of time in remedial classes that did not yield high school credit. In October of what should have been his senior year, Ricardo and his mother were summoned by the guidance counselor and informed that Ricardo was being discharged and referred to a vocational training center. His mother insisted that Ricardo needed more time to acquire the credits necessary to graduate and demanded her son's legal right to remain in school until he was twenty-one. Ricardo, too, wanted to remain in high school and promised to dutifully attend class and complete homework, in contrast to his recent behavior. The counselor responded by informing both student and parent that even if Ricardo stayed in school until his twenty-first birthday and dutifully fulfilled his obligations, he could not possibly acquire the necessary credits or pass the standardized tests required for a diploma. Ricardo left high school, attended the vocational training center intermittently for about a month, and then dropped out.

Is Ricardo a dropout? The question is much more complicated than it first appears. In Chicago, he would be considered a dropout, but in New York City he is considered a *transfer.* As a transfer, he will never be included in the dropout figures for the school he attended. High schools deliberately discharge students like Ricardo at alarming rates in this country, presumably to mask their high dropout rates. Where Ricardo lives, New York City, discharge rates are significantly higher than dropout rates and even higher than graduation rates. In 2001, New York City discharged more than 55,000 students, whereas 33,520 graduated and only 14,549 dropped out (Public Advocate for the City of New York, Advocates for Children, 2002). New York is typical in this regard. States across the country do not accurately track students who move out of districts, schools, and systems. Therefore, it is likely that students are often misclassified as transfers when they are actually dropouts (Rumberger & Thomas, 2000). Schools as well as states and municipalities also differ in their desire to accurately track discharged students. Manipulated discharge policies and practices are only one factor that contributes to suspect completion and dropout rates, which should be considered poor indicators of a severe urban problem.

Beware of Statistics

A major problem facing policymakers, advocates, and dropout preventionists is the inconsistent and conflicting figures on completers and noncompleters. The National Center for Education Statistics (NCES), which annually collects data from states on public school completion, warns its readers that state and local data collection policies have profound effects on the numbers of dropouts and completers reported by states (NCES, 2001). Much depends on how figures are obtained and who does the measuring. Consider the following.

U.S. Department of Commerce census data indicate that completion rates increased steadily until the 1990s and have since remained relatively stable at around 85 percent nationwide (Kaufman, 2001). However, according to the NCES data for 2000, approximately 75 percent of all high school students completed high school. Other agencies report a 5 percent to 9 percent national dropout rate. Figures from the U.S. Department of Education by state (with only 37 states represented) indicate that the dropout rate is lowest in Iowa, at 2.5 percent, and highest in Kentucky, at 9.2 percent (USDE, 2002).

Why are figures reflecting dropout and completion rates so discrepant? One reason for the confusion is that definitions of high school completers and dropouts differ depending on the data source. For example, *event* and *status* dropout rates are two measures used extensively, but they measure slightly different phenomena. *Event rates* provide the percentage of students aged fifteen to twenty-four who left school in the tenth through twelfth grades but had attended school the previous year. *Status rates* are higher because they include all dropouts between ages sixteen and twenty-four, regardless of when they last attended school (Kaufman, 2001). In 2000, the national event rate was 4.8 percent and the status rate 10.9 percent. This discrepancy is significant because it accounts for approximately 2 million teens and young adults in the United States. Acquiring completion and dropout rates from U.S. census data has the potential to yield accurate information but unfortunately underestimates the dropout rate because this method frequently misses minorities and the poor, who are more likely to have dropped out. Adding to the confusion is the fact that many data collection methods miss those students younger than sixteen years of age who drop out of school. This group is significant, since many academically at-risk students leave school during the transition between middle school and high school (Alexander, Entwisle, & Kabbani, 2001). Conflicting and inaccurate statistical data lead to misinterpretation of a serious urban problem but more acutely to self-serving interpretations of data that enhance individual interests. Schools want to present themselves in the best possible light for a myriad of reasons. Schools that fail to educate a significant portion of urban youth often manipulate dropout data to deflect attention from their failures.

Focus on What Matters

Figures should not obfuscate the one important fact: that dropping out of school remains an immense social and economic problem for urban youth from low-income and minority groups. Students living in major cities are twice as likely to leave school before graduation, and dropout rates from 30 percent to 60 percent are common in many urban schools (Alexander, Entwisle, & Horsey, 1997; Fine, 1991). High school completion disproportionately increases income for majority-group and middle-class citizens compared with minority groups and the poor, but the economic benefit of a high school diploma for all graduates is substantial (Fine, 1991). Today, the consequences of dropping out are so much more severe than in the past. Dropping out leads to a host of economic problems, including limited earning capacity, periods of unemployment, and greater reliance on public assistance (U.S. Congress, House Committee on Ways and Means, 2000). In the past, urban centers were able to absorb large numbers of dropouts into low-skilled manufacturing jobs. In cities where the cost of doing business has become prohibitive for industry, there are fewer and fewer jobs for low-skilled workers (Fine, 1991). The consequences of not completing high school are associated not only with limited access to employment but also with exclusion from employment-based benefits such as health care. Therefore, dropouts are likely to have more physical and mental health problems than completers (Gonzalez, Brusca-Vega, & Yawkey, 1999). Dropouts have a high rate of criminal activity and account for half the prison population (Educational Testing Service, 1995). In sum, dropouts are the least likely to participate in mainstream social, political, and economic life in this country.

Societal Influences on Dropping Out

Dropouts are often criticized for their character flaws, personal pathology, or poor judgment (Mehan, 1997). This discourse pervades the dropout literature and centers on student, family, and community culpability for educational failure (Swadener & Lubeck, 1995). Fine (1991) looks at the problem from a different perspective: "The bulk of the dropout literature obsesses on characteristics of individual students who flee rather than on attributes of the school from which they flee" (p. 22). She suggests that the intention of some is to deflect attention away from social failures and institutional injustices. In contrast, examination of the social influences related to dropping out encourages a perspective that avoids blaming the victim and places the responsibility for action on the institutions that serve urban children.

Minority-group membership, low socioeconomic status, nontraditional family organization, community instability, and limited English-language fluency are among the many conditions that increase the chances that students will attend schools ill equipped to meet their needs. When schools are unresponsive to students' needs, the risk of academic underachievement is increased, which is a major cause of to dropping out (Mehan, 1997).

The disparity of completion rates across ethnic groups is a major concern in this country, especially in light of increased immigration. In 2000, approximately 87 percent of all students completed high school: 95 percent of Asian Americans/Pacific Islanders, 92 percent of whites, 84 percent of African Americans, and 64 percent of Latinos (NCES, 2000). The graduation rates for African Americans and Latinos have increased in recent years, yet these two groups, along with Native Americans, disproportionately drop out compared with other ethnic groups. The dropout rate for whites shows less of a decline than that for African Americans. Latinos, especially those with limited English proficiency, drop out at extraordinarily high rates. A major study followed over 5,000 immigrant children from 1992 to 1996 in two major areas of immigrant settlement, southern California and Florida. A key finding was that a significantly lower number of immigrant students and children of immigrants dropped out of school than did students districtwide (Rumbaut, 2001). However, this trend masks the differing educational paths of several subpopulations of immigrant children, specifically those from Central America and Mexico. Understanding the issues facing Latino children in our schools is particularly important considering that the largest numbers of immigrants are coming from and will probably continue to come from Mexico and Central and South America (Ruiz-de-Velasco, Fix, & Clewell, 2000). Latinos face language, culture, and income challenges that result in high dropout rates.

Some arrive with significant gaps in their education and then enter schools that have generally low capacity to educate immigrants with limited English proficiency.

Poverty brings with it social problems within families that have the potential to compromise a young person's education. Dropout rates are highest among students living in families at the lowest income levels. Young people who face economic and social barriers are especially dependent on schools as well as community institutions for support, making it more tragic when schools fail to educate students from low-income families (Stanton-Salazar, 1997). Disruptive family stressors such as divorce, illness, death, and residential mobility are associated with low-income status. Whereas young children have little control over these events, older children are more challenged by these stressful conditions within families and more likely to drop out because of them (Alexander, Entwisle, & Horsey, 1997). Parental support and guidance are generally associated with academic achievement, but these aspects of family life are more difficult to achieve in homes under financial stress. Thus students living in such circumstances, often without optimal parental support and guidance, are more likely to display behavioral and/or academic problems. Children across economic groups generally do well in school when parents are optimistic and have high expectations for their children's school achievement; again these are stances that are difficult to maintain in financially stressed families (Entwisle, Alexander, & Olson, 1997). Nationally, single-parent homes rank lower on the socioeconomic ladder compared with mother-father arrangements (Alexander, Entwisle, & Horsey, 1997). Similarly, financial stress is more likely to occur in single-parent families, another factor making children more vulnerable to dropping out.

The effects of living in low-income neighborhoods are associated with teen psychological and educational functioning (Ray-Taylor, 2001). Communities plagued with substance abuse, violence, early parenthood, and homelessness present distractions for young people struggling with schoolwork. The decline in effectiveness of social institutions designed to support young people within their communities limits the availability of healthy role models who would encourage school completion. Many problems of low-income adolescents stem from the absence of jobs within their communities, which limits access to models with regular work hours and legitimate sources of income (Croninger & Lee, 2001). In these circumstances, children see little concrete evidence of the value of academic success.

There are certainly many students from minority groups who are succeeding in urban schools, but many others disengage from school manifesting poor attendance, behavior problems, and limited work completion that eventually results in dropping out or discharge. Among the most basic factors that influence a student's academic success or failure are the motivation to engage in schoolwork and the persistence to maintain engagement. Motivation and persistence are often subtle matters related to issues that arise from participation in majority group-controlled schools. Ogbu (1992) points to the meaning and value, voluntary and involuntary, that people from minority groups associate with academic achievement, which plays an important role in determining students' efforts in school. He argues that although many adults within minority-group communities verbalize the need to obtain good grades, there is actually minimal pressure exerted from these families and communities to do well in school. Indeed, many students from minority groups experience peer pressure discouraging them from adopting attitudes and behaviors associated with achieving good grades. For them, academic achievement means acceptance of the majority white American culture, which is viewed as a group of oppressors. Thus, those students who get good grades are usually isolated from other minority-group students. Fine (1991) presents what she calls a counterintuitive portrait of dropouts which supports, but does not exactly prove, Ogbu's theory. She studied a dropout population from a large, urban, comprehensive high school and found that they were significantly less depressed and more demonstrative concerning their rights than those who stayed in school. In contrast, students who remained in the school were more depressed, more conformist, and more likely to blame themselves for school failure. The dropouts were more likely to be psychologically healthy, critical of social injustices, and more willing to confront them than their counterparts who remained in school. The implication is that school completers suffer emotionally from not only the oppressive conditions found in many urban schools but potentially from outsider status within their adolescent world.

Influence of Educational Practices and Policies

Urban youth face many problems that pose threats to the likelihood of completing school, yet the most severe is access to a quality education. Dropouts report a variety of reasons for leaving school. They indicate that they do not like school, find schoolwork boring, do not get along with teachers, want a baby, have a baby, or need a job. However, the majority of high school dropouts frequently experience a long, slow, and often painful withdrawal from learning, their teachers, and the educational institutions that should support their efforts. Many begin school with differences between their skills and the skills required in kindergarten. The gap grows wider in years to come and results in a downward path. Many have not received the kind of education that might have reversed their downward academic trajectory. For many urban students, dropping out is not a discrete event but the culmination of a lengthy process resulting from the widespread failure on the part of schools to properly instruct a large group of mostly urban youth.

Structural characteristics of urban schools, such as their size and condition, influence the quality of opportunity for students (Duke, 2002; Rumberger & Thomas, 2000). Urban high schools tend to be large, yet research informs us that optimal capacity for high schools is between 600 and 900 students (Lee & Smith, 1997). Students in larger schools frequently feel more isolated and disengaged—

emotional dynamics that affect academic achievement and nurture noncompletion. During difficult times in students' lives, teachers should be a valuable source of emotional support and guidance. Such positive social relationships are powerful incentives to remain in school, but they are difficult to construct in large schools. Downsizing is important in elementary and middle schools interested in creating a sense of connection, but it is vital in high schools because this age group is more apt to leave school when there is little emotional connection. In addition to smaller schools, the physical condition of urban schools conveys an important message to students that relates to engagement. Students who attend run-down schools in impoverished communities get the message that they do not matter (Kozol, 1991).

There is little controversy concerning the positive contribution of quality teaching and limited class size to the completion rate (Rumberger & Thomas, 2000). In California schools, researchers confirmed that low teacher/student ratios combined with high percentages of teachers holding advanced degrees have a significant and positive effect on high school completion rates (Rumberger, Larson, Ream, & Palardy, 1999). For young children, a satisfactory transition from home to school is imperative for later schooling. Although the likelihood of a good transition depends on many contextual factors related to home, school, and community, quality teaching in the early grades facilitates a child's transition to academic life. In this critical period, good teachers assist children in building good work habits and foster the perception of young children as competent learners. In major cities where teacher shortages are common and novice and uncertified teachers fill vacancies in failing schools, urban children often do not receive support and quality instruction, which places them at risk for noncompletion.

Students placed on the low end of a tracking system often find school meaningless, increasing their likelihood of dropping out (Mehan, 1997). School success reflected in high track placement fosters students' beliefs in their own competence, which over time strengthens their attachment to school. Low-performing students, relegated to low academic tracks and retained in a grade, perceive teachers' differential treatment of them compared with high-achieving students. Frequently low-achieving students are called on less often, are provided with less wait time to respond to questions, are criticized more often for failure, are given less feedback, are interrupted more often, and are provided with few opportunities to learn new material. Children treated with low regard come to believe it and often fulfill low expectations (Acheson & Gall, 1998). Students in low educational track placements receive subtle, yet negative, messages implying low standing in the academic world (Alexander, Entwisle & Legters, 1998; Finn, 1989). This message is stigmatizing, adding to their detachment from school and eventual noncompletion.

Although consistent promotion from grade to grade hardly guarantees success for urban students, repeating a grade is associated with increased dropout risk.

Repeaters in Baltimore public schools make up 71 percent of all dropouts, and multiple repeaters make up almost 80 percent (Alexander, Entwisle, & Kabbani, 2001). Retained students do not do better than socially promoted students and have higher dropouts rates (Roderick, Bryk, Jacob, Easton & Allensworth, 1999). In a New York high school, students retained in ninth grade dropped out at a rate three times higher compared with their nonretained peers (Fine, 1991). Retention rates are high in urban schools, but educators rarely develop intervention plans to ameliorate the problems that retained students experienced the previous year. The attitude is that more time on-task will increase achievement, which is not always the case. In fact, retention is associated with many negative social and psychological consequences. Such policies make little sense for the individual students who require alternative teaching modalities or a nontraditional classroom structure in order to achieve academic success. However, retention does serve a purpose, albeit a sinister one. Retaining students in lower grades can accomplish the upgrading of overall test scores so that standardized test scores will look better (Haney, 2002). This procedure serves the school but places the retained student at greater risk for dropping out.

In the post-Columbine era, school safety has become a major source of public anxiety around the country. However, urban schools have been plagued for a long time with gang violence and the violence resulting from overcrowding, drug use, and discipline problems. A Nation at Risk, published in the 1980s, provided the connection between learning and students' perception of individual safety (Duke, 2002). Students perceive that their schools are safe when they experience well-managed classrooms, hallways, stairwells, and gathering areas. These are not the images common to urban schools, especially urban high schools. In 1982, the High School and Beyond study (National Center for Education Statistics, 1982) indicated that 7 percent of high school students did not feel safe in their schools. Following the 1990s, a decade of deadly violence in schools around the country, the percentage of fearful students has surely increased. School safety as a political issue ignores the reality of the student who must enter a large urban school each day, fearful of becoming the object of taunting, gun violence, or physical and sexual abuse. Concerns about safety impede learning and too often become so threatening that victims do not return.

The Contribution of the Standards Movement to Dropping Out

Christy, a seventeen-year-old, stayed at home. for 45 days in her senior year to nurse her sick mother. After her mother's death, Christy returned to school to learn that she had been discharged after her twentieth absence. Without the emotional energy or resources to fight the discharge, Christy took a job in a fast-food restaurant.

Jayden was discharged from high school after completing all coursework but failing the mathematics standardized test three times. He spent two months out of school and then enrolled in a general equivalency diploma (GED) program. Since the programs in his city are so popular and overcrowded, he spends the morning in class and goes home for the rest of the day.

Few argue the merits of the standards movement in education, but implementing a common curriculum and evaluating success within the curriculum with standardized tests will harm many students who have not been prepared in the early grades. Jayden's high school departure was neither voluntary nor preferred and had a profound effect on his self-image and life goals. High school students like Christy maintain little connection to large urban schools, so that when their lives are in crisis, they do not seek help from school counselors, teachers, or administrators. Many times, high schools discharge students for poor grades, bad behavior, or chronic truancy, and those discharged cannot find another school to accept them. Many poorly instructed students of low income and from minority groups are systematically excluded from academic programs and the social life of the school until they are eventually discharged (Fine, 1991). In a study of 100 public high schools in the late 1980s, researchers found that staff were pressured to reduce dropout rates by discharging students into GED or alternative educational programs (Rumberger & Thomas, 2000). Schools discharge the difficult-to-teach because these students compromise the school's ability to present itself as a normally functioning school (Riehl, 1999). Jayden and Christy are casualties of the current standards-based school reform movement, a major contributor to the dropout rate. Since schools more than ever need to demonstrate increases in test scores, one way to achieve this is to eliminate low-achieving and frequently absent students from their rolls. Benefits from the standards movement are political in that they provide the illusion that all students profit when held to a higher standard. This may be so in some places and with some students. However, students who do not meet the standard pay dearly.

Is the GED an Alternative?

Rachel informs her guidance counselor that she wants a fast track to a Navy career. She says, "The day I get my GED I will go straight to the recruiting office." Her statement indicates unawareness that all branches of the military require a high school diploma. Although this appears to be a sound plan from Rachel's perspective, she is unaware that the Navy no longer accepts the GED as evidence of high school completion.

Although percentages of high school completers have remained steady over the last decade, there has been a decrease in the number of students actually graduating from high school. This decline is a result of students' preferences or an involuntary push to complete high school through alternative means, typically the GED (Rumberger, 2001).

Dropping out, with all of its drawbacks, does not have to be an unalterable problem. The GED is gaining popularity as a viable alternative for students who cannot complete traditional high school. However, adolescents' access to the test encourages many like Rachel to seek the GED as an alternative to high school completion. Of the approximately 500,000 people receiving GEDs each year, 200,000 are younger than twenty years, and 50,000 are sixteen or seventeen years old. However, most teens do not actually go for the credential in their teenage years, since the majority of GED recipients are adults (Chaplin, 1999). Although there is a disparity in the depth of knowledge and employment skills between high school graduates and GED holders, more than 95 percent of employers indicate that they employ GED holders on the same basis as high school graduates, and 90 percent of colleges and universities accept the GED as equal to a high school diploma (American Council of Education, 2001; Brown, 2000). Although the GED may be an alternative to traditional high school completion, in reality it rarely leads to a four-year college education. Only 2 percent of GED holders actually obtain a four-year college degree (Chaplin, 1999). The GED credential is not as easy to obtain as many think. The January 2002 revision of the GED test better reflects competencies possessed by high school graduates. Therefore, as the credential becomes more difficult to obtain, the GED will not be the second chance it once was for dropouts.

Reducing the Dropout Rate

Before the discussion turns to approaches for reducing the dropout rate, the reader should understand that there are many initiatives currently in place designed to keep students in urban schools until graduation. A discussion of specific approaches would be too exhaustive for this chapter. Instead, I will present global approaches that educators interested in school reform can adapt into specific strategies to create socially just schools that motivate students to complete.

The dropout problem is so multileveled that comprehensive school reforms at every level of education are required to produce a significant increase in urban school completers. Traditional approaches to dropout prevention within conventional school structures are bandages that have done little to increase school completion. Societal reforms in the United States do not appear forthcoming in the current political climate. Therefore, it falls to urban educators to create equal access to quality education as well as positive outcomes for all learners.

In generally successful schools that have a small group of students at risk for dropping out, it is common to find supplemental services such as counseling, remediation, and social support within an existing school program. Unfortunately, there is little evidence that supplemental services influence the completion rate (Rumberger, 2001). In urban centers with large numbers of failing schools, reforms related to policies, practices, and structures are necessary to increase school completion. More powerful prevention strategies begin in the early grades, not as special programs designed for children at risk for dropping out but as naturally occurring components of quality education programs. There is no need for separate dropout prevention programs or alternative schools for vulnerable students if all schools provide students with quality instruction and necessary supports. Thus, urban centers need to create schools in which the problems of potential dropouts drive school structures, policies, and curricula. Such an approach involves fundamental changes in the way schools function and in attitudes of professional educators. Despite the difficulty in accomplishing such monumental changes, some schools have been successful in doing so and should serve as models for those interested in moving to a more socially just institutional position.

Effective dropout prevention strategies not only target students but simultaneously address the contextual issues within families, communities, classrooms, and school systems. One example is the innovative use of public schools as centers of community activity. School buildings need not lock the doors at the end of the instructional day but can stay open to provide services to the community. As community partners, schools could offer recreation, remediation, comprehensive health, mental health, and social support programs for students and families. The utilization of schools in such a way provides students and families with opportunities to build connections to their schools, a factor that is essential to school completion for youth from low-income and minority-group backgrounds. Families would benefit from such arrangements, in which they too could receive services and emotional support, which in turn improve the contexts of students' lives.

Dropout prevention needs to start long before students reach high school and long before educational failure and problematic behaviors become too entrenched. Prevention programs designed for middle and high school students with long-standing problems are the least effective. Early intervention is an initial cost-effective approach to dropout prevention (Rumberger, 2001). The High/Scope Perry Preschool study illustrates the potential influence of a high-quality preschool education. At ages three and four, youngsters living in poverty and at high risk for school failure receive a high-quality preschool education based on the High/Scope learning model. In adulthood, program participants have demonstrated a wide range of benefits, including significantly increased school completion rates (Schweinhart, Barnes, & Weikart, 1993). Research supports the idea that only high-quality preschool programs promote healthy development for young children. Implementation of what is known in regard to quality curriculum and teacher disposition is vital for the growing numbers of children attending preschool.

A quality preschool experience is only a first step in building a successful school life. The next step is to ensure that urban students finish school, by maximizing successful learning in elementary school and then in the stressful middle school years. Instruction in basic skills and critical thought needs to occur in a non-threatening, caring, and committed environment for learning, where individual teachers accept a personal responsibility for student success. The way students experience school is an important factor. Students must feel comfortable in their classrooms if they are to become successful learners. This occurs when schools acknowledge the realities in which students live and when diverse cultures are truly valued. Student comfort level decreases when curriculum provides a single dominant worldview that is incompatible with the values students receive in their homes. This is not to say that teachers and students must be from the same ethnic group or that ethnic-group membership should drive methodology design. Rather, schools and classrooms must be organized in ways such that students receive the instruction they require, delivered in respectful ways that best fit their learning and cultural styles. Lisa Delpit (1995) puts it this way:

> In any discussion of education and culture, it is important to remember that children are individuals and cannot be made to fit into any preconceived mold of how they are supposed to act. The question is not necessarily how to create the perfect "culturally matched" learning situation for each ethnic group, but rather how to recognize when there is a problem for a particular child and how to seek its cause in the most broadly conceived fashion. Knowledge about culture is but one tool that educators may make use of when devising solutions for a school's difficulty in educating diverse children. (p. 167)

In small schools with low teacher/student ratios and in smaller learning communities within large high schools, quality instruction is more likely to thrive. In addition, teachers would be in a better position to enhance school engagement by individually responding to students. Imagine a high school where teachers call parents to find out why a student is absent or to problem solve with them about a disciplinary issue. In smaller settings, there will be greater opportunities to provide students with this type of social capital.

A primary strategy is modification of the educational environment so that teachers become not simply aware of students' needs and employ appropriate teaching methods matched to them but continuously assess their own classroom practices and alter their instructional environments to ensure proper fit with students (Lunenburg, 2000). On a practical level, students presented with material that is too difficult or above their current skill level will become frustrated and turn away from learning. In contrast, when material is too easy or below the students' skill level, they become bored and similarly turn away from learning. Attention to this principle early on would provide the strong foundation that would reduce the need for remediation in the higher grades. The standards movement ignores this basic learning principle by presenting students with materials they cannot adequately process. Older students should be assisted in meeting higher standards in their classrooms by providing them with extra time, attractive catch-up activities, and respectful recovery programs to make up for weak skills.

In a multifaceted approach that encourages school completion, high school dropout prevention is not forgotten. The codirector of a successful urban high school with a 5 percent dropout rate articulates specific practices that support high completion rates in a school that serves students from low-income and minority groups (Rumberger, 2001). According to the codirector, classes should be small and organized into longer than traditional blocks of time so that teachers and students have the opportunity to engage in concentrated work and develop relationships. The school must articulate and maintain a clear mission and goal(s) aligned to its vision. Teachers are provided with relevant professional development. School improvement results from a democratic process of decision making. School culture should encourage staff risk taking, self-governance, and professional collegiality in a structure that provides for a low teacher/student ratio.

Armed with an understanding of why students drop out and the disposition to influence students' lives, educators can create comprehensive approaches that both assist individual students and improve educational settings for potential dropouts. Most educators are well-intentioned men and women. However, when they perpetrate unjust educational policies that permit poor instruction and push out students from public high schools, they damage a large proportion of our citizenry. In her attempt to establish socially just schools, Fine (1991) provokes educators with these words: "Intentions must be directed toward the disruption of what is and what appears inevitable, not toward well-meaning compliance" (p. 183). In other words, educators must commit to responsible action.

References

Acheson, Keith A., & Gall, Meredith D. (Eds.) (1998). *Techniques in the clinical supervision of teachers*. White Plains, NY: Longman.

Alexander, Karl K., Entwisle, Doris R., & Horsey, Carrie (1997). From first grade forward: Early foundations of high school dropouts. *Sociology of Education, 70*, 87-107.

Alexander, Karl L., Entwisle, Doris R., & Kabbani, Nader S. (2001). The dropout process in life course perspective: Early risk factors at home and school. *Teachers College Record, 103*, 760-822.

Alexander, Karl L., Entwisle, Doris R., & Legters, Nettie (1998, August). *On the multiple faces of first grade tracking*. Paper presented at the annual meeting of the American Sociological Association, San Francisco, CA.

American Council on Education (2001). *Who took the GED? GED 2000 statistical report*. Washington, DC: General Educational Developmental Testing Service.

Brown, Bettina L. (2000). *Is the GED a valuable credential?* Columbus, OH: Center on Education and Training for Employment.

Chaplin, Duncan (1999, November). *GEDs and teenagers: Are there unintended consequences?* Paper presented at the annual meeting of the Association for Public Policy Analysis and Management, Washington, DC.

Croninger, Robert G., & Lee, Valerie E. (2001). Social capital and dropping out of high school: Benefits to at-risk students of teachers' supports and guidance. *Teachers College Record, 103*, 548-581.

Delpit, Lisa (1995). *Other people's children: Cultural conflict in the classroom*. New York: The New Press.

Duke, Daniel L. (2002). *Creating safe schools for all children*. Boston: Allyn and Bacon.

Dynarski, Mark, & Gleason, Philip (1998). *How can we help? What we have learned from fed-*

eral dropout-prevention programs. Princeton, NJ: Mathematica Policy Research, Inc.

Educational Testing Service (1995). *Dreams deferred: High school dropouts in the United States.* Princeton, NJ: Educational Testing Service, Policy Information Service.

Entwisle, Doris R., Alexander, Karl L., & Olson, Linda S. (1997). *Children, schools and inequality.* Boulder, CO: Westview.

Fine, Michelle (1991). *Framing dropouts: Notes on the politics of an urban public high school.* Albany: State University of New York Press.

Finn, Jeremy D. (1989). Withdrawing from school. *Review of Educational Research, 59,* 117-142.

Gonzalez, Virginia M., Brusca-Vega, Rita, & Yawkey, Thomas D. (1999). *Assessment and instruction of culturally and linguistically diverse students with or at risk of learning problems: From research to practice.* Boston: Allyn and Bacon.

Haney, Walter (2002, October). *Revising the myth of the Texan miracle in education: Lessons about dropout research and dropout prevention.* Paper prepared for Achieve, Inc. and The Civil Rights Project of Harvard University.

Kaufman, Philip (2001, January). *The national dropout data collection system: Assessing consistency.* Paper prepared for Achieve, Inc. and The Civil Rights Project of Harvard University.

Kozol, Jonathan (1991). *Savage inequalities: Children in America's schools.* New York: Crown.

Lee, Valerie E., & Smith, Julia B. (1997). High school's size: Which works best, and for whom? *Educational Evaluation and Policy Analysis, 19,* 205-227.

Lunenburg, Fred C. (2000). *High school dropouts: Issues and solutions.* Huntsville, TX: Sam Houston State University. (ERIC Document Reproduction Service No. 448 239)

Mehan, Hugh (1997). *Contextual factors surrounding Hispanic dropouts.* La Jolla, CA: Sociology & Education. Website: http://www.ncela.gwu.edu/miscpubs/hdp/1/index.htm. Accessed November 7, 2003.

NCES [National Center for Education Statistics] (1982). *High School and Beyond.* Washington, DC: U.S. Government Printing Office.

—— (2000). *Dropout rates in the United States: 2000.* Washington, DC: U.S. Government Printing Office.

—— (2001). *Dropout rates in the United States: 2001.* Washington, DC: U.S. Government Printing Office.

—— (2002). *Public high school dropouts and completers from the common core of data: School years 1998-1999 and 1999-2000.* Washington, DC: U.S. Department of Education.

Ogbu, John U. (1992). Understanding cultural diversity and learning. *Educational Researcher, 21,* 5-14.

Public Advocate for the City of New York, Advocates for Children (2002). *Pushing out at-risk students: An analysis of high school discharge figures.*

Ray-Taylor, Rossi (2001). Closing the academic achievement gap: Successful strategies for educators, schools, and communities. *The CEIC Review, 10,* 1-2.

Riehl, Carolyn (1999). Labeling and letting go: An organizational analysis of how high school students are discharged as dropouts. In A. M. Pallas (Ed.), *Research in Sociology of Education and Socialization* Vol. 12; pp. 231-268. New York: JAI.

Roderick, Melissa; Bryk, Anthony S.; Jacob, Brian A.; Easton, John Q.; & Allensworth, Elaine (1999). *Ending social promotion: Results from the first two years.* Chicago: Consortium on Chicago School Research.

Ruiz-de-Velasco, Jorge; Fix, Michael; & Clewell, Beatriz C. (2000). *Overlooked and underserved: Immigrant students in U.S. schools.* Washington, DC: The Urban Institute.

Rumbaut, Rubén G. (2001). Children of immigrants and their achievement: Relating family and school to engagement, aspirations, and achievement. *The CEIC Review, 10*, 6-9.

Rumberger, Russell W. (2001, May). *Why students drop out of school and what can be done.* Paper presented at the conference "Dropouts in America: How Severe Is the Problem? Do We Know about Intervention and Prevention?" Boston, MA.

Rumberger, Russell W., & Thomas, Scott L. (2000). The distribution of dropout and turnover rates among urban and suburban high schools. *Sociology of Education, 73*, 39-67.

Rumberger, Russell W., Larson, Katherine A., Ream, Robert K., & Palardy, Gregory A. (1999). *The educational consequences of mobility for California students and schools.* Berkeley: Policy Analysis for California Education.

Schweinhart, Lawrence J., Barnes, Helen V., & Weikart, David P. (1993). *Significant benefits: The High/Scope Perry Preschool study through age 27.* Ypsilanti, MI: High/Scope Press.

Stanton-Salazar, Ricardo D. (1997). A social capital framework for understanding the socialization of racial minority children and youths. *Harvard Education Review, 67*, 1-40.

Swadener, Beth B., & Lubeck, Sally (1995). *Children and families "at promise": Deconstructing the discourse of risk.* Albany: State University of New York Press.

U.S. Congress, House Committee on Ways and Means (2000). *Overview of entitlement programs.* Washington, DC: U.S. Government Printing Office.

David Forbes

CHAPTER FIVE

What Is the Role of Counseling in Urban Schools?

The role of the urban school counselor today is to promote the whole development of all school community members as well as that of the school community itself. By *whole development* I mean not only the advancement of cognitive, intellectual, and academic abilities but also emotional, moral, social, spiritual, physical, and aesthetic ones. *All community members* means teachers, administrators, parents, and staff as well as every student. And by *school community* I mean the entire school culture as a living organism, including the quality of its relationships.

This holistic, compassionate counseling replaces the kind whereby counselors' primary function was to process students as raw material for future economic competition and bureaucratic efficiency, accommodating the employment needs of the market or the government. Schools too often have served to reproduce existing class relations. Given that calculus, with the loss of manufacturing jobs and the need for fewer and highly skilled workers, millions of urban working-class and poor students become relegated to the trash heap. Devalued and neglected, they are left with poor-quality public education that contributes to illiteracy, attrition, and despair. Today, however, it is no longer acceptable, if it ever was, to treat education and students as commodities instead of intrinsically valuable ends (see Miller, 1997). Counselors in urban schools no longer can afford to play the role of functionaries in an indifferent education bureaucracy that shortchanges the people it is supposed to educate. It is wisdom that enables the counselor to see the greater needs of the members of the school community and compassion that drives the counselor to help each and every one of them to become a whole person.

The emerging counselor role also does away with the old battle between two opposing counseling camps—those who would promote academic success while minimizing affective and interpersonal issues, and those who emphasize personal counseling at the expense of academic concerns. In this tired schema, politicians and bureaucrats narrowly define academic success through standardized tests, while emotional health becomes consigned to a privatized realm characterized by adjustment to the status quo. Both split off aspects of the whole person. Instead, holistic urban school counselors address multiple intelligences and the unique capacities of each individual. They advocate for quality education, social justice, and full citizenship based on everyone's interconnection with others everywhere. Unlike a teacher, administrator, or other specialized support professional, the counselor's unique position and responsibilities enable him or her to engage in the everyday tasks of the urban school as well as to step back and see the entire school as a system in need of care.

In a globalized, post–9/11 world, nothing less will do. This radical role requirement calls for the counselor to act as a "wizard" in a world of "muggles" (i.e., the rest of us, according to Harry Potter): a higher-order visionary with the wisdom and presence of mind to understand and respect the different levels of consciousness of both the parts and the whole and the compassion to help everyone evolve toward higher, more integrated levels. It means thinking globally and acting locally, and even thinking locally while acting globally (Beck & Cowan, 2002). It means being fully aware of an urban school's material and social limitations and of the varying levels of consciousness within it and succumbing to neither utopian idealism nor cynical despair. The counselor can do this because she or he knows that the world is of one piece and is constantly changing and evolving. Over and above the thinking of the standards bureaucrats and those who would commodify knowledge as a means toward material success, a mindful, compassionate counselor is attuned to this dynamic of change and growth toward wholeness, which is the very nature of learning and education itself.

An urban school is situated within an elaborate, multilayered nexus of values, goals, and behavioral patterns, with its own life conditions. This urban matrix both throbs with tensions and bursts with hopeful opportunities. Stress arises as cultural sensibilities and belief systems of groups from different parts of society and from the entire world come together in one place, rub against each other, and create friction; sometimes they ignite. Anxiety is heightened by the threat of terrorism as well as by a current presidential administration hell-bent on world military and economic domination. These compound the already existing stresses in everyday urban life: bare-bones essential services and maintenance-deferred infrastructures; competition for scarce resources such as housing, a decent wage, quality education, and cultural and recreational space; clogged streets, dangerous traffic, and inadequate mass transit; violent crime, gangs, drugs, and homelessness; public health epidemics both actual (HIV, asthma, obesity, infant mortality, lead poisoning) and possible (anthrax, smallpox, radiation from terror-targeted nuclear power plants) and noise and air pollution.

As a consequence, many urban students and family members live with low to moderate levels of posttraumatic stress on a day-to-day basis. They feel anxious and insecure, squeezed between the constraints of limited and uncertain economic resources and the relentless pull of pervasive media messages and images that glorify materialist consumption. A significant number suffer from unaddressed depression, grief, or sense of helplessness as a result of immigrant family dislocation, loss of a family member due to crime or illness, or being a witness to or victim of violence. Others exhibit self-destructive, aggressive, and impulsive behaviors, having been raised in chaotic, emotionally troubled families marked by authoritarian relations, overwhelmed caregivers, substance abuse, or domestic violence. Beneath the workaday bustle and cool pose of many students, urban school counselors often discern these kinds of problems.

At the same time, the potential for healthy growth here and now is enormous. With the ability to access instant information and establish worldwide networks through the Internet and advanced telecommunications, old, rigid systems of domination and ideology are being challenged and transformed. There is a growing planetary concern for the health of the entire biosphere. Human rights has advanced as an international political issue. More scientists recognize that the mind affects the body in terms of improving health, emotional awareness, and stress reduction (Goleman, 2003). Cross-cultural research on optimal human development shows that all children everywhere need the same things in order to thrive: healthy attachments, emotional literacy, a deep sense of meaning and purpose, the time to grow at their own pace, and caring, safe communities. Networks of educators and peacemakers who work on local and international levels are raising people's consciousness everywhere: More folks are realizing that real safety and security cannot come from the aggressive deployment of guns or bombs but only from genuine compassion for and understanding of one's self and of others.

This knowledge and its corresponding level of awareness are at the vanguard of social progress and have concrete implications for policy development and everyday practice. They stand over and above the retrograde educational policies that treat knowledge as a scarce resource for the privileged few and that seek to impose restrictive, dominant-defined standards on children without respect to their emotional and social developmental needs. This universal perspective also trumps the consciousness of those in government who assume that force, greed, and competition are the best and only means to motivate people and to ensure their safety.

In short, a higher-order global consciousness is out of the bottle. On a local scale this means that urban school counselors can draw from a worldwide knowledge base to help them assess what members of the school community need in order to maximize their health and happiness. Counselors then share the relevant knowledge and skills and make them more accessible to everyone. Some of the ways they do this are by: helping young men become more emotionally literate (for example, identifying feelings and learning to better recognize situational cues); encouraging African Americans, Latinos, and students from other under-represented groups to get on the college preparatory track; teaching schoolwide conflict resolution and peacemaking skills; leading workshops with parents on communication with their children and on participating in the school power structure; and running student discussion groups on relationships that promote higher moral reasoning and media literacy.

Armed with the proper education and support, the urban school counselor carries out these professional skills. What is most valuable, however, is the counselor's mindful awareness, the ability to hold a variety of contradictory thoughts and feelings at the same time, and to continue to act on what is right. He or she can be sensitive to the despair of people's lives and bothered by the social injustice that shortchanges students' access to quality education, all the while working with a calm, centered presence of mind and striving to create a realm of safety and compassion. Mindful counselors give from a full cup and also know how to replenish themselves.

Counselors choose not to operate from a deficit model that emphasizes people's limitations or focuses on mental pathology. Rather, counselors today help school communities and their members evaluate their strengths and resources. They encourage them to put forth a more evolved, positive vision of creativity, health, and happiness and to make it happen (Kessler, 2000). Despite many obstacles, most urban citizens the world over understand the value of quality education and desire it for their children.

For urban citizens to survive within and evolve from their complex urban matrix, a new order of school counselor is called for, one who embodies a more advanced, comprehensive consciousness and way of being. Gone is the image of the counselor who sits in the guidance office waiting for the principal to refer students for individual counseling or whose main task was to track students into vocational slots or perform class scheduling. In today's world, simple chores have given way to multitasking. Linear, print-media learning is being challenged by instant information that is targeted to whole-body, affective, and sensory processing. Those who can see the larger picture and can be flexible and creative in situations characterized by considerable uncertainty are replacing narrow, technical specialists. Proper education and support are required to bring these counselors into being.

Urban school counselors then must be encouraged to develop the capacity for higher-order, whole-brain thought and action. Rather than be captives of authority's agenda, they become the inventors of their work and creatively initiate and collaborate with members of the school community to create a common vision (Kegan, 1994). This requires that they embody a well-developed synthesis of conceptual, emotional, and interpersonal skills.

Counselors must be knowledgeable about the demands and limitations of academic standards and accountability issues, have insight into and facility with contemporary youth culture and the wider popular culture, have a working knowledge of parents' traditional cultural and class values, know how to read a student's body language as well as a report card, work with others to advocate for quality education for all, and have the capacity to listen to and help people learn to deal with feelings of anger, pain, and sorrow. In most cases they must do these things within a school that is poorly staffed, underfunded, lacking in essential supplies and equipment, and situated within a community where parents unfamiliar with school collaboration struggle on a day-to-day basis to survive.

With proper education in mindful urban counseling, counselors can best do all this in a conscious way. They move from one level of awareness to the next without getting stuck at any one place, all the while maintaining a vision of the whole. The counselor commits to being aware of his or her own experience at each moment. This means being open to the present and being fully present with each task and with the person before them. A contemplative educator, Judith Simmer-Brown (1999), suggests that in this approach one tolerates ambiguity and sets aside conceptual presuppositions about the other person. Such a stance, she says, relies on "the willingness to drop theory in order to experience more fully the actual flow of what one knows" (p. 105). With this presence of mind the counselor can be open to what is needed for all. He or she can avoid overidentification with one way of thinking or acting and maximize his or her capacity for compassion without burning out.

A mindful, open approach to experience is necessary in order for the counselor, or any educator, to be fully responsive and proactive. Without this openness to the living, changing nature of a school culture, everyday rituals and interactions become empty, deadened, and rigidified. Schools lapse into stupefied patterns. Individuals are not perceived as developing and changing beings but are cast in unbreakable molds: This child is the bright, successful student; this one is the loser and troublemaker. Learning, instead of being a vibrant process of wonderment, creativity, and exploration, is transformed into rote memorization and facts divorced from living relationships and nature.

Even reforms and innovative programs, if a spirit of presence does not embody them, become old and tired and lead to further despair. They become externalized fixes that reinforce the thinking that a new commodity or method is the answer, rather than cultivation of the courage to be aware of what is going on now. Without a mindful presence, purported solutions embodied by new curricular packages and programs, and even practice itself, become meaningless responses to the emptiness that much of urban education fosters in the first place. Unmindful program reform, by ignoring the living moment, prevents examining how people experience the meaning of what they are doing.

For example, Glickman (2003) suggests that successful schools are ones that regard themselves as sacred ground:

> These schools are not simply composites of classrooms, kind teachers, expansive hallways, and organized schedules. Instead, each school's attitude, purpose, activities, rituals, and demonstrations of student achievement have created an intergenerational institution of sacredness founded on democratic ideals. And within each of these schools, powerful symbols of progressive education live on in those who have participated in it. (p. 2)

Glickman describes some of these schools' rituals, stories, symbols, and ceremonies. For example, students in one school gather in a morning circle in which they share their work or provide support. Another school created a quilt that shows the history of its community. In a small, wealthy school at the end of the year, everyone participates in a ritual in which they place notes expressing feelings such as sadness, anger, and regret on a boat that then floats away down a river.

However, it would be a mistake for an educator to assume that one can pick and choose from this list and apply one or more of the examples to one's own school. The point is, as Glickman says (but does not emphasize), these activities connect with the heart and soul of the school's students over generations. They are alive because they continue to speak to the inner meaning of the members of the school community. Glickman, however, does not mention the need to be mindful of how these rituals are done, whether they are performed with a full heart, and he leads the reader to assume that practicing such rituals by themselves can contribute to educational improvement. But what happens when rituals are practiced in a mechanical way and when the participants experience them as empty and meaningless rather than sacred? How does the school address this issue and connect everyday rituals with the inner lives of the participants?

The inner life is a realm with which the urban school counselor is most familiar and for which he or she is most qualified to serve as guide. In this inner space the counselor promotes the quality of everyday learning and guards and nurtures the intrinsic meaning of education, which is nothing less than full human transformation. It is also here, in schools with paint-peeling halls, broken water fountains, and shabby libraries—schools surrounded by abandoned buildings and junk-filled lots, whose yards serve as recruiting stations for gang members— that the sacred act of learning and growing with others, for now, must occur.

Transforming Everyday School Life

Imagine that we have been following around an urban middle school counselor, Ms. Smith, for a day with a video camera, then freeze-frame a certain moment. Here is what we might see:

Ms. Smith is down the hall from her office talking with a new teacher, Ms. Brown, just outside Ms. Brown's classroom.

A student, Jason, walking past Ms. Smith and Ms. Brown in the hall, is calling another student a "faggot."

A student, Olga, thirteen, is waiting outside Ms. Smith's office to speak with her.

Inside Ms. Smith's office, the phone has lit up; it's the assistant principal, Mr. Jones.

A sign behind Ms. Smith and Ms. Brown announces a peer mediation group run by Ms. Smith, which is to start in a few minutes.

What follows is a deconstruction of these scenes, what the camera doesn't show us. It is the inner meaning of what the counselor does, which is both context dependent and illuminated by the mindful presence of Ms. Smith:

Ms. Smith is talking with a new teacher, Ms. Brown.

Counselors consult with teachers. They help them with classroom management issues and with individual students, some of whom the teacher refers to the counselor for assistance. In urban schools, there are a number of rigid, cynical, exhausted teachers waiting to retire. Some are also skeptical that children of color or those who need English language skills can learn much. Counselors can provide these teachers with empathy regarding their feelings of frustration and unhappiness. They then need to challenge them: If such teachers first feel heard and understood, they are more likely to be open to considering how their thinking and actions are not only toxic to themselves but harmful to the children. Counselors can try to get the teachers to consider other ways of thinking about the students and to offer them practical alternatives that work for both the teacher and the students.

There are also many new, idealistic teachers faced with scarce resources and overcrowded classrooms who are in danger of falling into despair and quitting. Their initial enthusiasm, creativity, and concern for children need to be rekindled. A counselor also would work with these teachers to provide them with support, encouragement, and a compassionate ear along with useful suggestions.

In this case Ms. Brown, a new teacher, has been seeking advice from Ms. Smith about classroom management. She has lessons to teach and test scores to improve and has been struggling with feeling frustrated and demoralized. In the beginning of the year the students' behavior ranged from sullen, bored, and alienated to angry, aggressive, and hyperactive.

Ms. Smith has been working with Ms. Brown on setting up a more responsive classroom. If the teacher can create a climate that addresses and meets more of the students' developmental and emotional needs, they are more likely to settle in and learn better. Ms. Smith has suggested that Ms. Brown adopt some group counseling skills within her classroom. As a result the students and Ms. Brown meet for a few minutes at the beginning of each class. They have established some rituals for greeting each other and for checking in on how they are feeling and sharing some news. Ms. Brown is open to Ms. Smith's suggestion that she create a time to make the classroom a sacred space, where even for a short time the children can know what it's like to feel safe and practice being at peace. Ms. Brown is experimenting with setting up an agreement about how the class will conduct itself with input from the students.

The students have begun to feel that they are being taken more seriously and that Ms. Brown cares about them. There have been fewer fights and disruptions. Ms. Brown has been able to lighten up and share in some of the students' humor. Ms. Smith cautions Ms. Brown, however, to go only as far as she and the students feel comfortable and safe with going. Not all students are at the same emotional level. Some cannot handle a certain level of disclosure and require highly structured, limited activities. Ms. Smith also encourages Ms. Brown to seek support from other colleagues as well.

Ms. Smith is also helping Ms. Brown find ways of connecting the course material with the students' lives: using the content of relevant rap songs for lessons related to social studies and writing, doing oral history projects with students' family members and neighbors, having the students keep a journal. Ms. Brown is considering Ms. Smith's suggestion that the students do more small-group work in which they are given a problem and are required to solve it with others.

Ms. Brown is puzzled by these early adolescents' self-consciousness and self-centeredness as well as their slavish conformity to peers. Ms. Smith encourages Ms. Brown to reflect back on her own early adolescence and reconnect with some of her own feelings of uncertainty, insecurity, and need for approval. More than just promoting different pedagogical techniques, she hopes that Ms. Brown can maintain her own sense of compassion. Doing so would allow her to reach out to her students and create a more meaningful and effective learning experience for everyone.

A student, Jason, walking past calls another student a "faggot."

Ms. Smith overhears the comment and stops talking with Ms. Brown. Ms. Brown has also heard it and rolls her eyes. "They're at that all the time," Ms. Brown says. "I've gotten to the point where I ignore it. It's like, what can you do? That's just what they say."

Ms. Smith, however, stops Jason and asks to speak with him. Because she has previously established an informal relationship with him by visiting his classrooms and engaging him and his classmates in discussions, it is easier for Ms. Smith to ask him to please come over. She walks a few feet down the hall with Jason away from Ms. Brown in order not to embarrass him.

"I'm not happy about hearing you call another student a hurtful name," Ms. Smith says. "What does the word mean to you?"

Jason says it's no big deal, all the students say it all the time. "It doesn't even means the kid's gay, it's just a word we use," he tells her.

"That's part of the problem," Ms. Smith says. "It is a harmful word. It hurts kids who are gay and have a right to be who they are. It also hurts straight guys because then they don't dare act in any way that might invite the name: no crying, no showing you feel hurt by anything, no hugging…" Ms. Smith stops herself and realizes she doesn't want to give a moral lecture, especially in the hall, to a captive audience of one squirming to escape.

"Think about it," she tells Jason.

Ms. Smith is concerned about not letting the school lapse into an unsafe, uncaring place, where people are unconscious of and indifferent to the thousand daily taunts, humiliations, and injustices that happen in the blink of an eye but that over time can generate incremental wounds. Unlike Ms. Brown, she is trying to not let the little hurtful acts go unnoticed, but neither does she wish to be repressive, judgmental, and hurtful in turn. Ms. Smith realizes at that moment that she cannot do this by herself and would be foolish to try. The problem also needs to be tackled at an earlier phase by leading discussions on this issue in the classrooms and possibly even in assemblies and workshops. The entire school needs to think about how everyone treats each other but in a safe, compassionate, respectful format, not in a harsh, punitive, moralistic one. Administrators, teachers, and staff as well need to be mindful of what kinds of messages they send when they speak and act in certain ways.

It is not a matter of repressing language or of being politically correct; that kind of rigid, zero-tolerance policy tends to backfire and create further acting out. A repressive approach relies on external fixes: Certain words are forbidden; punishment must be meted out and policies enforced regardless of the circumstances, as if that solves the problem of consciousness. For some, strong rules and policies are necessary and do provide a measure of safety and security for the school community. Still, Ms. Smith knows, there is a need to place the issue within a larger discussion, one that speaks to the heart of children's concerns and anxieties about gender identity, sexuality, acceptance from one's peers and oneself, and the need to feel safe. She promises herself that she will gather a task force of other school staff members, students, and parents to address the issue in a mindful way.

A student, Olga, thirteen, is waiting to speak with Ms. Smith.

Olga's English teacher referred her to Ms. Smith last week. Olga was acting aggressively toward other girls, and for an assigned composition she had written a story about a girl who self-destructs. The teacher has told Ms. Smith that Olga is very bright and speaks up in class. Ms. Smith has seen Olga once and scheduled her for a session tomorrow but told Olga to contact her if she needed to speak with her before then. Olga is hoping to catch Ms. Smith for a few minutes between periods.

Ms. Smith brings Olga inside her office and shuts the door. She tells her she has a few minutes now and gives Olga her undivided attention.

Olga is upset. This morning she had a fight with her mother, an immigrant from the Dominican Republic. Her mother has become mean and strict, she says. She won't let her stay with her friends after school. The mother is dating a man who deals drugs and whom Olga dislikes. Olga's father is in the Dominican Republic and she misses him, but her mother makes it difficult for her to contact him, she says. She begins to cry.

Ms. Smith directs her entire presence toward Olga. She turns her body toward her and listens with an open heart and a full intent to understand her. Ms. Smith knows that very few children, or even adults, receive the luxury of this kind of non-judgmental attentiveness, if even for a short time. Children in particular are sensitive to adults' cycles of attentiveness. Children require quality attention in order to thrive. Many adults are themselves distracted and unable to be with themselves in the present, let alone share this kind of presence with another. To make matters worse, many adults maintain their power over children by manipulating their attention, by focusing and then withdrawing their interest, and children are at their mercy in this regard. The Buddhist peace activist Thich Nhat Hanh encourages the practice of mindful listening in everyday life. He says that we often unintentionally harm those whom we love when we pay them only half a mind when they are speaking to us. Every time we tune out those we love, we destroy a piece of our relationship. We can understand that it is altogether easy to lapse into this habit amidst the infinite distractions of our complex lives; it is harder to set things aside and be in the present with someone. Yet it is a true way to establish and maintain genuine connections with others.

Olga senses that Ms. Smith is there for her. She relaxes somewhat and her breathing begins to slow. When Olga begins to cry, Ms. Smith hands her a tissue. She sees that Olga has a lot of things with which to contend in her life, involving her family, peers, school, and her sense of self.

"It hurts that you miss your *papi*," Ms. Smith says. "I wonder if you also miss your *mami* too."

Olga looks puzzled and says she doesn't know what Ms. Smith means; she's with her mother every day.

Ms. Smith suggests that Olga and her mother were probably once a lot closer. Now that Olga is growing up, she spends less time with her mother, who also has a new boyfriend.

Olga thinks about it. "That's true," she says. "It's different now."

Ms. Smith ventures to say that it's possible that her mother also misses Olga, her little girl, and still wants to keep her the way she was when she was younger. But she doesn't know how to act toward this young woman anymore. Her mother has already gone through some loss by moving here from her country.

Olga thinks about this too. Ms. Smith is cultivating Olga's sense of empathy and compassion, her ability to see others' points of view. But by the same token, she also encourages her to develop her own perspective, something that many girls begin to lose in favor of pleasing others. Ms. Smith tells Olga that she would like to invite her mother to come in for a family counseling session. Olga agrees to this. Ms. Smith tells her that she will see her tomorrow when they can talk more about her family situation. She also wants to speak with Olga about her work in school; she wants Olga to begin thinking about a good high school next year so she can prepare to go to college. She tells Olga about a group she is setting up for other girls and invites her to join it. Ms. Smith has seen a number of young women in the school act harshly toward their own self-image and toward others, and has heard them say that they are too fat and worry that they are not good enough to have a boyfriend. Ms. Smith also has seen many children of immigrant families struggle with establishing their autonomy, and rebelling against the traditional values their families hold. She wants to address this issue in her groups as well.

When it is time for Olga to go, Ms. Smith says to her, "You have a right to be happy." Olga smiles for the first time. Personal joy is not a luxury, Ms. Smith believes; it is a basic entitlement, no less for these children.

The phone is lit up in Ms. Smith's office; the assistant principal, Mr. Jones, is calling.

Mr. Jones oversees the school counselors. Because Ms. Smith is with a client, Olga, she does not pick up the phone and lets it take a message. She will call Mr. Jones back as soon as possible.

Over the course of her own development Ms. Smith has had to work hard to set limits on her time and efforts. She is better at it now, but it is still not a simple matter. There are many needy people in the school, and they each have good need of Ms. Smith's skills. If Ms. Smith were not mindful, she would run around all day, drop everything, and try to accommodate everyone. When she was younger, Ms. Smith had the tendency to do just that. At an earlier job, she had trouble saying no and maintaining boundaries. She soon became resentful of many of her colleagues and her clients. She often would come down with colds; her body was telling her she needed to do something to take care of herself but she didn't listen. Each time she returned to work, she was unable to change her pattern and soon found herself falling even more behind in her work; she was on the verge of burning out. Soon after, Ms. Smith went back to school and studied mindful urban school counseling.

From her counseling education program, Ms. Smith has learned to set appropriate limits with Mr. Jones and others. At times Mr. Jones has entered her office when the door was closed and she was meeting with a student, teacher, or even a family. She has spoken to him about this. She makes sure she closes the door and places a sign out front. She takes time for lunch as well; even the pop psychology books, she reminds herself, tell you that you're no good to others if you're no good to yourself. Mr. Jones has many crises; if he is short-staffed at times, he has felt that Ms. Smith needs to drop everything and substitute for the person who is absent. Ms. Smith has told Mr. Jones that she is willing to brainstorm other ways to help him solve his staffing shortage and to do some preventive planning to minimize the administration's lurching from one crisis to the next.

Mr. Jones pushes some of Ms. Smith's (emotional) buttons. He can be disrespectful and throws his weight around. He represents some of the narrow, bureaucratic values that Ms. Smith hopes the school will move beyond: a taste for petty and rigid displays of power, a penchant for seeing students as numbers rather than people, and an insensitivity and lack of awareness of the cultural background of many of the students. Ms. Smith has worked at being mindful of her feelings of irritability toward Mr. Jones. She has noticed that he is the kind of authoritarian male with whom she grew up in her family. She has tried to become aware of any negative thoughts or feelings that arise when she interacts with him, to acknowledge them, then breathe and let them go. She realizes she is the one with the problem and decided that she did not want to live with aggravation and give anyone that kind of power over her well-being and state of mind.

Over the course of time she has noticed that Mr. Jones has less of an effect on her equanimity. She also has come to better understand his way of thinking and the values he holds and has even developed some compassion for him. After all, he is under considerable pressure from administrators to raise test scores and to improve school attendance. She sees that he is hard on himself as well as others and does not seem to be a happy person. She also has noticed that some of the boys respond positively to his style and approach. They appreciate the clear structure and no-nonsense version of right and wrong he provides, his emphasis on a work ethic with its promise of rewards to come, and his gruff but at times playful demeanor.

Ms. Smith calls Mr. Jones back. He is tense over the phone. Mr. Jones has an upcoming deadline for a report, and he needs input from Ms. Smith. He needs numbers, research-backed data that show that the school is improving. The principal is on him, he tells her; he feels like the principal, the district superintendent, the city chancellor, the state commissioner all want a piece of his hide.

"I'm sorry to hear that," Ms. Smith says. "I know you're working hard, and it sounds like these folks don't appreciate your efforts."

Mr. Jones thanks her. He slows down a bit and asks her when she can get in her part of the report. Ms. Smith tells him, "You'll have it on your desk by the end of the week, before Monday's deadline." Mr. Jones is happy about that, and the way Ms. Smith put it somehow makes him feel more reassured. Ms. Smith has been working on ways she can help the school improve test scores and decrease truancy. She did some action research projects in which she collected data before and after implementing some counseling programs. She was able to show that involving the students and parents in certain school projects contributed to better test scores and higher attendance. In this case Ms. Smith had worked to ensure that her own motives dovetailed with those of the administration: By generating data she was establishing her own successful track record in order to justify funding and support for more counseling programs.

Ms. Smith asks about Mr. Jones's family. Mr. Jones waxes effusive about his son's first year at college and his daughter's grades in high school. Before hanging up, Ms. Smith asks Mr. Jones if he would consider following up on a concern of hers. She has been getting reports from some of the younger students that some of the eighth graders are fondling each other and possibly engaging in sexual activity in certain stairwells between classes. She asks that he follow up on this and coordinate an effort among the teachers, custodians, and guards to step up more hall monitoring. On her end Ms. Smith says she would like to identify some of the eighth graders and run a classroom workshop and a more extended group for them on sexuality, intimacy, and relationships. Mr. Jones agrees to act on her request.

Ms. Smith runs a peer mediation group.

The peer mediation group is one of Ms. Smith's favorite projects. Teachers and administrators require students who get into fights to appear before the group, which then helps decide how to resolve the conflict. Of late more students are referring themselves, a sign that students respect the group and find it helpful. A number of the boys and girls are popular leaders who were elected by their classmates to the group. They take the group seriously and already have had an impact on the overall climate of the school.

The group on occasion meets on its own without adjudicating a conflict. Ms. Smith has noticed that there are two dominant trends of thinking among the group that coexist but sometimes are in conflict. Both are of a higher-order level. One tendency emphasizes communal values. These students feel strongly that everyone is equal and has a right to be heard, that people who are different should be accepted, and that consensus and collaboration are necessary. Sometimes, however, the communally oriented students get too worked up about their principles and end up rigidly advancing them: No one can be better than anyone in anything; all differences are good and equal; everyone must participate; we must share everything; we must agree on everything; no one can be confronted, because it hurts their feelings.

The second tendency is more individualistic. These students feel that there are standards for success and that some individuals deserve more than others due to their hard work and mastery. They feel that a person's knowledge and abilities rather than consensus should determine who gets what. There are winners and losers, and people should be willing to compete; the winners get the goods, and the losers take their lumps if necessary. The individualists, in turn, sometimes adopt a greedy and selfish take on things. At times they insist on individual self-interest, calculation, and domination at the expense of moral obligation to others.

Today, two boys are appearing before the group. Both are on the basketball team and keep getting into fights. A teacher who is their head coach sent them to the peer mediation group. They both are egocentric and have limited ability to see another's viewpoint. They take every slight personally and can think only in terms of revenge and retaliation.

After hearing the two boys' sides of the story, those peer mediators who value a more communal approach suggest that the two continue to talk it out until they reach a mutual agreement about how to get along. The young men do not know how to do this; the strategy fails and gets them nowhere. The more individualistically inclined mediators encourage the two boys to make their best argument about why each one is right and let the best one win. This serves to rekindle their animosity and power struggle.

Ms. Smith intervenes. She realizes that the young men's level of development is such that they cannot yet do what either of the mediator positions suggests. They are in need of a more structured arbitration. Ms. Smith summons the group privately and tells them that they will have to serve as the external authority for these young men. She asks them by what social order or rule these two would best comply and why. After some discussion the group concludes that the two would feel guilty if they let their basketball teammates down; they are to be ordered to stop fighting for the sake of the team and even the entire school, which is rooting for them. The young men appear relieved. It is out of their hands, and they accept the decision.

In this case Ms. Smith is attuned both to what the young men and the group are able to understand and to what is needed. She realizes that the boys do not have enough autonomous ego strength or internalized social constraints to resolve their conflicts. They require a more structured social order to keep them in line. The factions within her mediation group, while operating at higher levels, still tend to think that their way is the only right one. From her perch atop the whole developmental spiral, Ms. Smith maintains an overview of everyone involved. She is flexible enough to move up and down through the various levels of awareness as required in order to maximize the students' growth.

Conclusion

Urban school communities and their members face difficult conditions and are in need of care. They require a new kind of counselor who is wise and compassionate, one who can visualize the entire multidimensional interplay of the system and creatively work within it for the full benefit of all its citizens. Such counselors themselves need support and specialized education in the complexities of an urban system, in understanding and working with all developmental levels of consciousness, and in mindfulness-based counseling. As higher-order "wizards," mindful urban school counselors can then help promote individual and communal development, academic and personal growth, and order and creativity all together. Such counselors bring about true knowledge because they understand and speak to the heart of what matters and are attuned to the wonder of the present moment. Ms. Smith is out there in the schools; we need others to join her.

References

Beck, Don E., & Cowan, Christopher C. (2002). *Spiral dynamics: Mastering values, leadership, and change.* Malden, MA: Blackwell.

Educational Leadership, 60, 34-39. Website: http://www.ascd.org/publications/ed_lead/200303/glickman.html. Accessed November 7, 2003.

Glickman, Carl D. (2003). Symbols and celebrations that sustain education.

Goleman, Daniel (2003). *Destructive emotions: How can we overcome them? A scientific dialogue with the Dalai Lama.* New York: Bantam.

Kegan, Robert (1994). *In over our heads: The mental demands of modern life.* Cambridge, MA: Harvard University Press.

Kessler, Rachael (2000). *The soul of education: Helping students find connection, compassion, and character at school.* Alexandria, VA: Association for Supervision and Curriculum Development.

Miller, Ron (1997). *What are schools for? Holistic education in American culture.* Brandon, VT: Holistic Education.

Simmer-Brown, Judith (1999). Commitment and openness: A contemplative approach to pluralism. In S. Glazer (Ed.), *The heart of learning: Spirituality in education* (pp. 97-112). New York: Tarcher/Putnam.

Luis F. Mirón

CHAPTER SIX

How Do We Locate Resistance in Urban Schools?

Like most institutions funded with taxpayer monies, public schools must honor the laws of the country. Beginning with passage of the Civil Rights Act of 1964, discrimination because of race, ethnicity, gender, sexuality, or religion has become forbidden. For example, it is against the law for any public school or university to deny admission to immigrants (legal or illegal) because of their noncitizen status. However, many building administrators and classroom teachers believe that if they follow the guidelines of federal laws, their schools will be protected from discrimination, racism, and prejudice. Educators assume that by following the letter of the law, the spirit of the law will be honored and respected. Research and knowledge of professional practice tell us differently. More precisely dejure desegregation is equated with educational equality.

Desegregation of Little Rock, Arkansas, public schools after the passage of the historic *Brown v. Board of Education* decision unleashed nearly a half century of externally generated reforms of urban public schools. Today public schools are situated differently as the global political economy, and the worldwide concentration of capital in particular, has caused a host of demographic and other pressures on urban schools (see Lipman, 2002). Urban schools are now resegregated and notoriously underfunded in comparison with their more affluent suburban counterparts. Furthermore, they are perhaps somewhat academically weakened owing in part to the influx of immigrant populations who arrive with limited English, low family incomes, and a lack of cultural support for learning. This context is similar to the historical circumstances of inner-city schools serving poor students of color; however, I want to argue that the pressures are exacerbated with waves of immigration from Mexico and Latin America as well as the heavy-handed role of the state in exacting academic standards.

Between 1993 and 1998, I conducted a qualitative study of four public inner-city high schools enrolling large percentages of students from ethnic and language minority groups in New Orleans. The study consisted of approximately 50 interviews with students lasting between 30 and 90 minutes (Mirón, 1996; Lauria & Mirón, 2004). In these interviews I sought to ascertain the extent to which students from similar socioeconomic backgrounds and varying school cultures (magnet vs. neighborhood) and with different levels of academic success (A's and B's vs. C's and D's) expressed widespread "resistance" to both the formal and the hidden curriculum and to pedagogical practices.

Drawing upon this research, I will attempt to answer the question, of how students resist in urban schools. In addition I summarize important demographic data on educational inequality in Chicago to provide a comparative glimpse of substantial contextual issues found in the majority of urban schools and districts nationwide. I begin by addressing the uniqueness of the urban school "problem."

Are Urban Schools Different?

Inner-city schools are different. Lipman (2002, pp. 385–389) paints a rich picture of public education in Chicago, the "dual city." As Chicago strives to become a "global city" like Los Angeles and New York, academic and social inequalities have deepened. Lipman cites the often-noted economic shift in the United States from a manufacturing to a service and knowledge base. As a result the country has a "highly segmented and increasingly polarized labor force." Lipman states that service jobs, for instance, are highly segmented by wage/salary levels, education, and benefits. Growth in highly skilled technical, professional, and managerial jobs at the high end are dominated by white males, while an abundance of low-end, low-skilled jobs are held mostly by women and people of color.

In addition, Lipman notes the widespread expansion of contingent, provisional labor: multitask, part-time, and temporary work performed mainly by women, workers of color, and immigrants who often hold down two, three, and even four jobs to make ends meet. A quickly growing informal economy employs primarily immigrant and women workers who provide specialized consumer goods and services for the well-to-do (designer clothing and live-in child care) and cheap goods and services for poor or lower-income households (e.g., unlicensed day care). He claims that there is little opportunity for gainful employment in the formal economy for large sectors of the population, specifically African American and Latino youth.

Paradoxically, as the global economy grows and capitalism intensifies, economic and social inequalities widen. For instance, the overwhelming majority of new jobs pay lower wages and offer less protection (heath insurance, pensions). Between

1973 and 1995 real average weekly wages for production and nonsupervisory workers decreased from approximately $480 to $395. More dramatically, the wealthiest 1 percent of households increased their wealth by 28 percent from 1983 to 1992, while the bottom 40 percent saw their income decrease by nearly 50 percent.

Like most "global cities," Chicago has experienced widening inequalities that are mirrored in geography. These social and economic inequalities, moreover, are vividly illustrated in the move to gentrify old neighborhoods with expensive upscale housing and restaurants, high-tech employment, and (central to our goals here) academically achieving public schools. (Although the site of my research [see Lauria & Mirón, 2004] is not a "global city," it too is not immune to the processes and effects of globalization.) These escalating inequalities linked to the worldwide consolidation of capital have been well documented. I argue that it is the intensification of educational inequality, on a meta level, that inner-city high school students most resist and resent. The processes of globalization deny them access to a quality education and thus the possibility of social mobility.

How does the global economy produce educational inequality?

Using secondary sources, Lipman (2002) documents the economic shift in Chicago from manufacturing to service/information employment. From 1967 to 1990, the number of jobs in manufacturing fell an astounding 41 percent, from a total of 546,500 to 216,190. In comparison, nonmanufacturing jobs rose by an equally impressive 59 percent, from 797,867 to 983,580. Most significantly, as the *Chicago Tribune* reported in 1999, the trend saw manufacturing employment with average salaries of $37,000 being replaced by service jobs whose wages paid only $26,000. Because 23 percent of workers in the city belong to a union, the impact on the working class has been even more severe, often resulting in the loss of health insurance and retirement benefits. This economic transformation led to what Lipman refers to as the "production of educational inequality."

In brief, the efforts of two generations of rule by the Daleys (Richard Daley Jr. was recently reelected to a third term) have resulted in the marketing of Chicago as a "world class" city that attracts businesses in the new knowledge economy. In order to "sell" the city to affluent and well-educated professionals who will staff the kinds of firms the city covets, Chicago has embarked on the most ambitious urban school reform agenda in the nation. This reform agenda, moreover, has created a system of high-stakes testing and accountability, college preparatory "magnet schools" as well as remedial high schools, and a pedagogical culture that rewards achievement on standardized tests. For example, in some of the schools in Lipman's study, nearly two months of the academic year were spent in preparation for tests, complete with cheerleading and pep (or prep?) rallies. These everyday practices are being reproduced in urban school districts besieged by underachievement all over the country.

The New Orleans Experience:
From Political Resistance to Political Agency

Unlike previous scholarly notions of resistance, the concept demonstrated in my work extends beyond mere moments in time or simple expressions of acting out. Resistance involves a discourse practice that is an expression of human agency. This expression may take the form of political agency. The question that ensues is, How can human agency become transformed into political agency? In this section I would like to outline a new conception of how a return to the political may develop. But first I need to sketch in broad strokes the conceptual (sociological) underpinnings of this move.

Social Structures

Sociologists have long indicated that social structures serve a dual function. At their heart is an understanding that they exist interactively with human agents. Social structures both (1) constrain the actions that agents can perform and (2) provide the space to act. This includes political (collective) actions. For example, social structures are neither organic, self-regulating systems nor freewheeling spaces where agents can roam without rules. The point is that structures are products of history—people acting in behalf of their beliefs—and, once constructed, tend to re-create themselves time and time again. So where do resistance and political agency come into play within this conception?

More likely to employ passive resistance, inner-city students in particular seem to lack the capacity to exercise political agency. Subjected in many instances to a prescripted curriculum and pedagogy, they lack cultural and historical knowledge of their social situation, their "situatedness." For example, many students I interviewed in the neighborhood high schools in New Orleans were unaware of how construction of interstate highways through the city in the 1950s devastated local communities and residential neighborhoods. People and families were displaced. On the other hand, inner-city students from approximately the same socioeconomic backgrounds enrolled in magnet schools were treated to a rich curriculum emphasizing cultural diversity, oral history, and writing programs that placed students at the center of pedagogy. Therefore, given a curriculum and instructional practices that ignore students' lived cultural experiences and history, political agency is almost nil. Social reproduction happens. Students do, however, resist these structures. I argue that this form of resistance largely results in high school students disengaging from school, often dropping out or, as the data indicate below, accommodating to teachers' busywork. Though these forms of resistance may seem similar on the surface, we should bear in mind that a strategy of accommodation leading to leaving school versus remaining in school—and choosing to graduate—obviously has different outcomes and should be kept analytically separate.

Inner-city students armed with culturally relevant knowledge and coming out of a school culture that places a premium on racial/ethnic pride are more free to act. They possess the capacity to exercise political agency, which means that in cities like Chicago and New Orleans, they can petition local school boards to establish schools such as Roberto Clemente High School, serving Puerto Rican students in Chicago, and programs like "Students at the Center" at McDonough #35 magnet high school in New Orleans, a writing program built on oral history and creative arts. Such students learn to view inner-city high schools as vehicles for local community development and lobby the school board to enact these curricular models in other high schools as antidotes to dropping out of school or, worse, incarceration.

It was not unreasonable to predict such intense student resistance, because the setting of our study—an urban center beset by economic restructuring and a sagging tourist economy—left high school graduates few prospects for employment besides working in fast-food restaurants or busing tables in one of the area's numerous upscale eateries. In short, high school students had few viable career options and thus little incentive to do well in school. Surprisingly, what my colleagues and I found was that all the students we interviewed were highly motivated to graduate from high school—many of them aspired to attend college. There was, indeed, student resistance; however, the forms of student resistance varied to a certain degree by the form of school organization and culture. At times, forms of resistance converged. In general, student resistance in this urban center characterized at the time by widespread poverty, illiteracy, and violent crime was directly tied to students' perceptions of their teachers' academic expectations and everyday practices of racial stereotyping.

For instance, African American high school students in particular often complained that teachers believed that all Asian American students (e.g., upper-class Vietnamese) were intelligent and highly motivated and enjoyed strong family support for learning. By contrast, African Americans (especially males) were seen as mostly hoodlums and disinterested in learning. Moreover, some of these students complained that the principals shut down student assemblies and cultural activities. In hopes of curbing actual and perceived student violence, school administrators disbanded clubs and organizations. On the other hand, students enrolled in college preparatory magnet schools (see Lauria & Mirón, 2004; Mirón, 1996) took pride in the caring school atmosphere, the challenging curriculum, and rich extracurricular opportunities. I call this pedagogical phenomenon *academic discrimination*. Furthermore, the kinds of student resistance I will disclose below are based on high school students' relationship to this form of discrimination and institutional racism, especially their perceived capacity for human agency, expressions of student voice, and their own representations of racial/ethnic identities.

Prototypes of Student Resistance

Based on the student interview data, students manifested two broad strategies of resistance: accommodation and mobilization. These strategies of resistance, moreover, were direct responses to students' relationship to the formal and hidden curricula. As we gleaned from the ethnographic interviews, their overall goal in both of these kinds of strategies of resistance was to secure their right to a quality education (Mirón & Lauria, 1998, p. 191).

What is most striking is that, like the Chicago school reform summarized above, school cultures matter. In magnet schools in New Orleans, generally characterized by an emphasis on "diversity," the curriculum differed sharply from that of the neighborhood public schools. In the magnet schools, we found a culturally relevant curriculum and a sense of racial/ethnic pride. On the other hand, students in neighborhood schools were seemingly denied a quality education owing primarily to a curriculum that emphasized busywork and a lack of student voice. The intensity of student resistance, moreover, as will be disclosed below, largely depended on the type of school organization and corresponding everyday lived culture. Urban students' capacity for agency—the ability to act on perceived alternatives—closely paralled the form of resistance.

Accommodation

For students at the magnet schools, accommodation meant being fully engaged in the rich formal curriculum, a sense of racial/ethnic pride, and a broad array of student activities. These students perceived the school-based activities as connecting them to the wider society by providing them with practical social skills as well as instruction in global affairs. In other words, their teachers made explicit connections between local context and the processes of globalization. Furthermore, teachers, administrators, and counselors fostered student voice, in the process "authorizing" students to have a role in curriculum policy and engaging them in the mission and cultural traditions of magnet schools. Students perceived that these connections protected them from the callousness of the outside world, a societal attitude that reduced African American males in particular to a nameless statistic.

By contrast, the widespread curtailment of student assemblies, organizations, and clubs obviously hindered student voice at the neighborhood secondary schools. There, a school climate existed that systematically disengaged students from the curriculum and from the broader school culture more generally. Some of these students enrolled in neighborhood schools employed a form of passive resistance, telling the interviewers that they "did what they had to do to get by." These students were not "silenced" and they were obviously not pushed out of school, as they maintained passing averages by the end of the year. Following Anthony Giddens' theory of structuration, I want to argue that these students were not merely passive victims. Just the reverse was true: They made the decision to remain in school and graduate, thus at least securing the possibility, however limited, that they could improve their life chances.

Mobilization

All of the students we interviewed made an important strategic decision: to remain in high school. I say that this was a *decision* because, at least in the neighborhood schools, there were keen pressures to disengage stemming from the low expectations of teachers, peers, and administrators. As I stated earlier, as researchers we tacitly bought into lowered expectations when we believed students would show evidence of giving up on school for economic reasons. Just the reverse turned out to be true. I argue that this decision represents a kind of human agency. At times this converts into political agency.

Deciding to remain in inner-city public high schools, despite a weak economy, constitutes a discourse practice. Most of the neighborhood students would voice this discourse as an "antagonism" expressed to the researchers. There was little opportunity to organize collectively, as leadership practices astutely separated students from one another, in effect enacting an extreme psychological paradigm of learning. Other students, however, mobilized on behalf of their civil rights, which they perceived entitled them to access to a quality education. In other words, they formed strategic alliances with parents, school board members, and community leaders to make their demands heard on behalf of educational justice. Many of these students told us again and again: "The teacher can't take away my grades. If she does, I will tell my mama. And if my mama can't change my teacher's mind, she will take it all the way to the school board if she has to." This mobilization was grounded in a collective ideology among African Americans in New Orleans in particular that their parents' and community's struggles for civil and human rights during the Civil Rights movement of the 1950s and 60s left them with a near moral obligation to succeed academically and give something back to their local communities. At one of the magnet schools, students frequently told us, "You must remember where you came from," and, "Our teachers remind us to stand on the shoulders of those who came before us." Resistance here was clearly tied to a sense of racial/ethnic pride, respect for elders, and a collective recognition that white society was a common "enemy."

The following narratives of student resistance illustrate the prototypical forms of resistance, which at once support the capacity for political agency and vividly demonstrate how the structures of inner-city schools constrain agency. The narratives are organized by actual interview questions posed to high school students in New Orleans.

1. What is everyday life like as a student in your school?

The first question in the interview protocol of this five-year ethnographic case study asked inner-city secondary students to describe what it was like to be a student in their school. Stark differences existed between the organizational cultures of magnet vs. neighborhood high schools. Yet these differences blurred a bit as we documented how students resisted. At the neighborhood public schools, students often complained of boredom with class activities. Furthermore, the administrative practice of curtailing student assemblies ("shutdown") exacerbated boredom and isolation.

The research uncovered an unexpected finding. When we coded the interview transcripts of nearly 1,000 pages, these emotions, coupled with an apparent distrust of students by their teachers in regard to completion of homework assignments, related to the conditions of violent crime, both at school and in the local community. This is ironic given the strong regulation of student behavior. Naturally students resisted these practices and social conditions, yet the form of this resistance was voiced in accommodationist terms. As the administration in the neighborhood schools moved to shut down student assemblies and therefore preempted student voice, the students seemed to get angrier. This may have exacerbated the conditions for violent crime, an ironic unintended consequence.

> The curriculum and everything else here is way below. I used to have a 3.9 average and [at my old school] they used to motivate us better than back here. Like the teachers here really don't teach. If you get it, you get it. If you don't, you don't. Well you didn't bring up anything about violence. One week we had four fights in one day.
>
> I think the African American students are treated fairly by the administration. I mean that if they do something wrong, then they will just have to suffer the consequences. African American students treat Asian American students very differently. I mean they would make fun of them because of the language that they use. I say there is no need to do that because if you came from another country and you couldn't speak fluent English either, you wouldn't want anybody doing that to you.

There were stark contrasts at the magnet high schools. The interviewers recorded few negative comments about what it was like to be a student in this kind of urban high school. More typical was this statement:

> It's fun, exciting. You get involved with a lot of community activities…. Especially being a black male like myself, you get a lot of prestige and a lot of pushing from your teachers and the principal. And I really enjoy that, especially from the principal. It's just a sort of love here—and it really helps a lot of children.

2. What is schoolwork like?

Since we found the curriculum to be much richer at the magnet schools and the pedagogy more tuned in to community concerns as well as global affairs, I will underscore this type of school:

> To be a student here, it's a lot of hard work, but after you get the hang of it, you know it's fairly easy if you do all of your work. You have to study, and once you study and catch up and you know the work, then you can go ahead of the rest of the students. Then it would be easier for you. The teacher explains it, and then you already know it.
>
> I try very hard because at my school there are a lot of people who make very good grades—and you want to be just like those people. I find myself up some nights until 3 or 4 in the morning just studying, you know, working the material in my head.

At the magnet schools, academic work implied an application of the competitive work ethic to students' studies in order to become successful. Students appeared to learn collaboratively from and to model themselves after other students (some of whom attended the same school) and to compete with students in their ethnic group for top honors.

By contrast, students at the neighborhood high schools tended not to push themselves as much. They often told us that they "did what they had to do to get by" and to graduate. Apparently they strategically chose not to do more. Some of the students actually blamed the teachers for holding low expectations, which did not require them to work harder or learn anything of substance. They frequently complained of busywork. We gleaned from these admonishments that students at these schools do in fact desire to compete academically.

On the one hand, students at the neighborhood high schools resisted: In our interviews with them, they expressed antagonism because they perceived that they were unjustly denied a quality education. But their resistance took the form of an accommodation to the wishes of their classroom teachers, who appeared to engage in an implicit (hidden) social contract of controlling students by holding out the carrot of a passing grade and eventually a high school diploma. More precisely, this form of student resistance was tied to students' notion of agency by accepting the quid pro quo of paying attention, completing seat assignments, and especially not challenging the teacher's authority in order to just get out of there. This strategy guaranteed them, in their minds, the prerequisite of completing high school as the first step in the long pursuit of a middle-class life.

3. With whom do you identify?

In trying to understand students' behaviors and relationships at school, at home, and in their neighborhoods, we asked them if they changed behavior in each of these social environments. We wanted to know whether they were able to move comfortably among "multiple identities" that were located in different discourses, for example, between studiousness and sustained focus in school and clowning around and hanging out at home and in the neighborhood. Could students from the magnet schools, for instance, keep discursively separate who they were at school from the peer pressures of the street? The most interesting finding was that 38 percent of all students—from both types of school—felt alienated from their neighborhood (had no friends, were fearful), whereas another 38 percent felt comfortable.

These results varied inversely between the two types of school organization. Among students at the magnet schools, 58 percent felt alienated in their neighborhoods and 25 percent felt comfortable. At the neighborhood schools, 16 percent felt alienated, while 58 percent felt comfortable. Furthermore we generally expected that the dynamics of students' identity politics would play out among their friends in the neighborhood. Therefore, students of similar academic performance (A's/B's vs. C's/D's) or similar social class background would express similar degrees of affiliation and identification with the home vis-à-vis the high school. This turned out to be false. The only students we found at the neighborhood schools who felt alienated from their neighborhoods were females. Inversely the only students from the magnet schools who felt comfortable in their neighborhoods were males. Secondly, when these students enrolled in the magnet schools, they had the feeling of escaping to a safer, less chaotic social environment. This was coupled with the prevailing ideology of the magnet school, i.e., that it provides a ticket to college admission. Paradoxically the magnet schools reproduced this dominant ideology, and there too the students willingly accommodated with apparent ease.

Students in the magnet schools seemed to experience greater difficulties separating their academic identities from their personal identities. Their peers who did not attend magnet schools, which offered academically rich and culturally relevant curricula, apparently could not understand why their friends changed. This caused conflicts. On the other hand, students in neighborhood schools felt less conflicted, as their friends generally attended less challenging schools as well. Of course, these are generalizations, as there is not space in this chapter to closely examine the nuances.

The interviews disclosed that at the magnet schools, students generally felt that teachers were there to help them academically, socially, and emotionally. Teachers cared. In sharp contrast, students in the neighborhood high schools generally perceived that their teachers treated segments of the student population differently. For example, black males widely perceived that their (mostly white) teachers discriminated against them by holding lower expectations for them and stereotyping most of them as hoodlums:

> Some teachers have their favorite student, but it isn't [necessarily] racism. My teacher thinks that I'm a hoodlum or a gang member. A lot of other teachers say that, though. I hear the other teachers say that.
>
> The teachers expect more from the Vietnamese students, that they are always smarter and stuff. It's like the Vietnamese student is always smarter, and my teachers never expect a black [male] student to be smarter than a Vietnamese student, you know. They always automatically think that we're dumb.
>
> From what I know, some teachers may think that, well, if a person is white, well, they are better than the rest, you know. If another [black] student makes a higher grade, then the teacher will say, well, the white student must have had a bad day. The teachers won't put them down or announce their grade in class, or anything like that. They will just keep it to themselves and come talk with the student privately.

These interview narratives disclose the perceptions among the students in the neighborhood high schools of the authoritarian school climate. Democratic practices, to say nothing of deep racial/ethnic democracy, are apparently void. Students felt stuck "back here" in their neighborhood schools, seemingly isolated from the wider society and even from each other. "Shutdown" was the norm. However, by accommodating, going along with, their teachers, students resisted. They specifically exercised their "situated" agency and made the one strategic choice available. They chose to pass their grade level and go on to graduate. This kind of student resistance obviously differs from that characterized by Robert Everhart (1983) and others as an escape from anxieties. I argue that this form of student resistance is inherently political and, perhaps more evocatively, "collective." It begins the pedagogical move from human to more political agency.

Toward a New Urban Pedagogy

Classroom teachers in inner-city public schools, whether they are white or teachers of color, find themselves in an unenviable position. They are daily besieged by the demands of the state to lift student achievement and struggle with the social realities of widespread inequality. Despite this contradictory location, teachers must strive to become transformative intellectuals.

Their first pedagogical imperative is to foster their students' racial/ethnic identity and pride. So as not to become mired in factionalism, however, classroom teachers must demand greater awareness of the identity of "the other." During these uncertain times, knowledge of the plight of Muslims, Middle Eastern women, and oppressed populations around the world is indispensable. Why is this important?

On ethical grounds alone, classroom teachers in urban centers must find the means to resist the increasing surveillance of schooling, and perhaps more perniciously the trend toward standardization of teaching and learning. These trends are clearly linked to processes of globalization and in particular the overwhelming propensity of the nation-state to converge upon neoliberal market ideologies. On pragmatic grounds, however, teachers coalescing around broader concerns, and linking these issues to global processes and events, make their political positioning stronger. They are less vulnerable. Students and teachers are thus partners in the struggle for democracy in urban schools—sites where the appeal of the "global city," like Chicago or Los Angeles, makes imperative the regulation of student bodies and teacher pedagogy through high-stakes testing and accountability.

In this regard Henry Giroux (1983) has argued that curricula that lay bare the colonizing legacies of western Europe enable classroom teachers to transform their roles. They become cultural workers who, together with their students, "take seriously the identities of subordinate cultures" (p. 154). Public schooling for racial/ethnic minorities in inner cities, therefore, can potentially assume a counterhegemonic purpose by becoming a site for cultural politics. Though institutionally rare, there are countless examples of these transformations, such as the Roberto Clemente School and other schools serving Puerto Rican students in Chicago. These schools have implemented a critical pedagogy based on the principles of Paulo Freire. Here I want to extend Giroux's argument and assert that procedurally, only by understanding how students construct their racial/ethnic identity—and finding pedagogical space to accomplish this task—is the transformation of teachers from bankers of knowledge to cultural workers institutionally possible. Schools are sites of both meaning and morality.

A Vision of Urban Student Resistance

The resources that urban students possess, as shown in our study, are uniquely situated sociocultural perspectives from their shared experiences relating to violence and the material hardships of poverty. Whether they are conscious of this or not, they share collective struggles for quality public schooling.

Educators should form coalitions with students to design interventions, forged at the national, state, or local levels, that confront (and, one hopes, interrupt) the perceived moral transgressions articulated in the student narratives. Specifically, principals and classroom teachers must deliberately foster a school climate or school/community partnerships whereby students may occupy safe pedagogical spaces and places to construct the production of meaning and morality.

This issue of creating safe spaces for student dialogues and collaborative learning environments may be more complicated than first imagined. Our data show that even when presented transactional opportunities for information sharing with teachers, the students in our study remained skeptical. Students' collective attitude, especially in the neighborhood schools, was, "What's in it for the teacher?" Building trust takes time, but it is our contention that teachers need to constantly remind themselves that sensitive issues such as teenage pregnancy, home difficulties, and ordinary adolescent angst are everyday concerns for students. Secondly, students should lead discussions of private issues and their relationships to the formal and informal curriculum. This will help prevent the perception that teachers gossip about personal concerns. Students would feel more comfortable. Classroom practices that facilitate the articulation of student voice, for example, those at Roberto Clemente High School, should be replicated.

In general, what the student interviews revealed as necessary, but perhaps insufficient, was a school climate that increased self-discipline and provided caring in a nonpaternalistic manner along with a more culturally relevant curriculum. Pedagogically, what seemed to distinguish the magnet schools most centrally was their relevant and engaging curriculum. Students at these two public schools, above all, were connected to the world. A common complaint voiced by students at the neighborhood schools was: "[The adults there] are ignorant on the subject, so therefore how can you teach somebody something you don't know?" Globalization was a process that meant something in the everyday world of student learning. Urban school curriculum architects need to keep foremost in mind the processes of globalization and issues that can potentially unite high school students with their teachers, for example, against global economic oppression.

Public schools are not institutional isomorphs. Classroom leaders and administrators understandably often function as if schools had no connections to the broader community and political economy. They do. Moreover, many of the high school students we interviewed voiced a desire to make these relational interconnections explicit in the curriculum. They wanted help in overcoming their class backgrounds and cultural biases. One student from a neighborhood school told us, "I don't live in the best neighborhood. I don't think society really cares about me."

What is crucial, I believe, from a pedagogical perspective is to authorize student voices as "learning subjects." Despite denied access to quality public schooling and high-paying jobs owing to the disappearance of work in the inner city, demonstrated income inequality, and persistent low wages for many racial minority groups, inner-city students nonetheless choose to remain in school. Nationwide, approximately 50 percent of students in urban centers do so. High school students in our study perceive that they have few material options other than to stay in school and graduate. Moreover, those students who do graduate and eventually enroll in college often must learn to navigate separate personal and cultural identities and set spatial distances from their everyday life in their residential neighborhoods. High school students in urban centers, especially those enrolled in neighborhood schools, often have to develop new academic self-images to succeed and gain admission to college. Potentially, these students could experience an inexorable estrangement from their nonacademically oriented peers, who may get pushed out of school as a result of policy structures and school practices. They must negotiate between, on the one hand, new identities located in academic discourses and spaces embedded in their "moral strategy" to obtain quality public schooling, and, on the other, broader social and economic connections to the world.

References

Everhart, Robert (1983). *Reading, Writing, and Resistance: Adolescence and Labor in a Junior High School.* Boston: Routledge and Kegan Paul.

Giroux, H. (1983). *Theory and resistance in education: A pedagogy for the opposition.* South Hadley, MA: Bergin and Garvey.

Lauria, Mickey, & Mirón, Luis F. (2004). *Urban schools: The new social spaces of resistance.* New York: Peter Lang.

Lipman, Pauline (2002). Making the global city, making inequality: The political economy and cultural politics of Chicago school policy. *American Educational Research Journal*, 39, 379-423.

Mirón, Luis F. (1996). *The social construction of urban schooling: Situating the crisis.* Cresskill, NJ: Hampton Press.

—— (1997). *Resisting discrimination: Affirmative strategies for principals and teachers.* Thousand Oaks, CA: Corwin Press.

Mirón, Luis F., & Lauria, Mickey (1998). Student voice as agency: Resistance and accommodation in inner city schools. *Anthropology and Education Quarterly*, 29, 189-213.

Mirón, Luis F., Bogotch, Ira E., & Biesta, Gert (2001). In pursuit of the good life: High school students' constructions of morality and the implications for educational leadership. *Cultural Studies—Critical Methodologies*, 1, 490-517.

Haroon Kharem

CHAPTER SEVEN

What Does It Mean
to Be in a Gang?

*It became clear that school labeling practices and the exercise of rules oper-
ated as part of a hidden curriculum to marginalize and isolate Black male
youth in disciplinary spaces and brand them as criminally inclined.*
(Ann Arnett Ferguson, 2001)

*True nerve exposes a lack of fear of dying...the clear risk of violent death may
be preferable to being "dissed" by another.... Not to be afraid...has made
the concept of manhood a part of his very identity, he has difficulty manipulating it—it often controls him.*
(Elijah Anderson, 1995)

For many teachers, gang life is a remote and terribly frightening concept.
For many Americans, in general, few things scare them as much as the possibility of running into gangs. Many of us have watched the movie *Grand Canyon*
and can relate to the fear that Kevin Kline's character experienced when his car
broke down in Los Angeles on his way home from a Lakers game. He faces the
scariest group in the United States—a group of young black men. He is saved from
death only by the intervention of a "good" black man, portrayed by Danny Glover.
Black men must always bear the consequences of such white fear. Indeed, one cannot understand American history without insight into the role that white fear of
black men has played in shaping the nation's institutions and its consciousness.

Too infrequently do teachers and students in urban teacher education gain
insight into what it means to be a black, Latino, or Asian gang member. Many of
the programs purporting to educate teachers and other citizens about gangs have
little to say about why young people feel the need to join them. Feelings of powerlessness, a lack of respect from others, and low self-esteem experienced by young
black men and women and the relationship between these feelings and gang
membership are not common insights among educators. So often the ostensibly
"random acts of violence" committed by gang members are directly related to
efforts to assert their self-worth, to demand respect, and to defend their dignity. In
the twenty-first century the only solution to the problems presented by gangs in
the cities involves building more prisons, installing metal detectors in schools, and
treating children as adult offenders. Such policies, however, have not worked, as

the number of black males in prison continues to increase. Incarceration rates for black males in the United States are five times higher than they were in South Africa at the height of apartheid.

From my vantage point as a black male who grew up as a gang member in Brooklyn, New York, I watch with amazement the ways that such policies are justified and implemented. Political and educational leaders often promote such policies with little effort to study and understand the experiences and perspectives of young people who grow up in urban poverty, with its attendant racism and class bias. Many of these policymakers have no experience working with or even talking to young people who face these realities on a daily basis. Without this knowledge, such policymakers make a career of responding to only the symptoms of urban social problems—not their causes. Urban schools spend millions of dollars developing more rules, hiring security personnel, buying metal detectors, constructing schools for at-risk children, and contracting anti-gang consultants. In these responses, students from gangs are viewed from outside the context of their lives and everyday experiences. Many of the answers provided to principals and teachers by anti-gang consultants never mention racism and poverty as factors that move young people to join gangs. They never ask what it might mean to be in a gang.

Such questions might produce information that could help political and educational leaders develop social and educational policies that actually work to solve the causes of gang-related problems. Students who are gang members many times speak with great insight about why gangs exist and often present very powerful suggestions about what schools can do to address the realities that create them. Such students are often far more helpful than paid consultants because they are not as concerned with telling school officials what they want to hear. Typically the only agenda such students are pursuing involves their struggle to be treated respectfully and with dignity. The knowledge they bring to school is the view from outside, the subjugated knowledge of institutions that is too often dismissed from our understanding of what really is going on in urban schools and the communities that surround them. A thirteen-year-old boy who is attacked daily on his way to school, for example, is a prime candidate for a gang. An anti-gang program that urges students to "say no" to gangs and study hard because it's the right thing to do has no meaning for the thirteen-year-old who is getting his teeth knocked out. The high moral tone of such programs can be offensive to those students who understand the complexity of moral choices involved in joining a gang.

To know the importance of listening to the voices of our urban students caught in the quagmire of poverty and racism is essential to being and becoming an urban teacher. Every urban teacher must understand the violence, fear, and sense of indignity that students bring to the classroom. Such understanding, I argue, cannot be separated from the curriculum of urban schools. While not all students experience these problems, those who don't have much to learn from those who do. New understandings of one another will emerge in the conversations that take place in this context. Teachers, principals, and educational policy-makers who listen in to these conversations may learn more than they expected about the fabric of the society in which they live. We all have a story.

Returning to East New York and Ocean Hill-Brownsville for the first time in over 20 years brought strong emotional memories as I drove to an elementary school not far from where my sister used to live on Sutter Avenue and Barby Street. I was saddened that the building she lived in no longer existed, that there was no memory of the families, the kids, and the fire that claimed the life of my niece and nephew during the Christmas holidays of 1971. My memory of East New York and Brownsville is of vacant lots, the Pitkin Avenue shopping area, walking down Sutter Avenue hearing cuts from Curtis Mayfield's *Super Fly*, Isaac Hayes's *Theme from Shaft*, Earth Wind and Fire's "Power" from their album *Last Days and Time*, or the Dramatics' *Whatcha See Is Whatcha Get*. You could go from one end of Sutter Avenue to the other and see people you knew.

My other memories are of the street gangs that lived in the Brownsville-East New York section. One constant that has not changed is the level of poverty and the look of struggle and frustration on people's faces. The people are not mean or nasty, but as they go from childhood to adulthood in Brownsville-East New York, the daily struggles begin to etch lines in their faces. The other constant is that gangs still fight over the same turf over which those before them fought, turf that none of them ever legally owned. Yet many young black males fought and died over a cement block that they loved and at the same time hated.

Street gangs have always existed for kids from poor, working-, and middle-class families in New York City. The early 1970s were no different than the present, except for the names of the gangs that ran the streets back then: the Savage Skulls, the Savage Nomads, the Black Spades, and the Tomahawks. They owned the streets of Ocean Hill/Brownsville/East New York, as well as the South Bronx. They fought each other for control of turfs and no doubt supplied the precursors of those who fought the crack turf wars of the 1980s. There were no drive-by shootings back then, but gang battles were brutal, and anything that could maim or kill became a weapon. This was a time when a black teen had to know how to "use his hands" in close-quarter fights, because that was how you earned respect. Hollywood has created an image of gang members as karate and kickboxing experts. I never saw anyone use karate or kickboxing in a fight. The violence in gangs today differs from our lifestyle. We did not spray a rival gang member's house with automatic-weapons fire (such guns were not available on the streets yet). We did not threaten or hurt the family of a rival gang member. The killing has changed—not only is it more violent, but bystanders and family members are also injured and killed. Ocean Hill-Brownsville gang wars took a toll on black youth as the funerals mounted and prisons became full of gang members from the streets. Mike Tyson was from our neighborhood; he was a little too young to become a Tomahawk, but probably admired us as he watched us walking and sporting our colors without fear of the police.

Street gangs require only a few unspoken codes, the violation of any one of which can demand dire penalties. Allegiance/loyalty is the most important ingredient. If you grew up with most of the members, you had more than a mutual allegiance. There was a familial love?love that bound the members to each other—and an inner silent pledge to protect each other, your turf, and your community from all outsiders. There is this assumption (especially promoted by the movie industry) that gangs harass the community. However, I remember that many shopkeepers in black and Hispanic communities knew most gang members, from childhood. If any harassment took place, it was usually the result of the shopkeeper's treatment of community members. The majority of the neighborhood people were not afraid to walk the streets, as everyone knew each other and the community was made up of extended family members and friends; in fact, many gang members kept the streets safe for the neighborhood. While the neighborhood had its collection of pimps and prostitutes, drug dealers, and other kinds of street entrepreneurs whom we knew on a first-name basis, we were not involved in those activities. In fact, some of the hustlers on the street were once in gangs themselves, and knew what lines not to cross. They were tolerated as long as their hustle did not harm any family members of gangs (mothers, fathers, brothers, sisters, even extended family).

While drugs were rampant in Brownsville and East New York, most gang members were not involved in selling drugs, as they are today—one could not be a viable Savage Skull, Savage Nomad, Black Spade, or Tomahawk and be on hardcore drugs. It is not to say that we did not consume drugs, but anyone becoming addicted to hardcore drugs lost any respect he ever had within the gangs.

As a young black kid in the Fort Greene section of Brooklyn, the first street gangs I remember were the Fort Greene Chaplains and the Mau Maus from the Marcy Projects on Flushing Avenue. As a kid in the first grade, we all looked up to these older gang members with awe—they seemed to sport their gang jackets (now called colors) without fear of the police. These were our heroes, the ones we wanted to be like, and we admired their stories, battle scars, their narrow escapes from the police, and their passage through the prison system. We wanted their approval and acceptance and waited for our turn to be able to join them and share our own stories of passage. Many of the older gang members were older brothers, cousins, or neighbors.

As I teach potential public school teachers, most seem to forget or not realize that when children leave the school premises, they have to survive in neighborhoods. They have to physically and verbally defend themselves and their family members. Some potential teachers believe, whether through societal beliefs or statistical data, that black children rarely make it into honors classes and should be relegated to compensatory or special education classes (Ferguson, 2001). I remember when we first moved into the Farragut Houses in Fort Greene, our building was right across the street from the Brooklyn Navy Yard. From my tenth-floor bedroom window I could see clear across Brooklyn. I can remember many nights when the gangs would fight the sailors and white workers from the Navy Yard. A sailor or worker verbally sexually harassing a teenager or young woman in the neighborhood drew immediate retaliation. This was always a major cause of the fights. My first trip to the store for my mother was an awakening experience that prepared me, as similar errands did for other kids, to know how to handle myself when I became older. I had to walk through the entire Farragut Houses projects to get to the store. This was a nightmare, as fear would grip me and many other kids, as we were always challenged by small roving bands of kids from the project. When I would reach the store, there were always older kids waiting for me to come out with change I supposedly did not have. Parents always sent their kids to the store to buy groceries or something they themselves forgot to purchase. To a kid in elementary school, it was either fun because you got to go outside (if you were being punished) or a nightmare if you ran into older kids waiting for you on the way to or from the store. Once confronted, you had two choices: You could give up the money and get slapped around a little or you could fight, and if you lost, you still lost the money. No matter what choice you made, you better not lose the money. If you did, you would have to face the wrath of an angry parent. Some parents walked with you back to the store to confront the kids who took the money and beat you. It was common to see a mother standing there telling her child that he better get their money back. Readers may think that mothers were too harsh on the kid, but one could not grow up in the projects and have his or her self-respect questioned. (When my mother took my brother and me anywhere, we had to be on our best behavior so as not to embarrass her in front of white people.)

Young black males are perceived as behavior problems in schools because teachers and educators fail to understand their cultural norms, that self-respect is highly regarded, and for some it is the only thing they have. The idea of having "respect" has caused so much death among black males, and yet it is the least understood quality of being a black male. Growing up in the projects, this "respect" was crucial to survival and dignity. Having respect made others leave you alone. Such respect was earned by how well you could protect yourself from physical violence through the use of physical violence. While this respect may generate pride within the individual and respect from others, it is generated by a fear that emerges at an early age. Young black males are forced to make decisions while very young concerning their survival and well-being. I remember a fight I had with a bigger and older kid when I was in the second grade. All day in class and at lunch, my only concern was the fight. I did not pay attention to anything the teacher said all day. My greatest fear was what would happen if I ran away. I knew if I shied away from the fight, I would have no respect at all from my peers, and I would be labeled a punk—a designation that would spread not only around the school but also throughout the projects.

Teachers need to understand that no child wants to be associated with being a goofy milquetoast, like Urkel in the TV sitcom *Family Matters* (a cartoon of a black intellectual). I remember that by fifth grade I was trying not to carry any books to school because when I got into fights, I hated to have my books sprawled all over the sidewalk. More importantly, it was not cool or hip to carry books. While I enjoyed reading and read books voraciously—as did so many other kids—I did not want to be seen as not being cool. Gloria Ladson-Billings (2001) tells the story of a young black male who felt that his sense of respect among his peers in the community was more important than bringing his books home to do his homework. The teacher who saw that the student was clowning in class and not doing his homework could have punished him but instead struck a deal with him that allowed him to complete his homework and maintain his sense of respect with his peers in the community (pp. 77-8). Culture is more than historical heritage in this case; culture here is also defined as how young black males see themselves and the world. More importantly, the teacher was sensitive enough to see that the problem was not necessarily a behavior problem. Buoyed by this understanding, the teacher allowed the student to maintain his dignity and in the process empowered him to complete his homework.

I have observed many elementary school-aged black males struggling to holding back tears as teachers and other school administrators berate and scold them for minor infractions. Such students are attempting to maintain their sense of manhood and respect. What often happens is that tension builds up inside until something or someone causes them to become violent. They strike out sensing that they have no outlet, no alternative. Many young black males have a sense that no one cares for them, so why should they themselves care what happens? Nathan McCall (1994) makes an important observation: "For as long as I can remember, black folks have always had a serious thing about respect. I guess because white people disrespected them so blatantly for so long that blacks viciously protected what little morsels of self-respect they had left" (p. 55).

Last year I witnessed a third-grade teacher scream at one of the black males in her classroom to the point that he left his seat and walked out. The teacher continued to scream at him into the hallway. I followed the kid into the hallway and waited until he walked back down the hall toward me. When I asked him if he understood that if he maintained this path of just walking out of the classroom he would be sent to the principal's office, he replied that he knew it and did not care. I continued the dialogue and asked, "If you keep this up as you get older, you know where you are going to end up?" He replied, "Yes, prison." I was not only saddened but angered, wondering how schools became training grounds for the prison system, that this third-grade student already knew where he was headed because no one cared enough to detour him from the path he was traveling. I understood that this young black male felt that the only recourse he had was to leave the class to hold onto what little self-respect he had left.

When I entered the third grade, I did not realize that I was part of the experiment of desegregation. I was bused, without my mother's permission, to a predominantly white school in the Fort Hamilton section of Brooklyn. The policymakers who passed and implemented the desegregation never allowed us black kids to tell them what we thought about all of this busing. Why was I taken from a school just across the street from our apartment to a school all the way across Brooklyn? Why was I forced to be outside to catch the bus at 7:15 A.M. every morning until the sixth grade? (By the way, kids from the projects did not have school buses—we were required to use public transportation.) Also, why was this desegregation just a one-way street? No white kids were bused into the Fort Greene or Red Hook schools where some of the other black kids came from.

In the classes in the school to which we were bused, we were not allowed to talk because many of the teachers did not think we had any knowledge to contribute to the class. If one of us raised our hand, he/she was passed over. This made me mad and stopped me from even trying to participate in the class lessons. We were always placed in the back of the classroom and punished more harshly for behavior problems. If we got into a dispute with the white kids, it was always our fault. Many of the black kids had physical altercations with white kids over being called a "nigger," and we always ended up in the principal's office for starting the fight. Everett Dawson, a black teacher in North Carolina in the 1970s, said that he attended in-service seminars on how to deal with black students who were coming to the predominantly white schools. The "experts" on black students told a group of white teachers that the "black students weren't going to be polite [and] were not going to bring in all their homework every day, and [warned] the white teachers [about what they] were going to have to accept from the black students once the schools were integrated" (Foster, 1997, p. 7). According to the narrative, the experts continued this for three days until a black teacher raised the question: "How are black teachers to get along with the white students?" Are potential teachers to assume that because a child is black, there will be problems? Are there workshops on what images and what societal beliefs a white teacher may bring to a classroom of black children? Does the term "at risk" (which really is a racial code word for a black or Hispanic child from a poor community) bring to the mind of the teacher an image of this child as one who cannot learn like any other child?

I remember vividly a geography lesson on the continents. When the teacher asked the class what kind of things would be found in Africa, all the students, even the black students, responded by saying jungles, elephants, gorillas, lions, and giraffes. There was no mention of people or cities, no mention of any civilization, because in their minds Africa was not a civilized place; it was the Dark Continent. I can remember most of us black students getting quiet in the class because Africa was not a place we wanted to be associated with in comparison with what was discussed in class about the European and North American continents. We resisted participation in the lessons on Africa because we did not want to be people of African descent. To be called an African was an insult, even though the Black Power movement was just getting under way. Any reference to Africa throughout my school life was always that of the jungle, of wild animals or seminaked people who were in need of civilizing. As David Livingstone wrote in 1867: "We come among them as members of a superior race…that desires to elevate the more degraded portions of the human family" (Coupland, 1928, p. 107). Why would we want to associate with Africa or its cultural norms if everything we were shown about the place we came from was primitive? As I write, the words of Carter G. Woodson, written back in 1933 come to mind:

> The same educational process which inspires and stimulates the oppressor with the thought that he is everything and has accomplished everything worthwhile, depresses and crushes at the same time the spark of genius in the Negro by making him feel that his race does not amount to much and never will measure up to the standards of other peoples. (Woodson, 1990)

Our teachers never realized that our silence and resistance to their geography lessons had connections to a racist ideology that celebrated Eurocentric paradigms while it disparaged who we were as children of African descent. I can also remember a teacher telling one of the black students who had raised his hand and yelled out the answer to put his hand down, that we needed to learn how to be obedient to the rules so that we could learn "how to be taught." I never understood what she meant, until years later. She was telling us that we needed to learn complete obedience to the school rules, but more importantly she was telling us that we (and our culture) were deficient and in need of correction. The cultural orientation and ideological teacher preparation she had received in college had informed her that black children were all part of a deficient culture whose language skills needed *drilling* in the rules of "proper" English. The teacher had been abstractly trained against racism but had not been trained in how to translate the abstract into actual experience. Her pedagogy was still paternalistic, and she delegitimatized our culture, history, and language.

Today, middle-class black teachers who refuse to identify with poor blacks have joined with those whites who believe that children from the projects are inadequate, pathological, and in need of civilizing. Recently, I was sitting in the office of a colleague when a former student came in to see the other professor. I asked her how teaching was and she responded with confidence, "They are animals!" I was surprised because within one year of teaching she had already come to believe that the kids in her elementary school were no better than animals that needed to be caged. When teachers can refer to young children and teenagers as animals, it is no surprise that within the course of the day there are many negative comments and few acts of encouragement. Many studies claim that the majority of the behavior problems in schools are caused by black males who need to be banished to the principal's office or expelled into the streets so that the other students can learn (Ferguson, 2001).

As I look back, I see bitterness among the black males who were bused to the white schools. By the time most of us were in the sixth grade, many hated going to the school. We had also become aware about race, and we knew we were not welcome in the white schools. Thus, we lived in a different world five days a week from 8 to 3. We were forced to live in a world where race was foremost in our consciousness, knowing as we did that the teachers thought we were unteachable. During lunchtime, when the white kids went to the store, we were not allowed to go, as the parents told the school they did not want us walking around their neighborhood. The other world was life in the projects, with its black and Puerto Rican families. Here we could be ourselves, as we were removed from the fearful microscope of white people.

By the time I reached the seventh grade, we were all in small gangs, or as they are called today, "crews." We were still being bused to the predominantly white schools in the Bay Ridge section of Brooklyn. Thus, we were still fighting white kids in school and on the way to the bus or train. Back in the projects, we mimicked the older gangs in our neighborhood. We would fight the gangs from Fort Greene over the smallest things just about every Friday night. However, these were only fistfights that were mostly caused by a kid from either project venturing into the other's project to see a girl or an argument at a party. Most of us were still going to school, even though we were beginning to skip classes, being sent to the principal's office more often, becoming petty hustlers, and beginning to hang with the older gang members.

By the time I had reached the tenth grade, I was no longer going to school and was living with my older sister. I joined the Tomahawks, who were small when I joined in the beginning but had the reputation as being one of the toughest gangs in New York City. As our reputation spread, we grew to over 500 members with chapters all over Brooklyn. The violence was constant, as we fought rival gangs from the South Bronx and other parts of Brooklyn. We periodically fought with a Crown Heights gang called the Jolly Stompers, who were kids from lower-middle-class/working-class black families. As I look back on all that we did as young black males, whether it was how we dressed, fought, or talked to girls, it always concerned our need for respect. The emphasis of the streets and our lives was rooted in respect. Some of the most brutal fights stemmed from petty incidents that embodied some affront to a person's respect.

The first part of my life having been spent on the streets of New York City, the second part has been spent correcting the consequences of the first part. As I attended college, I came to understand that many black males received two degrees: One was earned in college; the other was earned as we studied who we were as black men, reading about African/African American history, sociology, psychology, and every other discipline to gain the knowledge we needed to appreciate who we were. Some might say I have arrived in society having received a doctorate degree. While I have crossed over the poverty line into a world of scholars and professionals, my life as a black man in American society has not changed much at all. I still get stopped by the police and questioned, I still get those looks from some whites as to why I am driving or walking through their neighborhood. I still receive looks from people that say I am intimidating to them, no matter how unaggressive and unthreatening I act without losing my "respect." It amazes me that some white people hate it when black males act aggressively on the job, but yet at the same time demand aggressive behavior on the ladder to upward mobility. They want passive young black males in the classroom but then expect us, all of a sudden, to become aggressive as long as it does not threaten their position.

Negrophobia or the fear of the black man has a long history in the United States. It affects how black children are educated and prepared to become citizens in a country that consistently views them as a societal problem. For too long this negrophobia has caused the dominant society to tell us as black males that we are good for nothing, and we have internalized this and other opinions of the oppressor (our not being "capable of learning anything," our being "unproductive") to the point where we believe the lie ourselves. This negrophobia has caused a whole educational system to not expect much from black males. Instead, it has caused our society to construct and spend billions of dollars on massive prisons to house them rather than educating them.

References

Anderson, Elijah (1995). The code of the streets. *Atlantic Monthly, 273,* 80-94.

Coupland, Reginald (1928). *Kirk on the Zambesi: A chapter of African history.* Oxford: Clarendon.

Ferguson, Ann Arnett (2001). *Bad boys: Public schools in the making of black masculinity.* Ann Arbor: University of Michigan Press.

Foster, Michele (Ed.) (1997). *Black teachers on teaching.* New York: The New Press.

Ladson-Billings, Gloria (2001). *Crossing over to Canaan: The journey of new teachers in diverse classrooms.* San Francisco: Jossey-Bass.

McCall, Nathan (1994). *Makes me wanna holler: A young black man in America.* New York: Random House.

Woodson, Carter G. (1990). *The miseducation of the Negro* [1933]. Trenton, NJ: Africa World.

Eleanor Armour-Thomas

CHAPTER EIGHT

What Is the Nature of Evaluation and Assessment in an Urban Context?

The current reform movement, with its emphasis on standards and academic excellence for all, has heightened interest in and awareness of the seemingly ubiquitous problem of educating children and youth from diverse backgrounds. The problem is particularly acute in the urban setting, where population diversity is most pronounced and some of the most contentious debates have occurred about the appropriateness of evaluation and assessment measures for diverse populations. This chapter begins with an exploration of a number of issues related to the nature of evaluation and assessment. This is followed by an examination of population diversity as an important characteristic of life in an urban context and the challenges it poses for the validity and use of evaluation and assessment judgments for racial/ethnic/linguistic groups, particularly those from low-income backgrounds. The chapter ends with a commentary on the complexity of answering questions on evaluation and assessment.

The Nature of Evaluation and Assessment

Evaluation and assessment are data-gathering procedures or techniques that are used for making interpretative judgments about an individual or group's behavior or a program, curriculum, or instructional approach. These judgments may be used to inform the decision making on the well-being of the individual or group or the efficacy or effectiveness of a program, curriculum, or instructional approach of interest. Typically, information is embodied in a score, which Messick (1995) defined as:

Any coding or summation of observed consistencies or performance regularities on a test, questionnaire, observation procedure, or other assessment device such as work samples, portfolios, and realistic problem simulations. (p. 741)

The concept of a score as the basis for making judgments describes evaluation and assessment in quantitative terms and thus more precisely defines data-gathering procedures as measurement procedures and seeks answers to questions such as these: How effective is this program? How appropriate is this curriculum for this class? How well did Maria do on this exam? Did she do better than Philip on the same exam? However, not all evaluation and assessment judgments are based on a score. Indeed, some judgments are derived from the clinical insights of a service provider or significant other, such as a parent, a teacher, or a school psychologist. Such judgments are sometimes termed "expert" or "professional" because they reflect the wisdom of opinion based on years of experience with the phenomenon of interest. Different evaluation and assessment procedures yield different types of information that may serve different purposes. The list that follows is illustrative of the more common terms used in the literature.

Quantitative procedure. Provides the actual score achieved on a measuring device. For example, John achieved a score of 78 on a standardized test in reading.

Qualitative measure. Provides a description of the process by which the score is achieved. For example, John seems to be experiencing more difficulty with receptive vocabulary than with expressive vocabulary. Observations and interviews may be used to obtain this type of information.

Formative procedure. Used to ascertain areas of students' strengths and areas that need work before or during instruction or an intervention. The term *diagnostic* is sometimes used to convey a similar function. Such information may be used for planning and adjusting differentiated instruction. An example of a formative procedure is a pretest given before the start of a course or a curriculum unit. Or, the teacher may give a curriculum-embedded assessment after a few lessons in the unit to see which students are making progress and which are not, in terms of the overall objectives of the unit.

Summative procedure. Used for making decisions at the end of instruction or intervention about level of achievement attained. The information may be used to make predictions of future performance. For example, a final grade at the end of a course or unit of instruction may be considered a summative judgment on student performance, and a prognosis may be offered about the student's likely performance on a similar test given under similar conditions in the future.

Performance procedure. Provides direct information on samples of students' actual work. They are sometimes described as "authentic," a term coined by Wiggins (1989) to reflect complex, "real-life" performance. An example of performance assessment is a portfolio that may be used to showcase students' accomplishments as well as the process by which the accomplishments were achieved over a period of time. They are sometimes referred to as *alternative assessments* to distinguish them from traditional standardized tests of achievement or intelligence.

Standardized procedure. Provides indirect or inferential information about a program, individual, or group. It is assumed that such a procedure meets certain measurement criteria of reliability, validity, and fairness, and it is oftentimes used to make comparative judgments about the performance of different groups on a given construct such as intelligence, personality, language proficiency, and academic achievement. When scores on these procedures are compared with the average scores of others, the measurement procedure is termed *norm referenced* (e.g., the Stanford Achievement Test in mathematics). If, however, the scores are compared with a given predetermined criterion or standard of performance, the measurement procedure is termed *criterion referenced* (e.g., criterion reading; Hackett, 1971). The same standardized procedure may be used as a norm-referenced and a criterion-referenced measure.

These terms are not mutually exclusive. For example, a formative procedure may be considered qualitative in the sense that it provides information on the process of student engagement on a task or the quality of his/her effort expended on a given task. Or a performance measure may be considered summative if it provides information for making a final appraisal of students' accomplishments. As a third example, a standardized measure may be described as a performance measure if it meets the psychometric criteria of reliability, validity, and fairness.

The degree to which one can place confidence in the obtained results of an evaluation or assessment procedure depends on whether the procedure meets certain measurement assumptions. In the case of evaluation, the questions of interest are: Does the evaluation provide necessary and sufficient information to its intended users? Is the evaluation politically viable and cost effective and are its procedures practical? Is the evaluation conducted in a legally and ethically defensible manner with due concern not only for the participants involved but for those impacted by its results? And, finally, does the evaluation provide accurate information in terms of the worth or merit of that which is being evaluated? (JCSEE, 1994). In the case of assessment, the questions of interest share some similarity with those of evaluation: Does the assessment provide accurate and reliable information to its intended users? Is the assessment free from bias (e.g., gender, race, ethnic, language, class, exceptionality)? Is the assessment conducted in a legally and ethically defensible manner, and are there any negative consequences for participants due to the use of assessment results?

Because there are so many different types of information that can be provided from evaluative and assessment procedures for enabling different types of decisions, it is difficult to ascertain which measurement procedure to label *evaluation* and which *assessment*. The literature about these terms is not helpful in this regard. Indeed, some textbooks use these terms interchangeably, as in formative and summative assessment (Woolfolk, 1998) or formative and summative evaluation (Slavin, 2002). Others use the terms *standardized test* and *standardized assessment* interchangeably to refer to procedures that have in common an adherence to psychometric criteria of validity, reliability, and fairness. Yet, there are those who view testing as part of a larger process of assessment and therefore do not consider testing and assessment to be synonymous (e.g., Salvia and Ysseldyke, 1978).

Despite this ambiguity, there is a general tendency in the literature toward using the term *evaluation* for interpretative judgment about the effectiveness of a program, an innovative curriculum, or an instructional approach. In contrast, the general tendency in the literature is to define *assessment* as the use of multiple data-gathering procedures to make interpretative judgments about the behavior of an individual or group of students within a given domain on a variety of tasks in a variety of contexts. Because of the comprehensiveness of the information yielded from the use of multiple procedures and the meaning of the various interpretative judgments in terms of the total functioning of the individual or group, I prefer to use the concept of an *assessment system*. Such a system may include one or more standardized tests, observation protocol, interview, and a questionnaire.

Purposes of Evaluation and Assessment

Knowledge of the nature of evaluation and assessment is not very useful unless we also know the purpose for which such data-gathering procedures are to be used and the type of information they will provide to teachers, parents, principals, psychologists, and other professionals in enabling them to make appropriate decisions for students' well-being. Decisions vary in a number of ways.

Some decisions need to be made about the effectiveness or efficacy of an instructional program, curriculum, or instructional approach. A school district may be considering an innovative mathematics curriculum but wants to know whether children are likely to make better academic progress using this approach versus the conventional one. Similarly, funders of an after-school program for children falling behind in their schoolwork may want to weigh the benefits of the program vis-à-vis its cost effectiveness. Other decisions have to do with placement decisions. A school may have to decide who enters or leaves its programs for cognitively challenged or learning-disabled youngsters or who gets placed in low-track or remedial classes and who gets into the accelerated or honors classes. For these decisions, the decision maker will also need information that will help him/her predict how successful individuals and groups are likely to be in these placements. Sometimes, decisions have to be made about promotion, retention, and graduation. For these, decision makers need information about who has not completed a course of study successfully and who is ready for more advanced coursework. And finally, there are decisions that need to be made about the improvement of a program, curriculum, or instructional approach and of teaching and learning. For example, before proceeding with instruction, a teacher may need diagnostic information about children's readiness for the planned lesson. Later in the lesson the teacher may want to know which children seem to be on track for meeting the learning outcome of the lesson and which ones are not. And at the end of the lesson, the teacher would need to know who has attained its learning objectives.

The choice of data-gathering procedure depends on the type of decisions needed to be made and the seriousness of their consequences for intended users. Typically, for placement, promotion, retention, and graduation purposes, standardized measures are used (e.g., standardized achievement and intelligence tests). The term *high stakes* is used to describe these procedures, since the information may be used to make decisions with positive or negative life-altering implications for intended users.

Population Diversity as an Urban Phenomenon

The concentration of large numbers of people from diverse backgrounds is a distinctive feature of urban life. Due in part to immigration and technological advances in transportation, communication, and mass media, groups of people congregate in cities reflecting their linguistic, cultural, class, racial, and ethnic diversities. Typically, studies of urban education tend to focus on children and youth from low-income backgrounds and from racial and ethnic minority groups (primarily African Americans, Latinos, and Native Americans). Some studies document the seemingly chronic achievement gap between such populations and their European and Asian counterparts from middle-class backgrounds and speculate on the attributions of the disparity, such as inherited intellectual inferiority or the debilitating effects of inadequate socialization experiences. Other studies call attention to the special challenges of large urban school districts, such as academically inferior and overcrowded schools (Gay, 1997; Kozol, 1991) and the deleterious educational consequences of inner-city social isolation caused by the flight of middle-class families to the suburbs (Wilson, 1987). Still other studies lament the less than optimal conditions of teaching and learning for children enrolled in schools in high-poverty, minority-group areas. Consider, for example, the conclusion reached by the Education Trust (1998), which still holds true today in many urban school districts:

> [C]hildren are often taught by teachers who are the least prepared; children are less likely to be enrolled in academically challenging courses; they are too often treated differently in what they are expected to do and the kinds of assignments they are given and teachers often lack the resources needed to teach well.

Against this backdrop of urbanicity, what are the implications of human diversity for assessment? Some would argue that it has more relevance for pedagogical and psychological intervention than for assessment. After all, in a democratic society committed to equity and social justice, service providers such as teachers, psychologists, administrators, and support personnel have a primary responsibility for ensuring that opportunity for quality educational and psychological services is made available for all children and youth irrespective of their economic and social circumstances. But, to the extent that individuals and groups behave in certain ways as a function of their ethnicity, race, class, culture, language, gender, or other aspects of diversity, then such differences should be considered in assessment. It is well to remember, though, that although population diversity is essentially an urban phenomenon, it is by no means limited to cities. Indeed, rural and suburban areas have significant numbers of people from diverse backgrounds, who face similar challenges their counterparts in urban settings. There are at least two aspects of assessment that have proven problematic for children and youth from diverse backgrounds: (1) the validity of interpretative judgments from standardized assessments and (2) the use of assessment results in making decisions with life-changing consequences for this population of students. Each will be considered in turn.

Diversity and Threats to Validity of Standardized Assessment

Messick (1995) defines validity as "an overall evaluative judgment of the degree to which empirical evidence and theoretical rationales support the adequacy and appropriateness of interpretations and actions on the basis of test scores or other modes of assessment" (p. 741).

For more than three decades, critics of standardized assessments have questioned the validity of its interpretative judgments for children from diverse backgrounds, particularly those from low-income families. On virtually every standardized assessment measure (e.g., intelligence, academic achievement, language proficiency, personality), on the average, African American, Latino, and Native American students perform significantly lower than their Euro-American and Asian American peers, the majority of whom come from middle-class backgrounds. Although deficit explanations for the gap, e.g., whether genetic or societal in origin, have been advanced over the years, there are other explanations. In recent years we have become increasingly aware of the importance of some characteristics of diversity (e.g., language, race, ethnicity, class, gender) for identity and functioning and have argued that they should be considered when exploring attributions for observed differences in performance on standardized assessments. For example, Phinney (1996) identified three aspects of ethnicity that may have psychological salience for influencing behavior of ethnic groups of color (African Americans, Asian Americans, Native Americans, Latinos, Pacific Islanders):

- Cultural attitudes, values, and behaviors that distinguish racial or ethnic groups
- The perceptions of meaning associated with belonging to a racial or ethnic group
- Negative experiences associated with minority-group status in the United States (e.g., prejudice/discrimination, a sense of powerlessness)

Elsewhere, I have addressed similar issues that challenge the accuracy of interpretative judgments from standardized assessments for children from diverse backgrounds (e.g., Armour-Thomas, 1992, 2003; Armour-Thomas & Gopaul-McNicol, 1998; Gopaul-McNicol & Armour-Thomas, 2002). A summary of these concerns follows.

Nonequivalence of experiences. Some African American, Latino, and Native American children, particularly those from low-income backgrounds, have experiences in and out of school that are not conducive to doing well on standardized assessments. Exposure to watered-down curricula, ill-prepared teachers, inadequate resources are but a few institutional factors that contribute to their experientially disadvantaged status. In contrast, children from Euro-American and Asian American affluent backgrounds have opportunities and resources in and out of school that are conducive to doing well on standardized procedures, and therefore these children may be described as experientially advantaged. When both groups are administered a standardized measure of achievement or intelligence, erroneous judgments of ability are more likely to be made, on the average, for children of color than for their peers from more affluent backgrounds.

Unfamiliar sociolinguistics. Sociolinguistic variables are courtesies and conventions that govern verbal interactions. During the administration of a standardized assessment, examiners who are unfamiliar with the sociolinguistic patterns of discourse of children from diverse backgrounds may inadvertently make faulty judgments of the examinee's ability.

Variation in acculturation. The level of identification that some immigrant children have with the value system of their own culture may make adjustment to the host culture difficult. The adjustment may take longer if their families occupy a subordinate class position in the host culture. The performance of these children on a standardized measure (e.g., intelligence, personality) is not likely to yield accurate information about their performance or behavior.

Misdiagnosis of the source of language difficulty. Some English language learners exhibit behaviors similar to those observed in language-impaired monolingual speakers of English. An untrained examiner using a standardized assessment of language proficiency may inadvertently misdiagnose normal manifestation of second-language acquisition as poor language development.

Variation on language use. Many factors affect variations in the use of language, such as socioeconomic level, regionality, recency of arrival in a host culture, and differential or uneven exposure to school-like experiences. An untrained examiner using a standardized assessment of language proficiency may regard variations in language use as symptomatic of a problem more intrinsic to the individual and may consequently be led to an incorrect judgment of language proficiency (see Irish & Clay, 1995; Brereton, 1995; and Brice-Heath, 1989, for a more comprehensive discussion of language variation in certain linguistic/racial/ethnic groups).

Stereotypical belief system. A damaging effect of racism with relevance for performance on standardized assessments of intelligence is what Steele (1997) calls the *stereotype threat.* According to him, some children from racial/ethnic minorities internalize the stereotypical belief or myth of intellectual inferiority. When told that an IQ measure was assessing their intellectual ability, these students tended to perform less well than their Euro-American peers, for whom such information held no threat. For this reason, judgments about performance on intellectual measures may be inaccurate for children who are vulnerable to the stereotype threat.

Resistant belief system. Ogbu (1992) argues that some children from racial/ethnic groups (African American, Native American, Mexican American) hold an oppositional belief system as a way of resisting what they perceive as a one-way assimilation or acculturation into the dominant or mainstream culture. One aspect of this oppositional frame of reference is what Ogbu calls *cultural inversion*—the tendency to view as inappropriate or illegitimate certain forms of behavior, events, and/or symbols because they are characteristics valued by members of another racial/ethnic group (e.g., Euro-Americans). These are the children who chide their peers for "acting white" if they strive to achieve and who show poor academic effort themselves. For this group of children, relatively low scores on standardized assessments of intelligence or academic achievement may not be a true reflection of their academic or intellectual ability.

Diversity and the Use of Standardized Procedures

Another long-standing criticism of standardized assessments concerns the use of data in making educational decisions for diverse populations, particularly African American, Latino, and Native American children from low-income backgrounds. As indicated in an earlier section, a well-documented finding in comparative studies of academic achievement and intelligence is that these populations of children, on the average, do less well on standardized measures than their European American and Asian American peers from middle-class backgrounds. Relatively low scores on these measures are used to decide who gets tracked into low-level or honors classes, who is labeled gifted/talented or mentally challenged, who gets placed in special education classes for emotionally disturbed and learning disabled, and who gets placed in ESL (English as a second language) classes. The disproportionate number of poor children from minority groups who are placed in slow-track, remedial, and special education classes has given rise to the complaint against the use of standardized measures for placement purposes. Fueling the suspicion about the inappropriateness of the uses of standardized measures for these populations of students is the fact that many of them have unequal access to quality teaching and learning experiences conducive to the development of competencies assessed on standardized measures. Moreover, there is little reason to expect positive change in their performance on subsequent standardized procedures to the extent that the negative conditions for learning remain unchanged. Indeed, the case can be made that this cyclical process of standardized assessment, followed by placement, followed by standardized assessment may have the unintended but negative consequences of exposing children to unequal opportunities to learn.

Commentary

In this author's judgment, the question of the nature of evaluation and assessment in an urban context presupposes a series of other questions: What is the definition of evaluation and assessment? What are the assumptions of evaluation and assessment? Who or what is the focus of evaluation and assessment? What decisions need to be made on the basis of evaluation and assessment results? Are there negative consequences of evaluation and assessment for its intended users? In this chapter I have tried to address these questions, only to realize that they have given rise to more questions: What is the nature of evaluation and assessment in a society committed to equity and social justice? Who is responsible for evaluation and assessment? What is the relationship between evaluation and assessment and curriculum, instruction, and learning? Who are the stakeholders in the evaluation and assessment process (design, administration, and impact)? What is the role of culture in evaluation and assessment? Alas, these questions are beyond the scope of this chapter, but they serve as a reminder that evaluation and assessment are not neutral or decontextualized terms, and questions about their nature cannot be answered outside of moral, political, historical, social, philosophical, and economic contexts.

References

Armour-Thomas, Eleanor (1992). Intellectual assessment of children from culturally diverse backgrounds. *School Psychology Review, 21*, 552-565.

—— (2003). Assessment of psychometric intelligence for racial and ethnic minorities: Some unanswered questions. In G. Bernal, J. E. Trimble, A. K. Burlew, & F. T. L. Leong (Eds.), *Handbook of racial and ethnic minority psychology* (pp. 357-374). Thousand Oaks, CA: Sage.

Armour-Thomas, Eleanor, & Gopaul-McNicol, Sharon-ann (1998). *Assessing intelligence: Applying a bio-cultural model.* Thousand Oaks, CA: Sage.

Brereton, B. (1985). *Social life in the Caribbean: 1838-1938.* London: Heinemann Kingston.

Brice-Heath, Shirley (1989). Oral and literate traditions among black Americans living in poverty. *American Psychologist, 44*, 367-373.

Education Trust (1998). *Education Watch: The Education Trust state and national data book* (Vol. 11). Washington, DC: Author.

Gay, Geneva (1997). Educational equality for students of color. In J. A. Banks & C. A. M. Banks (Eds.), *Multicultural education: Issues and perspectives* (pp. 195-228). Boston: Allyn and Bacon.

Gopaul-McNicol, Sharon-ann, & Armour-Thomas, Eleanor (2002). *Assessment and culture: Psychological tests with minority populations.* New York: Academic.

Hackett, M. G. (1971). *Criterion reading: Individualized learning management system.* Westminster, MD: Random House.

Irish, J. A. George, & Clay, Coleen (1995). *Assessment of Caribbean students: A guide for assessing children from CARICOM nation states and dependent territories.* Brooklyn, NY: Caribbean Diaspora.

JCSEE [Joint Committee on Standards for Educational Evaluation] (1994). *The program evaluation standards: How to assess evaluations of educational programs.* Thousand Oaks, CA: Sage.

Kozol, Jonathan (1991). *Savage inequalities: Children in America's schools.* New York: Crown.

Messick, Samuel (1995). Validity of psychological assessment: Validation of inferences from persons' responses and performances as scientific inquiry into score meaning. *American Psychologist, 50,* 741-749.

Ogbu, John U. (1992). Understanding cultural diversity and learning. *Educational Researcher, 21,* 5-14.

Phinney, Jean S. (1996). When we talk about American ethnic groups, what do we mean? *American Psychologist, 51,* 918-927.

Salvia, John, & Ysseldyke, James E. (1978). *Assessment in special and remedial education.* Boston: Houghton Mifflin.

Slavin, Robert E. (2002). *Educational psychology: Theory and practice.* 7th ed. Boston: Allyn and Bacon.

Steele, Claude M. (1997). A threat in the air: How stereotypes shape intellectual identity and performance. *American Psychologist, 52,* 613-629.

Wiggins, Grant (1989). A true test: Toward more authentic and equitable assessment. *Phi Delta Kappan, 70,* 703-713.

Wilson, William J. (1987). *The truly disadvantaged: The inner city, the underclass, and public policy.* University of Chicago Press.

Woolfolk, Anita E. (1998). *Educational psychology.* 7th ed. Boston: Allyn and Bacon.

CHAPTER NINE

What Is Urban Education in an Age of Standardization and Scripted Learning?

"Urban education" comprises two words, one simpler to define than the other. *Urban*, we know, is the environment of a city: a complex hub of human endeavor, a place of dense population of diverse peoples, an important location for financial and governmental affairs, and a rich center of cultural imagination and artistic creation. Urban environments are some of the most contradictory areas of our world, where the extremes of our civilization coexist—the richest of the rich and the poorest of the poor, the most privileged and the most disenfranchised, live and work here in large concentrations.

The economic gap at the outset of the twenty-first century is felt in its full ferocity in our city neighborhoods. Individuals from around the globe are pressed together in urban environments, thrusting their disparate values and ways of knowing up against each other in constant daily negotiations. Some of the most exciting intellectual and artistic personalities are drawn to urban centers, as well as some of the most psychotic and manipulative. Each day in cities—the seats of financial and governmental authority and decision making—power plays itself out in fascinating and unsettling ways. Complex though they may be, however, we know exactly what we mean when we refer to urban centers and urban environments.

In contrast, the word *education* is far more elusive. It slips out from underneath precise and facile definition. Philosophers and scholars have debated the term for centuries. Certainly, we must agree that education is not limited to schooling. We must make, I believe, a clear distinction between education and schooling

(Greene, 2001, p. 7). Education is something that is received from parents, from peers, from media—from any part of our environment. In order to have any kind of intellectually satisfying understanding of education, we must put forth a rather broad, unfocused definition of the term to mean anything that shapes us, engages us, and makes us who we are.

It follows, then, that education situated amidst the complexities and challenges of an urban environment is a many-faceted, dense activity occurring continually in both intended and unintended contexts. Outside of homes and schools, which are arguably the most influential sites of education, young people in cities are educated by street culture, by places in the neighborhoods they frequent, by the people who surround them, by encounters with personalities and institutions in the city, by dominant societal ideologies, and by the media bombardment that occurs in extreme manifestations in urban centers. Urban environments are enormously stimulating—they are a sort of constant barrage of education, miseducation, information, misinformation, and contact with widely diverse people, ideas, and experiences. All of these things profoundly shape the lives of those who live there, especially the children.

The aspect of education that most interests me is the point at which a person's direct experience (whether it be an encounter with art, with media, with another person, with an idea, organization, or skill, etc.) is mediated with an intention or an orientation toward teaching and learning. This mediation might occur via text, person, or experience, but the intentionality is important—mediation with the purpose of shaping, changing, and deepening understanding. I do not deny that much important and profound education takes place outside the scope of intentionality, but it is within this intentional realm that ideas about teaching and learning concern me the most. I am interested in schools and other sites where education is formalized, but much more than that, I am interested in what it means to have the intent to teach and the intent to learn, what the complicated relationship between student and teacher (or student and other mediator) consists of, and what our responsibilities as adult citizens are toward the mediation of the experiences of our society's future adults.

Schools fascinate and excite me because they are filled with others who are also passionate about the ideas of teaching and learning. They frustrate me just as intensely because of the authority and power structures that govern their operations. Urban schools—in this instance, the New York City public schools—are bound up in a tremendously bureaucratic system that has increasingly narrow conceptions of what and how to teach and of what numeracy and literacy might actually mean. Ours is indeed an age of imposed standardization, teacher scripting, and, some would argue, schooling for social control. The system runs counter to some of the most basic principles of what schools in a democracy should aspire to. Amy Gutmann (1987), in her thoughtful analysis of the purposes of democratic schooling, believes that the skills and values of deliberation must be at the core of what and how teaching occurs in schools. She does not believe that anything is okay to teach, or that educators can be simply commanded to teach certain curricula in certain ways. She is worth quoting at some length:

> The value of critical deliberation among good lives and good societies would be neglected by a society that inculcated in children uncritical acceptance of any particular way or ways of (personal and political) life. Children might then be taught to accept uncritically the set of beliefs, say, that supports the view that the only acceptable role for women is to serve men and to raise children. A society that inculcated such a sexist set of values would be undemocratic not because sexist values are wrong (although I have no doubt that they are, at least for our society), but because that society failed to secure any space for educating children to deliberate critically among a range of good lives and good societies. To integrate the value of critical deliberation among good lives, we must defend some principled limits on political and parental authority over education, limits that in practice require parents and states to cede some educational authority to professional educators. (p. 44)

Gutmann clearly recognizes that rigid, top-down, "one-size-fits-all" mandates, often made by politicians and bureaucrats rather than educators, do not allow for the type of critical deliberations necessary in a true democracy. Furthermore, the limits of which she speaks are two: nonrepression and nondiscrimination (pp. 44-47). Nonrepression, in essence, means that no school should be able to use education to restrict any group within it from rational deliberation or consideration of different ways of life. Nondiscrimination really becomes a principle of nonexclusion: "No educable child may be excluded from an education adequate to participating in the political processes that structure choice among good lives" (p. 45).

In the eyes of many, both educational experts and laypeople, America's public school system violates the principles of both nonrepression and nondiscrimination. And our urban schools are perhaps the most blatant examples of what happens in the face of such violation. There are schools and entire districts in New York City where populations, often people of color from economically disadvantaged neighborhoods, are deliberately (though perhaps "covertly") excluded from certain knowledge and certain means of teaching and learning. In these schools, standards and scripts have a stranglehold on teachers, choking off both their expertise and their opportunities to provide experiences of critical deliberation and discussion. The students here are not educated with the purpose of becoming future important participants and deliberators in civic and cultural life. No matter how committed, how critically aware of dominant social and political ideologies, how theoretically grounded and brilliant in practice a teacher may be, within a criminal system, she will not be able to fully engage in democratic teaching and learning. While her curriculum is dictated, her practice prescribed, and she and her students evaluated with biased standardized tests (and I realize that these things occur within both blatant and subtle contexts), she will never be free. She will never be a free individual who uses her own experience to mediate the experience of her students.

So am I interested in urban public schools? Profoundly. Do I want to work under the authority that governs them? Never. Both my professional life and some of my greatest hopes for democratic schooling lie in bridges from the outside urban environment into schools. I am interested, more generally, in organizations that have their own conversations and make up their own minds about what teaching and learning might be. And I am also interested, quite specifically, in art—in works of art and artistic processes—and what engagements with art might mean in a student's life. I am interested in the processes of mediation—of teaching and learning—that might surround art making and perceiving. I work inside urban schools, but I do not work for them. No outside Department of Education authority looks at my lesson plans. Together with my partner teachers, I am able to design imaginative kinds of educational experiences—where the desks get shoved to the side and moving our bodies through space becomes a profound way of understanding ourselves; where we ask important, critical questions about why the world is as it is. John Dewey highlights the importance of imagination in how we view the world:

> [Imagination] designates a quality that animates and pervades all processes of making and observation. It is a way of seeing and feeling things as they compose an integral whole. It is the large and generous blending of interests at the point where the mind comes in contact with the world. When old and familiar things are made new in experience, there is imagination. When the new is created, the far and strange become the most natural inevitable things in the world. There is always some measure of imagination in the meeting of mind and universe, and this adventure is, in its measure, imagination. (Dewey, 1934, p. 267)

There is no standardized test for my students at the end of their experiences. But there is highly exacting rigor. I work for an institution in a cultural organization where artists and teachers come together to talk about skills of perception, interpretation, and imagination. We hold workshops on inquiry—on asking ever-deeper layers of provocative, penetrating questions—instead of "staff development" on how to perform scripted lessons. We discuss theories and methods of portfolio practice instead of creating labels that attach "NYS Learning Standards" to bulletin boards of predictable student work. As a community, we hold ourselves accountable for thoughtful, reflective practice. We create and then look deeply at all of our lessons, the purposes and the practices with which they are enacted. I am not saying that this type of meaningful educational conversation never occurs in public schools or that thoughtful, imaginative teachers don't work there. I simply mean that the profound, dictated limits that bound the possibilities of most public schools actually prohibit those who work within them from engaging in *enough* meaningful educational dialogue and practice of this type.

By partnering with an organization outside the direct authority of "the system," schools can create a space for principals, teachers, and artists to reimagine teaching and learning. As a teaching artist for an arts organization, I enter the school arena free of many (though not all) of its constraints. I am often able to change the nature of the conversation that I have with my teacher partners while I am there. The tightness of bureaucratic control certainly surrounds us, but together we are able to carve out a place where we mediate our students' educational experiences with our own ideas, with rich and often controversial "texts" (works of art) and with alternative ways of knowing the world. I can bring some fresh, unencumbered energy into the schools because I am nourished, fed, and "governed" by the institution for which I work and by my own artistic life rather than starved and "ruled" by the Department of Education. Without overdramatizing the metaphor, I often feel as though I am entering zones of starvation, where both students and teachers are hungry for the taste of intellectual freedom and rigor brought by imaginative, challenging teaching and learning in the arts. Maxine Greene has time and again written eloquently and passionately about the power of arts and imagination in a meaningful learning environment. Here she speaks to their centrality:

> The point of acquiring skills and the rudiments of academic disciplines, the tricks of the academic trade, is so they may contribute to our seeing and…naming. Feeling the human connection, teachers can address themselves to the thinking and judging and, yes, imagining consciousness of their students. A person's *consciousness* is the way in which he or she thrusts into the world. It is not some interiority, some realm of awareness inside the brain. Rather, it must be understood as a reaching out, an intending, a grasping of the appearances of things. Acts of various kinds are involved: perceptual, cognitive, intuitive, emotional, and yes again, imaginative. A perceptual act, for instance, enables a person to take a perspective on aspects of things in the sounding or appearing world. By attending, listening, gazing, a perceiver structures what presents itself. (Greene, 1995, pp. 25-26)

It is certainly not always easy. Teachers with whom I work are often beleaguered and bound by the system. But for extended moments, we are truly creators as we reimagine and enact what learning experiences can be for our students, how we can help them "reach out" toward the "sounding and appearing world." We are removed, or suspended, in large measure (though again, not totally) from the rigid authority (federal, state, local, district) that shapes most of the students' other educational experiences. It is possible that we have slid under the watchful eye of the Department of Education administrators because we are working in the arts. The arts don't really matter—they are not literacy or math and they are not (yet) widely tested. "The system" doesn't really understand art or care much what happens with it though it pays some lip service to believing that art is important.

Within the schools, however, I am very accountable for producing quality educational experiences. The teachers and principal would have little time for me, my organization, or art if they felt that the students were not growing, learning, interpreting, questioning, debating, and understanding more. The truth is, my organization finds that schools want us to be much more than just a service provider. They view us as an educational partner and source of expertise.

Given these circumstances, teaching artists and cultural organizations are in a uniquely important and potentially significant position. We are situated, in a very positive way, to subvert rather than reform the system. We have a rich and deep presence in the public schools, and we work with classroom teachers and students daily, yet we are also free of many of the strictures and structures that commandeer public school life. We mediate our students' lives by creating intentionally educative experiences rather than by executing somebody else's ideas of what and how to teach; the power of curriculum and the nature of instruction is in our hands. We can change both the quality and the substance of the educational conversation in schools and enact radical practice without having to report directly to the Department of Education to do either of those things. It is our own educational ideals and our school partners to whom we must hold ourselves accountable. This makes for delicious dangers and opportunities.

In cities, where there are a great number and variety of working artists, cultural organizations can gather some of the most wildly creative and accomplished people to bring into contact with students to mediate student experiences in the arts. Also, because arts education (with arts specialist teachers) within urban schools has, tragically, largely broken down, schools are actually seeking our presence. Since the 1970s, in the field of arts education, the idea of cultural organizations and working artists teaching in the schools has expanded widely. We hold our own conversations (as opposed to being forced to participate in Department vocabulary and agenda) about education, curriculum, art, teaching, and learning, and extend those conversations to our school partners. And we now exist as powerful educational forces in our own right, somewhat outside the existing local, state, and federal educational power structures.

This unique positionality carries with it great responsibilities as well as freedoms. It means that cultural organizations must be more than self-congratulatory for simply bearing the art and culture banner; it means that we must think deeply about our practice and, because of our important role in schools, begin to consider the democratic purposes about which Amy Gutmann and John Dewey write. Fortunately, we can think and talk about those purposes outside the purview of the Department of Education though ultimately we will be enacting our practice within the schools that the Department oversees—a complication, to be sure. Additionally, I believe that our unique position gives us both the challenge and the opportunity to look at schools as individual cultures rather than as a vast mass. Because we are working at specific sites, we can design specific programs—unlike the one-size-fits-all approach that often characterizes the Department of Education.

Within this context of urban education, I also feel particularly excited about being involved in the arts. The arts entail important ways of knowing the world, without privileging logical, rational modes. They provide experiences that help students learn how to integrate intellect with their bodies—with kinesthetic ways of knowing and learning, with rhythmic ways of understanding, with the mystery of color, with new ways of seeing, hearing, and reading the world's meanings, and with their intuition and expressive natures. It is vital that in a culture of standardized knowledge, which reduces so much about understanding the world to multiple-choice answers, we have active experiences for students that resist linear, testable, predictable explanations for the way things are. Elliot Eisner, a long-standing arts education intellectual, writes about the importance of the relationships among art, meaning-making capacity, and school:

> Education can be regarded as a process concerned with expanding and deepening the kind of meaning people can have in their lives. The construction of meaning depends upon the individual's ability to experience and interpret the significance of the environment, including the ways in which others have constructed and represented meaning…. The ability to secure meaning from [artistic] forms is not innate; rather, it is developed and this development typically is affected by a school's curriculum. (Eisner, 1998, p. 7)

Another important reason for studying works of art in our schools today is that there is no single correct interpretation of these works. There can be no multiple-choice test on how one understands a Martha Graham piece or a classical Indian dance, or how one hears a performance of Poulenc chamber music or of Japanese Kodo drumming. Certainly there could be tests that ask for contextual information about these pieces, but there is no exam for aesthetic engagement or interpretation that I know of. What there is is engaged dialogue within a classroom community, in which the multiple perspectives and multiple interpretations of students are shared, considered, turned over, critiqued, reconsidered, and respected. It is the kind of dialogue that is at the heart of what Amy Gutmann calls democratic deliberation. It is a kind of honing of the skills necessary for a hermeneutic or interpretive understanding of the world. All children, but urban children in particular—who are faced with such a constant barrage of signs, signals, visuals, and sounds—need to be educated in reading and interpreting their world rather than uncritically and unreflectively absorbing it.

Finally, amidst all of the talk about multiculturalism and diversity, I believe that the arts can create truly deep and authentic experiences for students, in which they are brought into "profound transactions" (Dewey, 1934) with cultures and values other than their own. To encounter the visceral rage in the Urban Bush Women's performance of *Stomp Dance* is a quite different experience for students than reading about slavery. I think we need both. But the dance asks of them a different kind of understanding, perceiving, and feeling. They will have a different conversation about the dance performance than they will in history class—the dancers' sweat and feet and bodies will ask students to make a different kind of meaning out of what it means to be an African American woman today in New York City. In urban environments where so many cultures and values bump against each other on the streets, we need to have school experiences that transcend textbooks and standardized tests in order to help students negotiate and understand their experiences. We need to educate—intentionally—in ways that nurture non-repression and nondiscrimination.

Experiences in urban education (and I speak here of the part of it that involves intentional teaching) within city learning environments provides unique opportunities for organizations that work with public schools but exist outside of them. My most deeply rooted passions and hopes for democratic educational practices and values exist within this sector of the urban educational scene—within the arts and cultural organizations and their school partners who dare to confront the challenges and rigors of imagining *and enacting* learning that reaches far beyond standardization and scripts.

References

Dewey, John (1934). *Art as experience*. New York: Minton, Balch, and Co.

Eisner, Elliot (1998). *The kind of schools we need*. Portsmouth, NH: Heinemann.

Greene, Maxine (1995). *Releasing the imagination: Essays on education, the arts, and social change*. San Francisco: Jossey-Bass.

—— (2001). *Variations on a blue guitar: The Lincoln Center Institute lectures on aesthetic education*. New York: Teacher's College Press.

Gutmann, Amy (1987). *Democratic education*. Princeton, NJ: Princeton University Press.

CHAPTER TEN

How Can We Transgress in the Field of Disabilities in Urban Education?

In the first decade of the twenty-first century, disabilities education is riddled with contradictions and complications. So many problems face urban educators who deal with disabilities and special education that practitioners in the field—myself included—often suffer from a form of professional schizophrenia. While I am dedicated to the work of educating individuals with varying forms of disabilities, I understand the problems facing educators in this domain. And, as education students in the field of disabilities know, there are plenty of students who need help in urban and other schools in the United States. In the contemporary era, there are over 5.3 million students who are involved in federally supported programs for children and adolescents with disabilities. About one out of eight students enrolled in U.S. schools is officially designated as possessing disabilities. A little over half of the elementary and secondary students so designated (51.2 percent) are diagnosed with learning disabilities. Of the remaining students, 21.2 percent have language or speech impairments, 11.3 percent, mental retardation, 8.7 percent, serious emotional disturbances, and 7.6 percent, other health conditions such as hearing, orthopedic or visual impairments and multiple disabilities (Kaye, 1997).

In light of these sobering statistics, we are confronted with the collision of two major trends in the domain of disabilities and special education. The first trend involves the movement for inclusive education over the last third of a century. The key element of the inclusion movement involves the effort to educate students with disabilities as close to general education as is pedagogically feasible. At first the impulse focused on students with more severe disabilities, but it has moved to include individuals with mild disabilities. The second trend involves the disturbing overrepresentation of students of racial/ethnic and/or linguistic minorities in special education. Because of the demographics of urban education, this second trend has become a very important issue in urban education in the United States. African American, Latino, and Native American students are especially affected by overrepresentation, especially in the category of mild disabilities—e.g., learning disabilities, mild mental retardation, and emotional disturbances. Issues of socioeconomic class also exert a profound influence in determining which students are included in categories of disability.

Such connections to race, ethnicity, and class should set off warning sirens for educators who are concerned with individuals with disabilities. Such warnings should alert special educators to the need to examine their field in larger social, economic, political, and cultural contexts. In light of all of the complications and contradictions that disability educators must confront, the one thing that I would hope we could agree on involves this contextualizing process. But such is not the case. Within disability studies and special education, there has existed a deafening silence on issues of social, economic, political, and cultural contexts. Even around issues of overrepresentation of the nonwhite and the poor in categories of disability, one can find little work on the influence of social factors. Indeed, research on the literature of special education has found that less than 3 percent of empirical research published in the major journals of the field examined findings across racial, ethnic, and social class lines (Artiles, Trent, & Kuan, 1997). A culture of silence exists in the field concerning such justice-related issues. Critical scholars must resist such positivistic reductionism and address the harm it does to students from minority-group and lower-socioeconomic backgrounds.

When such neglect is viewed in the context of the new standards movement and legislation such as No Child Left Behind, the news gets worse. Many analysts worry that students with disabilities will be harmed by administrators who pressure teachers to focus on test content to the degree that it leaves little time to support students with special needs who demand attention. The mechanism of the standards movement (Horn & Kincheloe, 2001; Kincheloe & Weil, 2001) constructs a "politics of difference" that enhances the performance of those from more privileged backgrounds while undermining the chances of those from marginalized spaces. The privileged are the "we" who work hard, speak proper English, and score in the highest percentiles of the standardized tests. The marginalized are the "other(s)" who "speak poorly," exploit the welfare system, have "bad manners," are "slow learners," and come to school dirty. The standards movement has operated to organize and "scientifically validate" such deficit perspectives on these students. Disability education in its overrepresentation articulation must not be co-opted by such ways of viewing marginalized students.

With these introductory ideas in mind, I was initially excited to write a chapter for this book on the question of whether or not special education is working in urban schools. Recognizing this as a loaded question, I wondered after extensive analysis whether I could succeed in addressing such a complex issue. After all, there are academicians in the field of disabilities who've spent their lives analyzing similar questions (e.g., Biklen, Bogdan, Cherryholmes, Meyen, Skrtic, Turnbull, to name a few), and in comparison with them, I'm just a neophyte. The advantage that I have on my contemporaries is that I concurrently work by day as a middle school facilitator within the New York City public school system and by night as an adjunct, and in between I pursue doctoral studies, which keeps my feet wet in both the practical and the theoretical arenas of education. With this profile I'm what Skrtic (1995, p. 603) would deem a candidate for a critical pragmatist—this being a good thing—because I'm motivated to engage in a pedagogical process of remaking myself to redefine discourse in alternative matters premised on expressing myself in new and interesting ways for coping within the field and the world.

My guess is that having someone like myself discuss my narrative might be a good thing in order to suture the rift between the academy and the practical world of education, while at the same time allowing my experiences and knowledge to come to voice. My voice is one of many within the field, and I make no claims to having *the* answers. In many ways I see my narrative as an entry point (for me and others who may relate to me) into unmasking a type of indigenous knowledge that's specific to facilitators working with persons with disabilities. As Semali and Kincheloe (1999) point out:

> [I]ndigenous knowledge…is an everyday rationalization that rewards individuals who live in a given locality. In part, to these individuals, indigenous knowledge reflects the dynamic way in which the residents of an area have come to understand themselves in relationship to their natural environment. (p. 3)

My narrative seeks to reflect upon the dynamic ways in which I have come to understand myself in relation to my environment—where *environment* in this context includes the academy, public school, working community, and home in Brooklyn, New York. My narrative is a glimpse of how and why I (and perhaps others) have come to organize knowledge, beliefs, and history to enhance my life and identity as a facilitator.

I said earlier that the question of whether special education is working in the public schools is a loaded one. I make this claim because, within the context of such a question, how do we define the notion of whether something is working? What does the concept of *working* mean? I'd have to say that *working* needs to be contextualized into a larger framework of impact. If I were to address the issues of bureaucracy and politics, or even teacher training within the field of special education, I would say that I don't see it working very well, because the culture and organization of schools often fail in their responsibilities, thus having an adverse impact. Basically, the public school system has been taken over to fulfill an agenda that doesn't necessarily provide what Public Law 94–142 (the Education of All

Handicapped Children Act) was championed for (i.e., for students with severe needs). As Bursztyn (2002) states so succinctly: "The system has been hijacked by other priorities":

> Most students served in special education are not those with severe needs, but rather are children with mild behavior and learning problems who are often difficult to differentiate from those not designated as disabled. Those children are at great risk of misdiagnosis because linguistic and cultural differences do not need new labeling categories or specialized services; they need caring and competent teachers who are supported within their school communities to address all challenges in the classroom. (p. 181)

In fact, Bursztyn would probably agree with Skrtic (1995) that there is a crisis in the professional knowledge that governs not only the organizational aspects of the field of disabilities but the facilitators as well.

For example, take testing/evaluation as a problem of professional knowledge. Who owns such knowledge and why is it used? One could write a book on this topic, and it wouldn't necessarily be specific to the field of disabilities, although it could be. Testing/evaluating children has become very questionable. Evaluations are meant to determine whether a child has a disability and, if so, what type. Evaluations were meant to help a facilitator clearly determine what type of curriculum was necessary for a child—including adaptations and modifications. However, within the literacy of evaluations resides a nomenclature that excludes the teacher from truly understanding how a child needs to be accommodated, serviced, and educated. Most evaluations are coded, and unless you've been indoctrinated into the field of school psychology or psychometrics, you stand little chance of deciphering the code. At times an evaluation is so comprehensive that the jargon will confuse a teacher because it's overly detailed, while other times it's oversimplified to the point where a teacher sees the evaluation as vague and practically meaningless.

Rarely has this researcher come across an accurate evaluation of a child, let alone one that actually helped me to prepare curriculum. For the most part an evaluation is so decontextualized that it only remotely resembles anything the child will accurately mature into. In fact, an evaluation, done every three years, is out of date no more than a few months after it's been done, due to maturation problems of the child. Of course, a determinant could be the level of training a teacher has in decoding an evaluation, but even the best-trained teachers, while able to decode, are in agreement on the lack of value an evaluation really has in helping a teacher determine curriculum and service needs.

So the question remains, Why use evaluations? Foremost, they are a legally binding contract that weighs heavily upon a teacher, school, district, city, and state. To serve the purpose of avoiding legal ramifications, an evaluation is purely perfunctory. I guess some theorist might go so far as to say that testing is used purely as the gatekeeper to monitor the upper versus the lower classes and to subjugate those who are not able—but I digress.

So, the topic of whether special education is working presents a dilemma for me because my immediate reaction is that special education doesn't work well in urban schools, which makes me wonder why some of us I have chosen to position ourselves in an area of education that on the surface is seemingly failing students, parents, and teachers. I would even go so far as to argue that we are set up to fail — but that's another paper. The mental imagery that primarily floods my mind about whether special education works is that of chaos, and I honestly feel the need to respond with an emphatic "No!" about whether it's working. Then I start to reminisce about some of the things that do work in the field, why I even got started in it, and how colleagues (teachers, graduate students, professors) and I function as facilitators to implement practices that do help students succeed. I begin to reframe my ideas in this manner and notice that what works in special education is the interrelationship between facilitators and parents and students, working together directly on a daily basis — despite whatever shortcomings we might have — and not the practices of administrators or "educrats" (i.e., educational bureaucrats). This doesn't imply that administrators don't contribute to what's successful in the field, but whatever they do contribute is rarely connected directly to the student and family.

This helps to restore some of my faith in the field, but the task of answering what works or doesn't work still worries me because of the scale and complexity of the problems faced (e.g., poor training, lack of resources, unsuitable facilitator personality and character, testing and evaluative methods used to classify students and indoctrinate teachers, integration and inclusion, to name a few). I realize that identifying problem areas in special education is practically a no-brainer (as I tried to exemplify in my discussion of testing), because it's usually easy to find flaws in things, and the flaws found are just as applicable to general education as well. At first glance, focusing on the shortcomings of the field doesn't seem to help it move forward, but it is precisely this type of critical lens that a facilitator needs in order to make changes happen.

Since I don't know it all, I figure that focusing on a particular problem within the field, and not all of them, is a better way to handle the assigned task. So, I stop my spotlight from probing for the moment to address what I see as the most important problem. In special education, the training (which includes content knowledge and educational paradigms) and psychosocial development of the facilitator are imperative because I see the urgency to promote agents of change in this field who have critically self-examined their purpose and intent. Bell hooks (1994) calls this "engaged pedagogy" and considers it more demanding than conventional critical pedagogy. Engaged pedagogy emphasizes the need for the agent to acquire and facilitate well-being as the imperative for freedom because "teachers must be actively committed to a process of self-actualization that promotes their own well-being if they are to teach in a manner that empowers students" (p. 15). In accordance with this process, I offer my history and experiences to those already in, or entering, the field of disabilities education, so that it might aid in promoting this particular aspect of their lives.

Framing the Problem

What's so *special* about special education? Why is "special" education the professional domain for facilitators who want to educate persons with physical and/or cognitive learning differences (i.e., disabilities)? Why can't special educators just be educators who are specialists within the general domain of education and not separated into another field? Why is there a dichotomy in the literature when discussing disabilities—as if those who are able and those who are not able exist in separate worlds? Isn't everyone able, and isn't it just a matter of the extent to which one is able, based upon a continuum of ability? If there is a continuum of ability, then the real question becomes, Who determines the cutoff point that differentiates those who are able and those who aren't?

Consider the fundamental notion behind such questions, which resides in a disjointed literacy. On the one hand, it speaks to the process of liberation and social aspects of educating people with learning difficulties alongside people considered "normal," who have no learning difficulties (as if *normal* were a truly attainable condition of existence); on the other hand, this fundamental notion thrives upon a deficit model replete with factors that practically dehumanize, marginalize, and box in the very people it seeks to integrate. In fact, my trying to express and resolve the disjointed literacy of differentiated learners is innately flawed because of societal proclivities to classify, group, and sort people into those who have and those who have not, those who are skilled and those who are unskilled, those who are able and those who are disabled.

Furthermore, the notion behind such questions also yields repeated bifurcations that branch out into so many areas of "specialization" within the field of special education that one might swear that facilitators need multiple degrees (law, medicine, education) to fulfill the obligations of educating children and adults who are classified as disabled. Obviously, fulfilling such a notion is unrealistic, despite the facilitator's attempt to acquire as much knowledge as possible, because the other areas are themselves professional fields that are built on positivistic models replete with the same factors that perpetuate marginalization. Thus, fulfilling obligations to educate children (especially those with disabilities) reduces many pedagogues to almost futile agents of hope because of the manic nature involved in assimilating such knowledge (Kincheloe, 1999, pp. 8-11).

The opening questions are just a few that I as a researcher and facilitator continue to ask myself because I witness the downward spiral of failed initiatives that the field of special education experiences year after year—mainly the debauchery of the implementation of inclusive practices in the New York City public school system. While fiscal crises that cut funding to needed services are a foremost obvious problem, I would argue that the way in which facilitators are indoctrinated into the profession fails to maximize their individual training to fully carry out their responsibilities as educators, hence leaving them with little confidence to meet the challenges they face.

When I ask colleagues (including professors) to respond to the aforementioned questions, I often get a shoulder shrugged at me, indicating that they don't know; or they throw the old reverse-psychology gag back at me, in which they ask, "What do *you* think special education means?" Still others provide some type of politically correct response, as if rehearsed, to protect their credibility as professionals in the field.

I am also often met with resistance to the questions, a reluctance to admit that the term *special* in education is often perceived as some type of clever euphemism to mean an education provided for individuals who are "crazy," "dumb," and "stupid," among other adjectives that seek to characterize a stand-offish or "inaccessible" personality. I need to clarify that while I judge my contemporaries based upon their responses, I do so in order that I might liberate myself by vicariously understanding my shortcomings and theirs as well. I've often fallen culprit to such misperceptions and responses as well—primarily when I entered the field a decade ago—and never felt good about admitting it; it's taken a lot of self-reflection to overstep my own boundaries, limitations, and superficial nuances of my persona in order to understand my role as a facilitator and advocate for persons with disabilities. By listening and reading, I learn from others in the field and see that I'm not that far removed from the perceived reality that is known as *the field of special education*, because there are more views and opinions shared among us than not.

Although I'm not sure that educators actually get past their limitations 100 percent, I do know that getting past limitations involves a critical look at one's self and identity in such a way as to prepare one to meet the moral imperatives of educating all children. Until now I've always sought opportunities to position myself in a formal work in order to address the problem of becoming a facilitator, not only for myself but more so for those facilitators either already involved or on the cusp of entering the field—and I would hope that what I have to say is equally important for those in other areas of education.

My endeavor is no easy task and must be considered a work in progress. I have a specific literacy of the world, through which I explain my ideas, just as many of you have. I can only hope that my experiences and words resonate well, specifically with teachers who are making the transition from being passive individuals looking to be taught "how to teach" to being active individuals ready to face the complexity of being educators and who are cognitively reflexive in order to motivate themselves and their students toward an emancipatory praxis. Unfortunately, schools of education train the pedagogue poorly, and emancipatory praxis is rarely the outcome:

> Most schools of education train teachers to become technicists who unreflectively embrace methods and approaches; they are in some cases either unwilling or unable

to prepare teachers to become intellectuals able to assume leadership through independent thought and action. (Macedo, 1994, p. 153)

A goal of this chapter is to accommodate teachers' understanding of their sense of *being*, of a transformation from merely dispensing prescriptive remedies to understanding their role as facilitators, who nurture individuality and welcome the complexity of engaging young minds to become knowledge producers rather than passive receptacles of information.

Should teachers undertake such a transformation toward being a facilitator, one can only hope that they will maintain an enthusiasm for being challenged by the complexities of knowledge production as they work with children who are at-risk or have disabilities in a system that has marginalized and failed them. Teaching professionals as facilitators for children with disabilities take on more than do general educators and must be able to maintain a chameleon-like reflexivity for accommodating individual differences. They must guard against the stagnation of buying into the dominant hegemony of deficitism and cookbook cures just to survive and keep a job in the public sector as a "teacher" (Giroux, 1997; Macedo, 1994) Being facilitative requires more of a person—it requires her to challenge ideological frameworks and the power behind them. The facilitator for children with disabilities needs to be political by nature, since the field's ideology is framed by laws that govern how schools must structure knowledge and conduct business (Skrtic, 1995). Being political in its strictest sense requires an activism that engages schools, communities, cities, states, and the federal government in a dialogue to help make changes that liberate the oppressed (Freire, 2000). Serving as an advocate for a parent who doesn't know his or her rights in a matter affecting a child's education is political, because being a facilitator secures some type of power that the parent doesn't have. Advocacy instills power into the hands of the powerless by not only pointing out the paths toward liberation, but building alliances that are reliable.

For the most part, I raise the issue of *being*, i.e., one's identity and sense of existence, as a central point around which to define what a facilitator needs to be able to do and become in order to succeed as a pedagogue in disabilities education in an urban school setting and perhaps in any other setting for that matter. The notion of being/becoming is the essence of ontological understanding, and crafting the necessary learning experiences to move one toward a pedagogical ontology is the art of teaching oneself (and others) how and why *transgressing* in one's role as facilitator needs to be done—as I myself try to fulfill this particular role in writing this chapter.

While this paper doesn't necessarily seek to explain exactly "how to" go about transgressing in the role of facilitator—although there are glimpses of such a methodology—it does seek to clarify why one might need to do it. Hence, the title of this chapter, I hope, becomes understood, as I attempt to unpack some ideas within the context of critical theory. Some may even consider this an entry point into a critical theory of pedagogical ontology for special education.

Critical Theory

An understanding of what a theory is, and what it means to be critical, is in order before addressing critical theory per se. Giroux (1997), in discussing the Frankfurt School's understanding of what the general idea behind a theory is, explains that a theory for social change, justice, and liberatory practices seeks mainly to understand three concepts: (1) how relationships exist in society between the particular and the whole, (2) how self-critique needs to reflect on historical and social factors that either broaden or limit growth, and (3) how a theory unmasks things that function to assert differences (pp. 41-42).

By understanding this idea of theory, an individual enters a dialectical mode that acknowledges that some bodies of knowledge are false, and the urgency to accurately identify where the problems reside is what is critical. The urgency to pinpoint problems of the economy, race, class, gender, ideologies, discourses, education, and religion is the critical aspect of the dialectic in order to understand how power and justice work to move toward a state of freedom (Kincheloe & McLaren, 2000). False knowledge needs to be changed via discussions about such particulars versus wholes, and enacting social change then puts theory into action, making it transformative. Therefore, according to Giroux, a theory that is critical is

> a transformative activity that views itself as explicitly political and commits itself to the projection of a future that is as yet unfilled. Thus, critical theory contains a transcendent element in which critical thought becomes the precondition for human freedom. (pp. 43-44)

What is critical theory? Critical theory takes many forms and is chameleon-like in its appearance. While the term *critical theory* is singular, the concept actually comprises a plethora of theories that look to challenge and unmask assumptions about how the world is historically and socially constructed, what constitutes knowledge, and the way in which relationships of self and world engage in critiques. Due to the evolutionary nature of knowledge, as well as ever-changing environmental and societal conditions, critical theory avoids too much specificity in order to allow room for growth. Kincheloe and McLaren (2000) point out that "fixed characteristics of [critical theory] are contrary to [its] desire...to avoid the production of blueprints of sociopolitical and epistemological beliefs" (p. 281). From a critical perspective, critical theory is devoid of blueprints because theories themselves are subject to interpretation, and the act of interpretation involves making sense of our perceptual observations of the world, which is an interpretation of the world in itself. Basically, written or verbal expression of one's interaction with the world is already a second-generation copy of what one experiences. This interpretative dimension within the context of critical theory is called hermeneutics (p. 285).

Pedagogical Ontology

Ontology, the study of being and the nature of existence, is based upon assumptions made via a philosophical endeavor to challenge theories about what kind of entities exist (Abercrombie, Hill, & Turner, 2000; MacIntyre, 1967; Teichman & Evans, 1991). Based upon Martin Heidegger's work, ontology seeks to explain "what character *being* must have if human consciousness is to be what it is" (MacIntyre, 1967). Similarly, based upon Willard Quine's work, ontology is concerned with what a belief in a given theory commits us to and "what relationships exist between intensional and extensional logic" (MacIntyre, 1967). Simply decoded, an entity has consciousness that manifests in some form. For the purpose of this paper, an *entity* can be understood as someone who embodies and enacts his or her consciousness for the sake of pedagogical development—i.e., is a facilitator. So, ontologically speaking, examining one's *being* as a facilitator is the nature of this role, challenging assumptions and beliefs about one's own existence. The key is to be aware of what relationships exist between one's beliefs (which occur within the self) and how they get enacted in the world as outward expressions and manifestations—hence fulfilling the intensional and extensional logic set by Quine.

From a sociological perspective, pedagogy is simply the art of teaching (Abercrombie et al., 2000). In what way(s) the art is enacted is the crucial element of whether teaching retains fidelity to the banking, or bank-deposit, model of education. The banking model is founded on the positivistic notion that children are passive vessels into whose minds discrete pieces of information, void of historical and social context, may be deposited (Freire, 2000; Giroux, 1997; Macedo, 1994). In this context, the teacher teaches and the student is taught; the teacher knows everything and the student knows nothing; the teacher talks and the student listens (Freire, 2000, p. 73). I say that the notion of teaching as an art signifies an emergence of literacies that work to liberate the teacher from this banking model, which by implication is its antithesis. Such an enactment of teaching moves from *teacher* to *facilitator*. For being a facilitator implies that one understands the manner in which others may, as we noted earlier, be guided to become knowledge producers and not just receptacles of information.

Moving away from the banking model requires one to be able to engage in dialogue with others as a means of inducing action and reflection to transform their lived experiences. This is an art of transformation indicative of pedagogues who are agents of change. Freire (2000) argues that a pedagogue needs to have love for the world and people; humility, not arrogance; and faith in the power of people to be able to create and re-create their destinies (pp. 89-91). Having such qualities will yield a mutual trust between dialogical beings and a hope that critical thinking will take place to truly communicate an educative process that builds upon knowledge that is historically justified for all that partake in the process (pp. 84-124).

So, a pedagogical ontology (i.e., challenging one's self-beliefs in order to engage in dialogue with others as a means of transformative action and reflection) is a never-ending process. Doing so moves one from being perfunctorily a teacher to being a facilitator and agent of change who ushers in liberation for all involved in the transformative process that individuals need to recognize and enact in order to be justified in their beliefs. Ultimately, being a pedagogical ontologist in the field of special education moves one even deeper, to assume the role of agent for those who may not be able to effectively participate in dialogical methods,which requires the most severe monitoring of the self so as not to abuse the privilege of power one has over another. Such a pedagogue uses critical discretion to advocate for others when necessary so as not to disrupt the balance of trust and hope that all participants have in the process we call freedom.

Self-Narrative

Being born and raised an only child in Brooklyn was no bowl of cherries! My mother, for the most part, raised me as a single parent during the 70s and 80s and wanted me to be something of a mama's boy, while my father wanted me to be a tough guy/jock type—she praising my obedient nature and school grades and he desperately trying to improve my athleticism and brawn. While having many qualities in both areas, I chose to start down the path of personal freedom. In doing so I became interested in the social dynamics of my life and took pleasure in trying to lead a bohemian lifestyle. In hindsight, I view my identity and life as paradoxical. Despite identifying with being a Hispanic male, I spent my whole adolescence in an Italian/Irish neighborhood, with mostly Italian friends. My acceptance by them was a challenge for me to prove myself, being a mixed breed. Experiences often entailed survival skills of wit and occasional brawn that became a confounded juxtaposition to my poor, pacifistic, religious homelife. I was lectured to do well in school, to not fight, to listen to Mom, and to go to church. Of course, this was enough to drive someone to drink—which I did as a rite of passage—and I generally lived by the motto "sex, drugs, and rock-n-roll."

Growing up left me asking many questions regarding my identity and purpose and sparked my inquiry into other individuals' purposes and why everyone else I grew up with had it better than I despite my privilege of race and gender. I was born into a low-socioeconomic background with many disadvantages. After all, I'm the product of West Side Story had Tony been able to marry Maria and have a kid. The color of my skin seems to have played a major role in preventing me from being marginalized—and knowing a few tough Italian friends didn't hurt either. I was always, and remain, intrigued by how so many different people, with so many beliefs, experiencing so many different crises, were expected to live among each other and do so peacefully. I wanted to seek out answers just like most teenagers, but many teenagers seemed to lack the motivation to do so. Many of my questions would remain unanswered until I attended college.

My elementary and junior high school years were fun and interesting, but my high school years remain the milestone of my life. I majored in music and industrial arts. I became a principal flutist and excelled despite the lack of formal training outside of school. I won the Levitson Medal of Honor for Industrial Arts and a state scholarship to teach industrial arts, but I had to decline the offer due to familial obligations—ironically, I would become a teacher anyway.

Concurrently during high school, my whole adolescence was spent being a Boy Scout. I was trained under a scoutmaster who had been a sergeant in World War II, so the Boy Scouts was more like military training—which I still find humorous; his name was Arthur Augenzucker. I blame him for all of my persistence and motivation to achieve—his persuasive size 10 ½ steel-shank boots often found their meaning in the most unwarranted locations. Abuse? Perhaps, but I always looked upon it as tough love and provision of what was lacking at home, with an overly complacent mother and a weekend dad. I was Artie's most highly decorated junior assistant scoutmaster at the age of sixteen, earning all skill awards, 36 merit badges, two religious medals, a purple knot, and a translator's strip for Spanish. Artie pushed me to aim high, to earn Eagle Scout. He provided me with a work ethic and a sense of responsibility.

Unfortunately, my mother fell ill and was hospitalized and sent off to a ward as I was finishing my Eagle project—I never made it. Mom lost it because her second husband died of leukemia and she couldn't face the world. I adapted as best I could to take on the role of "man of the house" while I was still a student in high school. These were the roughest years of my life, because I hit rock-bottom, becoming dissociated from life to some extent—I was an angry young man. Graduating high school, not making Eagle Scout, and having to be the breadwinner at such a young age was frustrating and confusing. The next couple of years after high school were devastating for me due to the enormous amount of responsibilities I had to face; but I persevered and obtained gainful employment within the film industry through my uncle, an animator/graphic artist for a postproduction house. This job paid well, which alleviated many of the stressors that I was experiencing at the time. At the apex of my career, the postproduction house fell into severe financial problems, and I was permanently "laid off." By then my mother had recovered, and I was able to live on my own and go to college.

The majority of my formal higher education was completed on my own, with hardly any help from friends or family. In 1990 I enrolled at Brooklyn College to study psychology, philosophy, and religion, and the acceptance letter left me with a smile from ear to ear—I couldn't believe I made it. I put myself through college on loans, college work-study, and two part-time jobs—I guess I was determined to obtain my degree and fulfill my lost childhood dreams. I graduated in the fall of 1993 and immediately found work in the field of psychology.

I started formal work in the field of disabilities nine years ago when I became a clinical intake coordinator for the Association for the Help of Retarded Children

(AHRC). I had just graduated with a B.S. in psychology and was ready to conquer the field. I found my job in the *New York Times*, as they say, in a small ad that seemed fit for someone first entering the field. After interviewing, I realized that I was about to become "a suit," i.e., a deskilled white-collar worker—something I dreaded becoming, but I figured I needed to start somewhere. My responsibilities were mainly clerical and perfunctory. I managed highly confidential "consumer" files and a database that tracked services provided. I used this information to coordinate meetings among consumers, social workers, psychologists, psychiatrists, nutritionists, and various other service providers. Weekly and monthly meetings were held to discuss how much money was being generated by analyzing reports I wrote tracking the number of visits to each service provider in order to determine overall costs and profits. Unfortunately, being an intelligent worker in a deskilled position often got me into trouble as I questioned and challenged the many objectives of my position—mainly why there was an emphasis on pushing services to generate more profit. The positivistic framework that delineated the direction of the department I worked in not only limited my involvement (which was inevitable, in hindsight) but ensured I'd be a deskilled laborer for the rest of my career in that position. So after ruffling some feathers, I pushed to be transferred to another department within the organization, which required taking a major cut in pay. Moving into the education department in an early childhood setting seemed rife with possibilities because I had made a conscientious effort to become a facilitator.

This decision was a milestone in my life that awakened me to new horizons because it forced me to enter a Masters program in special education that helped me to identify and shape my goals. I was extremely fortunate to have empowering and supportive professors who promised a challenging experience that ironically would propel me into the academy that has provided me the opportunity to write this chapter. Becoming a facilitator was more about liberating myself from the inequities that marginalized me, and by doing so I now feel obligated to return my knowledge to children who are disadvantaged on many levels. For me, the field of special education was a venue that harbored those who were not conforming and were resistant to the dominant ideology of school and society. Special education was a symbol of hope.

I worked for five years in a predominantly Caribbean community with adolescents of all abilities (general, gifted, and special education) in an inclusion program that I set up for the school I worked in. I currently work in a predominantly white and Hispanic community with adolescents categorized as learning disabled and emotionally handicapped. I've learned that *cultural diversity, disabilities,* and *teaching to the diverse learner with disabilities* are just catchphrases unless you consistently work on actualizing their meanings—they are not concepts you learn and are finished with, especially with adolescents. As I see it, diversity may be viewed either microcosmically as a matter of cause and *effect,* in which DNA and genetic coding predispose individuals to certain fates, or macrocosmically as cause and *affect*, whereby response to environmental conditions are learned, for better or worse.

Understanding my position, my moral imperative is to contextualize my experiences so that students may understand how they might survive a system that sets them up for failure. I've come to the realization that there are many facilitators who come from a greater position of privilege and may not understand what's so important about my experiences. All I can say is that my experiences are most definitely a product of growing up in an urban community and public school system. My lived experiences clearly help me to navigate my students and their families around a system that is disempowering. Because of my hardships, I can look students in the eye and tell them things that aren't contrived or pretentious because I've lived many of their experiences. I often relate well to my students because of this empathy, which helps to motivate them in the direction of hope—a hope that some will be able to actualize.

References

Abercrombie, Nicholas; Hill, Stephen; & Turner, Bryan S. (2000). *The Penguin Dictionary of Sociology* (4th ed.). London and New York: Penguin.

Artiles, Alfredo; Trent, Stanley C.; & Kuan, Li-Ann (1997). Learning disabilities empirical research on ethnic minority students: An analysis of 22 years of studies published in selected refereed journals. *Learning Disabilities Research and Practice, 12,* 82-91.

Bursztyn, Alberto (2002). The path to academic disability: Javier's school experience. In C. Korn & A. Bursztyn (Eds.), *Rethinking multicultural education: Case studies in cultural transition.* Westport, CT: Bergin and Garvey.

Freire, Paulo (2000). *Pedagogy of the oppressed* [1970]. Trans. Myra Bergman Ramos. New York: Continuum.

Giroux, Henry A. (1997). *Pedagogy and the politics of hope: Theory, culture, and schooling: A critical reader.* Boulder, CO: Westview.

hooks, b. (1994). *Teaching to transgress: Education as the practice of freedom.* New York: Routledge.

Horn, Raymond A., & Kincheloe, Joe L. (Eds.) (2001). *American standards: Quality education in a complex world: The Texas case.* New York: Peter Lang.

Kaye, H. Stephen (1997). *Education of children with disabilities*. Abstract 19. San Francisco: Disability Statistics Center/University of California. Website: http://dsc.ucsf.edu. Accessed November 8, 2003.

Kincheloe, Joe L. (1999). Trouble ahead, trouble behind: Grounding the post-formal critique of educational psychology. In J. L. Kincheloe, S. Steinberg, & P. H. Hinchey (Eds.), *The post-formal reader: Cognition and education* (pp. 4-54). New York: Falmer.

Kincheloe, Joe L., & McLaren, Peter (2000). Rethinking critical theory and qualitative research. In N. K. Denzin & Y. S. Lincoln (Eds.), *Handbook of qualitative research* (2nd ed.; pp. 279-309). Thousand Oaks, CA: Sage.

Kincheloe, Joe L., & Weil, Danny (Eds.) (2001). *Standards and schooling in the United States: An encyclopedia.* 3 vols. Santa Barbara, CA: ABC-Clio.

Macedo, Donaldo (1994). *Literacies of power: What Americans are not allowed to know.* Boulder, CO: Westview.

MacIntyre, Alasdair (1967). Ontology. In P. Edwards (Ed.), *Encyclopedia of Philosophy* (Vol. 5, pp. 542–543). New York: Macmillan.

Semali, Ladislaus M., & Kincheloe, Joe L. (1999). Introduction: What is indigenous knowledge and why should we study it? In L. M. Semali and J. L. Kincheloe (Eds.), *What is indigenous knowledge? Voices from the academy.* New York: Falmer.

Skrtic, Thomas M. (1995). The crisis in professional knowledge. In E. L. Meyen & T. M. Skrtic (Eds.), *Special education and student disability: An introduction* (4th ed). Denver: Love.

Teichman, Jenny, & Evans, Katherine C. (1991). *Philosophy: A beginner's guide.* Cambridge, MA: Blackwell.

Alma Rubal-Lopez

CHAPTER ELEVEN

Does Bilingual Education Matter?

Urban schools around the country are challenged by the existence of huge numbers of students who possess limited English proficiency. Almost four million students in U.S. elementary and secondary schools are not proficient English speakers, and about 75 percent of them are first-language Spanish speakers. The other 25 percent speak as their home language at least 200 other tongues. The effort to deal with these linguistic realities faces practical and political obstacles in the twenty-first century. On the practical level there are simply not enough qualified teachers to provide language education to many of these students. On the political level there is a widespread perception in the United States that bilingual education does not work and that English-only programs operate more efficiently and more in line with what is believed to be the English heritage of the nation (Lanauze, 1999). While the problems of language and education in urban schools are diverse, this chapter will focus attention on the 75 percent of the linguistically different population: first-language Spanish-speaking Latinos.

Urban schools of education must address the needs of the communities that their current student population will be teaching once they complete their course of study and become certified to teach. The populations in large urban centers in which such schools are located are more often than not composed predominantly of poor nonwhite immigrants who are culturally and linguistically diverse. In New York City, where the overwhelming number of graduates will most likely choose to remain, and in New York State with its numerous diverse cities, the urgent need to educate teachers of linguistically diverse populations becomes even more eminent.

This urgency is further underscored when one examines measures of academic achievement for Latinos, the largest linguistic minority in the United States and in New York State, which reveal that Latino students have the lowest academic performance on several measures, representing all levels of education from prekindergarten to college. For example, a profile of this population in New York State shows that Latino prekindergarten enrollment rates are the lowest compared with those of blacks and whites. Furthermore, results of the New York State Assessment Program, a standardized test given to fourth and eighth graders to measure English language arts and mathematics competency, reveal that Latinos scored the lowest on all tests for both grades. At the secondary-school level, they lead blacks and whites in having a statewide high school dropout rate of 7.6 percent, compared with 6.3 percent for blacks and 2.3 percent for whites. Furthermore, in the Big 5 school districts of New York State, Latino dropout rates are 47 percent in Yonkers, 22.4 percent in New York City, 3 percent in Syracuse, 20.4 percent in Rochester, and 6 percent in Buffalo. Their college education completion rates are also poor, with 8.6 percent of degrees conferred in 2000-2001 going to Latinos, compared with 11.2 percent for blacks and 67.5% for whites (NYSED, 2002).

For many Latino students, English is not their first language. They, therefore, need to be placed in English as a second language (ESL) classes or in bilingual education. In 1999 there were 148,399 students with limited English proficiency in New York City public schools, representing 15 percent of the student population. Slightly more than 65 percent of these students were Spanish speaking (Hernandez, 1998). At the same time, the number of qualified bilingual teachers fell way below those necessary to address the needs of linguistic minorities. On a national level, the anticipated shortage of such teachers within the next five years is 66 percent (CGCS, 2001).

Despite the aforementioned dismal statistics and the substantially high number of students from linguistic minorities in need of adequately trained teachers, efforts to create bilingual teacher training programs often meet with little enthusiasm, and much justification for the absence of such action is usually grounded in budgetary constraints. Institutions of higher education that pontificate about social justice and promulgate the views of Paulo Freire, bell hooks, Lisa Delpit, and others who write about the plight of the poor and disenfranchised but remain silent in the absence of appropriate and quality training to address the needs of linguistic minorities cannot speak with any degree of integrity. Their programs must adequately address issues of language diversity.

Oftentimes, the controversial nature of bilingual education in the public school arena plays a role in the low prioritizing of such programs in higher education. Unfortunately, schools of education interpret efforts in the political arena against bilingual programs as a sign that such programs will soon be done away with. Thus there is a constant anticipation that bilingual programs will be made obsolete with the swing of the pendulum, therefore indicating a lack of need for appropriate teacher education programs. This mindset has contributed to years of negligence and lack of resources, which characterizes bilingual teacher training programs.

In public universities where budget constraints are great, this is reflected in the lack of well-trained faculty members who can address issues of English language learners and in the lack of other resources necessary for the growth and strengthening of ESL programs. In some colleges, a Spanish surname immediately qualifies one as an expert in bilingual education, when in reality the complexity of the subject matter is of such a magnitude that few persons truly have the theoretical and practical knowledge across disciplines to fully understand the issues of bilingual education.

Thinking that views bilingual education teaching programs as fleeting and the product of outside forces is often reflected in the classroom, where bilingual education is viewed as a topic to be covered rather than a concern that should permeate every class in every course throughout the education curriculum. Bilingual education is often presented in the classroom discourse in a simplistic positivist manner. The pros and cons of bilingual education and the various models of such a course of study are reviewed and seen as sufficient to understand the totality of such an issue.

Such an approach provides limited information about the teaching of linguistic minorities and does little to challenge many negative preconceived attitudes about bilingual education. Graduates from such programs find themselves with perspectives that view bilingual education as temporary, designed only for a particular population, and not part of the "real curriculum," adding to its devaluation. These attitudes, in turn, are played out in the classroom in the ways that bilingual children are marginalized and in the quality of programs that are created for them.

Even in schools of education where issues of social justice, diversity, and equality of opportunity permeate their mission, faculty oftentimes find students' attitudes toward bilingual education to be formed prior to entering teacher training programs and unaltered at the completion of such a course of study.

While classroom discussions centering on whether bilingual education programs should exist or not and the kinds of bilingual programs that should be implemented are important, such considerations are often addressed from a perspective that views ESL programs as an accommodation for immigrant groups. This leads to viewing bilingual education as having one purpose, namely, the attainment of English competency. Therefore, the classroom discourse becomes a debate about what is a faster and more efficient way to attain English competency rather than an examination of what is most beneficial for the cognitive, psychological, and social development of all children.

The stress on English fluency and hence the subsequent marginalization of linguistic minorities from the mainstream population are reflected in how these students have historically been addressed, with such labels as *limited English proficient, nonspeakers of English,* and more recently *English language learners* (often styled as a proper term with all initial capital letters). Such labels also negate any prior knowledge that students bring with them because of the unidirectional mindset with which they are seen.

Any conversation of approaches used in bilingual classrooms or a discussion of whether bilingual education should be eliminated, limited, or expanded should be undertaken after a lengthy discussion of the sociopolitical, cultural, and historical forces impacting on bilingualism and bilingual education in the United States. Without such a discourse, Christina Bratt Paulston explains: "We will never understand the consequences of that education" (quoted in Baker, 1996, p. 166). While the future of bilingual education and methodological concerns are important, their premature consideration in the absence of substantive knowledge concerning language acquisition, cognition, and a worldview of multiculturalism, among other critical issues, can lead to hollow and incorrect decisions about how children from linguistic minority groups should be educated.

The decontextualization of bilingual education results in it being viewed as a "Latino thing" or a special accommodation for linguistic minority groups without any basis or connection to economic, social, or historical factors. Hence, the classroom discourse becomes a debate about nonacademic concerns using a vernacular of personal opinions rather than a consideration of what is best for the student based on historical, investigative, philosophical, psychological, and social factors and concerns.

In the public policy and political arenas, the same sterile and hollow arguments and issues are discussed with the same results, namely, little gain in the understanding of bilingual education and the continuation of unfaltering negative attitudes regarding the need to make accommodations for immigrants. The feeling is that these persons have chosen to come to the United States and should become English speakers as quickly as possible. In this domain, where constituencies and political interests prevail, decisions about monetary allocations and the kinds of bilingual education to be funded (usually those that are transitional and most cost effective) become clearer, since recipients of such programs are children of non-English speakers who might also be illegal immigrants with little political clout.

The lack of interest and commitment to bilingual programs can be attributed to some extent to the narrow purview of information presented and considered, which disregards a multitude of variables that play a part in language learning and focuses on cost-effective and quick results. Such a discourse speaks to *how* without understanding *why*. Thus a rigorous, complex, and critical discourse, as proposed by Joe Kincheloe in chapter 1 of this book, does not take place in classrooms, legislatures, or boards of education.

Moreover, in the absence of such information, being bilingual is not seen as knowing more about the world or having an educational enhancement. It is viewed as a problem to solve. What should we do with this population? How can we make them English speakers? Such thinking leads to a path where knowing less is valued over knowing more. This thinking leads to not recognizing the importance of being able to communicate in more than one language and to appreciate the music, literature, theater, and other cultural forms of non-English cultures, which inability seems to characterize the majority of U.S. citizens. This stance of "knowing less is better" is then translated and upheld in policy.

Decision makers are once again caught making judgments about our children without the rigorous, scholarly, and complex considerations that such decisions warrant. Knowing two languages is seen as a detriment, something that there is no place for in our education. These educators and policymakers who pride themselves on valuing education, frown upon the watering down of American education, and welcome the standards movement now find themselves with their pants down and on the side of less education, on the side of monolingualism or knowing less. As Macedo (1994) explains, such persons view the learning of English as education itself.

To avoid this outcome, an initial discourse on bilingualism (whether in the classroom, legislature, or board of education) should include the social, cognitive, racial, and economic forces that impact on and result from the use of two languages as opposed to a focus on bilingual education as solely a discipline, treated narrowly, with an emphasis on its mechanics. By engaging students of education in such a dialogue, the role of these future teachers shifts from one of being technicians to that of bringing forth expertise in an area of study that is expansive, universal, and interdisciplinary. The rigor, complexity, and critical analysis proposed by Kincheloe in chapter 1 of this volume could be attained and students provided with the understanding and knowledge that will help them make intelligent decisions about the role of bilingual education in the school system. This will equip them with the knowledge necessary for leadership roles.

The shift from a discourse on bilingualism that is grounded solely in pedagogy to one that is inter/multidisciplinary in nature often results in students contemplating and engaging in inquiries about the linguistic, sociolinguistic, and psycholinguistic benefits and dynamics of knowing two languages. Furthermore, teacher students find themselves wishing to know why bilingual education programs are not created for everyone and why access to such programs for English first-language speakers is often restricted to private schools, recognizing that Americans are one of the few populations in the world that do not have a working knowledge of at least two languages upon completion of high school. Bilingual education would shift from having the marginalized status of a remedial program to being truly valued in a universal sense and as part of the mainstream. More importantly, bilingualism would be seen as something that is favorable and beneficial for the individual.

Any discourse on bilingual education that attains the rigor, complexity, and scholarship proposed by Kincheloe in chapter 1 must be grounded in various disciplines. Since this is beyond the purview of schools of education, the arts and sciences must take responsibility for educating our future teachers—in this case, about the role and nature of language and how the social, cultural, historical, and political contexts shape its use. A foundation that includes knowledge of history, philosophy, political science, psychology, and sociology, along with linguistics, is needed in order to understand the many issues surrounding the bilingual education controversy.

Such a knowledge base will allow for the conceptual connections that are essential to develop a worldview and a vision of educational purpose that all teachers should have. With this scholarship, intelligent decisions about what should occur in the classroom can be made, rather than desperate ready-made approaches that will most likely prove to be of little value.

To shed some light on the need for strengthening cooperation between schools of education and the arts and sciences, as well as bringing to the forefront the interdisciplinary nature of bilingual education, several issues relevant to the understanding of this topic will be discussed. While these do not exhaust the possible issues related to bilingual education, they do represent a smattering of disciplines in the arts and sciences that are important in understanding it, illustrative of the multidisciplinary and interdisciplinary nature we endorse.

The study of bilingual education is a long journey with many connecting roads. Each road brings us closer to an understanding of a particular issue, only to have more questions emerge and the need to take another road. One such path concerns the role that language has as a unifying force in society and ideological reasons why bilingual education might work against the philosophical foundations of the United States. In addition, bilingual education is seen as something that has been created recently to try and solve linguistic problems faced by our current immigrants. To address these issues, one must examine this subject from a historical perspective on a national and international level.

Such examination reveals that bilingualism and multilingualism are early phenomena of human societies (Lewis, 1977). Furthermore, the presence of a monolingual society is most likely an indication of political subordination by a hegemonic group. Not surprisingly, there are few existing monolingual sovereign nations.

Students are also surprised to learn that bilingual education has existed in one way or another for more than 5,000 years (Mackey, 1978). In reviewing the history of the United States, students are surprised to find that bilingual education existed as early as the 1800s and was promoted by the founders of the country. Bilingual education programs existed in some form or other throughout many regions of the United States. In *The American Bilingual Tradition*, Heinz Kloss writing in 1977 noted:

In the midwest in 1900 records show that at least 231,700 children were studying in German in public elementary schools. Moreover, in New Mexico, Spanish or English or both could be the language of a school's curriculum. In addition, during the second half of the 19th century, bilingual or non-English-language instruction was provided in some form in some public schools as follows: German in Pennsylvania, Maryland, Ohio, Indiana, Illinois, Missouri, Nebraska, Colorado, Oregon; Swedish, Norwegian, and Danish in Wisconsin, Illinois, Minnesota, Iowa, North and South Dakota, Nebraska, Washington; Dutch in Michigan; Polish and Italian in Wisconsin; Czech in Texas; French in Louisiana; and Spanish in the Southwest. (Quoted in Ovando and Collier, 1985, p. 24)

Students are further astonished by the absence of any mention of an official language in the United States Constitution. The reason for this omission reflects the linguistic diversity that existed in the initial days of the country and the recognition and acceptance of this diversity. Students are reminded that language diversity was at the very foundation of the young nation, and the founders of the country recognized the divisiveness of imposing an official language upon its citizens; therefore, they omitted such a clause.

Discussion of our constitutional rights inevitably leads to an examination of language and the law in the classroom, followed by a presentation of the court decisions that have impacted bilingual education in the United States. Such a conversation can oftentimes lead to a discussion regarding the Official English Movement and the English Only movement in favor of, respectively, making English the official language of the United States and making English the sole language in the classroom. Hence the debate that usually occurs is about whether language choice is a constitutional right and the forces that have fueled some persons to think that language can be legislated.

Further examination of the English Only movement reveals a void regarding its advocates' claims that being educated in English will improve the education of students from linguistic minority groups. According to Macedo (1994):

The proponents of "English only" also fail to raise two fundamental questions: First, if English is the most effective educational language, how can we explain over 60 million Americans being illiterate or functionally illiterate? Second, if education in "English only" can guarantee linguistic minorities a better future, as educators like William Bennett promise, why do the majority of Black Americans, whose ancestors have been speaking English for over two hundred years, find themselves still relegated to ghettos? (p. 126)

An understanding of the forces underlying these movements must address the growth of economic prosperity in the Southwest and the fear that many have of the rising political and economic power of the Mexican American population there.

These concerns, in turn, give rise to the debate about whether it is language, race, or economics that is the true fragmenting or divisive factor in the United States. After much discussion, it is usually agreed that in the United States it is unusual, although not unheard of, for a person to be discriminated against simply because he or she speaks two languages. However, if one of these languages is a marker of being Puerto Rican, Mexican American, or Haitian—usually associated with people of color who are more often than not poor—discrimination in housing, employment, and other domains may very well emerge. In this case, race and economics are the divisive factors.

On the role of language in promulgating intra- and international conflicts, Marshall and González (1990) write: "Few nonexperts know if this often-touted idea has any validity. The reason the problem is so difficult to study is twofold: First, there are very few, if any, monolingual countries in the world; and second, the research for finding possible answers is spread across a plethora of disciplines, including sociolinguistics, sociology, political science, language planning, social psychology and economics, among others" (p. 29).

According to Fishman and Solano, as cited in Marshall and González (1990), it seems impossible to find any conflicts that are based solely on language differences per se. Usually, the issue revolves around recognition for the demands of an ethnic minority or "nationist" concerns (Fishman, 1972) such as border issues, fishing rights, or other nonlinguistic issues.

What we do know is that national unity is strained when one group feels dissociated and perceives itself as unequal in political, economic, or social power. It is most likely that that group will become self-conscious of its ethnicity and, through this consciousness, become a possible source of sectionalism and political strain.

Moreover, a nation's unity is threatened most when it denies what is considered to be a human right. The discussion now shifts direction to a conversation about the definition of human rights and the role of education in attaining such a goal, followed by a philosophical discussion of the rights of all human beings and a look at the Universal Declaration of Human Rights, adopted by the United Nations in 1948, which acknowledges that everyone is entitled to all the rights and freedoms set forth in the document without distinction of any kind, such as language. Particular attention is given to Article 26, which states:

> Education shall be directed to the full development of the human personality and to the strengthening of respect for human rights and fundamental freedoms. It shall promote understanding, tolerance and friendship among all nations, racial or religious groups, and shall further the activities of the United Nations for the maintenance of peace. Furthermore, parents are acknowledged as having a right to choose the kind of education that shall be given to their children. (United Nations, 1995)

Consideration of such a document expands our discussion to include the role of parents in education, how education strengthens respect for human rights, and what "full development of the human personality" entails. The role of language in education in achieving these goals and how use of one's mother tongue can best help to realize them now become part of the dialogue.

In such a discussion, students often give examples of grandparents and parents who came from various European nations and were able to attain their rights by assimilating, without having to go through bilingual education. This brings up questions: What were the experiences of past immigrant groups? What were their educational experiences? Upon examination of the school completion rates of past immigrants, we find dismal results. Hence, the question that arises is whether bilingual education could have made a difference. The "sink or swim" policy adopted by public schools in the first half of the twentieth century in response to the education of new immigrants showed significantly more immigrants dropping out of school compared with native-born whites. Andrew D. Cohen, cited in Brisk (1998), shows that a 1911 survey of 30 U.S. cities found that 28 percent of American-born students and 27 percent of foreign-born English speakers were behind grade level, but 43 percent of foreign-born non-English speakers were behind grade level. When broken down by nationality, 51 percent of German students, 59.9 percent of Russian Jews, and 76.7 percent of Italians were behind with respect to age and grade level. Furthermore, Pearlman, cited in Brisk (1998), shows that in a 1908 survey of students who reached high school in five major cities, the children of immigrants who did not speak English at home had significantly lower educational attainment rates than their monolingual counterparts. For example, in Boston, nearly 70 percent of white students overall reached high school compared with only 38 percent of the students whose home language was not English. In Chicago, the respective rates were 42 percent and 18 percent; in New York, 32 percent and 13 percent; in Philadelphia, 27 percent and 13 percent; and in St. Louis, 27 percent and 10 percent. These findings did not include African Americans.

The figures cited show that past immigrants had a very difficult time in school, and many opted to drop out and join the workforce. In fact, many of these individuals did not attain full participation in American society until the third generation, something that proponents of bilingual education are trying to prevent current and future immigrants from enduring. In this case, bilingual education is not a means to overcome barriers but a way to get rid of the educational barriers facing our current and future immigrants.

The question that now arises is whether the current populations of non-English speakers have the same economic options of joining the workforce that past immigrants enjoyed. Such an inquiry requires an examination of New York City's labor market and statistics regarding the city's ever-changing economy. During the latter part of the last century, New York City's economy lost many industries to other states and foreign countries, resulting in a shortage of jobs for nonskilled laborers. This lack of lower-skilled or entry-level jobs impacts significantly on immigrants, who often are not literate in English.

Many students discuss the occupations of their grandparents who worked in the garment industry or other industries that no longer exist in New York City. Usually a consensus about the different economic challenges met by both present and past immigrants is reached. In essence, the economic reality of today is very different from that of the past. The United States is currently a technological society that requires literate persons for its workforce. In the past, immigrants were able to be absorbed into the workforce without much education because of the nature of the economy at the time, which was grounded in industry and did not require high skills or literacy.

Further sentiments revealed regarding linguistic minorities view immigrants as individuals who are benefiting from being in the United States but are unwilling to assimilate. A look at studies addressing the linguistic patterns of our current immigrants indicates that such views are not substantiated. As cited by Veltman (1983) and Amastae (1990), non-English speakers are shifting to English as rapidly as they always have. Hispanics, however, ontinue to speak Spanish in the home. Such a discussion leads into the reasons for this difference in the linguistic patterns of both past and present immigrant groups and the forces that have transformed the United States from a melting pot into a pluralistic society.

Prior to the revision of immigration quotas in the 1960s, immigrants to the United States were mainly white Europeans with ready access to assimilation into mainstream America. Their linguistic assimilation was the price they had to pay for admission into mainstream America. Since past immigrant groups were predominantly white, issues of race did not play a prominent role.

In contrast, current immigrant populations, originating from the Caribbean, Latin America, and Asia, are persons of color; therefore, race does play a significant role in their assimilation patterns. In cities like New York, color plays a crucial role in where you live, which school(s) your children will attend, and what intimate relationships you will maintain. For persons of color, ethnic enclaves very often characterized by languages other than English are more often than not the only available residence offered.

Census surveys in areas of the city attest to the use of Spanish in the home in community school districts that reflect high percentages of Latino students. Many persons realize that choices are limited and that complete assimilation is not in the cards. This is evident when trying to purchase a house, rent an apartment, or even select a decent school for one's child, an experience that I can personally attest to.

The immigrant, not out of choice but because of racial constraints, finds himself with no alternative but to maintain his culture and the ability to survive in his community as well as outside of his ethnic enclave. Furthermore, unlike past immigrant groups, who originated from Europe and arrived by boat, many current immigrant groups originate from countries that are geographically close to the United States. This distance is further shortened by the access of phone and air travel, resulting in the strengthening of ethnic ties.

Current immigration does not reqiure a complete severing of ties from the homeland, a common pattern for immigrants who rarely returned home because it was simply too far away, combined with monetary constraints.

In essence, both the social reality of being a person of color in a racist society and the accessibility to one's homeland play significant roles in maintaining one's ethnicity and the need to be bilingual. Bilingual education meets the needs of these immigrant children by providing them with the linguistic tools to survive in their communities as well as within the larger society. Thus the question that emerges is, What other advantages does being bilingual or being educated in bilingual classrooms have?

To answer this question, we must turn to studies on bilingualism within the fields of psycholinguistics and bilingual education that reveal that there are numerous cognitive, social, and psychological advantages to being taught in one's native language and being bilingual.

One of the first comprehensive studies to address language in education was conducted by the United Nations Educational Scientific and Cultural Organization (UNESCO). Findings indicated that children educated in a language that was not their home language experienced difficulties in the classroom (UNESCO, 1953). According to this monograph, written by international experts, one's mother tongue is the best linguistic medium of instruction because it serves as the vehicle through which the cultural environment is absorbed. According to these authorities, the mother tongue should be used for as long as possible.

The UNESCO report stipulates that competency in the second language can be attained if the mother tongue is the initial medium of instruction. The report also acknowledges that the use of one's mother tongue/home language facilitates literacy development, in addition to the learning of content areas and the strengthening of ties between the home and the school.

To have a better understanding of the detrimental effects of being educated in a language other than one's mother tongue, one merely needs to look at many of the Anglophone former colonies in which instruction has been conducted in English. Mazrui and Mazrui (1996), in discussing the education in English of children in Uganda and Kenya, speak of the dismal state of affairs in the school systems of both of these nations and the lack of English competency despite years of promoting English as a medium of instruction. Despite the use of English at the earliest possible levels of education in Uganda and monetary investments put into the promotion of English, it was found that there existed falling standards of English as reflected in the results of the Uganda National Examination Board. In Kenya, results from the national examination indicated that English use was falling, while Kiswahili use had shown an improvement. Many students in public universities in Kenya, according to the vice chancellor of Egerton University, are functionally illiterate in English. The role of English in former British and American colonies is further elaborated by Fishman, Conrad, and Rubal-Lopez (1996), who extensively address the role of English around the world.

Any discussion about the linguistic situation of a nation is incomplete without noting the status and functions of the languages spoken and the domains in which they are spoken. Who speaks what language to whom (Fishman, 1972) is the concern of the sociology of language. Not surprisingly, this is a significant and necessary discipline in understanding the societal use of language.

If being educated in a language that is not your mother tongue can be detrimental, then the question arises about what the benefits of being bilingual are. To address this, one must turn to research conducted in several disciplines which indicates that being bilingual has been found to have a positive impact on intelligence. Studies prior to the 1960s were often conducted on few subjects and did not include measures for degrees of bilingualism, socioeconomics, and other important variables that were not controlled for. Nonetheless, research conducted during the past 50 years indicates that there are cognitive advantages to being bilingual.

In international and cross-cultural studies conducted in Malaysia, Ireland, eastern Europe, Singapore, the United States, Mexico, and Canada, among other countries, it was found that bilingual speakers were superior to monolingual speakers on divergent thinking tests (see Ricciardelli [1992] and Baker [1988] for a review of these studies).

Other research attesting to the advantages of bilingualism have found that fluent bilingual speakers have greater metalinguistic awareness than their monolingual counterparts (Ianco-Worrall, 1972; Ben-Zeev, 1977a, 1977b; Bialystok, 1987a, 1987b; Bialystok & Ryan, 1985; Galambos & Hakuta, 1988). Such research addresses the ability to think about and reflect upon the nature and functions of language. This has been interpreted as the possibility that bilingual speakers may be ready slightly earlier than monolingual speakers in learning to read.

Additional findings have also found bilingual speakers to have greater communicative sensitivity than monolingual speakers (Ben-Zeev, 1977b; Genesee, Tucker, & Lambert, 1975). These studies have found that bilingual speakers have an increased sensitivity to the social nature and communicative functions of language. This can enhance one's communicative ability.

Other research on bilingualism and its relationship to cognition found that bilingual speakers were more field independent than monolingual speakers. The importance of this is that field-independent individuals tend to achieve higher scores academically than those who are field dependent. While these findings attesting to the advantages of being bilingual are important, they foster issues regarding degrees of bilingualism, ages when these advantages emerge, and many more related inquiries. In essence, consideration of these studies will now propel our attention to still another aspect of bilingualism and bilingual education and down a new road of inquiry.

One such path is the affective component of learning a second language. Exploration of such an issue provides us with information about the emotional variables that play a part in language learning and how these factors can impact on what happens in the classroom and, therefore, is invaluable in understanding the importance of learning in one's native language.

While research on the advantages of being bilingual provides us with reasons why bilingualism should be for all and promoted by a system that usually does the opposite, it does not alone explain why bilingual education is important. The variety of issues discussed here as well as others not attended to (including an array of constitutional, demographic, economic, political, and international issues) have taken us on a journey down many roads. Each road brings us closer to understanding how children from linguistic minority groups should be taught based on a complexity of factors found in the arts and sciences. In the presence of such a discourse, appropriate and meaningful pedagogical decisions can now be made by our future and current teachers.

References

Amastae, Jon (1990). Official English and the learning of English. In K. L. Adams & D. T. Brink (Eds.), *Perspectives on Official English: The campaign for English as the official language of the USA* (pp. 199-209). Berlin and New York: Mouton de Gruyter.

Baker, Colin (1996). *Foundations of bilingual education and bilingualism.* Clevedon, UK: Multilingual Matters.

—— (1988). *Key issues in bilingualism and bilingual education.* Clevedon, UK: Multilingual Matters.

Ben-Zeev, Sandra (1977a). The influence of bilingualism on cognitive strategy and cognitive development. *Child Development, 48,* 1009-1018.

—— (1977b). The effect of bilingualism in children from Spanish-English low economic neighborhoods on cognitive development and cognitive strategy. *Working Papers on Bilingualism, 14,* 83-122.

Bialystok, Ellen (1987a). Influences of bilingualism on metalinguistic development. *Second Language Research, 3,* 154-166.

—— (1987b). Words as things: Development of word concept by bilingual children. *Studies in Second Language Learning, 9,* 133-140.

Bialystok, Ellen, & Ryan, Ellen B. (1985). Toward a definition of metalinguistic skill. *Merrill-Palmer Quarterly, 31,* 229-251.

Brisk, María Estela (1998). *Bilingual education: From compensatory to quality schooling.* Mahwah, NJ: Lawrence Erlbaum.

CGCS [Council of the Great City Schools] (2001). *Educating English language learners in the nation's urban schools.* Washington, DC: Author.

Fishman, Joshua A. (1972). The sociology of language. In P. P. Giglioli (Ed.), *Language and social context* (pp. 45-59). Harmondsworth, UK: Penguin.

Fishman, Joshua A., Conrad, Andrew W., & Rubal-Lopez, Alma (1996). *Post-imperial English: Status change in former British and American colonies, 1940-1990.* Berlin and New York: Mouton de Gruyter.

Galambos, Sylvia J., & Hakuta, Kenji (1988). Subject specific and task-specific characteristics of metalinguistic awareness in bilingual children. *Applied Psycholinguistics, 9,* 141-162.

Genesee, Fred; Tucker, G. Richard; & Lambert, William E. (1975). Communication skills of bilingual children. *Child Development, 46,* 110-114.

Hernandez, L. (1998). *Facts and figures: Answers to frequently asked questions about limited English proficient (LEP) students and bilingual/ESL programs.* New York: Office of Bilingual Education.

Ianco-Worrall, Anita (1972). Bilingualism and cognitive development. *Child Development, 43,* 1390-1400.

Lanauze, Milagros (1999). *An overview of the United States educational system and language education across the nation.* Website: http://www.sgci.mec.es/usa/seminario/pdf/seminari01999/report19.pdf. Accessed November 9, 2003.

Lewis, Evan Glyn (1977). Bilingualism and bilingual education: The ancient world and the Renaissance. In B. Spolsky & R. L. Cooper (Eds.), *Frontiers of bilingual education.* Rowley, MA: Newbury House.

Macedo, Donaldo (1994). *Literacies of power.* Boulder, CO: Westview.

Mackey, William Francis (1978). The importation of bilingual education models. In J. Alatis (Ed.), *Georgetown University roundtable: International dimensions of education.* Washington, DC: Georgetown University Press.

Marshall, David F., & González, Roseann Dueñas (1990). Una lingua, una patria? Is monolingualism beneficial or harmful to a nation's unity? In K. L. Adams & D. T. Brink (Eds.), *Perspectives on Official English: The campaign for English as the official language of the USA* (pp. 29-53). Berlin and New York: Mouton de Gruyter.

Mazrui, Alamin M., & Mazrui, Ali A. (1996). A tale of two Englishes: The imperial language in post-colonial Kenya and Uganda. In J. A. Fishman, A. Conrad, & A. Rubal-Lopez (Eds.), *Post-imperial English: Status change in former British and American colonies, 1940-1990* (pp. 271-303). Berlin and New York: Mouton de Gruyter.

NYSED [New York State Education Department] (2002). *A profile of Latinos in the New York State education system from pre-K to Ph.D.* (Chapter 655 report). Albany: Author.

Ovando, Carlos J., & Collier, Virginia P. (1985). *Bilingual and ESL classrooms: Teaching in multicultural contexts.* New York: McGraw-Hill.

Ricciardelli, Lina A. (1992). Creativity and bilingualism. *Journal of Creative Behavior, 26,* 242-254.

UNESCO (1953). *The use of vernacular language in education.* Paris: Author.

United Nations (1995). Universal Declaration of Human Rights [1948]. In *The United Nations and human rights, 1945-1995.* New York: Department of Public Information, United Nations.

Veltman, Calvin J. (1983). *Language shift in the United States.* Berlin and New York: Mouton.

Elizabeth Quintero

CHAPTER TWELVE

Can Literacy Be Taught Successfully in Urban Schools?

I AM FROM...

I am from rolling pins and Bollywood Films with Aishwarya (actress) here
    and Shah Rukh (actor) so dear.
I am from sunflowers and skushed berries.
I am from Patel Brothers grocery store with lots and lots of spices.

I am from Mama and Papa, ... and JJ (my brother in-law), with Jaanu (means
    heart and soul in Hindi)
I am from "are beta, are beta, are Resha (my nickname), are are"
I am from bhindi (okra in Sindhi) papata (potatoes in Sindhi) and mani
    (bread in Sindhi)
I am from the mandir (Temple in Sindhi/Hindi) and gurdwara (Sikh temple)
    with my sweet sweet karan (food offering you get at a gurdwara)
    and peace of mind.
                                    (Teacher Education Graduate Student, 2003)

What about literacy in urban education? Isn't language a part of literacy?
Which literacy? Literacy for academics or literacy for love? These are profoundly complex questions. Teaching and learning occur in meantingul ways in
the language/literacy curriculum.

Okay, I do have something to say about all of these. What I believe is that
teaching and learning occur in meaningful ways in the language/literacy curriculum when three necessary conditions are met. The first condition is respect.
Learners and teachers have to respect each other—where we come from, how we
speak, what we do for work and fun. Secondly, the learning and teaching must be

participatory. All learners and teachers must communicate through dialogue, reading, writing, and listening while learning new information from each other. Thirdly, transformative action must happen. This means that learners use literacy to do something to make their world a better place. This action can be as personal as a love note or as political as the Lysistrata Project, in which hundreds of thousands of antiwar activists around the world participated in readings of the Greek play by Aristophanes. A woman from New Mexico was quoted in the *New York Times* as saying of the anti(Iraqi War effort, "There's a lot of people here who just want to do anything they can to keep it going" (March 4, 2003).

These conditions compose a context for what some of us teachers call critical literacy. We sometimes define critical literacy slightly differently from each other. For me, *critical literacy is a process of constructing meaning and critically using language (oral and written) as a means of expression, interpretation, and/or transformation through literacies of our lives and the lives of those around us.*

I use critical literacy for literacy instruction with children and for workshops and classes with preservice teachers, more advanced practicing teachers, and graduate students. When I use critical literacy with students, it takes the form of problem posing with activities centering on listening, dialogue, and action. This method combines reflective thinking, information gathering, collaborative decision making, and personal learning choices. By using problem posing, with its reflective and personal components, the learners are participating in a complex form of autobiographical narrative. I believe that this combined approach allows students to move beyond a neutral conception of culture in discussions of their relationships with schools and families and toward a better-defined conception of culture in a pluralistic, multicultural society.

I am a teacher and a writer with a perspective about learning and literacy which frames the ways I work and conduct research with all ages of learners from many different backgrounds. I study issues of literacy (and literacies) in urban schools, and I study families "at promise" (families whose diversities in language, culture, and lifestyle are strengths, not risks). I am fascinated by the use of language and critical literacy in the context of students' home culture and in the culture of learners' new learning environments in both schools and communities. I use a postformal perspective (Kincheloe & Steinberg, 1997), which demands that the politics of knowledge and the origins of sustained inequities of modern society be examined. Such a perspective grants us a new conception of what "being smart" means. "Postformalism is concerned with questions of justice, democracy, meaning, self-awareness, and the nature and function of social context" (Kincheloe, 2000, p. 83).

Who Are Our Students?

Mary Pipher (2002) documents that refugees from Russia, Serbia, Croatia, Bosnia, Hungary, Ethiopia, Kurdistan, and Somalia have come to Lincoln,

Nebraska. Poet Suheir Hammad, born in a refugee camp in Jordan and moving to a working-class neighborhood in Brooklyn, New York, at age five, represents the variety of histories and perspectives in an urban multicultural milieu. Her first book of poetry, *Born Palestinian, Born Black* is entitled as a homage to June Jordan, the late black poet. When asked about why she identified so much with African American literature, she said, "I think part of it is that I read so much as a kid, and African American literature is the outsider literature in the American canon, especially for poetry." She commented in an interview with a *New York Times* writer about her increased visibility, "I'm thankful. I'm doing this for a little girl somewhere in the middle of America with fuzzy hair and yellow skin, who will see my name and the power of an Eastern name that is not Osama bin Laden or Saddam Hussein" (March 14, 2003, B2).

A high school English teacher in a New York City school thinks a lot about who the students she teaches are. She notes that her students experience dilemmas of identity that are characteristic of teenagers. And she also notes that many of her students are immigrants, or children of immigrants, who feel trapped in that void between here and there: They belong nowhere. They are members of "the other" — Latino, Chicano, Hispanic, "Arab," "Asian," etc. This teacher also respects their community ties and their individual tenacity. She wrote about one of these students who uses her language and her art to show her self-respect, to participate, and to transform her world:

> The power of J's poem lies in her honest exchange with herself, her identity, and her audience. Though J neglects to hand in most writing assignments, or to show up to school most days, she clearly found personal meaning and inspiration in this assignment to write a poem to someone in particular…. She is at ease with her words when writing poetry, and can translate her verbal fluency into writing. She is moving beyond herself, discovering the world around her and how she fits into it, or rather, deciding whether or not she wants to fit into a world that does not accept her as she is. If teachers allow her to further explore this topic in a genuine fashion, she will hopefully move toward greater fluency in a range of linguistic styles, becoming more subtle and complex, exploring different voices, styles, forms, gaining confidence as a writer and a thinker. By simultaneously exploring her identity and her language, she has become more comfortable with both and is learning about herself and her words.

> What if…?
> What if you don't believe me?
> Will you not accept me if I was to tell you that
> I am black?
> Would it make a difference?
> Do I have to have that
> Mocha color skin,
> Hair in desperate need of a perm,
> Africa chantin,
> Reggae listenin'
> Incense burnin,'
> Roti eatin,' Project livin,' welfare recipient,
> "Black people habits."

Do I have to go to the extreme to please you?
What if you don't believe me?
Will you not accept me if I was to tell you that
I'm white?
Would it make a difference?
Do I have to have
Blonde hair, Blue eyes,
Pale skin,

A size 5 waist,
Shop at Abercrombie & Fitch,
Drink Evian,
And waste money as if I've got
Shitloads of it?
What if you don't believe me?
Do I still have to be what you want me to be?
Are you going to tell me that I,
Puerto Rican,
Dominican,
Cuban,
Or some other kind of Hispanic race that I have to fit
In order satisfy your qualifications
As to who you think I am?
What if you don't believe me?
It doesn't really matter because as long as my heart
Is able to beat faster and faster,
Just know that all you see, is ME!

Another woman, studying to be a literacy teacher, speaks of growing up in New York City:

I'm Chinese American, and in the Chinese community I would be described as a *jook-sing*, in other words, a child born in America who has adopted many American customs and characteristics. Being Chinese was not something I was proud of when I was younger, and because of that I failed to learn as much of the language as I could have, which I feel is a big part of being Chinese. Through this language I am able to have conversations with people who can fill me in on what being Chinese is all about. But because my ability is limited, I am often shy with my relatives who speak only Chinese. I don't want to be branded a *jook-sing* although I feel I am one. I am proud to be Chinese but when people ask me to tell them details about Chinese culture I'm afraid that I may fall short in explaining the complexity of it all. This aspect of me is important, it connects me to my family and their values. I am the way I am because of my ethnicity. I have accepted some of these beliefs and values as my own but I have also rebelled against some values that clash with my understanding of the world. I feel the latter aspect of myself can be attributed to my Americanized side. I don't tie my ethnicity to a particular place. I bring it wherever I go. However, I will say this, I feel my Chinese-ness the most if I am the only Chinese person in a particular place. I rarely feel this way in New York because of its diversity. Mostly I carry both plates in my hands wherever I go, but the people and the place will determine which one will be heavier.

A woman studying to become a literacy specialist from an urban area in Texas, spoke of her identity:

When I think of my ethnic identity, honestly I think of so many things, I don't know where to start. My family came from all over the place, actually, so I don't really know which ethnic group I identify myself with most. My mother is American by birth, as is her mother. But my grandmother grew up in Mexico, as did my grandfather. My grandmother's family was from Mexico. My grandfather's father was from Greece, his mother from Mexico. My father, born in Mexico, is of European descent. His father was born in Stockholm, his mother in San Antonio, right next to the Alamo. My grandmother also has Swedish and German ancestry. And while he is not Latino, my father grew up in Venezuela. These are all of the things I think of when I think of my ethnic background. I tend to relate more to the Hispanic side of my family, because I grew up in San Antonio, where there is such a large Hispanic population. I guess that would be the place my ethnic identity is tied to. Everyone in my family speaks Spanish; all my grandparents, aunts, uncles, etc. While the history of Mexican people has not played a large role in my upbringing, I know some of it, mostly what I learned in school and from my surroundings. People in San Antonio are very aware of Mexican culture, and this is shown in various ways throughout the city. Even though I am American, I relate to the Mexican culture most out of all of my backgrounds because it plays such a vital role in my everyday life.

Problem-Posing Critical Literacy

I believe that our students in urban schools, with their diverse strengths and needs, make the three criteria of respect, participation, and action even more important than ever. These criteria are best addressed through a problem-posing method, based on a critical literacy perspective. This method is powerful because it situates the participant as the activist in the dance between lived experience and new information. The method encourages what I see as a natural movement from reflection toward action. I stress that I use this problem-posing approach not as a prescriptive lesson planning format but as a way to facilitate student choice and generative work related to students' lives, whatever their age or contexts.

Problem-posing teaching, particularly when it incorporates multicultural literature and literature and the arts from the communities the students represent, nourishes an integrated curriculum which supports young students' meaningful learning. The problem-posing method was developed by Paulo Freire (1973) and critical pedagogists, initially for use with adult literacy students. The method leads students of any age, experience, or ability level to base new learning on personal experience in a way that encourages critical reflection. This method has not been widely used with younger learners, but lends itself well to integrated early childhood literacy development as well as to use of multicultural children's literature, oral storytelling, and poetry as a way to enact respect for students and their communities.

This methodology, with its strong theoretical and philosophical underpinnings, encourages teachers to NOT limit their teaching to units and lesson plans. It encourages teachers to use as a point of departure the background funds of knowledge (Mollet al., 1992) that the children bring from their lived experience rather than a written form of normalization. Personal narrative lets us listen to the voices of all the participants—students and authors, in their cultural contexts—as they tell about their experiences and explain ongoing efforts at agency and transformation.

Problem Posing for Preschoolers, Elementary, and Middle School Learners

My students and I address the possibilities and problems that critical literacies offer to classroom teachers. In creating a pedagogy for critical literacy, teachers use local knowledge of their particular sites and draw on a range of theories. What a critical perspective does is offer teachers a way to think about what it is that students are learning to read and write.

The method encourages students of all ages to write about their own lives and use their home languages with self-respect and pride. In the area of language development, we now know that children at age six have not yet begun to complete full cognitive development in their first language (Collier, 1989). When children's first-language development is discontinued before cognition is fully developed, they may experience negative cognitive effects in their second-language development; conversely, children who have an opportunity to learn in their native language and then learn a second language reach full cognitive development in two languages and enjoy cognitive advances over monolingual speakers (Collier, 1989). Making the issue of learning in a student's first language more urgent, research now shows that it may take as long as seven to ten years for nonnative speakers to reach the average level of performance by native speakers on standardized tests.

An undergraduate student majoring in early childhood education wrote about an article on second-language acquisition in relation to the strengths of a young child in her field placement:

> In regard to the article, there is one second-grade student, Andre, who deals with this issue. Because he was born in Norway but came to America at an early age, Andre is able to speak his native tongue and English equally well. I only realized that he was able to speak two languages through reading his "About the Author" at the end of one of his 'published' works. He was eager to point it out to me, which showed me that he was proud of his bilingualism. Indeed he should be proud, because it is a major accomplishment. Knowing two or more languages furthers communication. Having more words to choose from allows the opportunity for exact expression. I wish that my parents spoke to me in Italian. It is only now through my college course work that I have taken up the language. In knowing the Italian language, I feel more connected to my culture.

Another student in the same undergraduate early childhood literacy class personalized in terms of her own childhood the information in the same article:

> There are a few things that struck me while reading this article…. I personally related to this. As a child I was not encouraged to cultivate my home languages of Spanish and Italian in school. I would refuse to speak anything other than English because I felt that was the "right way" and that is what everyone else in school spoke. As a result, similar to what the article stated, I lost the ability to communicate well with my extend-

ed family. Sadly, I am unable to converse with my grandmother who speaks only Italian. This principle also relates to the classroom I am currently student-teaching in. There are a few students from different nations, and the teacher is well aware of this. Every morning during "meeting time," the children read what is written on the board. In both English and another language (usually Spanish), the words for 'good morning' are written and read out loud by all. This is an example of one way teachers could cultivate and help students appreciate bilingualism. It shows acknowledgment and respect for other languages and cultures, but more importantly, communicates that to the children.

Problem posing provides an arena for activities in which students can use their home languages, cultural stories, and traditions while learning English and competencies in a "standard curriculum." A few weeks after having participated in problem posing with multicultural children's literature, I gave the students examples of this method in a Head Start class and a first-grade class. Both examples are based on use of the book *The Whispering Cloth: A Refugee's Story* by Pegi Deitz Shea. The examples below using this children's story show how a work of literature can be used with activities developed for various age levels. My teacher education students see that participation is instructive for younger learners too. With young children, a problem-posing approach can enrich and maintain the student-centered integrity of scaffolding needed for younger learners. I will give only the experience from the first-grade class, below.

Example from a First-Grade Class

The following lesson was in a first-grade classroom in an urban school in a large Midwestern city. The teacher is a twenty-year veteran in the district, of Irish American descent. The student teacher with her is a Hmong male who is from the community where the school is situated. The students in the class consist of sixteen Hmong children, three African American children, and one child from South America. For this lesson, the teacher uses the storybook *The Whispering Cloth*.

Listening:

The teacher begins by gathering the children around her in the classroom central area where she unfolds several quilts. She reminds them of previous discussions and stories they have shared about quilts. Then she shows a weaving from Ireland and explains that it is from the country her family comes from. Then, she holds up a large, colorful "storycloth" which was been made by one of the school staff's relatives who is Hmong.

Dialogue:

The teacher asks, "Do you think a quilt could tell a story? Do you think you can hear a story from a cloth?" The children discuss briefly what they think about the question.

Action:

Then the teacher passes the folded cloth around the circle, so that each student can "listen" to the cloth. She shows the class the book and tells them just a little about it. "It is a story about a Hmong girl and her grandmother who live in a refugee camp in Thailand. Grandmother is teaching Mai how to make storycloths and Mai creates one that tells her story." Then the teacher shows the bilingual glossary in the book with Hmong words and English translations and explains that she will read the story in English in a few minutes, but first the student teacher, Mr. Z, will read it in Hmong.

Listening:

The story is read in Hmong. The students who do not understand Hmong nod their heads, stare at the pictures, and reflect the expressions on Mr. Z's face. They appear to be fascinated by the words in spite of not comprehending.

Dialogue:

The teacher then asks, "Can you guess what the story was about based upon Mr. Z's intonations, the pictures, and so forth?" The Hmong children make a few comments in English about the story.

Action:

Then the teacher reads the story in English.

The student teacher explains to the students that he has written a letter to their families explaining what they are learning about. The letter was written in English, Hmong, and Spanish. In the letter, the teachers ask the parents if their child can share either a storycloth, quilt, or other artifact that tells a family story. When the items are brought to school, extension activities are implemented.

The class makes a storycloth with a contribution from each student's drawing and writing (native language or English or both) during the following days.

After we (my preservice early-childhood-literacy teacher education class) spent time analyzing the examples of problem-posing lessons using *The Whispering Cloth*, the students began to work on their own problem posing with young children in their classrooms.

The following examples show two student teachers planning for preschoolers and second graders and one practicing teaching using the method with middle school English language learners.

Students Planning Problem Posing

1. Problem Posing with Pre-K

Rough Draft

For this lesson, I have selected a collection of 22 bilingual poems written by the Mexican poet Francisco X. Alarcón, *From the Bellybutton of the Moon and*

Other Summer Poems. In preparing the class for this lesson, the poem "From the Bellybutton of the Moon 1 & 2" should be posted up on opposite walls of the classroom. Pictures made by the children of activities they do with their family or special trips they have taken with their family should be posted next to these poems. The making of these pictures can be a separate activity done in advance. The children will be eager (especially in my class) to share pictures of their family/trips and are in fact even doing them now. There is only one girl in my class who is Mexican, Sofia-Elena, who is part Mexican and part Cuban. I think that she will definitely be able to relate to the lesson and be excited about sharing her life with her classmates. It is also important to incorporate this lesson into the general curriculum of the class. The children are learning about where they come from. They have studied babies, their school, their neighborhoods, and now they are learning about their homes. My cooperating teachers are now conducting home visits where four or five students visit the home of their classmate. During this visit they learn about their classmate's home life, family, and culture. The collection of poems I have chosen is particularly relevant because it is about Alarcón's childhood and what he learned about Mexico from his family. The children are given 45 minutes during the morning to participate in work time. They are given several options to choose from for their daily activity. For this lesson, I would like to incorporate Alarcón's poetry and/or readings from Mexican culture in each of the activities. If at all possible it would be an added benefit to have someone from Sofia-Elena's home come and speak to the children. This would have to be discussed and worked out by the cooperating teacher.

Listening:

During morning meeting, before the children begin work time, I will take down or call their attention to the poems posted on the walls. I will ask them to:

1   Talk about the pictures they made of their family and trips, and

2   Remind the class about what the poems were about. The poems will have been discussed in the preliminary activity.

Next, I will take out a tape that I recorded of myself reading the Alarcón poems section by section in Spanish and English and play it for them. I will also have created illustrations to complement the story. The children will listen to the story and look at the pictures as I hold them up for each section of the story. The poems are "Green Grass," "Sunflower," and "Rainbow."

Dialogue:

At the end of the poems, I will stop the tape and ask Sofia-Elena, my four-year-old coteacher, to share an object (or maybe a person) that is special to her and that reminds her of Mexico. I will ask the rest of the students, "What do you think of when you hear the words 'home' or 'school' or…" and follow the lead of their responses and questions. This discussion will lead the class toward an opportunity to express their thoughts in various work time activities.

Action:

There will be several options for work time. Sofia-Elena and I will explain them. These choices will be posted in print and with a picture so that Sofia-Elena will have an easier time remembering what they are when she announces them.

Audiovisual: Students may take turns recording their own poems, beginning with the words, "Whenever I say…"

Reading: Students may read some of the other poems in the book or choose from other bilingual books that have been put on display in advance.

Dramatic play: The children may take turns acting out some of the poems.

Writing: The students can write their own poems about their families and culture.

What Happened?

This student reported that on the day of her work with this lesson, it was raining and stormy, so she couldn't take the children outside before the lesson as she had hoped. She brought in a big sunflower plant in a pot (to go with the "Sunflower" poem) and a huge green "grass" plastic mat (like the artificial turf used in sports games) and asked the children to take off their shoes and pretend that they were outside in the grass (to go with the "Green Grass" poem). Then she conducted the lesson as planned in her description. She brought in to our class three of the poems created by the four-year-olds, which they dictated to her as a part of the "Action" section of her lesson. The poems show the children's involvement.

Spring
by KJ and C.
There's a sun in a flower.
A bird came in the flower and
took the sun away.
And the bird put it up to the sky.
The rain came down
and the bird got wet and he
rushed home and he
broke the sun's heart.
And the sun was never the same again.
The next day it wasn't raining
and the bird came back
The flowers bloomed
and the sun came back
He said, "Oh, what a gorgeous day."
When the sun came back he jumped
for joy and sang his song.

KJ's Poem	C's Song
When you see me in the Spring time	Once there was a kitten
I always see you.	and every night he liked to curl up in
You should say my name.	the bed and one day the kitten
I will love you.	tripped off the bed.
You should say what I say	He tried to jump back on but couldn't.
It never is the truth	
to say ma . . . ah.	
Oh . . . oh . . . oh . . .	
Halleluiah.	

2. Problem Posing with Second Grade

Another student planned this exercise for the second-grade students she was working with. She used the book *Isla* by Arthur Dorros:

> At the school where I am student-teaching the second-grade class, our study for the year is the history of New York City. The students just finished a section on immigration. The focus of my problem-posing lesson further explores this concept.

Listening:

I begin by saying, "I know a few of you have come here, to the United States, from another country. By a show of hands, let's see who you are. Does anybody have parents who have immigrated to this country? Raise your hands. I have to raise my hand too because my parents came from Europe. How about grandparents? Does anyone have grandparents or great-grandparents who have immigrated here? Or does anyone know neighbors or friends who are immigrants? Remember, your friends in class count. What about immigrants we don't know personally? Who are some immigrants who are in the news or on TV or in the movies?" I allow a few children to respond after each question.

Then I explain, "The grandmother of the girl in the story I am going to read is an immigrant, and she tells her grandchild about her homeland. The storybook is *Isla* by Arthur Dorros. Some of you may be familiar with another of his books, *Abuela* [show them]. *Isla* is a 'sequel' to that book, which means it's like part 2 of the book."

I read *Isla*.

Dialogue:

A discussion is held revolving around these questions:
In this story, how did the little girl come to appreciate the homeland of her grandmother? What are the kinds of things that we found about La Isla?
If we wanted to find out about the homeland of immigrants we know or even about the homeland of people we don't know but would like to know about, what kind of things would you like to find out? (List responses on chart paper)

Action:

I then ask the children to partner up and interview each other about their homeland or the homeland of someone they know. I say that if they don't want to share, they don't have to; they can listen in another's interview. I remind them to look at the chart we made, to get ideas for their questions. I want them to try and ask about at least two things. I give examples: for instance, if I were interviewing L., I might ask him about the kinds of places there are to visit in the Dominican Republic and what kinds of foods there are. I explain to the children that after their interviews, we will come back as a group and share some things that we learned. Then we will have time to draw some pictures. I will have them draw (or write) something about their homeland or the homeland of someone they know. If they can't think of anything to draw, they can draw something about their homeland here in New York. I remind them that immigrants have two homelands, the homeland of the country they moved from and the homeland of where they live now.

What Happened? (Excerpts from student journal)

Isla was a hit. Although the lesson did not go exactly according to plan, the outcome was better than expected. Students were very engaged. My personal belief as to why this lesson was successful is related to its interactive design. Because students took an active role in the experience from the beginning, personal meaning for each student was given to the concepts behind the lesson.

Each part of the lesson allowed students to take initiative and develop the details. During the reading, we stopped at points where interest was high or at points where questions arose and held a brief discussion. After the reading, students were able to brainstorm a long list of things they could find out about another's homeland. Some items included what the place looked like, what kinds of stores there were, what kinds of things there were to do, and what kinds of clothes people wore. After the brainstorming session, students used the list to interview each other. Then, time was given for the students to draw.

Originally, I had intended to hand out interview worksheets to the students to guide their thinking. Because of time constraints (only fifteen minutes was allotted for interview time), I changed my plan at the last minute and decided to ask the students to interview each other without a planned worksheet. The interviews went well. The students did not follow the directions exactly, but the basic concept of learning about the homeland of others was accomplished. There was a steady flow of conversation, and the children enjoyed talking about themselves and their families.

The only other part of the lesson that did not turn out as I expected was related to the extension activity. I had hoped that more students would draw a picture of their native homeland, but because I gave the choice of drawing New York, a majority of the children drew New York. Even so, I would not change the lesson design if I had a chance to do it again. I did not want students to get hung up on figuring out what to draw—I wanted them to enjoy the experience while making a concrete representation of what a homeland means to them. This, I believe, was accomplished.

I don't want this to sound all poshy and prettied up, but truthfully, the lesson went well. The students were able to extend on their theme study (related to immigration to New York), learn about a number of different countries, and develop an appreciation for the differences among them. When I have a chance to implement this sort of lesson in my own classroom, I will probably follow the same approach, as well as implement the original lesson I had intended (where the students would interview a person outside the classroom and conduct a miniresearch of that person's homeland).

3. Problem Posing with Middle School

Finally, I include a teacher using the method with her seventh-grade class of English-language learners. The school is in a large Midwestern city in a neighborhood that is home to many recent immigrants. In this particular class, the majority of students are native speakers of Spanish, from the United States, Mexico, and Central America. There are a few Hmong speakers, one speaker of Burmese, and one speaker of Somali.

Cummins (1994) outlines a framework for English-language learners that highlights distinction between conversational and academic communication. He notes that persuading another person of one's point of view and writing an essay demand cognitive skills necessary for academic language use. This teacher's use of problem posing provides opportunity for both conversational and academic communication.

Listening:

The teacher shows the class a photo of herself when she was seven years old and then pulls out a map of Minnesota. She shows them the small northern Minnesota town where her own immigrant family (from Serbia) lived when she was a child. Then she tells a story of how when she was seven, her father lost his job on the railroad, and there was no other work in their town. So the family decided to move to California. Her dad went first and saved money, and then sent for the family some months later. Her mother, with her four young children, flew on an economy flight leaving at midnight and arriving in California at dawn. "I still remember how impressed I was by the sight of the toy city below…and how happy my dad was to see us," the teacher recalls.

The teacher then shows the drawing she made in four parts that visually tells her story, drawn on one large sheet of butcher paper.

Dialogue:

Here the teacher asks the students, "What are sentences to explain each of the pictures?" Students work on keeping the story in past tense and have to learn a couple of new words like *airport* and *toy*.

Action:

The teacher then gives the students a lesson guide that includes the following instructions:

YOUR STORY ASSIGNMENT

1. Write a story about your childhood in your first language. Write the story in the past tense.

2. Write the same story in English. Divide it into 4 parts to go with 4 drawings.

3. Draw 4 pictures that show the 4 parts of your story.

4. Tell your story in English to 3 other students and a teacher.

5. Rewrite your story in the present tense.

6. Hand everything in to your teacher to get a grade.

This guide, along with the required task of reading their stories to others, satisfies an important component of providing opportunities for the development of academic English.

A student who had emigrated from Mexico to Minnesota told her story first with pictures, then she wrote the story in her native language of Spanish, and then she wrote the story in English. A student from El Salvador told his story of going from El Salvador to Mexico to the United States. His first work sample was in the form of a drawing; the second was a story written in his native language of Spanish, and the third a story he wrote in English.

Conclusion

Problem posing helps us to look at alternative ways of knowing, through students' real experiences and achievements. I maintain that with the help of the authors of literature, community storytellers and poets, and families who are encouraged to share lived experiences, learners of all ages can use critical literacy concepts in a profound way. The Listening/Dialogue/Action structure for literacy education considers the student as an individual who is part of family and community. We teachers create the context for learners to pose questions and encourage the consideration of the strengths of students and their families as well as the barriers they face daily.

Eduardo Galeano (2002) writes that graffiti on walls of many of our urban centers are much more thoughtful than advertising and other print which we are bombarded with in the environment. Some examples he gives are:

- Is living alone as impossible as living with someone?

- Does love die or just change residence?

- Will I be a poet when I'm a child?

- If the prisons are full of innocent people, where are the criminals?

- I hid what I was thinking so well that I don't remember it anymore.

- So much rain and so few rainbows.

- What if there's a war but no one goes?

I believe that these graffiti are meaningful to the writers and the readers because they come from life—from within. I believe problem-posing literacy has the potential for us to build on the strengths and the wisdom of our students and their communities. What are we waiting for?

References

Collier, Virginia P. (1989). How long? A synthesis of research on academic achievement in a second language. *TESOL Quarterly, 23,* 509-531.

Cummins, Jim (1994). The acquisition of English as a second language. In K. Spangenberg-Urbschat & R. Pritchard (Eds.), *Kids come in all languages: Reading instruction for ESL students.* Newark, DE: International Reading Association.

Freire, Paulo. (1973). *Education for critical consciousness.* New York: Seabury.

Galeano, E. (2002). Talking walls. *The Progressive,* p. 17.

Kincheloe, Joe L. (2000). Certifying the damage: Mainstream educational psychology and the oppression of children. In L. Soto (Ed.), *The politics of early childhood education* (pp. 75-84). New York: Peter Lang.

Kincheloe, Joe L., & Steinberg, Shirley R. (1997). *Changing multiculturalism.* Philadelphia: Open University Press.

Moll, Luis; Amanti, Carol; Neff, Deborah; & Gonzalez, Norma (1992). Funds of knowledge for teaching: Using a qualitative approach to connect homes and classrooms. *Theory into Practice, 31,* 132-41.

Pipher, M. (2002). *The middle of everywhere: The world's refugees come to our town.* New York: Harcourt.

CHAPTER THIRTEEN

How Can Urban Students Become Writers?

I know it's been forever and a day since I e-mailed you, but that's mainly because I've been wrapped up in these stupid classes. Let me say class (English). (sic)

I received the above e-mail from one of my former students. Her name is Kenesha Vassell. I was then at the midpoint of this chapter. She is a freshman/sophomore in Florida. I suspected her note was a call for help. The following night I received another e-mail. It read:

> I'm…send(ing) you two of the essays that I had to turn in, one which was due today. I know they might sound a little bit on the stupid side, but that's only because I really don't like doing her essays. She puts too much emphasis on little things. Not to mention how uninteresting the…topics are…. Her intentions may be to teach us to write, but it is difficult to write about things that are retarded. (LOL). Well, here they are….

I was more than a bit shocked. Kenesha Vassell had been a prolific writer both in my sophomore global history class and in her junior year, in which she graduated. Moreover, two years after graduation she had been instrumental in encouraging my "current" students. They had started a journal like the one Kenesha had edited while in high school. Acting as a coach of sorts, two years after graduation, she contributed an article to the new publication. Her commentary was well received by students two or three years her junior. Her crisp and provocative writing style spawned a mini-debate within the group.

I began asking myself, What had gone wrong? If this student was really an effective writer in high school, why was she having such difficulty with compositions in college? If one of my more stellar students was having so much difficulty with college writing, how credible was I in writing about how to teach writing to urban students?

I thought about her predicament. She was being asked to write about things that were to her "retarded." The topics weren't personal and emotional. When topics are personal and emotional, students find meaning. They write. I reflected on my very own difficult experience with college writing. Outside of the classroom I wrote profusely. Within the classroom my English professors thrashed my writing. Rather than accept my high C's, I would argue/challenge the professors and end up with different grades: high D's and low C's, except in one speech course. For most of my college friends, science was the bugbear. For me writing, or so my professors would have me believe, was my Achilles' heel. There was a double irony at work here. At the time, I couldn't understand how I could be so mediocre in English (writing) but do so well in speech. It was as if my speech teacher were saying to me: "Although the other English professors don't think you know how to write, you certainly know how to talk and transcribe it."

Yet, all that is written is worthwhile. All that is written should be accepted and praised. Suggestions can be given as to how it can or should be improved. This way the teacher builds on what the student offers and encourages rather than demoralizing and silencing the student.

I was the first in the family to attend college. There was no one to at least inform me of how to navigate the English department or to temper my speech. I could get better grades in college writing and other courses in which critical speech, or talking back, was a potential liability. Kenesha was like that also. She had an outspoken, fiery, tell-it-like-it-is disposition. I realized that I had to come up with "thought experiments" that could perhaps allow her to discover ways of navigating and surviving her college professor of writing.

In writing this chapter (outlining a framework on how to teach writing to inner-city high school students), communicating with her became a part of the process. I e-mailed her. I reiterated what I had always told her, that she could write. I shared my college writing experience with her so that she could realize that while she may have problems with the professor's approach, this did not necessarily mean that there was any major problems with her writing.

My task, then, was not so much to help write her paper but to find a way to further demonstrate her writing prowess so that she would disabuse herself of the notion that she couldn't write. Two weeks passed. I thought that Kenesha had reclaimed her former writing prowess. Then I was confronted by this e-mail:

Subj: I need help
Date 3/6/03 10:50:32

Mr. Holder

I have a report due on Wednesday, but I can't figure out a thesis statement. I'm pretty sure, well at least I would hope that you know what that is. It's supposed to be a compare or contrast essay and I can't think of anything. Nothing political (LOL). I'll give you an example of what someone wrote. The thesis was: Although having roommates does have advantages, when it comes to sharing a bathroom, living alone is the better choice. And then her three topic sentences were: When living alone, the chance of having to take a cold shower is much more than when living with roommates. When living alone, someone barging in on you while in the bathroom is not such a dilemma than it is when living with roommates; Running out of bathroom supplies happens more often while living with roommates than while living alone.

I will be greatly appreciative if you could help me find one.

Nesha.

After rereading this e-mail, especially the last sentence—about helping her find what was already present in her writing—I became even more convinced that the key to unlocking Kenesha's predicament was hidden in plain sight before our very eyes. And it was while reflecting on an appropriate response that I recalled Freire (1997) saying:

> The pitfall of a linguist is to believe that writing words is freezing them in time. Writing fixes the force of orality in time but the reader, in engaging with that force, is continually reinventing and redialoguing, and so the text remains alive and unfrozen. (31).

This realization led me to think of a way not only to concretize my assertions about her ability to conceptualize and write but also to devise a mode for her to revisit, reengage, and reclaim her words which were frozen in *Crossing Swords*, the high school publication of which she was a member of the editorial collective. So, titling my e-mail, "Much Ado about Little," I wrote:

Nesha:

There's very little that your professor is requiring of u that you did not do in high school. Reread your writings in *Crossing Swords,* especially the following essay which you wrote in your junior year and evaluate it 2 determine to what extent (if any) it conforms with your professor's desire 4 a thesis, topic sentences and development, etc.

Remember what I've always said that u r an intuitive writer and that you are familiar with, and use many of the writing techniques/conventions that your professor may be introducing as something esoteric…. After rereading your essay I want an answer to my questions…. Have u been writing within or outside the convention?

In the essay, "Classroom Melodies: Giving Voice to the Voiceless," that I attached to the e-mail, Kenesha had written:

Finding a classroom where it wasn't the same routine of entering, answering the "Do Now" and for the rest of the period copying notes, came as a shock and surprise to me. I wasn't used to debating and I never enjoyed participating in class. For, I wasn't accustomed to being in a classroom where students' voices were given such respect. The "calypso classroom" is how I would describe my tenth grade social studies class. I use this term because calypso is a form of music where different instruments and beats are used to form one melody. Although all instruments are not always in harmony and sometimes appear to be fighting each other for dominance, the mix always provides a beautiful end-product: harmonious music.

As our classroom was filled with students presenting different opinions and points of views this often led to frequent heated debates that weren't always harmonious. But in the end, after debating, our ideas either enlarged those of our opponents or we were able to help each other to see and appreciate another side of an issue. This constant give and take is what made the class so different.

Learning is supposed to be enjoyable as well as informative. Even though learning does not take place only in the classroom, it begins there. So part of the responsibility lies with the teacher to make students want to learn. *In order for students to learn, the classroom cannot be conducted as a dictatorship where students' voices are silenced and the teacher has all the say.* If it is that way all the time and students are not able to question the teacher's "facts" or ask why or how, students may not be excited about learning. Instead, they would be forever asking themselves: "Why is my answer wrong? Why won't the teacher listen to what I have to say?" As a student, I have noticed that some teachers just don't care anymore. Part of the problem is that some teachers don't know how to get students involved. They seem not to know how to engage and excite students about learning.

Although I was lucky enough to find a good teacher who actually loves to teach, what about the other students who may not be as fortunate? Why should they be stuck with a teacher whose motto is: "I don't care if you don't want to learn because I could just sit here and get paid?" How can you expect someone to want to learn in an environment where the teacher doesn't care or where he or she doesn't know how to make the classroom interesting? Maybe if these teachers would stop worrying about getting paid and put their interest into teaching, then students would want to learn. Then classes would be more interactive, as in the calypso classroom, and fewer students would cut classes because they will now have something to look forward to.

Teachers do have a greater impact on their students than many people believe. For example, before the calypso classroom I never wrote anything beyond what was required in the classroom. *It wasn't until my history teacher encouraged me to start writing, not just in the classroom but also about whatever was on my mind, that I began to pay closer attention to my environment and began writing on a daily basis. And I've been writing ever since!*

Because we are teenagers, too many adults sometimes underestimate our knowledge and interests. They think because we hang out a lot or we may be chillin' in the hallways before class that we are unconcerned youth who don't know what's going on in our surroundings. That's one of the most serious problems with some of the adults. They like to stereotype us and put us into their narrow categories when all we need is someone to tell us that we're good and encourage us to reach for the stars. Everybody has a talent or skill! All we need is someone, even a teacher, to pull it out from us.

In the classroom I began to notice that my social studies teacher, the adviser, had a talent for pulling information from students by presenting topics in a way to involve the entire class in discussion. Even the "bad" students were interested. Everybody got a new identity from debating and writing. If you were a hall walker or a class cutter, you weren't known as that in the class, but as the person who either wrote a particular essay or made a unique point in a discussion.

The discussions and writings in the calypso classroom gave everybody a chance to be in the spotlight. It gave everyone the chance to voice his or her opinion and to appreciate the reaction of classmates. It created a sense of community because rather than condemning one another's viewpoints, we started to appreciate and learn to see the other side of an issue.

Writing gave me a new identity. As I walked through the hallways, many teachers, security officers, and even students whom I didn't know told me that they read something I wrote. Writing has also enabled me to get involved with positive activities such as the Society for Social Analysis and my school journal, *Crossing Swords*, of which I am now the senior editor.

Writing has also been a way for me to express my feelings and voice my opinions on many issues that are of concern to me. Like Garfield McNeill, my fellow classmate, once wrote, "The pen is mightier than the mouth!" and I would definitely agree. Just saying something verbally may account for very little, because as fast as you say it, that's as fast as it may be forgotten. It's when you write that you actually make and leave your mark. People start to notice and understand you and that's when the voice of the voiceless is finally heard.

Does this essay read as coming from someone who would be unsure of her ability to come up with a thesis and supporting data for a college composition? I well remember Kenesha's words when she submitted the essay to me: "Would you believe that I never write such a long essay in English where I get credit for writing, but here I am writing my behind off for no credit for you and your magazine?"

"Since when do you write for me?" I asked.

"A'ight, don't give me another lecture about Rosemarie."

"Yes, always remember Rosemarie Dunbar's words: 'Do we write only for our teachers and ourselves?' No. We must begin thinking that we write for an audience beyond the teacher and the classroom."

"Okay, Mr. H, I get it."

Kenesha's essay not only resonates through time but also captures the feelings/sensibilities of the generations of students before her who wrote in the journal. Why did they write so much when there was not the tangible or traditional benefit of credit and grades? Students had not only discovered a voice but also a vehicle to freeze their texts in space and time so that future generations, even themselves, could "(re)read…the(ir) written texts," envisioning it as "the reinvention of oral speech."

It was only after reflecting further on both her essay and our March/April 2003 dialogue reproduced above that I realized that far from "teaching" students any techniques of writing, my classroom and the after-school project it spawned had actually provided students with what Postman (1996) refers to as "an inspired reason for schooling"(p. 18), one that disparages the reductionist focus on grades and preparation for passing tests. Instead, students discovered the joys and rewards of dialogue and discovery, as Kenesha so vividly underscores in her essay above. Moreover, by displaying a willingness to move along a "path where the effort of the thought was justified not by the finding but by the seeking" (Boorstin, 1999), they were displaying a commitment not merely to "answering questions but to questioning answers" as my friend, Danny Weil often says.

Hence, embedded within the writings of Kenesha and many of my students who mentored me was the notion that rather than *teaching* students how, or even motivating them, to write, what we were in fact intuitively doing, unknowingly, was fomenting an *urge* within them to write. Indeed, it was as if we had stumbled upon Freire's view that "technique is always secondary and is only important when it is in the service of something larger. To make technique primary is to lose the purpose of education" (Freire, 1997, p. 304).

However, to better understand this dialectic and drama, as it evolves, we must turn to students' very own words, especially since, as Kincheloe, Slattery, and Steinberg (2000) note, "often missing in the literature written for teacher education are student[s'] thoughtful discussions of teacher (mis)education" (p. 242). As a corrective, then, we must reinscribe students' distinctive voices where they can be most helpful: in discussions of the theater of urban education. And what better way to create reflective teachers than by facilitating interactive settings wherein we become students of our own students and classrooms? Indeed, it was a rereading of Kenesha's high school essay and her explanation of how I encouraged her to celebrate the poetry of everyday life in her writings which led me to refocus this chapter from teaching writing to fostering a community of writers. Key to this reconceptualization is our ongoing dialogue, serving as the source text for this exegesis/contribution.

Perhaps no better resource fosters this sense of self-reflection more effectively than students' reflections or confessions on educational issues. Fortunately for us, between 1988 and 2000, each new generation of students and I published more than 1,700 pages of student commentary on almost every facet of the human experience: war and peace, poverty and profligacy, communism and its demise, teen sex and its consequences, sense and nonsense, effective teaching and its antithesis, apartheid, truth commissions and reconciliation, military interventions and resistance movements, racism and its palliatives, shock and awe, and on and on.

How, then, did we get students to write so insightfully and profusely? Did we infuse the classroom with writing techniques or was there a simpler narrative at work, creating communicative communities across space and time akin to Chaucer's *Canterbury Tales*? Can there be many dissenting voices to the proposition that students compose more freely, creatively, and profusely when they envision writing simply as tale telling—as practiced uninhibitedly in their natural environments in the lunchroom, ballpark, or when chillin' with friends? In these theaters of resistance, people do not dare censor their rap as they venture, sometimes unwittingly, on a literary pilgrimage to self-knowledge.

However, before we interrogate the writing of a few more students, perhaps it would be best to isolate from Kenesha's essay some of the key ingredients that, in her view, foster a community of writers:

- Respect for students and their ideas (unsilencing of student voices)
- Questioning that engages, excites, and involves the entire class in discussion

(a reason or purpose to look forward to being in class)

- Discovery of new self (from debating and writing)
- Sense of community in which robust dialogue is encouraged and welcomed
- Joy of movement away from routine or ritualized work to transforming, self-affirming engagements

Kenesha's 2000 essay may well have been the most extensive treatment of the nature and drama of the engagements in our classroom. But when, in the fall of 1998, as a sophomore, she was first placed on my roster, she entered not merely into a classroom but, like her contemporaries, into a living tradition by participating in "the ongoing conversations that incorporate our past and shape our future" (Applebee, 1996, p. 3).

How was this conversation fashioned? From the start, were students and I aware of what we were getting into? Perhaps the adult reflections of one of the very first students who set the tradition in motion may provide some insight into how a community of writers evolved, perhaps unwittingly. Writing in the very last issue that was published before the school was unceremoniously closed in 2001 due to its consistent failure in all aspects of education and the fact that there was no redeeming qualities to the school., Ann M. Green in her essay "Moving Shadows: Retrospective and Prospective" wrote:

One day I found myself in a strange and large place called high school. Over the years this large place became a comfortable and familiar place I now refer to as Hale (Sarah J. Hale High School). Even more familiar and equally memorable is the Society for Social Analysis and the journal that arose from it, *Crossing Swords*. The history of the Society and the Journal is intriguing.

It all started with a small group of students in pursuit of a medium to express their creativity. Under the guidance of a persistent social studies teacher, affectionately known as Mr. Holder, even to those of us now in our late twenties, the group bonded together to form the Society for Social Analysis. During the first few weeks, the group experienced great turbulence as we tried to organize our inexperience into a corporate-like organization. We did not know at that time that our mentor had no idea where the collaboration of such terrific energies would lead, as he later admitted. However, like the intellectual development of young people, we each contributed something different and combined our contributions to create another step on our way to the pinnacle of our potential.

We were given the opportunity to do something that would endure for years and we took it. Fortunately, yes fortunately, we did not know that it was an opportunity to train us for the future. Like most teens, I was simply hoping to finish the year of class that I had to endure with a teacher who wanted me to read, analyze, and react to some form of literary piece. Could anything be more frustrating than to have to write a few paragraphs or an essay five days a week for two semesters? *I was being forced to be my own teacher, teacher to my teacher, and to my fellow students as they were to me. Could it get worse—developing my thinking skills?*

So it continued week after week. *We wrote, read the writings of others, edited their works, and typed them.* The developments that came later were incredible. Not only were we thinking and acting like journalists and researchers, we had to go public with our work. Time went by quickly, we had a journal ready for the public to read, and we were organizing a small gathering of fellow students, parents, and teachers to introduce our creativity, ability, and potential. *This was our moment to affirm ourselves as productive people.*

We never had a public speaking class on our high school schedule, and so Mr. Holder must have thought it necessary that we be "thrown" into one. We were out front introducing people, singing, and reading our works. Even more inconceivable, on a few occasions we were radio personalities on WLIB (1190 AM) and WBAI (99.5 FM). There we were telling a listening audience about our views on a wide variety of topics and how we came to be an "organization." What was happening to our quiet public school?

It seems like it was a good thing, because over twelve years later I am still speaking in front of people and the Society and the Journal are still going strong. I still marvel at some of the ideas and the way we formulated them into words. Recently [June 11, 1999], the Society had its Twelfth Annual Celebration and I was honored to be present.

Have you ever walked in on a speaker after the introduction was made and felt captivated by the ideas that were unfolding? Or, perhaps you've picked up a magazine with the cover missing and started to read something, anything. You might not know who the speaker is or what publication you're reading, but still you are deeply caught up in the depth of thought, imagination, and passion that went into the piece. This is what I got from the meeting and from the Journal. These young people are writing what they live, what they want, and they are speaking it, and more impressively they are doing it professionally. Professionally enough to use any cover on our unknown magazine. It could be *Time* magazine or *Jet* and we could certainly introduce [students] as Langston Hughes or Maya Angelou. But for the good of posterity we'll call the journal *Crossing Swords*, and we will call each author by (his/her) own name.

Roll call! Please stand up when you hear your name or when I say achiever or winner. Rosemarie Dunbar (my opposing sword), Vernette Olive, Mauricia O'Kieffe, Rabyaah Althaibani, Lakeisha Hudson, Shilue Johnson, Kenesha Vassell, Garfield McNeil, Natalie Aime Bien, Anicia Dalhouse, Ade Nicholson, Anicia Dalhouse, Ade Nicholson. ACHIEVER, ACHIEVER, WINNER, WINNER, and I will keep calling until all of the children (young and old) stand up. I hope that you will echo the call for me. I hear one reply so far. Yes! That's my own voice. (*Crossing Swords*, 2000).

Like the teenage Kenesha, Green, no mere Generation X materialistic conformist, provides an up-close view of the writing community as it took shape.

In more ways than one, 1991 was a watershed year. It marked the end of an era for the founders of the journal. The first generation of students graduated. After four years with the project, did students and I have a sense (or appreciation) of the nature of the writing community flowing as it did from our classroom without borders that was evolving, almost imperceptibly? Let's revisit two impressions from 1991. With graduation around the corner, Rosemarie Dunbar seized the opportunity to literally say "Adios!" She wrote:

Act I: Freshman

Everything new and different. Life had practically changed. No! Life had changed. Imagine my being in Sarah J. Hale for four years. Well, my four years are now winding down. **My long jail term is almost over**. For, what was four years of my life went by real quick.

Act II: The Advisor

A short persistent *man* who for me continued the interest Mr. Boles, my eighth-grade social studies teacher in Junior High School, started. The Advisor,…a man you can speak with the human thing present in the beginning of the conversation. A man, unlike many others, who will say: 'Yes, you have a point." Yet, not saying you're wrong or even right. But just saying, "You have a point Ms. Dunbar." But, the Advisor, a man who, if you listen to him, puts education in a 'nutshell' and pushes you to develop, sharpen, and even to reject your point.

Act III: Social Studies

I liked it in junior high school and still do. For me, social studies has been my dream and fairy tale. It is my favorite subject and what I hope will be part of my adult life. I have experienced fairytales, drama and mystery in the classroom.

Social studies, a love I started with Mr. Boles, has intensified. It's the well-rounded part of my curriculum. I can travel from English to math through science and long to come right back to social studies.

Act IV: Crossing Swords

Crossing Swords—especially the first issue—is a combination of the three persistent parts of my whole as a student, friends being a part of my whole. For me, **Crossing Swords has been my commander, my critic and my complaining and sounding board. This journal is the first solid piece of granite cast in what some may call my young life and serves as a release and a vehicle for my voice, my anger, my joy, and my all.**

As a graduating senior, looking back on four years at this school, I am proud of our creation—a unique journal. Topics in each issue capture the joy and magic of the debates and events that have occupied me **while I was imprisoned here.**

Epilogue: Thanks

I thank Vernette Olive, The Advisor and the library, across the street from the school, for providing the setting that helped in the development of a path-breaking journal and allowed me to walk away a young Black female with a hell of a lot to be proud of. Adios! (*Crossing Swords* 1991, pp. 12-13).

Education is more circular than linear. Though students' confessional narratives often reveal deep appreciation for teachers, we are as much beneficiaries as students. If, as Kenesha Vassell sings, "I never wrote anything beyond what was required in the classroom," I too must note that before immersing myself in the writing community, I never wrote anything that was interesting. True, I wrote numerous graduate papers, which a few professors suggested that I could have easily, with a bit of revising, submitted to scholarly journals. And I even had a few articles published in newspapers and in wrote odd monograph or two, but the more I read students' works the more I realized how much of my earlier forays into writing lacked flair, pungency, and edge. So with 1991 being such a pivotal year and after reading Rosemarie's and a few other students' reflections, I realized that theirs was a tough act to follow. Still, the resiliency flowing from our arena pushed me to rise to the challenge of writing something, anything:

The summer of '87 had ended. When they came to the school, the leaves had begun to turn brown. Their faces were bright, but hesitant. In the classroom, they would produce bright moments.

Every class produces gems. Sometimes, it's the creative use of a word or phrase hidden in a mass of sentences. Or, a student's unique view may spark a heated exchange, spawning flashes of brilliance.

Too many moments of brilliance are lost. Lost from our collective memory. Should these impassioned classroom voices be treasured? Can creative minds be nurtured? For four years, students had with no hesitancy answered with a resounding "Yes!":

"Write! Write! You never know where your writings may end up!" A student's rhetorical question lingers: "How can we write ten paragraphs of facts when we are provided with inaccurate and inadequate 'facts'?" Discovery of the rewards of going beyond classroom text inspired these scholars-in-formation to ponder complex issues.

If the premiere issue of *Crossing Swords* encapsulated the language of a student "uprising" against lethargic and inappropriate education, and the second volume served as the springboard from which students—at different points on the achievement spectrum—launched a "search for meaning," then in 1990, through "dialogue and discovery," they transformed classrooms from an area of darkness and silence into an enlightened arena of clashing viewpoints. This legacy is sure to inform and instruct the future.

In this issue, writers explore continuity in their thoughts and discover discontinuities. The range of topics is wide, yet the discerning reader will detect a single underlying theme: human creativity and the search for truth and social justice. Captured in this publication, then, are not mere words and phrases from discursive pens, but the essence of contributors' concerns and aspirations. By engaging parents and others—beyond the school—in discourse, students continue to break down the partitions insulating grade levels, subjects, teachers, and the community-at-large.

And now, as spring turns into summer, the pioneering contributors become the class of 1995. Undoubtedly, many will look back and view their high school accomplishments as inconsequential when compared to future achievements. Still, present and future contributors, standing on the shoulders of giants—the ninth graders of 1987/88—will continually discover and develop latent talents while crystallizing the tradition of robust dialogue.

To be sure, this repository, "that we...creat[ed] from scratch and not in the image of any other magazine in existence," facilitated the birth of ideas and movement away from partial truths and allowed participants to blaze their own trail while collectively making an individual mark (*Crossing Swords*, 1991, p. iix).

Today, it's fashionable to speak about creating parent centers and encouraging community participation. Yet, within the first four years of our writing community, more than twenty parents had participated in a variety of tangible ways in the classroom by typing students' work, proofreading, providing critical feedback on student writings, chaperoning students to weekend civic activities, accompanying students to a live radio interview, attending and addressing after-school functions of the Society for Social Analysis. In short, by the publication of our 1991 journal, of more than 180 pages, our instrumental classroom was well on the way to constructing an indelible bridge, or a triad of hope and renewal among students, teachers, and parents/community. Indeed within the first four years of publishing the journal more than 25 educational officials—including teachers, the principal, the superintendent, and college professors—in addition to fourteen parents and friends from the community, published critical, though supportive, evaluations of students' writings.

Two adult views suffice as a snapshot of the dynamic between our writing community and the community at large, which not only provided a protective shield for our battleground but also nurtured students' writing skills. Kester Alves, then a Hubert Humphrey Fellow at Boston University, opined:

> *Crossing Swords* marks a relevant, constructive and timely contribution to the evolution of a genuinely participatory approach to education, which should be popularized and emulated throughout the system…. The ultimate result will be the development of a self-confident, intellectually aware and expressive citizenry so essential to the maintenance of a dynamic and, indeed, a truly democratic society. (*Crossing Swords*, 1991, cover)

Reader, are you still there? Can you imagine the sense of fulfillment that students felt once they realized that their words were not, as Shilue Johnson observed, "squandered and tossed like pennies in the air" (*Crossing Swords*, 1997, p. 159) but were read with gusto in corridors way beyond the school? This may well have been belated confirmation of ninth-grader Rosemarie Dunbar's dictum: "If you think what you have to say is important enough to be said, then someone will think that your writing is important enough to be read." As such, by creating a lively writing and reading classroom community, students' work after circulation within the school was then critically appreciated by a burgeoning community of adults committed to facilitating, encouraging, and engaging students' distinctive voices while emoting concern for their developing social consciousness. In that sense we were in fact discovering that our classroom no longer had borders. It was against this backdrop that community activist Jane Califf, then chair of the Brooklyn Clean Air Committee, noted:

> It's terrific that students critique each other's essays. I haven't seen that before in collections of students' writings. That's surely a way to make students think. (*Crossing Swords*, 1991, back cover)

The preceding two views were based strictly on a reading of students' works. One can only wonder what readers' reactions would have been if they had actually met some of the students or even if they had had the chance to visit the classroom or the after-school meeting of the group, as Clara Williams, an adult, repeatedly did over the 1989-1991 period. Reflecting on her interactions with the group in a piece in which she challenged students to "Carry The Torch," she wrote:

> The last of the student founders of the Society for Social Analysis will graduate this June (1991). Will the journal, *Crossing Swords*, continue? Recently I attended an after-school meeting of the Society for Social Analysis and was struck by similarities with meetings of the past. Some of the founders/seniors were offering input, but Opal Bablington, a ninth grader, chaired the meeting. I saw this as the passing of the baton of leadership and felt proud.

But I couldn't help but wonder whether the new guard at the journal would have the same zeal as the old. Would the Friday after-school meetings of the society be the priority of the new members? Would they — if need be — do as I saw Ann Marie Green do many times, hobble to school at the end of the week on crutches to attend the society's meetings?

You see Ann Marie had been injured in school and had to have a leg cast and in-home tutoring. She did not have to attend school, but because of her commitment to the society and its work, she came to meetings on crutches. Once, a snowstorm canceled a Friday meeting—but no one told Ann Marie—can you believe she came? That's commitment!

> No longer can S. J. Hale students say "No one cares about what we have to say," or "No one even listens." *Crossing Swords* is yours. Use it; to fight back (against) the "adults," small minded enough to think of you as "failures." Use it! If you don't, who else outside of your teachers will hear you? (*Crossing Swords*, 1991, p. 150)

What was particularly moving about Clara Williams' contributions and interactions with the group was that although her niece had transferred from the school in 1990, she continued arranging her work schedule to attend meetings of the group and for two years served as de facto coadvisor to it. No condescending educational bureaucrat had to tell her and the many parents who continuously supported the group what real education looked like or *train* them about how to facilitate and nurture intellectual stimulation in their children. And in spite of all the claims from on high about how "it takes a village" to educate a child, few of the proponents of this view could recognize "the interlocking layers of the village" if it were in their face. Ms. Williams, an ordinary citizen, made extraordinary contributions to sustain our literal village, which was visible to all but the elite who utter nothing but vague platitudes while many urban teens wither away as the system atrophies.

Being a central link between community and school, Ms. Williams was in more than a unique position to chart the evolution of the writing community. In the 1989 journal she observed:

> Our future is safe! There is an abundance of future leaders. Our children are receiving what Dr. Carter Woodson described as a "real education...to inspire people to live more abundantly, to learn to begin with life as they find it and make it better." How do I know? I have seen the student contributors to the journal, *Crossing Swords*, in action.
>
> My first visit to the after-school meeting of the Society for Social Analysis was a result of my niece having attended one of the Society's sessions and saying that she did not intend to attend another. It didn't make sense. I had read the first volume of *Crossing Swords* and thought it to be phenomenal. Several of my niece's essays were included and social studies was her favorite subject.
>
> Where was the logic? To find it, I thought I would visit just once—drop in and drop out as parents/guardians are supposed to show a little concern—and see for myself what went on during meetings. I was in for a pleasant surprise. I didn't expect to see students governing themselves and Mr. Holder, the advisor, doing just that—being overruled when offering advice the students did not agree with. Strange? I thought so, too.
>
> I experienced the joy of students voicing their opinions without being intimidated by sharp disagreements. I was impressed with the level and intensity of discussion: Students holding fast to their views and sometimes changing their opinions when confronted with their colleagues' more forcefully reasoned positions. I was also fascinated by their ability to criticize each other's writing and concerning themselves with the message and not the messenger.

The rotation of leadership roles was another pleasant surprise. Although there is a president, all members got the chance to chair meetings. Democracy in action? Was I dreaming? Since conducting meetings is a skill which needs developing, some meetings went smoother that others. Should they discard the practice of rotational leadership in the interest of "perfect" meetings? One member (Mauricia O'Kieffe) rationalized the situation: "Just because something is difficult to perfect, that doesn't mean we should stop trying."

My first visit was so fascinating that I had to return. Since then I have attended meetings frequently. I feel certain that the members and the contributors to this journal are making our society better, now and in the future. (*Crossing Swords*, 1989, p. 60)

Ping. Ping…

Subj: My essay due 2morrow
Date: 4/8/03 11:40:30 PM Eastern Daylight Time

This is the essay that I am turning in tomorrow. I just wanted you to tell me if i could write the intro the way i did, with the convo. I've been working on it all day, so I'm almost done.

Just from the tone and heading of Kenesha's e-mail, I sensed that she had recaptured her old self. So without even a bit of trepediation I downloaded the essay and began reading:

"So what did you do last night?" says Kelly.
"Nothing much. Just talked on the phone to Kevin," replies Jan.
"You're always on the phone with that loser. What you need to do is drop that zero and get with a hero," John interjects from way across the room.
"O.K., class, quiet down!" a booming voice shouts from the front of the classroom.
"So you going to the club this weekend? Kevin's friend will be there," says Jan.
Kelly replies, "O' word, I'll be there of course."
"Did anyone finish reading the chapter I assigned?">GET NAME OF BOOK< the same voice echoes.
John interrupts once again, "Man, that club is going to be crazy, I'll see you there, right, Jan?"

This is a typical conversation that may take place in a classroom. The voice that veers from the front of the room is a teacher trying to take control of her class. Many students would have probably figured that out, because this is nothing out of the norm.

All I could say to her after reading this far in her essay was: "Way to go, sis! Rage on!" I could feel the vibes oozing from her pen and the space from which she composed her narrative. If art mimics life, then how many white swans must a skeptic see before conceding that swans are white? What, then, is the likelihood that at the very same time Kenesha was composing her introduction, I too was struggling with a similar construction?

Vignettes: Promoting Reading/Listening, Speaking, Writing, or Class Conflict?

> You…broke the rules. You started that store, made room for black men and women, and didn't take no collection, and didn't tell' em what to think. You…opened your heart. That's revolution, brother, rebellion against the rule. Walter Mosley, *Always Outnumbered, Always Outgunned*
>
> Mr. Holder pushed us to talk. That's what we are doing; we are talking in the journal. Rosemarie Dunbar, WLIB 1988 radio interview (*Crossing Swords*, 1989, p. 104)

A specter is haunting American education — the specter of indigenous knowledge. All the prowesses of the miseducated elite have entered into an unholy alliance to exorcise this specter: educational czars and their charlatans, administra(i)tors and sycophants alike.

It is high time that those autochthonous educational change agents openly, in the glare of the shock and awe of the establishment, publish their views, their intuitions, their inclinations, and meet this nursery tale of the specter of indigenous knowledge with the banter and cantos of the dialectics of the oppressed.

To this end, disempowered students of all learning dispositions and disinclinations, in collaboration with recalcitrant teachers, have sampled pages from their rhyme books and produced this critical dialogue, encapsulating at times the spectacular vernacular of Ebonics, the language of resistance. The educational system, misguided by its philosophy of poverty that stunts students' intellectual, creative, and emotional growth, is rearing its own gravediggers.

The history of all hitherto authoritarian classrooms is the history of class struggles. Serenity and impatience, fluidity and rigidity, stasis and mobility, *autonomy* and dependence stood in constant opposition to one another, carrying on an uninterrupted didactic monologue in the theaters of discourse, discord, and dystopia.

It was against this backdrop that one afternoon during the 1989-90 school year, as students ambled into the room and took their seats, I went to the chalkboard and began writing:

DO NOW: Explain each viewpoint and state to what extent you agree or disagree with each:

Viewpoint #1: "'And there would come a time when nations would beat their swords into plowshares' (Isaiah). Finally we are at that time!"

What are plowshares? Did you see the Grammies last night? Isaiah tore up the place! Nah. You mean…. Which Isaiah? Isaiah Thomas, the Pistons guard? Be serious, don't you know your Bible? And, what you know 'bout the Bible? Wait up, I'm no nonbeliever. What are plowshares? Ignoring the voices behind my back I continued writing.

Viewpoint #2: "A great democratic revolution is taking place in our midst; everybody sees it, but by no means everybody judges it in the same way."
De Tocqueville

Talking intensified. So I said: "I hope you know how to copy and talk and think and listen at the same time and…" *What's wrong with him, springing names and words on us just like that? If we never heard of Toc…whatever, how can we know what he means? It was the bomb! What? The Grammies. I don't have time for this! His "Do Now" is a simple statement, just read it and even you might understand. Don't try to play me or else it's on. Every day is the same thing. You hold me back when I want to absorb info like a sponge. Can I hold the pass? Hi cutie, can I have your digits?* That's enough! Settle down and consider the statements and give it your best shot. That's all I ask. *But how can we when we never heard of them?* I have one more. *Are we supposed to answer them all?* Yes! *You ODin' or what? Why not give us a break?*

Viewpoint #3: "You never judge a system by its adherents; you don't even judge a religion by its believers. You shouldn't judge socialism by its adherents, judge it by its principles."
Kwame Toure (Stokely Carmichael)

We work every day, why not lighten up? Okay: Rows 1 and 2, respond to Viewpoint #1; rows 3 and 4 do Viewpoint #2, and row 5 do Viewpoint #3 and #2. *Why two for us and we have the least people?* Because you can bear the burden.*

No way am I doing two for the same credit as everybody. Don't you know he doesn't give credit for busywork? Later for him then! Who is Kwame what? That doesn't even sound like a real name. And on and on. Until, from the back of the room, I heard a student who rarely attended classes shout out, "What kind of history teacher are you, and your students don't know 'bout Stokely Carmichael and Black Power?"

I responded, "Why not tell us more about Stokely Carmichael?" The student obliged us for a minute or two. I asked the class, "What then do you think Toure means by the statement?

Discussion ensued until someone said, "If a priest does wrong, that does not mean one should give up on religion."

I interjected, "So if there are problems in socialist states, what does that mean?"

---

* Throughout the term I had noticed that row 5 often refrained from participating in class discussions. The "strategy" employed here was one of many spontaneous ways of continuously challenging students to talk and then write. After all, isn't any talk better than disengagement?

A near unanimous response: "Communism is bad! But…"

Next we moved on to a discussion of Isaiah's statement. After a few questions, someone was able to ask, "Is the statement saying that nations would, instead of preparing for war, prepare for peace?" *Make food, not war!* Someone from row 5 retorted, *You mean 'Make love, not war'?*

Then I asked, "Which New York building do you think would be the most appropriate to place Isaiah's statement on?" *The Empire State Building. Why? It's the tallest building, so everybody would be able to see Isaiah's graffiti. Be serious, it should be on the Twin Towers. That's the tallest building. Why not on the library or the Pentagon?* A student from row 5 quickly retorted, *When did it move to New York?*

Again the student at the back of the room put up his hand and said, "It should be on the United Nations building."

I asked, "Why?"

"Duh. Isn't that what the UN is about, making peace?"

Writing in her skillfully entitled "Classroom Hysteria" and reflecting on her 1997-2000 classroom experience, Anicia Dalhouse may well have captured the timbre and flare of the intellectual battleground that was the classroom, noting:

> The environment in that classroom was different from all of my other history classes. All the teachers seemed to be so uptight in the classrooms, to the point that it contributed to kids not wanting to learn. But my sophomore teacher left room for hysteria in the classroom. He truly realized what was necessary in order to teach teenagers. There had to be times for hysteria, but he knew when enough was enough.
>
> Throughout the term my friends and I who sat in the back of the classroom used to complain about the room being too cold, whether [or not it actually was], just to cause a distraction from doing the work, but the teacher outsmarted us by telling us that we had an air conditioner in the back of the classroom. That was one of our everyday laughs.…
>
> After being in the classroom for a while I began to realize that the teacher wanted to see kids achieve in school and he complimented us all the time about our good answers or the good essay and even the good point that was made in class yesterday. I think that was one of the teacher's key characteristics in motivating me to do well in his class. I was a talkative child in school—the one with the smart remarks who pointed out every joke. So it was a miracle that my social studies teacher caught my attention. Everybody knew that I hated school and hated work, especially writing essays, because they required too many paragraphs.
>
> My friends and I used to often joke that Mr. Holder only gave us essays because he wanted writings to put in *Crossing Swords*. But the more I wrote, the more the teacher complimented me about my ideas and writing. [H]is ability to listen to students, no matter how small their deeds may be, and make that child feel motivated to learn is what makes him so unique. His keenness to encourage children's ability to express their thoughts on paper and to motivate them to learn history is what makes the teacher so special. It was my history class that motivated me to excel in school. (*Crossing Swords*, 2000, p. 32)

Suddenly, a student whose head had been on the desk—as if sleeping—from the beginning of the period shot up and, without even waiting for me to acknowledge her hand and pronouncing *Tocqueville* flawlessly, said, "I get it. He was talking about the revolutions in the Soviet bloc against communism." After placing

Tocqueville in historical context and making a mental note to present the students with an excerpt of his writing, we considered the breaches in the Soviet Union's former iron curtain. But, before we consider the responses that were written stemming from the classroom discussion, we present the introduction to the section of the journal in which many classroom essays were preserved:

> It's ironic to think that what took decades to build could have been easily destroyed in a matter of seconds. This just proves how effective organized masses of people can be.
>
> As you may know, the world has been going through tremendous changes: South Africa, Eastern Europe, Panama, just to name a few countries [sic] where important changes have taken place within the last year. The people in these countries with the moral support of the world fought the injustices they were experiencing [from] their governments.
>
> Right now I believe the world is just watching and listening as if it were a sleeping giant. People are forging bonds and this is most essential to provide a better future for future generations.

In this section you will find various controversies as students discuss the changes in today's world. These students decided to share their views on the world with the world. (*Crossing Swords*, 1990, p. 95)

This was the way that Nikki Burton, a senior, introduced the section "As the World Turns and Warms Up, Walls Crumble!" which dealt with world issues. Writing in that section, Judy Forbin, then a sophomore, offered "What's LEFT? Communism's Sinking Ship?"

> It is…two and a half times the size of the USA. Located on the…Eurasia landmass, most of it has a midlatitude wet and dry cold winter climate. If geography serves us well, we are talking about the Soviet Union.
>
> Russia's geographic factors have had a large impact on its history. Because it had few natural barriers it was easily invaded. In earlier times the Mongols invaded. This kept Russia out of the Renaissance and pushed it further behind culturally than the other European nations.
>
> At the beginning of the twentieth century Russia was ripe for revolution. The wide gap in living conditions led people to fight for land reform, food, and social justice. By 1917 the Russian Revolution was successful and communism was introduced. After the revolution there was civil war (1917-1921).
>
> In 1917 Vladimir Lenin became the leader of the…world's first proclaimed communist state. Lenin decided to adapt the ideas of Karl Marx, the father of communism. Ever since that time the USSR has pursued the goal of establishing a workable communist state….
>
> In 1985 Mikhail Gorbachev became the leader. He was from a younger generation and apparently had a more liberal outlook. He espoused a policy of *glasnost*, which means a new openness, in Soviet society. He took small but meaningful steps to increase citizens' individual freedom. He also freed political prisoners.
>
> As a result of this openness, the people of Lithuania and other republics are fighting for their freedom from the jaws of communism. Even in the Soviet Union, as all over the world, especially in Eastern Europe, people are realizing that the "great" communist Empire is falling around the ears of its fathers: the Brezhnevs, Khrushchevs, Gorbachevs, and all the other 'chevs.'
>
> Gorbachev developed the idea of *perestroika* to deal with the economic problems. By this policy he intend(ed) to lessen the role of central planning, or total government

control of the economy. Certain capitalist economic policies will now be allowed.

In foreign policy issues Gorbachev has taken a hands-off policy in internal events in Eastern Europe. No longer is the Soviet Union willing to "preserve communism" at all costs. This "democratization" of Russia's foreign policy is the greatest change of all.

In the past, countries of Eastern Europe were forced to live under very oppressive governments and conditions. This relaxation of power allowed the people to rise up and change their governments. The falling of the Berlin Wall in August 1989 was the straw that finally broke the camel's back. Then the domino effect took place. Countries like Hungary, Rumania, and others began demonstrating for a democratic government. The people of Eastern Europe want freedom; freedom of speech and religion and the ability to trade and travel as freely as other peoples of the world.

I hope that the march to democracy continues and just maybe it will be the end of communism. Many people now realize that communism does not work!

From today's standpoint, where can we find students' impressions of some of the earth-shattering events of the last fifteen years of the twentieth century? In this sense, we were creating not only a writing community but also a repository—a time capsule, if you will—of students' developing internationalism and civic consciousness. No to be outdone, junior Tricia Parris spoke about the "Triumph of Democracy or Collapse of Communism":

COMMUNISM! What is it and what did it do to people? Can we do without it? Why has it faded?

In *Webster's New World Dictionary of The American Language* communism is defined as "any theory or system of common ownership of property." It is socialism as formulated by Karl Marx and Lenin as well as many other individuals….

In August 1989, the Berlin Wall, which separated communist East Germany from West Germany, was opened after 26 years. Today some people refer to it as a gate of peace. The gate became a symbol of peace and hope as East and West Germany came closer together. This celebration of happiness showed that there was indeed an end to communism in Eastern Europe. Now people are concerned about the power of a unified Germany. Can Germany bury its past?

In the 1940's the communists came to power in Rumania. The government was able to quickly establish total control over the society. Despite an orderly society, the people faced numerous hardships; food shortages, denial of basic rights and the ability to practice one's religion and freedom of speech. These were a few of the many hardships which citizens faced for almost a half century.

In December 1989, Rumanian citizens got rid of their leader, or, should I say dictator? At first the leader was able to get away…. However, they later captured and executed the dictator. Some people who were fighting to overthrow communism said that if they lose the war, then they would lose their lives. The people won. You could see the joy on their faces. A sad era had ended. They were cheerful and hopeful for a better life.

…As I look at the global village, I see people breaking away from communism in Poland, East Germany, Hungary, and now Rumania. Is the USSR next?

As can be seen, students demonstrated intense interest in worldwide struggles for freedom, going beyond a mere concern with grades and passing tests. They, therefore, were not merely recording history as filtered through their collective eyes, but also making history. The intensity, passion, and insightfulness with which they were following and recording their interpretations of world events reminds me of

Friedrich Engels' reaction to Marx's *The 18th Brumaire:* "This eminent under-standing of the living history of the day, this clear-sighted appreciation of events at the moment happening, is indeed without parallel."

To be sure, given the symmetry of students' impressions of communism, one can easily dismiss these views as merely a knee-jerk reaction to press coverage of the time. How then should we interpret their views on the invasion of Panama, on apartheid, and later on the Gulf War that sometimes run counter to the popular/official view? By demonstrating such clarity of expression and prescience, weren't they turning history on its head?

They were writing at a time, during the waning years of the Cold War, when many felt that peace between East and West was on the horizon. And this led to the coining of a new term to capture the hope of the post-Cold War era; in the media and wherever issues were discussed, there was talk of the "peace dividend." It was within this setting that I circulated news articles in addition to much of the writings from the 1988 journal to serve as source texts for the 1990 discussion. Chsauna Jenkins' "Dividends of Peace? Watching and Waiting!" (in which she engaged in metacognition, thinking about her thinking) was framed by a note from the editors:

> *In the spring 1988 issue of* Crossing Swords, *Chsauna Jenkins, Ann Marie Green and Cindy Holley opined: "Poverty is a very sad situation. [It] is far more important than a few nuclear threats!…Governments and citizens of the world should put forth a greater effort to aid those in need." In the following essay, Chsauna reflects on the original article in light of the lightning world changes.*

> Over the years we have watched as AIDS and the homeless plagued the cities in our great country. We have also watched as the bridges began to wear and crumble down. At the same time we have watched as the country spent billions of dollars on instruments of war and on such "urgencies" as sending men to the moon while poverty encircled the inner cities.

> It's about time that the government started worrying about helping the people in our country so that when we do need defense, the country will have people to defend it. It's also about time we started being more concerned about life on earth instead of what's not on Mars.

> Now that the tension between the USA and the USSR has been eased, both governments are beginning to cut back on military and defense spending. Now that there is less chance of war between the superpowers, each has realized that [it doesn't] need to spend as much money on weapons of mass destruction.

> If the changes—movement away from communism—were not taking place in Eastern Europe and the Soviet Union, I wonder if cuts in the military budget would have been possible. For it is the money which normally would have been spent on weapons of war, which is referred to as the "peace dividend." Everybody proclaims that we are a step closer to peace. Are we really?

> If we weren't a step closer to peace, would people and the government have been calling for increased funds for social programs to help the people of our country better themselves, and the country? How much longer would we have had to wait? More important, how much longer will we have to wait before we see some real progress in the inner cities? The government, the media and everybody can talk and talk about dividends of peace and the desire to make changes, but when will we actually see changes?

> The government has some nerve. For years they have been spending billions of dollars on so-called military defense, and it is only when relations are improving with the Soviet Union that the leaders think about solving the wars, which have been going on for years, within their own country. I am still waiting to see the rewards of peace. (*Crossing Swords*, 1990, pp. 101-102)

Chsauna, demonstrating remarkable forethought and reading of the tenor and trajectory of world history, dismissed the notion of the "peace dividend" even before it caught on. And how on point was she.

Students' interest in world affairs knew no boundaries. As citizens developing with a deep sense of civic virtue and a commitment to preparing themselves to become knowledgeable and committed members of society, they debated the issues that were engaging the public.

Writing in opposition to the 1989 U.S. invasion of Panama, senior Natalie Bowen opined:

> It is not surprising, then, that there is a lot of anger, tension and resentment towards the United States government by Panamanians, especially amongst those who live overseas…. In 1983 the USA also invaded Grenada, dismantling its government and crippling the island. By these acts the United States successfully proved itself to be lawless and is thus looked upon as such by the majority of Latin American nations. (*Crossing Swords*, 1990, p. 107)

The nature of the forum that we had created was such that the writing field was equalized in that students in lower grades felt able to contest the views of seniors. Sophomore Andrea Fennicks challenged Natalie's views:

> In the essay "Removing the Mask," Natalie Bowen argues that the U.S.A. had no right to intervene in Panama…. I disagree with her views….
>
> If President Bush didn't defend our country and its citizens, people would have criticized him. Yet when the president acted, some people are still not satisfied! How else could the president have acted? He acted the best way he saw fit. (*Crossing Swords*, 1990, p. 108)

And, the debates continued: from year to year and topic to topic. Through it all it was students' desire not to remain passive receptacles of teachers' or the media's predigested truths which kept the dynamic of the discourse afloat.

The Gulf War was a defining moment of the early 1990s, and, as was to be expected, students followed it assiduously. Within the classroom, I often shared different viewpoints on the issue as the springboard for classroom discussions and students' own developing civic consciousness. Indeed, we used two opposing views to frame the section of the 1991 journal, which presented views on the Gulf War. So, the section was presented thus:

> "I object to those who would say that we lack patriotism. (N)obody in this House [of Representatives] or in this country is going to browbeat me about disagreeing with the President." Charles Rangel (D-NY)
>
> "If opposing injustice anywhere obliges [the United States] to become involved everywhere, then only a fool would not prefer involvement nowhere." Charles Krauthammer, *Time*, March 4, 1991

These then were the epigrams that cast a distinctive glow on Patricia McGlashan's "After the War: What Happens?"

Why does America stick its nose all over the world? To this day the American government has yet to give a valid reason for rushing into war without thinking fully of the consequences at home and abroad.

At first the government claimed that economic reasons justified its presence in the Arabian Gulf; then our presence was said to be needed in order to safeguard American values. Later still we learned that the real reason was to safeguard Saudi Arabia; then it was to defeat a dangerous, Hitlerite dictator. And, now we are learning that the real reason is for the preservation of economic stability and "our way of life."

Since [Saddam] Hussein did not pull out of Kuwait on January 15, "mother hen" decided to protect her chick although many of her [other] chicks could have been roasted alive in the war fields of the Middle East.

The thousands of soldiers in Kuwait named the crisis the "mom's war." Taking pictures, memories and lots of fear of not returning home, many female soldiers, some of whom are also moms, went to do their patriotic duties and left behind children and families. By law, women can't serve on the frontline, but who's to say where the frontline is?

The frontline is everywhere! These soldiers are not only filled with fear of not returning home, but afraid of a poison gas attack. Before the attack on Iraq, soldiers were depending on George Bush to keep the peace in the Middle East.

America has yet to lay down that image it has as a superpower. America has to be on top of everything. Whether at home or a million miles away, the government is always willing to risk the lives of innocent people to keep this image alive. No matter what the cost, the government wants to continue this image as world policeman.

Having passed through so many wars, one would think that the U.S. would know better than to rush into another one. According to Mr. Bush, he went "the extra mile" to prevent war. I did not see the extra mile. What I did see, however, was five months of war preparations rather than peace preparations.

Completing this section in mid-March 2003 as the United States administration silences and marginalizes the United Nations, it seems as if with very minor adjustments Patricia's essay can be read as if written today.

It would also appear that our patience with Saddam Hussein ran out before we got to the bargaining table. I never saw the United States running to defend the same freedom that millions of Africans seek, year after year, in South Africa. Neither did they declare war on the racist South African regime five months after declaring sanctions on them that did not work. So, why the rush to war with Iraq? Is oil more valuable than blood?

I thought this was a democratic society in which people had freedom of speech and the right to dissent. Did this change while I was asleep? If not, why are attempts made to silence opponents of the war, who are also dismissed as unpatriotic? If citizens cannot express their dissatisfaction with the war in the Gulf, pardon my lack of patriotism.

Opponents of the war are just facing reality. There are serious problems on the home front for which the government says there is no money. Needed programs have been cut; teachers are being fired; class sizes are increasing; there was no money to save Freedom National Bank and major cities are going bankrupt. Yet, within a five-month period we had enough money to afford a billon-dollar-a-day war.

Were you reading this essay blindfolded—with the cover of the magazine missing, as Ann M. Green suggests we sometimes do—wouldn't you have been hard-pressed to date it, much less correctly identify its source?

> The U.S. needs to get its priorities straight because when the war with Iraq is over the government will be faced with the same problems it tried to avoid, only the problems would have increased.
>
> If our society thinks we have problems now, just wait until our troops come home to find limited opportunities, if any. It's possible that when many soldiers return home, they will discover that the government that sent them to war does not care whether or not they are homeless and destitute. They will be like veterans of wars past; sitting and wondering why the country they love and fought for turned its backs on them.

Patricia's essay sparked heated discussion in the classroom and in the meetings of the Society for Social Analysis. As always, whenever I was on the brink of thinking that there was unanimity of views on any issue, there were contrary voices compelling the class to continually rethink assumptions and positions.

Sophomore Maria Ayala challenged the senior, in her essay "The Reality of Fear":

> Patricia McGlashan argues that the American government "does not mind its business." I disagree with Patricia because all America is trying to do is to protect Kuwait from Iraq.
>
> At first I didn't agree with what the president was doing. However, since the war has started I agree with him and support the troops one hundred percent. (*Crossing Swords*, p. 50)

And Diana Garcia, a junior, employed poetry to fashion her statement on the war:

> Serve your country
> Dressed in green
> Die fighting for peace
> Buried with the flag
> Triumph in enemy's eyes
> Swords raised in honor
> Today you're remembered
> Tomorrow enlists another. (*Crossing Swords*, 1991, p. 50)

Still responding to Patricia's essay, sophomore Kerri Thompson wondered about "Names on a Wall, Again":

> The president keeps saying that the war against Iraq will not be another Vietnam. Does he know that for sure? Further, America had no right in Vietnam either….
>
> Are we going to have to build another wall with all the casualties written on it again? I don't think that authorities are thinking about the many people who may die. They are just concerned with maintaining America's strength.

Even after the war was over, discussion still raged in the classroom and in the pages of the journal. Responding to the preceding student commentary and writing as if she were composing a political pamphlet for mass distribution, NurJahan Simmons, a junior, asserted in her provocatively titled "Freedom and Its Denial":

I believe that "black gold" was the real reason for the war. Thousands of African Americans were put under tremendous life-threatening situations because of OIL. While we, in America, lived and breathed, this outrageous action took place.

Some people stated, "We (Americans) are fighting for the freedom of Kuwait and for our own freedom." My question is: When they say "our" freedom, who are they talking about?

Today African Americans are not treated equally. For anyone to believe otherwise, in my opinion, the person must have a selective perception of reality. In many inner cities, African American youth cannot walk the streets in a group without the police slowing down as they pass by and harassing us. Many times when we enter stores in our own neighborhoods, we are followed....

Often we are not only accused of crimes we did not commit but are often stopped in the streets and accused of stealing cars we drive, and own. Furthermore police brutality is a frequent occurrence throughout the ghettoes of North America. In addition, there is always an undercurrent of racism to the point that you can't go into certain neighborhoods to look at a used car (Yusef Hawkins).

The undercurrent grows stronger as powerful forces continue to condone this type of biased attitude. The media is a good example: how they seemed to play a big role in the "Central Park Jogger Case," "The Bensonhurst Trial" and the "Teaneck Case." The irony of these examples is that they were not all given the same amount of press coverage or the same type of "viewpoints" (donated by the press). Instead, these viewpoints were fashioned to fit the needs of a predominantly "white press."

With all these facts one wonders: How can African Americans, in good conscience, fight for a country that denies us so much? (*Crossing Swords*, 1991, pp. 53-54)

Do vignettes, adages, counterfactual statements, and the like really facilitate robust dialogue? Maybe not. Nevertheless, enlarge Erasmus' adage "MAKE HASTE SLOWLY!" into a poster. Remove all other posters and decorations from the room. Hang the adage above the chalkboard. Wait for the discord.

Zeitgeist: Engaging the Spirits of the Times

[W]e were creating [*Crossing Swords*] from scratch and not in the image of any other magazine in existence. Mauricia O'Kieffe, editor-in chief, *Crossing Swords*, 1989

Reflecting on her involvement in the writing community, Vernette Olive-Carboin wrote "Therefore I Think":

It has been approximately ten years since the birth of the Society for Social Analysis and *Crossing Swords*, of which I am proud to have been one of the founding members. This journal is one that played a major role in my life. It...taught me nonconformity to the norm, to doubt, question, reason, research, think independently, respond positively to any issue in our society and voice my substantive opinions. These variables are critical to the formula of success.

Sometimes we limit our self-expression and are ashamed of the ideas that are within us because we see the false security of conformity. Most people believe that conformity to the norm is virtue while non-conformity is consequential. It is very difficult for anyone to bring new, creative ideas to the majority because it usually upsets that which has already been established.

In other words, man is usually fearful about going against what the majority believes. He would rather quote something ancient or repeat what has been said for centuries rather than speak those powerful words, "I doubt, I question, so therefore,

I think." For thousands of years man has been doing certain things, and when new thought emerges, coming in the form of an individual, it uproots, it confuses, and it shakes all that was thought to be significant.

I pray that the Society for Social Analysis will exist for many years to come and I hope that more students will take *Crossing Swords* seriously. This journal has certainly enabled me to think beyond the norm....

In order to break the bonds of the mass mind, you must begin to doubt, to inquire, to question and to think independently and positively. The Society for Social Analysis was one motivational tool that inspired me to do these things. Therefore, I can truly look in the mirror and admire the one looking back at me. (*Crossing Swords*, 1997, p. ix)

Writing in *The Tipping Point*, an extremely fascinating book with profound implications for education, Malcolm Gladwell (2000) considers, among other things, the indispensable role that "[c]onnectors...people with a special gift for bringing the world together" (p. 38) play in social epidemics or the spreading of an idea or information. It is within this context that we can envision *Crossing Swords*, the students' very own self-created journal as their connector or "agent of infection" (p. 88) and writing communities as the "virus" we were spreading. Moreover, in celebrating the writing community reflected in their journal, weren't Kenesha, Ann, and Vernette really alluding to its valve as a connector in spreading a writing epidemic?

"Where are the boys? Why are there no boys with you?" asked Kay Thompson, of radio station WLIB (1190 AM) on June 23, 1988. Facing her on our first live radio interview were ninth graders Rosemarie Dunbar, Ann Marie Green, Vernette Olive, Nikkitria Roberts, Senyal Walton, sophomore Mauricia O'Kieffe, and Senyal's mother, Ms. Walton. Though I was taken aback (especially since I had intended to defer all questions to students) by an issue so transparent to everyone but me, I nevertheless replied, "Quite a few guys wrote but none volunteered to come."

On reflecting after the interview I realized that the reality was a bit more complex. Of the 140 students who passed through my classes over the 1987–88 school year—the period over which the first journal was completed—42 students contributed to it, of which only 6 were males. And there was no male in the editorial collective of eight students. Clearly, then, though the school and my classroom could have been about 70 percent to 75 percent female, males were demonstrably unrepresented in the developing writing community.

This was the case in spite of my having made continuous outreach to all students, even calling parents to encourage their children to get involved in the journal or other extracurricular activities. This was the sentiment behind the student-crafted opening statement of the journal, which was signed by the editorial collective. It read:

We of the Society for Social Analysis would like to welcome you to our journal. This journal is made up of essays and stories written by students you may know as classmates.

The object of the journal and organization is to open the eyes of the "blind" to show them how much students are willing to do.

We would like to encourage all students to become actively involved in any one of the numerous clubs in our school or in the community where you live. Involvement in a club can be rewarding. (*Crossing Swords*, 1988, p. iii)

Reading this statement today I still marvel at students' prescience and enhanced sense of civic consciousness and of inclusiveness. To be sure, it was a hard sell convincing them of many of the merits of creating a community of independent thinkers and writers. Many balked at the possibilities inherent in such a venture. Still, we persisted in trying to "break the bonds of the mass mind." Little wonder, then, that Ann Marie, building on Vernette's vision of a sustainable writing community, skillfully re-created the "turbulence," intensity, and uncertainty of that critical period. Miriam Sauda Perez also touched on the drama of the early days of the project. Her remarks from the *Crossing Swords* Annual Symposium, Friday, June 11, 1999, are quoted at length:

Good afternoon. I graduated from Hale in 1988. I want to thank Mr. Holder for inviting me to speak to you…. I applaud all the students who read. It was really inspirational. I want to say a bit before I read two of my poems.

Mr. Holder was the first person to encourage me to write. I never had a teacher who encouraged me to pursue anything before Mr. Holder. So he is very important to me, even though I really haven't kept in contact the way I should have. He's real important to me. Anyway, I'll read, then maybe I'll have more to say.

The first poem I'm going to read is "Rumba for My Children."…And the next poem is called "Sweet Jazz, Bitter Blues."

Bitter blues play
\In the streets below/
'Black on Black'/
Suicide/
Becomes our sour/
Tune/
Man—caught up in a/
Master plan/
Women—barter vile soul/
For a five dollar vial/
Children—soldiers/
In a chaotic self-righteous street/
Corner harmony/
Of gunshots/
And voices wailing into the night/
Coltrane blows/
Jericho walls crumble…

As I was saying, Mr. Holder inspired me to continue writing. I was in his history class and I wrote an essay for an exam that he really liked:

I arrived in the Thirteen Colonies and was greeted with the stroke of a whip and the shout of the word 'nigger.' I was quite disappointed. Things weren't like in 1988 from which I had just been transported. Here in the eighteenth century my ancestors were still in bondage.

I went to praise my Lord Allah and they called me a devil. I went to the local shop and they asked me whom my owner was. By this time I was really fed up. I began to preach to my people and to organize them against the prevalent injustices. The wicked authorities locked me up and I had no right to speak the Truth.

They had just violated three of my 20th century constitutional rights: Freedom of speech, freedom of religion and citizenship rights for blacks, at least on paper. I was naive. I was shocked. Even though I had read about the wickedness of these times in my social studies textbook, I was not prepared.

I was happy, when, at my trial, they found me guilty and transported me back to 1988. [*Crossing Swords*, 1988, p. 25]

…And he tried to convince me to write for the journal. And I was like—you know how some teenagers are—not that there is anything wrong with being a teenager, but I was like "I don't have time for this!"…He called my house, and I never had a teacher in high school call my house. So I said to myself, "This man is crazy! He's calling my house to get me to write!"

And upon my graduation he gave me some books, one of (which) was Gil Noble's autobiography. I still have the book today. I read it and it inspired me…. It talked about people I didn't know. I didn't have people inspire me that way.

Anyway, I decided a year after I graduated to go to college and I have been working as a writer while attending college on and off for the last ten years. I don't really like going to school. I like learning but I don't like sitting in class, but it is something I have to do. So I went and finally I graduated this June [1999 from Brooklyn College]…. I'm not going to hold up the mic any longer but I thank you for having me. And to all you young writers, keep writing. [Sustained applause.] Thank you. (*Imprints*, 2000, p. 304)

And sophomore Kenisha Minott, who cohosted the event, underlined Miriam's comments by telling the audience of some 70 people (including her grandmother, who had just arrived from Jamaica) packed into the vestibule of the school's library, "As you can see, the book is really legendary" (*Imprints*, 2000, p. 4).

During the 1988-89 school year as discussion raged in the classroom, I kept hearing, like a stuck record, Kay Thompson's question in my mind, "Where are the boys?" Though convinced at that time that growth, emotional and intellectual, can't be compelled or legislated, I nevertheless toyed with the idea of viewing boys' receptivity to writing, and even learning, within the popular framework. Being unschooled in psychology and unfazed by the fads of the day (e.g., different learning styles of blacks and whites, girls and boys), the very theater of the classroom convinced me to continue viewing writing as an organic outgrowth flowing from the inner soul. As such, even before stumbling upon Alfie Kohn in Janice Hale's *Learning While Black*, I was operating from the framework that all students can write and will write when

intrinsic motivation is developed in learners by attention being paid to the notion of *artistic teaching*, in which children are motivated by the interesting manner in which content is presented, are given opportunities to explore ideas and content in meaningful collaboration with their teachers and peers, and are presented with choices in curriculum. (Hale, 2001, p. 123)

If intrinsic motivation isn't what both students and adults quoted throughout this chapter have outlined, then a few more voices may clinch the issue. However, throughout students' entry into the tradition of a supportive, nonjudgmental environment in which active listening is central, as organic intellectuals in formation they have been documenting their own transformations and transfigurations. As such, entry into the conversations allows them to discover and record facets of their world to themselves and the world.

Are students keen observers and critical listeners of the worlds they inhabit? Can we create settings in which they respectfully consider contradictory viewpoints while discovering the power of critical listening as a precursor to synthesis? Can students teach teachers about what works for new, developing, and seasoned writers and why it does? As teachers, are we humble enough to listen to the dialects and dialectics of youth as they tell tales of how they navigate and try to master their classrooms and world? Let's listen in on Garfield McNeil's reflections as he talks about a "Soul Saver":

> Because of *Crossing Swords*, I know that true boundaries are not set until they are broken. When I first came to *Crossing Swords* I was a new poet with a lot of hidden talent, but because of my past I did not realize my true potential.
>
> I can still remember my first poem. It was entitled "Who Shall Govern the Governors?" To this day I don't know what took hold of me the first time I wrote for the journal. The Society for Social Analysis brought peace into my life. It brought a sense of love with every meeting we held.
>
> Although, compared to the Society (as a whole), my contribution is small, the group taught me that no matter how big or small the body of one's work is, what is important is the effort that was made. Sometimes I used to say to the advisor, Mr. Holder, "This kid only wrote six lines," to which he would reply, "At least it is six more lines than he wrote before."
>
> It took me two years to grasp the concept. I now realize that before many of us came to *Crossing Swords* we had no idea of our gift. I think that the Society was an ignition for some and a hope for others.
>
> If I had to describe *Crossing Swords* in two words, the words would be: soul saver. When we met on Fridays the group sustained itself because the advisor constantly challenged us. Our burning desires to realize what the skeptics say can't be done by teens is what kept us coming back for more (as some may put it).
>
> Personally, the Society has given me a sense of pride and acceptance. I think I would have just remained complacent and careless if it were not for the Society. When I first saw the words "Associate Editor" next to my name, all the years of pain seemed to just freeze and a sense of elation filled my spirit.
>
> Despite my environment, writing slowly became a positive addiction for me. I remember how I used to bring in pages of poetry, and even though I am an individual, when I read my work I read it as part of a collection. I saw kids my own age actually looking and listening to me. The trust that was developed in the group gave me a sense of security.
>
> Indeed, the journal has been an outlet for creative thoughts and heated debates. I remember at the beginning of the 1999 school year that we used to have debates in the classroom. Perhaps our heated debates would have seemed peculiar to an outsider, especially since we got along very well with each other without even the notion of violence. (*Crossing Swords*, 2000, p. 26)

Are we really serious about encouraging writing as an essential, sustainable, life-affirming, and transforming activity in urban centers? How else can students memorialize classroom lore and their very being and, yes, according to Ann Marie, provide avenues for affirmation of self? Are the powers-that-be really concerned about leaving no child behind, while classroom budgets are cut and expert consultancy thrives? Isn't the latest mantra merely the fad of the day, allowing expert writers to crisscross and engulf the inner cities dazzling audiences with their doublespeak while leaving victims no different than they were? Do these educational experts ever really rub shoulders with the masses and try to connect with their space? How come urban centers have been the brunt of so many studies, reports, and initiatives but so very little transforming? Will more talk-shops and tank tops—oops!—I mean, think tanks pacify the masses, or shouldn't committed educators adopt and try to infuse intellectual courage as the key to individual, social, community, and ultimately national transformation?

How essential is it to create a space where student writers can publicly share and ventilate views? Would the community even care about what our youth have to say? Do those who ru(i)n the system care enough about the boats stuck at the bottom? What about the media and their frequent "exposés" on education? Do they ever get it right? Why should we even bother?

These are excerpts from the *Crossing Swords* Annual Symposium, held on June 11, 1999, which was cohosted by sophomore Kenisha Minott and ninth grader Shana Bryce.

KENISHA MINOTT: I'd now like to call upon Mr. George [former assistant principal of security) to present the next award.

MR. GEORGE: Good afternoon. It's a pleasure to be back here. I left but I never really left.… This place will always be in my heart, and it's a pleasure to see that Mr. Holder has for twelve years maintained *Crossing Swords*.

He has put a lot of time and many long nights into the journal. Many times Mr. Holder would call me at four o'clock in the morning to ask advice about a poem or to review a poem and other aspects of the journa.…

The award that I'm going to present is to a young poet, a very promising poet. When I read his poems, the depth, the passion, and the intensity of the writings of this young man moved me. So I told Mr. Holder that the poems express such deep emotions and intelligence that I felt that I had to present this award.

Garfield McNeil is that rare young poet who comes along and dazzles us with depth, passion, and intensity. He handles very diverse and challenging themes in a very original and unique way. For example, in the poem "Who Shall Govern the Governor?" he raises some serious and troubling questions about morality, authority, and religion.

Ultimately he forces us to think about the question of who our elected officials have to answer to if they do not, as he feels, answer to the people. If it is a higher authority or morality, then, as he says: "Now the question at hand is: / Who shall govern the gods?" In these lines we hear echoes of the perennial question posed by the Greek dramatists Euripides and Aeschylus, as they confronted the capricious gods of their religion.

This poet's range is wide. His grasp of the nuances of language is evident in the poem "Imagine," in which we hear echoes of John Lennon's classic song "Imagine" as well as the Dub poet Muta Buraka's poem "Dis Poem," with its similar ending refrain: "Dis poem will live in your mind / you shall never forget dis poem."

McNeil is an intelligent and insightful poet who tackles such universal themes as justice and death with clarity and vision.

Based on his originality of thought and his brilliant poetic achievements, Garfield McNeil is hereby honored with the Langston Hughes Award for Outstanding Poetic Contributions to *Crossing Swords* 1999." [Sustained applause]

GARFIELD MCNEIL: In my life there are a few people who'll stand out in my mind. Even when I pass high school and pass college, when I'm 117 years old, with my kids and grandkids, Mr. Holder will be one of those people, for he inspired me to write…. There are just not enough words for what Mr. Holder has done for me. He's brilliant. He motivates you, he makes you think, he captivates your mind. And I would also like to thank Hadassah Neepaul. Throughout the school year she has been a friend to me. [Applause.] Thank you. (*Imprints*, 2000, p. 11)

Do events like these help forge communities of writers? How are connections established and sustained by these interactions? Do public readings before an appreciative audience of classmates, teachers, parents, friends, even enemies, deepen the urge to be heard and to write? Let's consider two reactions to this series of genuine questions.

Giving the featured address at the Annual Symposium was Dr. J. A. George Irish, director of the Caribbean Research Center at Medgar Evers College. Note the structure and flow of the spontaneous and unrehearsed student-run function:

(HOST) SHANA BRYCE: Thank you Mr. Molofsky. Before I introduce this next person. I'd like to read [one of my] poem[s] that the advisor insisted that I read:

Life's Necessities
It has always been said that your necessities
for life are food, clothing and air. What about
an education? Is it a necessity in my future?
Education…
Is the sweet air I breath,
The food that
Satisfies my soul.
It is my shelter from ignorance.
It is the eternal river
That forever flows
From the mountain of knowledge.
Knowledge is the never-ending story! [*Crossing Swords*, 1999, p. 56]

[Sustained applause]. Now I would like to introduce Ade Nicholson, our editor at large.

ADE NICHOLSON: Good afternoon.... I would like to call on Dr. George Irish to come forward.... Dr. Irish, on behalf of the Society for Social Analysis I would like to present you with a copy of our journal, *Crossing Swords*. [Applause.] Would you be kind enough to say a few words?

DR. GEORGE IRISH: Thank you. Greetings, sisters and brothers. On occasions like this I'm dumbfounded. I say that because sometimes when we get invited to functions, we don't know how to prepare. One of the things I have learned to do in life is to come with an open mind—an open spirit—and to respond to the environment, the ambience, and the mood of the occasion. And that's the way I'm going to respond today.

Even though I've had the privilege of reading many of these poems before coming here today, there is nothing as rich or, as touching, as hearing an author recite or read his or her own writing, because there is something that you cannot capture on the written page as opposed to when it is presented directly from the soul of the person from whom the art work originates. [Applause.] There is something that touches you in a very sensitive way. And this afternoon I can't swear for the rest of you in the audience, but I've certainly been touched. Touched to the point where I found that I was getting a little emotional, and I've been trained not to let my emotions come out around people. I should let my intellect control my behavior and my responses.

But that's one of the sad things about the way we teach when we make students believe that the only way to respond to the realities of life is through some objective lens. And you distance yourself and come up with some objective analysis. But I've found that for the realities of life, the true response is one that has been touched and tinged with your personal sensibility. And so this afternoon as I listened to the poems, particularly of those who graduated and, interestingly, those who are in the process of development right here in the school, I feel moved as a father, as a teacher, as a preacher, politician, and all the numerous hats I've had to wear, to say to you young people that what you have committed to paper here is more than words. [Applause.] It's more than just ideas. It's a vision: A vision that very often people don't associate with the people of your age, your neighborhood, your school, your race, and your color. But it's a vision, a message for the world, the universe. [Sustained applause.]

You are not speaking to Sarah J. Hale High School. You're not speaking just to your classmates; you are speaking to the universe. You are saying to the world that there is something bottled up inside. There is something you feel so profoundly about that you share it with someone. And, it takes courage to do that, specifically the sentiments you share with us today—so deep, so moving, delicate sometimes. Your hurts, your fears, your anxieties, your ambitions, and your aspirations—you share them and it takes a lot of courage. Because very often we prefer to hide our true feelings, and we give the teacher the version of what we think they would like to hear. And we give to our parents some of the statements we think they'll like to hear.

But when you start committing yourselves in literary form, in poetic form, you are saying to the world, this is who I am. This is where I am. This is the real me and I am leaving it for generations to read—for generations to hear, for other students to understand; somebody passed through this world that went through certain challenges, who had certain agonies, certain discomforts in life. But out of all of this, there is a message. And I thank you for the message. And the message that I would like to share with you is wrapped up in five words.

As you go forward into life, as you face the millennium I hope that you continue to pursue excellence in all things. But there are five "A's" in particular that I want you to cherish, hold on to, and pursue.

The first of them is *aptitude*. Find out what your personal ability is, what your strength is because, many other people are going to want to tell you what your strengths and weaknesses are. Many people are going to want to tell you what direction you should go toward in life, and what you should avoid in life. But you personally have got to know what your true aptitude is, what the skills are that you are blessed with, the talents that God has endowed you with. Know them, understand them, and try to discover how you can develop them. You have that first "A" on your transcript and you're on your way to success.

The second "A" that I want you to pursue is not in geography or history or political science or mathematics. It's an "A" that speaks to cultivating the right *attitude*. Because you may have the aptitude, you may have the ability, you may have the skills, but you must have the right attitude toward your parents and other humans. If your attitude stinks, no matter how many skills you have, how much money you have, no matter how much brains you have, you are a nonstarter. So let's cultivate productive, constructive attitudes.

The third "A" I want you to pursue in life is related to *aspirations*. If you discover the right aptitude and cultivate the right attitude and you have learned to dream and understand that it is okay to dream, then you are on to something great. I've been to too many schools where children think that to be a "nerd" is a crime—to aspire to high achievement and excellence is something to be shameful about. I get the impression from this group, the *Crossing Swords* group, the Society for Social Analysis, that you're not in that group, that you understand that in order to succeed in life, you've got to set yourself your own goals and aspire to achieve them. Without that element of aspiration in your life, your soul will dry up. These dreams make our goals come alive, and that makes us practice the things that will make our dreams become reality.

The fourth "A" is *application*. You can dream as much as you like, but if you don't have the discipline to apply yourself to the task that can make these dreams become real, you are a loser. So get the aptitude, cultivate the attitude, pursue the application, practice the application, and the end result is the highest level of *achievement*. That's the fifth "A." [Applause.]

May God bless you as you go forward in life. I wish to compliment you, compliment your advisor, your principal, and all those who have inspired you in life. Never get trapped in the circumstances around you, but let your vision transcend the superficial realities so that you can discover the deeper realities, which are going to be the alternative measure of your stature as a person. [Sustained applause.]

SHANA BRYCE: Thank you, Dr. Irish, for your powerful words of inspiration.

In terms of envisioning a structure and orientation to facilitate writing, I need but underscore the salience of emotion in educational theater. What, then, do we have here if not a journal which connects students of different grade levels and eras, all through construction of a writing community that continuously reinvents itself to face the challenges of each new era. Further along at the June 11 Annual Symposium, we find:

KENISHA MINOTT: I'd now like to call upon Lakeisha Hudson, a 1997 graduate and former editor-at-large of *Crossing Swords*, 1995-1997, to present the next award.

LAKEISHA HUDSON: Good afternoon. Before I introduce this next award, I would like to say that I was only introduced to [this recipient's] writings a short time ago and what struck me about one piece of her writing was that it inspired an entire section in this issue of *Crossing Swords*. And the title of this section is "Witness to History." One thing that stood out was that she spoke about the changes and the challenges that the students are going through with the number of principals that they have had in a very short period.

I think that history is repeating itself. I graduated in 1997, but when I started in 1993 we went through the same thing, such as the walkouts and the changing of principals. We were fed up with what was going on, but we overcame it. We made it with the help of teachers, fellow students and [others]. We overcame the changes and the challenges, and you can do it as well. As someone said, students now have to play a major part in the rebuilding process of the school. [Applause.]

I started writing for the journal during that time of the school crisis in 1993, and Mr. Holder constantly called upon me to write articles, so I continued. I'll be starting my third year of college, and all the writing has really helped. When you are up all night writing papers, sometimes till 3 in the morning, sometimes three or four papers a week, you would really check back and say, "I'm glad that I let someone help me improve my writing." It's going to really pay off, and you'll say over and over, "Thank you Mr. Holder. Thank you for inspiring me." So I'm just here to say to you, "Just keep writing, just keep doing it." I know you're going to say it's hot, and you don't feel like sitting here writing, but just keep doing it. The last day of school when I was graduating and everybody was getting ready for the prom, getting their nails done, I was sitting in a classroom writing this final essay for Mr. Holder. All my friends left me and went to the nail place, but I stayed. And it will always be in my memory that I stayed and completed the essay.

Like I said, the one essay of the student whom I am going to present this award to inspired all these students to write about the changes and the challenges that are taking place in the school. Personally, I know her. She is a great student. Mr. Holder constantly tells me how much she reminds him of me. And I am honored to present the Paulo Freire Award for Exemplary Analytical Skills to Monique Scott. [Applause.]

The education system is renowned for providing manuals for this and that. This mandate is another ruse that educators use to convince themselves that they are doing something tangible. Most manuals end up in the dustbin of history. In this chapter it would have been quite easy to prepare free flow charts featuring graphic designers, T charts, or Venn diagrams, and even borrow a few ideas from the workshop ,odel and present findings that are impressive.

Just as I was about to ambulate down that road, I was struck by two sayings: "Students get amazingly excited when they produce knowledge that has an audience in the school and community" (Kincheloe, 2001), and "If we do not have some knowledge of children's lives outside the realms of paper-and-pencil work, and even outside their classroom, then we cannot know their strengths" (Delpit, 1996). Both statements instruct us to seek out alternative, even nontraditional, and nonscripted ways of engaging the texts, students, and the classroom, that site of teeming conflict. What are the implications for the teaching of writing, rather, fostering the urge to write within students? Throughout this chapter, by unfreezing tales from a journal, I have attempted to allow students and the adult members of their borderless classroom, to tell the story behind their writing. One may argue that it was luck and chance, which sustained the writing community. If that's the case, why are we so unlucky in other areas, such as clean and uncrowded classrooms, adequate supplies, and on and on?

Looking back on all that students wrote over a relatively short period of time, I can't help but marvel at the serendipitous discoveries that I was fortunate enough to recognize. If each vignette tells about a different piece of the puzzle of how to, knowingly or unwittingly, foster a setting for the release of ideas on paper, then my story could fill in a small piece. At the 1999 function I was introduced thus:

KENISHA: I call upon Mr. Holder to present the next award.

MR. HOLDER: This is a very special award. I don't remember who it was but, I think it was Keisha who said that like most ninth graders, when she came into my class, I gave her a magazine to read…. But a strange thing happened last term. This group of ninth graders came in and I gave everybody a copy of

Crossing Swords, and the following morning a ninth grader came to me and said, "Mr. Holder, may I have another issue?" I was a bit perplexed so I asked, "What do you mean?" And the student replied, "I read all of it [210 pages]." Not wanting to question her further, I gave her the 1994 edition of the journal, which was about two hundred and twenty pages. The next day, she came to me and requested another issue, and for that entire week the student read five issues of the journal. More than one thousand pages! [Applause.]

That isn't all. She immediately knocked her way into the group. I mean she would come and volunteer to type early in the morning before school began. Sometimes when I got to school at 7:45 she would be waiting by the classroom. And whenever I arrived at 8 o'clock she'd inform me, "Mr. Holder, you are late." But the thing that really touched me about this student is once she said, "Mr. Holder, the writing in the journal is brilliant but there is one piece that really, really moved me." "Which article?" I asked, and she replied "The piece about 'The Will to Survive.'" Once she mentioned that article, it brought back memories, for it is a stunning piece of writing indeed. And she went on and told me that she would like to meet the student who wrote it. So may I call on Mr. Shilue Johnson to present this award? [Applause.]

SHILUE JOHNSON: It's good to be back. On behalf of the Society for Social Analysis and *Crossing Swords*, I present the Mary McLeod Bethune Award for Exemplary Analytical Skills to Sasha Pringle. [Applause.] It's a pleasure to meet you.

SASHA PRINGLE: I am delighted that I finally got the chance to meet you. Thank you.

SHILUE JOHNSON: Mr. Holder would like me to say a few words. What can I say? I graduated in 1997 and this year I'll be starting my junior year at Plattsburg University in upstate New York, about twenty minutes from Canada. And to tell you the truth, it is one of the best universities in upstate New York, although you may never have heard of it.

Writing for *Crossing Swords* has been absolutely the best thing I ever did in high school. I'd personally like to thank Mr. Holder, because without all the writing he encouraged me to do, I may not have survived in college for the last two years. [T]o tell you the truth, those of you who are about to graduate, college is no joke. It's not like high school, where you have to wait for teachers to put notes down. To tell you the truth, it's not easy. It's good to back. Thank you.

References

Applebee, Arthur, N. (1996). *Curriculum as conversation: Transforming traditions of teaching and learning.* University of Chicago Press.

Boorstin, Daniel, J. (1998). *The seekers: The study of man's continuing quest to understand his world.* New York: Random House.

Delpit, Lisa (1996). *Other People's Children: Cultural Conflict in the Classroom.* New Press.

Freire, Paulo (1997). A response. In P. Freire with J. W. Fraser et al. (Eds.), *Mentoring the mentor: A critical dialogue with Paulo Freire* (pp. 303-330). New York: Peter Lang.

Gladwell, Malcolm (2000). *The tipping point: How little things can make a big difference.* Boston: Little, Brown.

Hale, Janice E. (2001). *Learning while black: Creating educational excellence for African American children.* Baltimore: Johns Hopkins University Press.

Imprints: Documents of the Society for Social Analysis. 1988-2000. Brooklyn, NY: Sarah J. Hale High School.

Kincheloe, Joe (2001). *Getting Beyond the Facts: Teaching Social Studies/Social Sciences in the Twenty-First Century.* New York: Peter Lang.

Kincheloe, Joe; Slattery, Patrick; & Steinberg, Shirley (2000). *Contextualizing teaching: Introduction to education and educational foundations.* New York: Addison Wesley Longman.

Postman, Neil (1996). *The end of education: Redefining the value of school.* New York: Vintage.

Vanessa Domine

CHAPTER FOURTEEN

How Important Is Technology in Urban Education?

Most respond to the question of technology in urban education with the complaint that "poor" schools don't have sufficient access to computers. Given the current digital age and the tumultuous history between technology and public schooling in the United States, the misguided definitions of technology as only computers and of urban communities as merely "poor" are not surprising. What is particularly problematic is the overarching assumption that computer access alone can address the challenges (overcrowding, high dropout rates, low test scores, inadequacies in teacher preparation) and opportunities (racial, ethnic, cultural, and linguistic diversity) within urban settings. While the use of computers can address some of these challenges on some level, their haphazard presence in the classroom more often than not indicates a dysfunction in the ideal of technology as consisting exclusively of computers and the Internet, and the lack of attention to the real needs of urban school teachers.

Thus, my answer to the question of how important technology is in urban education has to do with renewing our commitment to urban education while downplaying the technologies. I do not wish to diminish the importance of technological proficiency, as it plays a significant role in achieving educational innovation. However, success within urban education requires an authentic and ecological approach to schooling. In the context of student learning, urban schools are merely one component within a larger system that includes family, community, and government. In the context of teaching, technology is merely one component within a larger system that involves professional development, leadership, communication, assessment, and ongoing support. From this perspective, the excessive pursuit of computers and Internet access is another attempt to find a technological panacea for perceived "ills" of education, while shifting the attention away from the political, economic, and social motivators that compel urban education.

Moving Beyond Access

Over the past ten years, the United States has spent more than $40 billion to place computers in schools and connect classrooms to the Internet. In 1997 the government subsidized a $2 billion program called Educational Rate (E-rate) to help schools and libraries obtain Internet wiring and services. E-rate provided up to a 90 percent discount to schools with the largest number of poor children. The goal of E-rate was to increase equity of access or bridge the "digital divide" across poor and wealthy communities within the United States. Amidst controversy over widespread "fraud and abuse" within the administration of the E-rate program (Reuters, 2003), approximately 99 percent of schools (not classrooms) in the United States have access to the Internet. While nearly all schools have some level of Internet access, the digital divide remains a reality in the homes of many students within urban communities. Only 25 percent of the nation's poorest homes have Internet access, compared with 80 percent of homes with annual incomes above $75,000 (Dickard, 2003). The double-edged sword of E-rate is that the poorer school districts that obtain subsidized access without the funding support for professional development or technical support also have increased access to failure. The emergent inefficacies of technology in the classroom perpetuate myths of the teacher as Luddite and of low-performing students as inherently inferior. The lessons of E-rate teach us that urban education in the United States is still very much a complicated issue, despite federal efforts to operationally define educational success as access to computers and wiring. Widespread lack of professional development poses a serious risk to the nation's investment in educational technology, as many teachers have neither the experience nor the skills in using technology in meaningful ways that support, rather than detract from, their curricula. The federal government only recently realized that equipment and wiring are not enough for the successful integration of technology within schools.

Access to information is inarguably the first step toward knowledge. However, as humans, we need to do more than just access information. Any teacher who has received a cut-and-paste essay from students who conducted "research" on the World Wide Web realizes that students need a framework for understanding information. Such a framework extends beyond the practical skills of technological literacy and encompasses *media literacy*, the ability to access, analyze, evaluate, produce, and communicate information using a variety of technologies (Aufderheide, 1992). Cultivating media literacy among students requires acknowledging the constructed nature of information. It also requires an awareness of ownership in the sense that those who control our technologies influence the information we have access to and therefore determine social, political, and economic power. Conversations at the policy level about technological literacy therefore need to move beyond student acquisition of a set of technical skills to include habits of mind that allow students to thoughtfully navigate the mediated world in which they live. Given this broad view of literacy, access to the technology is important—but it is only the first step.

The Myth of Technology

Addressing the importance of technology within urban education requires us to establish a shared understanding of the word *technology* and its relationships to urban education. Not until the Great Exhibition of 1851, in the Crystal Palace in London, did technology become associated exclusively with machines. Beyond the technical lies a philosophical dimension that denotes a methodology, or a process of doing things, that lends itself to a particular way of thinking (Ellul, 1980; Finn, 1972; Winner, 1986). Technology is therefore ideology and a way of looking at the world. From this perspective, it cannot be limited to one specific machine or discipline of study or even a course subject area. Rather, it embodies political, social, and cultural ideologies that are woven throughout all bodies of knowledge, throughout all of education, and even throughout our daily lives (Downing, Mohammadi, & Sreberny-Mohammadi, 1995). Thus, conversations about technology cannot be separated from conversations about curriculum, teaching, learning, or the purposes of education. Do our attitudes about computers within urban schools assume that if students can just get access to information, they will learn and excel? Do teaching and learning occur through the mere delivery and reception of information through value-free tools?

It is not until a specific technology is employed within a particular context, such as classroom instruction, that it serves as a medium for communication. Books, television, and computers are more than just tools for delivering information. They are mediators of information that influence students' lives both inside and outside the classroom in ways that are commercial, cultural, political, and social. The experiences of urban youth are commodified and commercialized through the cultural capital of clothing, video games, compact discs, cell phones, and pagers. In one sense, these technologies provide students with a common culture. In another sense, the languages of these technologies are, to a certain extent, constraints that create distinctions or divisions across youth. Stereotyping is one example of a shortcut to meaning that is inherent within the conventions of television, film, and the Internet. How then do we reconcile using these technologies in meaningful ways that value diversity in urban education? To address this, we need to look not just at tools or machines but more broadly at the wider mediated environment of teaching and learning.

Reframing technology as ideology calls for intellectually rigorous conversations about the ways in which technologies-as-media shape information and alter the ways in which individual students learn and individual teachers teach. Using technology in educationally significant ways requires teachers and educators to transcend the technical into a realm that, although mediated through technology, is driven by social and political consciousness. This paradigm shift renders obsolete the traditional role of the computer teacher and instead positions all teachers as educational leaders who orchestrate a variety of technologies to support personal, professional, and pedagogical goals. This view of technology empowers teachers to select what media will shape the classroom environment and how it will impact individual students beyond the four walls of the classroom. Authentic technology integration in the classroom calls for an abandonment of the technological elitism associated with computers in the classroom and an understanding that higher-level thinking skills can and should occur across older print and video as well as newer digital technologies. In this sense, student empowerment has little to do with the mobility associated with laptops and wireless networks and everything to do with social and political mobility into a world of the student's own creation.

Given this rigorous definition of the role of technology within urban education, it is not surprising that conversations about ideology are few and far between. It is much easier (although equally problematic) to talk about the tangible equipment than to articulate and then examine our ways of seeing education, technology, and the world around us. Despite its arduousness, questioning the impact of technology on our lives is essential to our survival as humans and relegates conversations about computers and wiring to the back burner—if only temporarily.

An Ecological Approach

The continuous pressure for educators and administrators to keep an eye on the moving target of technological innovation distracts us from what should be of paramount importance to education—the students themselves. The pendulum of history has swung from individualized student learning back to subject-matter emphasis. The inability to reconcile the two is illustrated in the current achievement gap that dangerously isolates the student in terms of individual achievement, race, and ethnicity. The gap refers to the disparity in school performance (e.g., grades, test scores, course selection, college completion) according to racial and ethnic differences. In 1996, several national tests found African American and Hispanic twelfth graders scoring at roughly the same levels in reading and math as white eighth graders (Johnston & Viadero, 2003). The designation of this disparity as an *achievement* gap implies inherent deficiencies in student performance and simultaneously ignores as possibilities the failures of teachers, educators, and leaders charged with supporting student achievement. In addition, aggregating testing scores in this manner perpetuates the stigma that race and ethnicity are valid determinants of success or failure. Yet, the achievement gap is not exclusive to urban education. Reported "gaps" exist in cities, suburbs, and rural school districts alike, suggesting that disparity of student achievement is symptomatic of a more serious condition within the larger system of public education in the United States.

In an effort to bridge the achievement gap, the federal government enacted the No Child Left Behind (NCLB) Act. Enacted in 2002, NCLB requires every identified racial and ethnic group to perform at grade level or make "adequate yearly progress" toward that end. If schools or districts are unable to prove successful performance or progress, they are threatened with mandatory tutoring and even privatization (U.S. Department of Education, 2002). The NCLB legislation mandates that every student in the United States be "technology literate" by the eighth grade. The U.S. Department of Education through NCLB funds the costs of standardized testing while cutting funds to the preexisting Technology Innovation Challenge Grants and the Technology Literacy Challenge—both national funding streams that support thoughtful and integrative uses of technology in schools and communities. NCLB and the achievement gap hauntingly echo E-rate and the digital divide in ignoring the fundamental principle that increased access to and accountability for student achievement and basic technological proficiency require *systemic* support and cannot be accurately measured in terms of standardized test scores and quantities of computers.

Educational policy avoids the commitment to use technology in the service of urban education. Ironically such a policy stance does not directly support the belief in diversity of race, ethnicity, culture, and language as the greatest asset as well as challenge to urban education. For a teacher, generating and coordinating multiple thinking styles and ways of seeing the world are central to achieving pedagogical excellence and student achievement within the four walls of the classroom. The greatest potential source of strength for accomplishing this lies in the insight and commitment of educators to see the bigger picture of schooling as one component of a larger system that includes families, housing developments, community centers, schools, religious organizations, libraries, universities, and business professionals. After all, urban communities face challenges associated with conflicting cultural identities, poverty, drug abuse, and disease before some children ever enter the classroom. The goal is not to derive a formulaic vision or template for technology to then apply to all urban settings or even urban education. Rather, the value of technology is in facilitating and supporting a shared purpose within the larger urban community and a felt pedagogical need within the school classrooms.

Herein lies the value of computers and the Internet for urban education: strengthening localized communities through a strategic use of communication technologies, such as e-mail, discussion boards, and/or live chat. One urban high school principal in Detroit was inspired by the technological savvy of her college-age children and chose to acquire computers and Internet access specifically for increasing parental involvement in schools within the district (Means, Penuel, &

Padilla, 2001). The principal creatively assembled Title I funding and business partnerships to build electronic networks between district schools and neighborhood housing developments. This orchestration of funding included monies for a technology coordinator and two computers labs—both in schools and within housing developments. The principal supported community professional development in which parents, teachers, and families collaborated on webpages for their classrooms and schools. The webpages announced school activities and hosted discussion threads for interaction among teachers, students, and parents. What is particularly powerful about this systemic approach to technology integration is its insight into the importance of parental and even whole-family support in student achievement. Also insightful is the reframing of professional development as a communal activity that includes parents, teachers, and students.

Another powerful example of using technology in the service of urban education is the Bilingual Excel Grant at McKinley High School in Buffalo, New York. Teachers faced the challenges of linguistic diversity among students as well as lack of student knowledge and awareness of their larger community and its cultural agencies:

> Students planned a tour of their community using a variety of modes of transportation. Through field trips in which students visited the public libraries, the art and historical museums, horticultural gardens, and a butterfly conservatory, they learned to describe and differentiate among the functions of each of these agencies and sites while improving their effective social communication in English. They gained an understanding of the social, historical, and cultural diversities within their communities by using various print and technology resources. Students applied learned technological knowledge and skills to design a Web page with the assistance of a consultant. As a result of working cooperatively with other students throughout this project, they developed cross-cultural skills and an understanding as well as an appreciation of one another. (Kearney, 2000, p. 153)

Although many urban schools do not have the funding for student transportation and technology consultants, similar efforts can be replicated by bringing cultural institutions to the school setting through volunteers, guest speakers, and Internet websites. Whether these connections happen through face-to-face communication or digital communication (or both) is secondary to the larger goal of building bridges between students and the communities in which they live.

Given this emphasis on technology in the service of urban education, the more fruitful questions to ask are: What are the authentic educational needs of the school community? How might teachers marshal the available print, video, and digital resources within the schools and the surrounding community to support such needs? Privileging the diversity of media forms afforded through technology is key when thinking about ways to support classroom curriculum. Although sometimes painful, critical conversations about technology are the only means by which an educational community can establish a common purpose for education and technology. Community-based decision making invites members to determine which technologies are appropriate, empower, and represent an urban community.

Whose stories are told and whose stories are left untold by history textbooks, live and online museum exhibits, or instructional films? What publishers, producers, and corporations are most likely to support the goals and interests of this particular urban community, and less likely to commercially exploit it? Within urban communities, it is incumbent upon school leaders to elicit from teachers, students, parents, and community leaders expectations for teaching and learning, to more thoughtfully guide the uses of technology within the classroom.

Redefining Pedagogy in the Context of Technology

Just as schools are one component within a larger community system, so teachers are one component within the larger school organization. Unfortunately, too many of these teachers are compartmentalized by the bureaucratic characteristics of attendance, discipline, testing, grading, and class schedules. A more holistic approach to classroom teaching situates the teacher as an empowered orchestra leader who uses a variety of resources to create a classroom environment that supports a consistent vision for teaching and learning. Among the sources of support are school leadership, communication, professional development, standards and assessment, and technology resources. In the context of technology, the educational commitment lies not just with the equipment, but also in building and sustaining a network of direct support for the pedagogical goals of the classroom teacher.

For urban schools that have existing imbalances within their educational communities (e.g., high dropout rates, low parental involvement, discipline problems), adding technology haphazardly runs the risk of perpetuating the cycle of putting blame on teachers and students for the lack of technology skills or performance. Technology integration is more complex than simply using technology in the classroom. It's about having the widest possible repertoire of instructional media and technologies available and selecting the most appropriate for use depending upon goals for students and pedagogical preferences. This approach does not pressure teachers new to either curriculum or technologies (or both) to immediately change their teaching philosophy. Instead of thinking up ways to blame teachers for the lack of technology integration, we need to ask, How can we support teachers in their felt need for technology within their classrooms?

Teachers' professional development and technology integration need to be reframed in terms of how technology directly supports teaching and learning by its variety, not just in the form of computers. Just as the uses of technology should privilege diversity within communities and among students, they should also privilege diversity of technologies and teaching styles.

In the context of the classroom, privileging diversity requires intervening among individual students' understandings and the texts and technologies of instruction. For example, a teacher may require students to read an essay, visit a website, or view a documentary about the Civil War. Regardless of the medium, the teacher should ask students to consider: Whose story is being told? Whose story is being left out? To what extent is this information representative of your own experiences? Specific to the medium, students should also ask: Who is the author and what is his/her motive for telling this story? Why did the author use print/digital/video format? How did the author construct this essay/website/film? Who has access to this essay/website/film? The culminating pedagogical act is to then ask students to express alternative views of Civil War history, choosing the content and medium for their (re)production. On a more grassroots level, students might access and analyze crime statistics within their neighborhood and look at news media portrayals of crime within the larger community. What information about the community is *not* reported? How do these representations compare with those of other communities? Are such portrayals accurate? Are they fair? It is within this progression of access, analysis, evaluation, and communication that the uses of technology can meaningfully support both media literacy and cultural diversity.

Using technologies in the context of student-produced media requires reconfiguring time and space in relation to pedagogy. Many urban schools have neither computer labs nor computers in the classroom and therefore struggle with equitable access and technological literacy for all students. Hands-on production work requires students to immerse themselves in the content and to experiment with the technology. Therefore, such teaching and learning demand extended blocks of time — not the 40-minute standard during the school day. Since many students within urban communities do not have access to these technologies at home, the opposition to such project-based work is almost insurmountable. The question arises, What is the most valuable use of classroom time? From a technological standpoint, the classroom is biased toward community. That is, there is great potential for student interaction, group discussions, and collaboration — despite traditional alignment of desks in rows. Although overcrowding is prevalent, a source of strength for student learning can be the classroom community. From this perspective, it does not make much pedagogical sense to use face-to-face classroom time for students to sit behind a computer, other than for live technical demonstrations or a formal class presentation. If students have neither school nor home access to computers, then how will such technological proficiencies be achieved in urban communities? What other technological resources can students and teachers draw from within the community? Can public libraries, community centers, and nonprofit organizations collaborate with teachers to compensate for the lack of equipment? If such partnerships can be forged and equity of access to computers and the Internet can be accomplished by combined efforts and technologies within homes, libraries, churches, and community centers, then the possibilities and resources for classroom teaching and learning with technology are virtually limitless.

Professional development is not training, but rather a transformative process that begins with experimentation at a basic level and grows as teachers gain experience with using technology with students in enacting curriculum in the classroom. Teachers need time and the freedom to experiment with a variety of technologies to discover authentic pedagogical strategies that are grounded within the real needs of the classroom and curriculum—that are linked to communities outside the classroom. Thus professional development must entail thinking about curriculum and the technologies that can (and cannot) successfully support it.

Rethinking professional development calls into question the value of one-day district workshops in which teachers are "released" to address issues pertaining to teaching, learning, and administration. Yet such a model is punitive, as it decontextualizes teaching. A new model for professional development involves continual practice, experimentation, and ongoing support in the uses of technology. Off-campus technology training sessions should be community based, where teachers can forge connections and cohorts within the surrounding community. Cohorts of curriculum design teams can meet on regular bases as a companion to ongoing (individual or group) uses of technology within the classroom. Such conversations are grounded in the reality of daily teaching experiences and allow for immediate transformation of what happens in the classroom. Fostering experimentation allows for daily occurrences of planning, design, integration, assessment, and redesign. In sum, the theory and practice of technology integration need to be inextricably connected to the processes and products of curriculum development.

To view the challenge of technology within urban education as merely one of access to computers and the Internet is to dangerously view the issues as involving technological uses of education rather than authentic educational uses for technology. Ultimately, the focus must shift away from merely accessing computer equipment to embrace a more holistic and humanistic framework that privileges diversity of all kinds—including technological diversity. The successes and failures of technology within urban education will be measured by the (in)ability of educational leaders to forge connections between schools and their communities. Ultimately, the school principal is responsible for bringing together all the elements within the educational community to support schooling. This leadership role requires the vision of education as a social, political, and economic responsibility that is enacted locally through the integration of families, schools, and community institutions. It is incumbent upon teachers and teacher educators to set their sights on developing authentic models of teaching and learning using a variety of technologies that support a shared, communal purpose instead of surfing the next technological wave.

References

Aufderheide, Patricia (1992). *Proceedings from the National Leadership Conference on Media Literacy.* Washington, DC: Aspen Institute.

Dickard, Norris (Ed.) (2003). *The sustainability challenge: Taking edtech to the next level.* Washington, DC: The Benton Foundation.

Downing, John; Mohammadi, Ali; & Sreberny-Mohammadi, Annabelle (Eds.) (1995). *Questioning the media: A critical introduction* (2nd ed.). Thousand Oaks, CA: Sage.

Ellul, Jacques (1980). *The technological system.* Trans. from French by Joachim Neugroschel. New York: Continuum.

Finn, James D. (1972). Automation and education: Technology and the instructional process. In R. J. McBeath (Ed.), *Extending education through technology: Selected writings by James D. Finn on instructional technology* (pp. 141–160). Washington, DC: Association for Educational Communications and Technology.

Johnston, Robert C., & Viadero, Debra (2003). Unmet promise: Raising minority achievement. *Education Week, 19,* 1, 18–19.

Kearney, Carol A. (2000). *Curriculum partner: Redefining the role of the library media specialist.* Westport, CT: Greenwood.

Means, Barbara; Penuel, William R.; & Padilla, Christine (2001). *The connected school: Technology and learning in high school.* San Francisco: Jossey-Bass.

Reuters (2003). *House panel expands probe into E-rate program.* March 13. Washington, DC: Reuters News Service.

U.S. Department of Education (2002). *No child left behind.* Website: http://www.nochildleftbehind.gov. Accessed November 8, 2003.

Winner, Langdon (1986). *The whale and the reactor: A search for limits in an age of high technology.* University of Chicago Press.

Koshi Dhingra

CHAPTER FIFTEEN

How Should Science Be Taught in Urban Settings?

How we think of the nature of science and scientists shapes the way we teach and learn science. It becomes important, therefore, to consider our own views as well as those of our students before attempting to list pedagogical approaches appropriate to urban classrooms. A not uncommon view of science is that it is an objective, fact-laden, impersonal discipline and that scientists are precise, logical, extremely bright, somewhat asocial or antisocial, and frequently eccentric individuals (usually white and male) who spend most of their time working on their own. This view, not surprisingly, distances many of our urban students from scientific pursuits and from identifying themselves as scientists.

Far from being a solitary activity, science possesses a significant social dimension. Three aspects of the social character of science are distinctive. First, members of the various scientific disciplines depend upon each other for the conditions (ideas, instruments, etc.) under which they practice. Second, initiation into scientific inquiry requires education from those who already practice it. Third, scientific practitioners are part of society, and the sciences depend for their survival upon society's valuing of what they do. The context of assumptions that supports reasoning and the sociocultural context that supports inquiry are directly related to knowledge construction (Longino, 1990).

The scientific method is typically described as a sequence of steps taken by all scientists during their investigations. However, most textbook descriptions impose limits on such key factors as personal interest, social influences, and relationships with the subject matter or test organisms. "Nonscientific approaches" such as Barbara McClintock's practice in coming up with the idea of "jumping genes," for which she was awarded the Nobel Prize in medicine and physiology in 1983, are important points of consideration when thinking about the question of what science is. McClintock's feeling for her study organisms, developed over time, had everything to do with the emergence of her insights about transposons, or jumping genes (Kirkup & Keller, 1992). Development of a personal relationship with study subjects is not only a natural outcome but also a strength of scientific inquiry; we can therefore invite our students to be scientists—which means bringing their whole selves into the classroom. Their ideas, beliefs, and feelings all become extremely relevant as they engage in scientific practice. Their assumptions about the natural, social, and political worlds, the values they place on various phenomena, activities, or ideas are all relevant to authentic scientific activity in the classroom—just as it is in the scientific community.

What Is Scientific Literacy?

Scientific literacy for all has been defined as an important goal by a range of national reform documents (American Association for the Advancement of Science, 1993; National Research Council, 1995). Bybee (2001) recommends that the goal of achieving scientific literacy for all can be most rapidly advanced by combining the efforts of both formal and free-choice education sectors. Literacy involves a familiarity with both language and culture; it involves a linking of all concepts that constitute a person's worldview. Again, this points to the need for the whole person to be engaged in science classroom activities, with room in the classroom agenda for student worldviews and their links to personal beliefs and experiences.

What is meant by scientific literacy? One analysis of the notion of scientific literacy distinguishes between three types. First, *practical scientific literacy* consists of knowledge that can be immediately put to use to help solve practical problems; second, *civic scientific literacy* enables citizens to be more informed on science and science-related issues in order that they may bring their knowledge to bear upon those issues; third, *cultural scientific literacy* allows people to know something about science as a major human achievement (Shen in Lucas, 1983). Science teachers would probably like to address all three types of scientific literacy whenever possible. We now can consider strategies that best facilitate the construction of these literacies in our students.

How Should We Teach Science in Urban Settings?

First, we need to be true both to the discipline and to our student population when we teach. This means that the factors that drive instruction must be what science is and who students are. Thus,

- students need to be engaged in authentic science activity and discussion, and
- students need to understand that their personal beliefs and experiences are relevant and welcome in the science classroom; they need to see the relevance of what they are learning to their own lives and community.

Second, there are two different models of the school world that drive teacher behavior and approaches (see Figure 1). I argue that Model B is what we need to move toward and use to drive our teaching.

	Model A	Model B
Nature of science	It is a body of correct knowledge. It is a set of precise thinking skills.	It is a set of tentative knowledge claims that are defended by arguments and that have been accepted by scientists as useful.
Nature of learning	It is the imprinting on a blank slate of information from: teacher books observation (experience) manipulation (experience)	It is an active learner-driven process of selecting and translating information via what the student already knows, resulting in idiosyncratically encoded linked words and images.
Nature of learners	Learners are mostly deficient with respect to learning, lacking skills. The task of the teacher is to correct or introduce skills and knowledge.	All learners are knowledgeable and can learn when the concept is encountered with respect to prior knowledge, and can learn metacognitive skills to become more efficient learners.
Implications for teaching	Must have correct knowledge. Must give clear message, blackboard pictures, experiences. Must wait for proper time or teach content-independent skills. Must diagnose degree of deficit, stream, accept that some kids cannot, make curriculum simpler.	Must know claims, present arguments, ask students to argue and evaluate theories. Must pose situations, ask students to argue about it, create conceptual conflict. Must give tasks that engage prior knowledge, require building of metacognitive skills (i.e., learning how to learn), and generate new knowledge. Teacher should avoid a "right answer" view (that there are singular right answers that exist in the teacher's head or in the textbook).

FIGURE 1: Models of the School World That Drive Behavior of Teachers

Finally, in order to be supported in these efforts, urban teachers need to explore the rich resources they have available to them that lie beyond the classroom. The urban environment has rich educational resources that are frequently both free and very accessible to science teachers. Examples of free-choice science settings that can enrich and facilitate such instruction or experiences include such accessible and free resources as museums, parks, the school's physical environment and community; discussions about relevant television programs; and websites with relevant materials.

Planning Authentic Science Activity

In a class I observed, fourth-grade students in a public school in Brooklyn, New York, had spent several class periods (over several days) working on a science project on plants. The project consisted of each student cutting out magazine pictures that related to plants and gluing them onto a piece of paper. Students chatted quietly as they worked; the task before them was clearly not in the least challenging or stimulating. The students each completed their plant-related collages after about a total of an hour and a half of cutting and pasting. My question was, "What had they learned in that span of time and in what way did cutting and pasting magazine pictures for this span of time resemble authentic science activity?"

In the postobservation discussion I had with the teacher after this class, it became apparent to me that her perception of what "doing science" meant and her understanding of "hands-on science" had limited her planning of this activity. The term *hands-on science* is used so widely that I think an important distinction to make is between "hands-on" and "minds-on" science activities. When planning authentic science activities to engage our students, the focus needs to be on the cognitive skills and domains which are connected to the activity. In other words, a hands-on activity must also be minds-on. Perhaps the teacher wanted students to learn about the variety of products commonly used in society derived from plants; perhaps she wanted them to appreciate the diversity of plant life that exists. For students to make such connections with their classroom activity, they needed to perhaps share and discuss their collages in groups with a few guiding discussion questions and/or present them to the whole class. My point is that this could have been a fruitful activity if the lesson design had been considered with a focus on the two points bulleted under "How Should We Teach Science in Urban Settings?" above. Think of ways that you would modify this activity so that it resembles more what you would consider to be authentic science activity.

In the next two sections, I will discuss two examples of resources that are very accessible in urban settings. A significant aspect of one's professional development when it comes to teaching science in urban settings is to take the initiative to locate and use the plentiful resources available beyond the school setting. In doing so, you can make science cross borders so that our students see that scientific activity exists and is relevant beyond the classroom setting. Further, the classroom then becomes a venue in which to discuss and question science-related experiences students have in a variety of settings (home, community, and other institutions such as museums).

Teacher Perspectives on Museums

In this section, I will present the perspectives of a few teachers who participated in a science teaching methods course at Brooklyn College. They were all elementary, middle, or high school teachers at different public schools in Brooklyn. The course was a collaborative effort between the American Museum of Natural History (AMNH) in New York City and Brooklyn College, so that college faculty taught the course in the museum using museum exhibits and resources consistently.

Stella, who teaches the ninth-grade Living Environment curriculum and Advanced Placement Biology has several years' teaching experience in Brooklyn. In her time as a teacher in New York, she has taken advantage of the high-quality free-choice science educational resources that the city offers. Among the places that Stella had taken students to in the past were the Brooklyn Botanic Garden, the New York Aquarium, the AMNH, the Dolan DNA Learning Center at the Cold Spring Harbor Laboratory, and outdoor settings near the school. However, Stella did not feel supported by the school administration in her efforts to include informal science learning. Transportation issues, paperwork, time constraints, substitute shortages, and low parent interest were all mentioned by her as representing significant obstacles. Stella also spoke of her sense that there was an underlying feeling amongst many faculty and administrators at her school that organization of field trips for students was a wasted effort. Her sense was that many of her colleagues perceived a difference in museum culture versus their students' culture. This tension between the perception of the museum as "high" culture and the students as consumers of "low" culture angered Stella, who perseveres in her own efforts to have her students experience science in a variety of settings.

From my discussions with many public school teachers in New York City, this was a common theme. Four teachers from the Brooklyn College-AMNH collaborative course spoke at length about their plans to take their class to the museum or to other informal science learning locations such as the Botanic Garden in April or May, once the rounds of testing were completed at their respective schools. School administration, they felt, would not support taking trips—perceived as nonacademic activity—in the face of the need for concentrated test preparation, perceived as in-class activity.

Susan, an elementary school teacher who said that she had not taken her class to the museum since she took the methods course there the previous summer, commented:

> The climate at my school is…test oriented. Although we are encouraged to include social studies and science in our programs, we are required to teach reading and lan-

guage arts for the first three periods of the day and two periods of math. There is the sense that the children must be prepared for the test, yet at the fourth-grade level they are also required to take a science test. I don't believe our administrators realize how important the other curriculum areas are to children's mathematical and language skills.

In Susan's school, the predominant view seems to be that children need to spend most of the day learning and preparing for the tests, which focus on language arts and mathematics. Further, the view is that the way in which children can best prepare for these tests is by in-class activity. The fact that there is a required science test at the fourth-grade level does not receive as much attention, perhaps because that is not an immediate issue.

Edward and Janelle both teach at SURR schools—schools under registration review—because students are not meeting the standards. They felt that as such, the possibility of trips to informal science centers for their students anytime before May was precluded. Edward added that there was a vigorous turnover of teachers and principals at his school, making it difficult to get a sense of stability and a sustained outlook on issues such as the value of informal science experiences. The principal of each school gave teachers the clear message that they were to concentrate on academics. Edward also spoke of his desire to have his class gain more access to the Internet so that they could visit the website of the AMNH and of similar institutions. He added that most of his students and their parents were probably unfamiliar with the museum and that such Internet access would be helpful in increasing exposure and building student identity as museum visitors and, therefore, a connection to museum culture.

The methods course at AMNH that these teachers took seemed to help them think in new ways of the museum as a teaching and learning resource. James, who is a learning leader at a middle school, spoke about his own learning during the science methods summer course:

> I've been fascinated by the museum for a long time. But I never really knew what to do when I got there…. I've learned some things about developing…different projects so that when students go there, they'll have questions instead of just saying I'll look at that, I'll look at that.

James feels that if students visit the museum with their own personal agendas and come prepared to resolve some questions, they will enjoy the experience and find it meaningful. He added that most of the teachers in his district—which is the same district that he went to school in—were probably not trained in what they or the students could do when they went on a trip. For them, "a trip is just a day out in the field and hopefully you'll learn something." This notion of a field trip as an isolated activity, separate from classroom learning, is one that is commonly held. However, like any other teacher-organized learning experience, well-designed activity and assessment that is connected to meaningful cognitive skills and domains and clear expectations are critical components.

Olivia's experience during a rock-sorting activity in the museum classroom was positive. She considered the importance of having this type of experience before attempting to attach unfamiliar labels (the names and definitions) to the rocks. She came up with new extensions of the activity that she would like to try with her own students, such as having them note color variations and relating that to chemical composition, having students determine density and identify the rocks based upon density, and so forth. She wrote in her reflections about an activity at a museum exhibit in which she participated after having completed the classroom activity:

> We then went to the hall of meteors and the hall of gems and minerals, where we were asked to try and find our rocks. Mine was formed when a meteor struck the Earth. It was not part of the meteor but instead it was heated up by the meteors when they hit Earth and then it cooled rapidly, thus getting its round shape. We were also asked to find a rock that interested us and to become an expert on that rock. I picked spodumene. Its chemical makeup is $LiAlSi_2O_6$: one part each of lithium and aluminium to two parts silicon and six parts oxygen. Its name comes from the Greek word meaning "burnt to ashes." This was a nice activity, except that I kept having trouble finding information on the first two rocks that I decided to look for, so I finally settled on a rock that had a lot of [text] next to it so that I could finish the assignment. I think I would like students to get rocks from different groups (calcium, carbon, etc.) so that we could go back and have a discussion on the different types of rocks (each could have his or her own rock as long as it came from the same group). I would probably group students together instead of having them work alone, so that everybody would have help finding information on their rock.

Organizing collaborative work groups and providing meaningful assignments for them is often a constructive strategy in many settings, including free-choice learning sites such as a museum.

What if your school culture is such that you are unable to visit a free-choice site with your students? Institutions such as the AMNH have high-quality and abundant teacher materials available. Reference to such venues and encouragement of students to visit these settings in their own time could help address the perceived gap between the "high" culture of the museum and the "low" culture of the students, as pointed out by Stella.

Television-Mediated Science Learning

Television remains a primary source of scientific and technical information for Americans (National Science Board, 1998). It is therefore important for educators to recognize that television-mediated understandings about the nature of science and scientists are part and parcel of what students bring with them into the classroom. The 63 student participants in a previous study (Dhingra, 1999) varied widely in their responses to television science, indicating that they bring rich and differentiated schema to the interpretation of what they see and that television viewers construct their own understandings. They saw a range of different programs as dealing with science—from *Bill Nye the Science Guy* to the highly popular dramatic series *The X-Files*. The large number of students who recognize the relevance to science of dramatic programming such as *The X-Files* and *E.R.* points to the idea that science on television, as in the real world, is not a segregated entity. If we want students to bring themselves into the classroom, then we need to find ways for their worldviews to have access to classroom agendas. The notion of worldview, with its tight links to language and culture, makes it difficult to define science as a separate entity and to prescribe scientific literacy as a list of agreed-upon scientific concepts. Recognition of the centrality of student worldviews in their learning implies that educators concern themselves with those social and cultural institutions and phenomena that shape worldviews and, thus, student conceptions of science.

Guided participation in discussion and activities grounded in the context of television programs that students are familiar with would increase student perceptions of the relevance of school science in their everyday interests and lives. The book on *The Real Science Behind* The X-Files (Simon, 1999), written by the science consultant to the program, is an example of attempts to achieve such a goal. However, if teachers are not open to the use of such material, they will continue to feel that school science has little to do with their everyday world. Television represents the everyday world; there are characters and situations on television which many students are familiar with or relate to. The medium is a tremendous resource as motivation, point of reference, or basis for critique in the classroom.

What are some effects of interactions between informal, television-mediated education and formal classroom learning? How do students view such interaction and how do they compare school science with television science? Two eleventh-grade students commented on related issues in an interview (Dhingra, 2002). Elizabeth talked about the times when television was discussed in class:

> I kind of like it because it's fun but it's one of those things where you have to be careful what you say because any minute the teacher could be, like—OK, focus now—and then you feel stupid.

Alison added:

> When you talk about something that you both [teacher and student] have in common, it's just like a supplement to class…. I feel like I participate more.

For both these students, talking about television programming in the context of class seems to be a different type of learning than they were accustomed to in school. The relationship between teacher and student shifts in such conversations because, as Alison pointed out, they are discussing something that they both have in common. No longer is the teacher necessarily the knower and the student the one with less knowledge. However, Elizabeth is aware that this situation is not the normal relationship, and consequently a part of her holds back from full participation, since the person who is talking when the teacher realizes the shift that has taken place is the person who will be made to "feel stupid." The conversation is seen by the teacher as being tangential to the formal science education, which it is her responsibility to facilitate. Informal talk about television science is not considered to fulfill that responsibility.

Although there are significant differences between the nature of school science and the nature of science depicted on television, it seems that the act of bringing in the outside world by reference to popular science viewed on television would motivate these and other students in the classroom. Some ways that teachers may do this include asking students about the ways in which classroom-mediated science relates to other experiences; assigning homework or projects based upon students' careful consideration of the science they view on television in which they need to question, discuss, and critique what they view; including classroom discussion of science in popular culture in order to assess what students think about the nature of science and scientists in general as well as particular scientific concepts.

The interaction between the meaning worlds of science in informal or free-choice settings (such as museums and television) and school science helps us expand and deepen student experiences with science. Such interactions are critical in a classroom that views science as a complex sociocultural phenomenon and students as individuals whose learning is mediated by a wide range of experiences, both inside and outside the classroom. Although as teachers in urban settings we deal with daily shortages of resources in many of our schools, we need to expand our thinking of the classroom to include the many rich offerings the city possesses to which our students have free access.

References

American Association for the Advancement of Science (1993). *Benchmarks for scientific literacy.* New York: Oxford University Press.

Bybee, Rodger W. (2001). Achieving scientific literacy: Strategies for insuring that free-choice science education complements national formal science education efforts. In J. H. Falk (Ed.), *Free-choice science education: How we learn science outside of school* (pp. 44-63). New York: Teachers College Press.

Dansinghani, Rashmi M. (2003). Unpublished raw data. New York University. New York.

Dhingra, Koshi (1999). *Ethnographic study of the construction of science on television.* Unpublished doctoral dissertation, Columbia University, New York.

—— (2002). Thinking about television science: How students understand the nature of science from different program genres. *Journal of Research in ScienceTeaching*: in press.

Kirkup, Gill, & Keller, Laurie S. (1992). A feeling for the organism: Fox Keller's life of Barbara McClintock. In authors (Eds.), *Inventing women: Science, technology, and gender* (pp. 188-195). Cambridge, UK: Polity.

Longino, Helen E. (1990). *Science as social knowledge: Values and objectivity in scientific inquiry.* Princeton, NJ: Princeton University Press.

Lucas, Arthur M. (1983). Scientific literacy and informal learning. *Studies in Science Education, 10,* 1-36.

National Research Council (1995). *National science education standards.* Washington, DC: National Academy.

National Science Board (1998). *Science and engineering indicators—1998*. Arlington, VA: National Science Foundation.

Simon, Anne (1999). *The real science behind* The X-Files. New York: Touchstone/Simon and Schuster.

Roymieco A. Carter

CHAPTER SIXTEEN

Can Aesthetics Be Taught in Urban Education?

The answer is not as simple as the question might imply. The word *aesthetics* is loaded with history and meaning which for some may stand diametrically opposed to "urban education." In this chapter, I examine tradition, time, and social practice in order to contextualize our understanding of aesthetics. The chapter also discusses the myriad of new ways in which aesthetics is understood and taught in urban education.

Aesthetics and the Traditional Voice

How do we understand the nature and value of everyday objects and experiences? How do we go about distinguishing the relevant from the irrelevant? Can we understand the purposes and meanings of experiences within objects? Are we able to place value judgments on the perceptions of these objects and experiences? From where do we draw the resources to defend our judgments? Should the same standards that were constructed to mystify heroic painting, classical theater performance, and traditional literature serve as the mold for creativity, expression, and beauty for the contemporary urban student? The student in the current urban educational setting is accustomed to viewing the urban public space as a visual battleground. The urban public space houses modes of expression and representation that would have been far from imaginable by the "fathers" of the traditional standards of aesthetics. The urban student is assaulted by imagery utilized for activism, propaganda, and advertising. These representations become the filters for the lived experience in the urban public space. The cultural attitudes and selected tolerances for language, expression, and literacy administered by the ambiguous social administration provides the urban student with the need to find alternate expressions of language and image. The new forms of expression are able to communicate the connected thoughts and emotions of the student in the urban public space. The barrage of visual messages forced on the urban student is complex, mixing manipulation and desire. The pressure from the outside inward on the individual is different from the traditional position of observation and disconnectedness. This change in direction makes it difficult to pass a blanket judgment on the quality of vision and aesthetic value of the urban student. When teachers in the urban setting are faced with the challenge of teaching aesthetics, rarely is it understood and presented from the outside inward. Urban education must rethink the principles of aesthetics and its purpose before teaching the value system to the urban student. The eighteenth-century bourgeois aesthete has transformed into our savvy, grounded urban student. Where once the site for viewing the transcendent image was the salon, now there are billboards on gritty subway trains. Along the route to school, the student is repeatedly confronted with overlapping social and corporate visual messages. The urban student is not expected to have the aesthetic "ascension into the divine." The new aesthetic messages through billboards warn of the dangers of AIDS alongside the horror stories of teen pregnancy. These messages are using the history of visual art to strengthen the encoded social messages for the urban student. On the opposite end of the spectrum, in the urban neighborhoods, the elaborate use of text and image is intended to deliver a different type of message. This urban gallery is the street. It becomes the canvas for the urban student to see resonating images of his or her life. The graffiti become the record of important individuals, borders, practices, and events that make up the urban space. Graffiti also serve as a backdrop for the expressions of individual style. These styles change rapidly in order to avoid absorption into mainstream culture. The urban atmosphere thrives off the energy and aesthetic vision of the urban youth culture.

There are complex historical and contemporary philosophical debates about aesthetics. One of the most famous historical debates between teacher and student was that of the teacher Plato's lack of interest in the art object as the ideal of beauty and truth versus the student Aristotle's belief that the art object can improve upon nature because it possesses the ability to reveal the essence of nature. These same philosophical debates have continued through the halls of the academies and caused the fragmentation of artistic practice in museums and galleries throughout the world. However, the basis of this inquiry is to address the aesthetic as a key that connects fundamental knowledge production to the lived experience.

In order to use this key, we will need to ease or release our grip on the reins that control the historical standards of aesthetics. It is important to note that this is not an abandonment of the traditional debate but rather a reconceptualization. Aesthetics, as with any production of knowledge, needs contextualization, in this case through the urban space. The challenge is to allow it to collapse underneath its own weight and history. Let's begin by entertaining the idea that the study of aesthetics, as a tool of critical inquiry, can provide a nontraditional framework for teaching concepts of beauty and value to the urban student.

There are two main approaches to the study of aesthetics: the conceptual and the formal. Conceptual study of aesthetics concerns itself with the nature of beauty, truth, value, and taste. These concepts are constructions of social interactions and exchanges. They are subject to change over time and become reflections of the cultures and classes that define them. Where in history, the concern for "truth" in representation is fueled by ongoing popular debate, the marginalized embodiments of "truth" for urban students are reflected in their names, clothing, relationships, responsibilities, and experiences of pleasure found in the urban lifestyle. On the other hand, the formal approach focuses on the rules of composition and the visual principles and elements that operate as the composition's building blocks. The formal aesthetic critique places judgment on the arrangement of line, shape, color, light, balance, proportion, order, rhythm, and patterns within the composition of the art object. Urban students are well aware of the principles that build a quality hip hop track. They have no problems identifying a quality wall of graffiti. The urban student finds it easy to comprehend and respond in the appropriate style, whether it is visual or behavioral. The urban stage has already provided the student with tools to build a critique of aesthetic quality. This view must be recognized and respected. The urban student is expected to adapt to the aesthetic standards as historically defined by the institution of school. But does the school look to adapt and learn the new aesthetic qualities and values embodied by the urban student?

If we accept the statement that any activity pertaining to the nature of art and its experiences is rationalized through the philosophy of aesthetics, then the teaching of aesthetics will have to reference the traditional forms of art but also the new forms that are specific to the digital age. Students of the digital age have seen paintings move, dancers defy time and gravity by using computers and digital sensors, buildings being walked through and experienced before they have even been built, and music made without the use of voice or instruments. Urban students might find themselves in disagreement with the traditional aesthetic view. How is the urban student able to apply the traditional qualities of popular cultural aesthetics to the subcultures of hip hop, trance, or industrial music when the rules that govern the limits of quality never realized the transformations of music over time? We are all too aware that contemporary jazz is still fighting for its place at the aesthetic table. These connections can be portals to understanding new art forms. Urban students construct bridges that illuminate the pathways from the door of the academy to life in the streets. They freely interpret and manipulate the traditional art forms. The path between expression and the experience becomes the new "truth" that is beauty. Maxine Greene (1995) illustrates connections students can have through the aesthetic experience:

> They can be enabled to realize that one way of finding out what they are singing, feeling, and imagining is to transmute it into some kind of content and give that content form. Doing so they may experience all sorts of sensuous openings. They may unexpectedly perceive patterns and structures they never knew existed in the surrounding world. (p. 137)

Such aesthetic experiences present the urban student with the privileged information necessary to form an academically useful value structure. The critique is established in the context relevant to the urban student, and then it is applied to the external practice or experience. An aesthetic critique operates with a purpose of identifying, appreciating, and evaluating the sense of beauty. Kant defines the 'beautiful' as that which, apart from a concept, pleases universally (Kant, 1928). This statement carries two fundamental conditions just beneath its surface. The first condition is that the urban student needs to make his or her judgment of taste as a product of subjectivity. The other is the condition of universality, which requires consensus and mainstream agreement. Based on Kant's criteria for beauty, the urban student's subjectivity must reflect the ability to experience pleasure/displeasure when faced with the work of art. The student will also need to experience pleasure/displeasure without desire in order to be an aesthetic critic of taste and judgment. Kant's definition, void of sensory perception, is an alien concept for the urban student. To see/gain pleasure in beauty is not problematic, yet making it conditional to being free of "desire" goes against the social messages of the urban environment. This understanding of pleasure in a Kantian framework of beauty places the observer (in our case, the urban student) in a position of being "disinterested." This means that a student viewing the work of art cannot experience pleasure in viewing the work of art, nor can the act of looking at or creating a work of art produce in itself the experience of pleasure.

Many urban students will find it difficult to see their life experiences and personal interests reflected in this definition of beauty and with good reason. Kant positions beauty in the safekeeping of the exceptional individuals who meet his criteria for possessing taste. These traditional restrictions need to be understood but also challenged. We need to be aware of the risks involved in subverting the use of the traditional view of aesthetics in order to know how best to maximize the uncharted territories of aesthetics, pleasure, and the urban space. In addition we also need to understand this traditional/historical critique, which usually alienates urban students from the aesthetic and convinces them that their artwork or experiences are devoid of beauty or value. However, teaching an expanded view of aesthetics provides students with the ability to realize the nature of the urban space and how it is unique to them as a reflection of the personal, social, and experiential.

Urban students are often asked to observe and analyze the representations of concepts, themes, and interpretations present in their everyday experiences. These events in the students' social interactions can be understood as works of art. Asking them to reflect upon their immediate surroundings in order to make judgments based on social values is a common practice that relates directly to the nature of aesthetics. The reflection of these events is shaped by the comparison of the lived experience and the social standards identified by the lesson plan or curriculum unit. These social standards or privileged analyses regulate the potential educational benefits. The observed work of art through the canonized aesthetic standards is valued for an alleged intrinsic beauty/meaning, not an interpretative or experiential one. The significance of a work of art is considered fixed and innate, not something that shifts from viewer to viewer. It is this limited perspective of teaching aesthetics that shortchanges the use of aesthetic understanding for urban youth. The lack of flexibility and depth in this type of lesson plan or unit truly truncates the urban student's use and discernment of aesthetics.

Educators can transform students' relationship to aesthetics by reconstructing the curriculum. A prime focus of this reconstructed curriculum is the students' environment, their assessment of it, and discussion/outline of the value structures of that environment. Without pushing students to evaluate their environment, they are left to judge objects and interactions of their lives against a value structure that is not relevant to the way they move through the world of popular culture. Beauty/aesthetics becomes a relative condition based primarily in the urban student's decision-making process. If urban students are targeted with social messages by the academy, businesses, or activists, they should have the ability to see them with clarity and inquiry. In a traditional classroom, urban students are asked to evaluate the aesthetic in an experience or object. They are usually given only the standard definitions of beauty, trust, value, and logic, which further alienates the urban student from understanding and benefiting from aesthetic experiences. Curricular spaces must be constructed in the classroom to contest, debunk, and re-create aesthetic pedagogy. Understanding can be achieved through conversations among the student, the event or object, and the many variations of aesthetic theory. In teaching aesthetics in urban education, urban students should be exposed to the traditional tools and discourse while asked to critically question these constructions. The teacher must encourage the urban student to create new tools and languages for the understanding of aesthetics. The major objective is to use students' reflection on the imagery of the urban space and its aesthetic value while developing critical insights to better prepare the urban student to negotiate the complexity of the urban environment.

Urban students' ability to connect aesthetic value to lived experience increases their learning of social attitudes, personal knowledge, and critical thinking skills. Encouraging students to discover connections among objects, theory, and lived experience uses aesthetics to transform rather than inscribe knowledge for the urban student. Having students create dialogues between themselves and art objects and using their dialogues to challenge the popular academic definitions result in the students discovering new senses of possibility. If we are to believe the canonizing statement which declares that the quality of a civilization is judged by its art, then we also have to know that the driving bass lines of hip hop, the synthetic repetition of trance and techno, the athletic contortions of street dance, the juxtaposition of styles in apparel and visual imagery, the emotion-filled voices of the slam poets all come together as parts of the new definition for quality of the current urban civilization. Transformative teaching practices place an importance on encouraging students to create aesthetic debates that peel away stale fabrications of reason that no longer reflect the current urban social attitudes.

Many of the traditional art forms (music, painting, literature, architecture, theater, and dance) have experienced shifts in meaning and use. Why hasn't aesthetics changed as well? Teaching students to "see" the art object and also to "see" the shifting of associated meanings of the art object informs them that reproducing the objects and arguments of privileged debates does little to move knowledge production forward. In a traditional context, students are asked to focus on their sense reaction to artwork. This aesthetic employs reason as a way to encourage students to reproduce but not to take responsibility for the application of the defined value system. This also implies that the students need to maintain the aesthetic perspective by creating a distance to objectify the judgment in order to inscribe the appropriate value onto the art object. This aesthetic distance places students outside of the subject/object and asks them to critique the representation against the traditional aesthetic standards in determining its value. The privileged aesthetic position for viewing art objects and experiences stunts personal discovery and produces disinterest. A nontraditional use (a shortening) of aesthetic distance would invite students to be engaged in the deconstruction of the subject. The challenge is in helping urban students see their reflection in the representation to solidify their connection to the art object. The student's connection to aesthetics is placed in jeopardy by focusing strictly on constructions of the formal composition, without also addressing the relations that the objects and experiences have to the individual or his/her meaningful relation to the intrinsic purpose or origin of the objects/experiences. Personal involvement is not a part of the traditional aesthetic perspective. The conflict of aesthetic distance versus engagement in the current urban setting does not allow for the necessary connections of utility, socioeconomic value, and personal emotion. Locating urban students within the work of art will reduce their disinterest and apathy in discussing aesthetics in the urban environment. Aesthetic distance can be shortened if we engage the urban student in the critical inquiry of the

- purpose of the transmission
- object or experience as "engaged moment"
- position of the receiver
- realization of the author (intent)

- technique of delivery
- conditions of the object/experience
- relationship of the object/experience to the local, regional, and world community.

The current teaching of aesthetics must work very hard to extend beyond the purely sensory-based, empirical, and logical approaches. Teaching the urban student to observe the created image, object, or experience only through the formal use of visual elements removes the art object from its communicative value. Students are discouraged from identifying the purpose, origin, subject matter, appeal, character, style, or expression associated with representation of the humanistic qualities embedded within any work of art. All of these questions are necessary to experience the work of art as an engagement of social knowledge production, not as sites of exclusion and alienation. The basis of engaged critical inquiry for an aesthetic critique should ask students to:

1   Identify how the author has presented an interpretation of an object, event, or concept. What are the point of view and communicated meanings presented by the author?

2   Understand the shift of meanings based on the location of the art object and how different viewers of the same art object will create variations of the interpretation. What evidence can students identify in order to substantiate their interpretation of the art object?

3   Identify a major thread of thought or theme within the art object. Is the art object part of a larger collection? What other art objects reflect common techniques or ideas that aid the viewer in the understanding of this piece of work?

4   Ask whether the art can object be connected to other nonaesthetic fields of study in order to advance the pluralistic dialogues of the art object and the transformative production of knowledge.

Does Time Shorten the Aesthetic Distance?

The cornerstone of teaching aesthetics in urban education exists within understanding the communicative components of representation. So, what is representation? Is representation the tacit concept of the art object that illuminates its aesthetic value, or is it the explicit perception of the object that gives the work of art its value? Rudolf Arnheim asks a similar question; he outlines the differences between "thing-oriented" (motoric) and "idea-oriented" (conceptual) styles of expression. In his description, he uncovers that the two styles do not operate independently of one another. Motoric acts will also resonate conceptual meanings, since in order to engage in or to act upon the world (making art objects), a student must be aware of the situation (understanding the use of representation) to respond to it (Arnheim, 1965). At its core, representation is the embodiment of codes utilized for communication. Urban students use slang as an in-group marker. It identifies the social borders between the urban student and the academy. The academy has a preoccupation with the identification and promotion of all that is quantifiable and formal. The student is well aware that the use of slang is informal and rejected by the educational system. The students empower themselves by deciding the levels of engagement by code switching. The rules for popular aesthetics and the vibrant urban student subculture reflect this same dynamic. Code is the language shared by the transmitting object (artwork) and the observer, that is, the understanding and interpretation made by the observer (urban student) of the artwork. The sophistication of visual languages is tempered only by the ability of the observer to understand these languages. The urban student will freely be able to decode the graffiti of Futura 2000, Phase 2, or Vandal, but the encoded messages of Gabriella Munter, Franz Marc, or Wassily Kandinsky appear alien and unapproachable. All art forms utilize and recognize constructions of pattern, and we refer to these representations as *expressions* or *styles*. Both the graffiti artists and the artists of the Blue Rider use color, shape, texture, and an expressive style to convey complex, thoughtful, and humanistic ideas. The observer of the work of art attaches the object to observations, ideas, and experiences that are outside of the experience of observing the art object.

The new aesthetic pedagogy must forge these connections and not perpetuate the traditional required distance between observer and observed:

> This distanced view of things is not, and cannot be, our normal outlook. As a rule, experiences constantly turn the same side towards us, namely, that which has the strongest practical force of appeal. We are not ordinarily aware of those aspects of things, which do not touch us immediately and practically, nor are we generally conscious of impressions apart from our own self, which is impressed. The sudden view of things from their reverse, usually unnoticed, side comes upon us as a revelation, and such revelations are precisely those of Art. In this most general sense, Distance is a factor in all Art. (Bullough, 1912)

Suppose an urban student, who accepts that he or she is incapable of creating a work of art that measures up to the aesthetic "greatness" privileged in the classroom, is exposed to the work of Diego Rivera. After researching Rivera's work he/she realizes that Rivera chose to describe his history and his observation of everyday life. The student realizes that to appreciate Diego Rivera as an artist, he or she needs to understand Rivera's creative attitude and originality constructed through the ways he chose to "see" the world. His murals, his use of color, light, shape, and pattern become dialogues between the personal and the social. The connections of the feelings, the messages, and the experiences of Rivera resonate with those of the student. This reduction of aesthetic distance is essential to students' learning. A pluralistic approach to aesthetic judgment is needed if we expect students in an urban environment to be able to utilize aesthetics as a component of knowledge production. The new approach is multidirectional; it will need to abandon fears that are associated with misinterpretation and complexity. "The consummatory function of the aesthetic," as explained by Eisner (1998), "provides delight in the inquiry itself. The durable outcomes of schooling are not to be found in short-term instrumental tasks. Such outcomes must penetrate more deeply" (p. 43). If students are expected to engage the art object for the purpose of understanding, creating, and/or defining its value, it becomes more important to understand the familiar, reflect upon it, then move on to the unfamiliar. Why take this approach, and what is its relation to time?

Observing a work of art from a familiar point of reference is intended to center the student in the area of inquiry, bringing him/her closer to it. The issue of aesthetic distance has a dual reality. We find a deep satisfaction when the art object is centered within our reflection. In order to get optimal clarity in what we are attempting to understand, the process of inquiry needs to develop under supportive conditions allowing time for incubation between exposure and critique. To illustrate this point, we need only to observe Maya Lin's public monument, the Vietnam Veterans Memorial. We can see the names inscribed on the wall within our reach. The wall's span, color, and texture are all immediately accessible to the viewer. In order to get the peripheral information from our field of vision, we need to scan, shifting our focus along the way. We make connections to the event, catalog the names, and contemplate the conceptual meaning of the composition during the observation of the monument. We are left to contemplate the event of Vietnam. The communicative use of the grave black granite patterned with thousands of soldiers' names becomes fundamentally important to our perception of the wall. When we are asked, what did you see? the answer will be much richer and with greater clarity because the act of observation encompassed the reflection, the time, and the raised awareness due to the representation. If we are predisposed to a packaged "objective" definition of the monument, asked to look at the monument, then with very little time for inquiry or engagement probed for the answer, the connection and insight will most likely be superficial. The response will not be a deep reflection of thoughtful critique. It will be a recording of the formal objects that we were able to observe. Bullough refers to this as a case of "underdistancing"; it results in what he labels a response that is "crudely naturalistic," "harrowing," and "repulsive in its realism" (Bullough, 1912). Aesthetics helps the urban student to observe connections and respond with a clear view of responsibility and understanding to the environment. The reflection of the student in relation to the work of art will raise the student's awareness of the subject matter. The aesthetic distance is short and the reflection is clear.

The next step is to allow enough time for students to ask the necessary questions to gain satisfaction, understanding, and closure. The connections are made and the preliminary answers are more insightful, while new and more challenging questions are being constructed. Confronting aesthetics this way becomes a motivating practice for students. It facilitates defining the purpose of inquiry while assisting students in a shift of vision to comprehend the aesthetic value of art. The ambiguity and disinterest usually accompanying aesthetics begin to fade for the student. The urban student's questions and engagement with art uncover the "aesthetic modes of knowing" that are often the purpose of works of art and reveals the intended message built into their construction. The conversation between art object and observer becomes a plan for action. The student is placed in a position of responsibility for the newly uncovered information. They become owner and catalyst for the activity of knowledge production not only in art but also in life.

It is no mistake that the context set for aesthetic judgment is heavily dependent on the types of representation put to use in the art object. The mode of representation is as important to the students' understanding as the subject matter of the representation. The way in which artists choose to use materials and techniques to express their character and mood has a direct relationship to the way observers conceptualize their comprehension of the message. The representation of an idea can take any of three basic structures:

1 *Representational* (realism, imitation, mimesis). This type of work characteristically utilizes a visually accurate portrayal of the world. The objects within the composition will appear in the work of art just as they appear in nature (Rader, 1938).

2 *Abstract* (expressionism, impressionism, cubism). This type of art object uses symbolic references in order to communicate concepts and ideas to the observer. The key to abstraction is that while it does not reflect nature, the visual components in the work of art can be connected back to their references in the world.

3 *Nonobjective* (field painting, texture painting). In this type of art object, the subject matter and technique do not represent or imitate visual reality or objects that are recognizable in nature (Hammacher, 1964).

Critical aesthetic analysis is highly but not solely dependent on the observer's ability to decode the expression of the artist in the art object. As an inescapable component of art making, expression is the artist's constructed attempt to alter, reflect, or intensify the internal feeling and emotions of the observer. Students asked to assess the aesthetic value of a work of art will need to reference the use of expression in the art object. This practice exposes the contextual nature of the subject matter. The artwork communicates the concept, object, or event central to its purpose as its subject. Alone, the subject matter operates as a notation or recording of a particular point of view. The expressive form in the artwork frames the point of view of the subject matter. This is often a challenging and uncomfortable component of the aesthetic judgment. In a traditional aesthetic structure, students would have to demonstrate a privileged ability to decode, then pass on their discovery to the waiting masses who lack such gifts. This model does not take into account how the world has changed and the possibility of multiple interpretations.

The technology that mediates nearly all of our current visual information is transparent and often taken for granted. We enter our homes and turn on our televisions, DVD players, CD players/stereos, and computers without a conscious thought to how these devices affect the ways in which we see. Our aesthetic responses to these are seen as natural and ordinary. Students surf the Web on the subway train or on their way to school. They are able to send symbolic messages to their friends without any forethought or assumed trade-offs. They have an idea; they pick up their cell phone and share the idea instantaneously. Never before has it been this easy to communicate ideas. Each of these devices alters the ways in which we see and construct aesthetic critique. The immediacy of these experiences affords all sorts of possibilities for aesthetic reflections. Though we are able to use these devices immediately, the understanding of how they change our ways of seeing comes through time, use, and application of traditional aesthetic principles in new spaces. At least three modes of communication are still relevant as channels for aesthetic experience through technology:

1   *Narrative.* If an idea is dependent on structuring a series of related events, the viewer of the structure will see the pattern rather than the individual events. In most narrative structures, the sequences will reflect a social, moral, or cultural logic.

2   *Image.* Any attempt to record, capture, mediate, or imitate reality can be understood as an image. Images are the most widely used mode of representation.

3   *Language.* The structuring of the world through a socially agreed-upon set of smaller components for the desire of communication.

Representation of an art object through one of the new technology-driven art forms is still subject to aesthetic judgment. Students can apply aesthetic values to the new forms and decode transmitted messages, subsequently redefining and discovering the aesthetic experience in the everyday urban environment instead of the museum, gallery, or public monument. Students can see the opportunities and challenges of decoding expression on a daily basis.

Why do we sit in movie theaters or in front of the television mesmerized and meditating on acts of romance, danger, kindness, heroism, violence, pleasure, and happiness, if the art object is able to reveal itself only to the privileged objective observer? How do we recognize the difference between digital media art objects and the electronically transmitted data intended to sell a concept, product, or service? How are we supposed to teach students to know when the digital art object is presented for appreciation or is a reflection of a biased political, social, or moral agenda, given the extreme commercialism pervasive in the urban environment? These tensions are the very reason for aesthetics to be taught in the urban environment. Students need to be exposed to the political, social, and moral agendas. They need to critically analyze how pleasure and desire are mobilized through the new media aesthetic. The urban environment is the landscape for the reconceptualized aesthetic curriculum.

The media aesthetic, as part of the urban landscape, is a new form of aesthetic critique. New technologies become familiar parts of the lived experience, so they become easily overlooked as a delivery system for the art object. Due to the transparent nature and familiarity of the technology driving the recognition of the art object, urban students will not distance themselves from the technology. They focus on the art object and do not take into account how the representation is affected by artificial lighting, the digital properties related to the screen, and the limited amount of colors available for screen display. All of these screen properties and the transparent inundation of these devices in our everyday lives affect what we see, where we see it, and how we value the objects themselves. Urban students face a new challenge: The art objects of everyday life are requesting them to alter their moods, and their points of view constructed by authors who are not immediately identifiable. The constructions of reality are easily recognized, but the meanings and purposes are becoming dangerously vague representations of a false logic, precisely in need of pedagogical utility.

The builders of these art objects may find it to their benefit to maintain viewers' ignorance of the practice as long as they are responding appropriately. The problem is that although the recognition and response to expression is a part of the everyday, the urban student is not consciously aware of or focused on the motivations for the work of art or the results of the contextualizing elements of the subject matter. The elements of expression are complex but discernible. The student willing to uncover the motivations that state how the subject matter intends to be seen needs to realize only a few simple concepts:

1   The art object is a product of a constructed message.

2   It is encoded with meaning and purpose by an author.

3   It uses common languages such as color and light.

4   The symbolic imagery is often an edited exaggeration of reality.

5   It is directed at "me" as a potential observer, and "I" am intended (by the author) to place how "I" feel above "my" observation of an analysis of the construction.

Recognition of and reflection on these concepts give the urban student a critical shield against the art objects that aim strictly to convince the observer that the author's intentions and moods are exact representations of the popular.

How Can Aesthetic Judgment Be Taught?

Aesthetic judgment relates mutually to the ability to think critically about the artwork and to place value on it. The challenge to teaching aesthetic judgment is not that of drawing conclusions about subjective likes or dislikes of the urban student. It is not the rationalizing of formal visual properties as they pertain to the work of art. Teaching students to place aesthetic judgments on art objects in an educational system that privileges the stance of collective agreement and correctness is counterproductive in locating the interpretative voice of the student. The balance and juxtaposition between the subjective judgment and a judgment derived strictly from reason will culminate in the production of new knowledge. This new knowledge/insight is a bridge to the institution from the social and personal location of the urban student.

In addition to exposing urban students to aesthetic critique, the educator needs to engage them in their own art making. Imagine the following scenario: The teacher has just finished a formal explanation of how to create a work of art. There is a bold statement just about to bubble forth from one of the corners of the room. A student proudly states, "I am going to change all that. I will make people change the way they think about this work. My work will be something new, something never seen before." The teacher smiles while standing in silence, waiting for the student to realize how difficult this task will be. The teacher, so as not to extinguish the burning enthusiasm of the student, then responds, "How do you plan to begin this redefining of art?" The student stumbles to find an answer worthy of his/her previously announced statement. This one statement has brought the urban student face to face with everyone who creates, judges, and values beauty. At this point the real learning of the aesthetic begins. There are a multitude of possible responses the teacher can issue that will stimulate the urban student to pick up the self-proclaimed challenge and move forward in her aesthetic sensitivity and production of knowledge. The teacher has the benefit of knowing what challenges lay ahead for the inexperience and youthful enthusiasm of the student.

Students may challenge definitions and rules because they are understood as limitations being issued by structures of authority. Teaching students to conduct aesthetic judgments means placing them in situations that challenge what is important about the definitions of taste, beauty, and pleasure. Urban students live within a commercial landscape. External pressures are constantly being applied to the image they carry of themselves through the world. In the practice of building filters for these pressures, these students are encouraged to use aesthetic judgments. The negotiation of subjectivity and universality is the condition of popular taste that enables students to decide the value of the art or other forms of expression that they encounter in their everyday experiences. This new analytical skill allows them to become critical of political, commercial, and activist imagery that attempts to inscribe new values upon them. Teachers and students may approach the act of expression and representation with differing views of subjectivity and universality. Students experience art making and the recognition of expression with the ability to appreciate its beauty, although their response may not be formed on the grounds of logic, reason, or authority. The teacher, however, has been trained to reason and to therefore identify and communicate the formal expressive properties structured within the work of art, in order to have it seen as a proponent of beauty. The teacher has already answered to definitions set out by the structures of authority. They have worked through many of the complexities that the urban student has yet to encounter. Another great benefit the teacher can offer urban students is that the teacher operates as a guide through the institutional universality that accompanies the formation of aesthetic judgment. Kant illustrates the complexity of negotiation that is needed for subjectivity and universality in aesthetic judgment:

> But when he puts a thing on a pedestal and calls it beautiful, he demands the same delight from others. He judges not merely for himself, but for all men, and then speaks of beauty as if it were a property of things. Thus he says the thing is beautiful; and it is not as if he counted on others agreeing in his judgment of liking owing to his having found them in such agreement on a number of occasions, but he demands this agreement of them. He blames them if they judge differently, and denies them taste, which he still requires of them as something they ought to have; and to this extent it is not open to men to say: "Everyone has his own taste." This would be equivalent to saying that there is no such thing at all as taste, i.e., no aesthetic judgment capable of making a rightful claim upon the assent of all men. (Kant, 1928)

Through dialogue, teachers can provide vocabulary and definitions to situate a foundation for a student's attitude, judgment, and values regarding art. This is a strategic positioning of subjective reasoning. The challenge is not to settle into the staunch position of institutionalized authority illustrated in Kant's example. Urban students need to be supported and assisted but not forced to have the judgment of authority overshadow the ways they have learned to appreciate music, language, dance, architecture, theater, painting, and sculpture found in their lived space. An inclusive view of aesthetic judgment will meet the desired goals for producing knowledge that transforms traditional constructions of value, taste, and beauty. The new understandings/interpretations make it possible for urban students to value and create new ways of seeing.

When asked to confront the principles of aesthetic judgment and knowledge production, urban students are asked to replace what they understand about art objects in their everyday life with popular definitions from sources unfamiliar to their reality. The definitions of aesthetic judgment are only a starting point of inquiry, not the end of knowledge production. The dialogue and inquiry that follow static definitions become the new assessment of value for the art object. For example, when urban students are shown a representation of their city, they are likely to see more than the regional borders, markings for neighborhoods, transit patterns, or population scales. Imagine what other issues can be uncovered if the students are encouraged to discuss the aesthetic judgment they place on the city as a work of art. Given motivation and guidance, they will make use of personal, economic, cognitive, moral, religious, and political experiences to express their aesthetic connections to the city as a work of art. These areas of value directly shape the urban student's aesthetic judgment. The teacher may place aesthetic value on the logical, defining it as the solution to avoid misinterpretation by the observing students. The map (as information) may not have any relevant aesthetic value to the student. Urban environments are rich with experiences that students are aware of but not able to address because of determined solutions instead of free association of the art object to lived experience. Aesthetic judgment can be formed only if urban students are allowed to recognize its aesthetic value.

The art object, as the focal point of aesthetic judgment, arguably has no intrinsic value if we take the stance that value is the way an object is used in the world. The art object takes a renewed position of importance in the way we understand our social and personal selves. The usefulness of the art object is in the dialogue of the observer and the work of art. Underscoring why students will need to work from the teaching definition outward into the lived experience makes the work of art useful in helping urban students understand and link themselves to complex life experiences. The human condition does not exist in isolation. We label our heroes based on our desires. We celebrate and admire acts of devotion and trust. We also fear events and experiences we do not understand. There is no lack of these themes and many others in the art objects throughout history and into the far-reaching future. Allowing urban students to find the aesthetic value and determine the aesthetic judgment for a work of art in their everyday lives repositions the value of the work. The new aesthetic refocuses the gaze from the traditional objects to experiences that are contextual, meaningful and relative, and highlights art and expression as the products of human interaction in the material and immaterial world.

Art and Social Practice: A Way of Understanding

The teaching of aesthetics in urban education is better understood if tied to lived experiences within the urban environment—its people, languages, homes, neighborhoods, families, authorities, actions, and exchanges that take place between these and other facets that illustrate experience as the reflection of understanding for the urban student. The various of experiences brought to the institution of education become valuable tools in the teaching of aesthetics in the urban space. The aesthetic is approachable as a lens for the observance of social practices such as ritual, work, habit, and pleasure in everyday life. It is also a formal practice for the discussion of morality and value within the social atmosphere. The new aesthetic engages a social consciousness and awareness.

The urban environment is flooded with varying social practices that are prime for aesthetic investigations and insights. Urban students are oftentimes deprived of traditional aesthetic experiences and discussions. This reconceptualization of aesthetics places them in the center of the new media aesthetic. Traditional aesthetic standards are studied and challenged as they are applied and discovered within new urban public spaces. Urban students become the new aesthetes. The people, spaces, and objects in their everyday experiences become treasured embodiments of beauty. While learning to value these experiences, students also learn the freedom and responsibility of understanding.

References

Arnheim, Rudolf (1965). *Visual thinking*. Los Angeles: University of California Press, p. 204.

Bullough, Edward (1912). 'Psychical distance' as a factor in art and as an aesthetic principle. *British Journal of Psychology*, 5, 87–117.

Eisner, Elliot W. (1998). *The kind of schools we need: Personal essays*. Portsmouth, NH: Heinemann.

Greene, Maxine (1995). *Releasing the imagination: Essays on education, the arts, and social change*. San Francisco: Jossey-Bass.

Hammacher, Abraham M. (1964). *Mondrian, De Stijl, and Their Impact*. [Art exhibition catalog.] New York: Marlborough Gallery.

Kant, Immanuel (1928). *Critique of judgment*. Trans. J. C. Meredith, Oxford: Oxford University Press. http://etext.library.adelaide.edu.au/k/k16j/part3.html. Accessed November 18, 2003.

Rader, Melvin (1938). *A modern book of esthetics*. New York: Henry Holt.

Leah Henry-Beauchamp and Tina Siedler

CHAPTER SEVENTEEN

Why Is Health an Urban Issue? Asthma: A Case in Point

We never signed up for this e-tour of duty. I knew being a parent was going to be hard. It was expected that our children would get sick, but the hospital, the medicine, the worry was never what we had in mind.... I hate asthma! Asthma makes me feel helpless in my ability to help my own son. It's terrifying when taking a simple breath becomes a chore.

Mother of a four-year-old

When students enter a teacher education program, they expect courses in curriculum, methods, and content knowledge. Colleges of education place emphasis on meeting the needs of teacher certification for individual states, preparing students for exams and assessment, and, on occasion, teaching about diversity and cultural difference. Preservice teachers do not enter a program expecting courses on or even mention of issues of health and safety. The occasional mention of urban health usually centers on problems with drugs and alcohol. In fact, images of the bad health of urban dwellers are obsessed with the consequences of addiction, crime victimization, and/or the dangers of sexual encounters. Issues like low birth weight, infant mortality, lead paint poisoning, poor diet, and the dangers of transportation are ignored. Teachers who plan to teach in urban areas must become well versed in the identification and treatment of both symptoms and diseases that are endemic to the city environment. In this chapter, I will discuss only asthma and its ramifications on young children. This chapter should serve as a model for teacher educators and teachers in what details are needed in order to educate those who are attempting to educate our urban children. I encourage readers to collect equal information on other ailments that are particularly serious in our cities.

Asthma: The Specifics

Asthma is a serious health issue that affects millions of urban children. The number of children diagnosed with asthma has steadily increased over the past ten years. Estimates from current research indicate that over one quarter of all African American children in urban areas have asthma. Despite various educational programs and efforts, there continues to be a growing number of children with asthma who are in need of services. It is crucial that parents and educators are familiar with the basics of asthma, including signs of an attack, potential promoters and triggers, and methods of treatments and prevention. With a general understanding of asthma, adults will learn to feel secure and confident in treating a child with asthma at home or in the classroom.

Asthma is a chronic lung disease which is caused by an increased reaction of a person's airways to various stimuli (ALA, 2003a). Asthma is considered a chronic condition because the lungs of a person with asthma are always inflamed. Asthma is also an episodic disease, causing attacks to occur when a person's inflamed lungs are constricted to the point where normal breathing is difficult or sometimes impossible. Attacks usually occur after a person with asthma comes in contact with a trigger and can consist of episodes of wheezing, coughing, shortness of breath, and a tightening in the chest. These attacks vary in intensity and may start suddenly or take a few days to develop (Butler, 2000). If asthma is not properly treated, it can cause death.

The statistics for pediatric asthma are alarming. It is estimated that 7.7 million children under the age of eighteen have been diagnosed with asthma; 3.8 million had an asthma episode in 1999 (ALA, 2003a). The numbers of children with asthma have contributed to its being the leading serious chronic illness among children and the leading cause of missed school days due to chronic conditions (ALA, 2003a). Most children have mild to moderate cases of asthma which can be treated by medication and monitoring. For some children the illness can be more severe and cause multiple hospitalizations and other complications. For children under the age of fifteen, asthma is the number one cause of hospitalization (ALA, 2003a). The estimated annual costs of treating asthma in children under the age of eighteen are estimated to be $3.2 billion (ALA, 2003b).

When asthma symptoms become exacerbated, children may not be able to attend school. These symptoms cause children to miss 10 million school days each year (AAAAI, 2002). Loss of a child's school day can lead to a parent or caregiver missing a day of work:

> I have missed so many days of work because of asthma. What am I supposed to do? My kid can't breathe—literally. My boss at first was sympathetic, but now that he realizes the reality of having a kid with asthma, I get no sympathy. A cold is one thing. The chicken pox is completely understandable. Even a high temperature or vomiting. Those are the kinds of excuses my boss understands. He does not understand asthma…. A couple of times, I have to admit, my child has told me he can't breathe and I have corrected him saying, "No baby, you just can't breathe well today!" I sent my sick child to school, just to keep that job. I love my kid. I hate the job. I really need the money. Tough choice. Asthma forces me to make calls like that.

This decrease in productivity among parents and caregivers has an estimated annual value of $1 billion (Butler, 2000).

A person does not grow out of asthma: It is a chronic condition. Asthma is a hereditary disease. The odds of having a child with asthma are three times greater in families that have one parent with asthma and six times greater if both parents have it (Butler, 2000). However, as people with asthma grow older, they become more accustomed to warning signs of an attack, how to avoid triggers, and the best treatment options for them. Asthma can become a manageable condition for many. However, for young children, it can be dangerous:

> The scariest moment in my whole life was March 26, 2002. Our second child was a month old. I remember parts of that day so clearly. It was such a beautiful winter morning. The whole world seemed to be blanketed in snow. My son had been coughing and wheezing for days. I had taken him to a doctor and had religiously given him the prescribed medicine. At any rate, I needed to change my daughter and I did not have a diaper downstairs. I left my son alone in the family room and quickly ran upstairs with our daughter in my arms to get the diaper. The whole thing took a total of 60 seconds. When I got back downstairs it was silent…. Time started doing that thing—you know, go real slow. My son was lying face down in a pool of clear vomit. I panicked. He was sheet white and barely conscious.
>
> It has been a year and I still cannot tell you how I managed to get the three of us to the emergency room at the hospital…. We laugh now, but my husband wanted to know why I wasn't embarrassed being in the hospital with my pajamas and slippers on. But at the time all I was thinking about was my son. Seven days later he was released from the hospital.

Because of their age and inexperience, children in urban settings will not always be aware of triggers and how to avoid them. If they are infants or toddlers, they will not be able to communicate their symptoms to their parents. In these cases it is the responsibility of the parents to be extremely vigilant and aware of their child's health behaviors. There is also the concern that it is not "cool" to use an inhaler and that children and youth can be teased and bullied when it is apparent that they have asthma.

Promoters and Triggers of Asthma

There is no one definitive explanation for why asthma continues to affect so many children, but there is research as to why asthma and asthma attacks happen. Without promoters and triggers, a person with asthma would never experience an asthma attack. Asthma *promoters* are things such as allergies, tobacco smoke, and respiratory infections, which cause the hypersensitive lungs to become inflamed (ALA, 1997). Asthma *triggers* include tobacco smoke, exercise, weather, medications, emotions, and chemical irritants, which cause an asthma attack in the already inflamed lungs. In urban areas, air pollution from motor-vehicle exhaust, dust, dirt, and poor ventilation contribute greatly to the increase in asthma. It is important for children, parents, and educators to understand and be aware of these promoters and triggers, so that they can take the necessary precautions in preventing asthma attacks whenever possible.

Smoking is one of the most dangerous promoters and triggers for children with asthma. The American Lung Association found that wheezing attacks in children could be reduced by 20 percent if parents didn't smoke in the home (ALA, 1997). For a child, secondhand cigarette smoke can serve as a promoter and trigger. The smoke irritates the lungs, causing them to become inflamed. Once inflamed, the smoke can then cause the lungs to constrict further, resulting in an attack of wheezing. An estimated 200,000 to 1 million asthmatic children have had their asthma condition worsened by exposure to secondhand smoke (ALA, 2003a). Parents of an asthmatic child should not smoke around that child or allow visitors to their homes to do so.

The most common promoters of asthma are respiratory infections, including influenza and cold bugs common in children. Viruses invade the airways and cause inflammation. Children with asthma should avoid people with the flu or colds. Parents may want their child to receive a flu shot each season. Ironically, the difficulty of getting flu shots in the large city contributes to the increase in asthma. Health clinics are difficult to get to, are not always staffed or open, and are poorly advertised, and many caregivers have no release from work in order to get children to the clinics for shots.

Once promoters have inflamed the airways of a person with asthma, the person is primed for an attack. It is at this point that the triggers do their damage. The triggers signal the airways to constrict beyond the point at which normal breathing can occur (ALA, 1997). It is important that children with asthma, their parent(s), and educators be aware of triggers:

> I guess as a parent you worry about your child's first day of school. It seems silly to think that I spent so much time worrying about the wrong things on my son's first day. Would he make a friend? Would he like his teacher? Would the kids tease him? I never would have thought to worry about would the teacher be wearing half a bottle of perfume. I never in a thousand years thought to worry if the teacher, in her mad scramble to get her room and bulletin boards set up, would be spraying adhesive when my child was in the room. And I certainly never thought to worry that the teacher wouldn't even realize that my son's uncontrollable coughing was the beginning signal of his respiratory distress. I never thought my son's first day in pre-K would end up with a four-hour stay in the emergency room and one steroid shot later to control an asthma attack. And I was not prepared for my son telling his father "school made him sick."

Asthma has different triggers. Walking to school or taking a subway or bus can contribute to triggering attacks. Exercise is one of the most obvious triggers. During most types of exercise, about 80 percent of people with asthma may experience a tightening in the chest, coughing, wheezing, or general discomfort (ALA, 1997). When people exercise they are required to breathe hard and fast, and this is difficult for a child with asthma. However, this does not mean that children with asthma should not or cannot exercise. If they can learn to control and be aware of their asthma symptoms, exercise should not be a problem. In fact, many doctors feel that regular exercise combined with asthma control may actually result in better long-term breathing (ALA, 1997).

Many children with asthma also suffer from allergies to substances like pollen and molds. Most develop what is called allergic rhinitis, more commonly known as hay fever (ALA, 1997). Children with allergic rhinitis release histamine that can trigger an asthma attack and cause a runny nose and watery eyes. An increased amount of pollen in the air can irritate the airways. Parents and educators should be observant of pollen counts (widely available in the media and on the Net) and keep children with asthma inside when the count is high. If possible, during days of high pollen counts, windows should be closed at home and in school and air-conditioning used if an option (ALA, 2003c).

Many children with asthma are allergic to dust mites, which are common in homes and classrooms. City schools that lack adequate ventilation and good custodial services are breeding grounds for mites as well as molds. The feces of the mites are inhaled into the lungs and are irritants to the airways, triggering an attack. To take control of dust mites, parents should put their child's mattress and pillows in airtight covers, wash the covers weekly in hot (at least 130°F) water, vacuum the child's bedroom at least once a week, and store books and toys that can collect dust in another room (ALA, 2003c).

Pet dander, or tiny pieces of skin that flake off of a domestic animal, is well known as a trigger of asthma attacks. Dander of cats and dogs can be an especially potent allergen, causing wheezing attacks in children (ALA, 1997). Rodents and birds can also cause a problem. If possible, parents should remove pets from their homes, as should educators from their classrooms. If pets cannot be removed, they should not be kept in the child's bedroom or near the child at any time. If there is forced-air heating in a home with pets, air ducts in the bedroom should be closed (ALA, 2003c). In addition, parents should wash pets weekly and avoid visits to places where animals are present.

Some triggers that occur in households and buildings are not so obvious. The presence of asbestos or lead-based paints is often found in public housing projects and old buildings, and these are triggers that dangerously affect asthmatic children. Excess kitchen smoke from cooking can irritate the airways of an asthmatic. Windows should be opened or a circulation fan used during cooking to prevent the smoke from getting too thick. Household products such as hair spray, talcum powder, perfume, paint, and deodorizers also have strong odors which can irritate the airways of an asthmatic child (ALA, 2003c). Again, parents should take the necessary precautions when using these products around their children who have asthma.

Perhaps an unavoidable trigger is that of air pollution, which includes ozone (smog), nitric oxide, acid aerosols, and diesel exhaust fumes. Researchers recently found a strong correlation between smog and serious asthma attacks (ALA, 1997). The inner city in North America is a haven for the complex fumes and smokes that harm our children. These pollutants inflame the airways and leave them more sensitive to a host of other allergens. Children with asthma are reportedly hit harder by air pollution than are adults. When the level of ozone and exhaust particles is very high, some hospitals have indicated that visits and admissions of children with asthma become 20 percent to 30 percent higher than usual (ALA, 1997).

There has recently been a debate over whether asthma can be triggered by emotional episodes. During emotional crises, a child may cry, yell, or hyperventilate, thus triggering an attack because of the force of air passing through and irritating the airways. While these episodes may have this effect, it is important to remember that asthma is not a psychological disease (ALA, 1997). In addition to emotional episodes, stress may trigger an attack because of the chemicals released by a person's body in response to it, which can also cause the airways to constrict.

Treatment for Children with Asthma

Parents of children who are asthmatic need to work in partnership with their doctor to develop an asthma treatment program that meets their child's needs. Parents of very young children with asthma need to be extremely vigilant of their child's symptoms and be able to communicate them to their doctor. Because these children are so young, they will be unable to express their symptoms or recognize the signals of an asthma attack. It is the parents' responsibility to serve as the voice of their child during this critical time of early development. It is also their responsibility to intervene early in the course of an asthma attack with medication to arrest and reverse airway constriction (ALA, 1997). As children get older, they become more involved in managing their asthma and eventually are able to recognize signals of an attack and administer medications independently. It may be up to a teacher to point out to the caregiver that a child is symptomatic of asthma. It is also essential that teachers be aware of conditions, the location of inhalers, and their use in the event of an attack.

Many of the medications used to treat adults with asthma are used for children. However, the doses of asthma medication for children are often lower than those for adults. Children with asthma may require special delivery systems for their medication. Very young children may require a nebulizer or a metered-dose inhaler with a spacer and face mask. A nebulizer allows a child to receive the medication by inhaling a mist through a mouthpiece or face mask. Nebulizers are a good alternative treatment for those children who cannot master the use of a metered-dose inhaler. Metered-dose inhalers require a child to be able to coordinate their use.

Devices such as spacers and face masks were developed to eliminate some of the problems children may have in medication administration. Spacers are tubes attached to the end of a metered-dose inhaler which collect the medication mist before it is inhaled (ALA, 1997). They make it easier for children with asthma to coordinate the metered dose, and they also put children at ease during the medication process. Face masks can be attached to mouthpieces with nebulizers and metered-dose inhalers. When used with a nebulizer, a face mask allows the flow of medication to be continual. With every breath, the child is inhaling asthma medication (ALA, 1997). When used with a metered-dose inhaler, a face mask must be used with a spacer. This combination is effective in training a child to use an inhaler. Once again, the "trendy" or "coolness" index is not usually met with asthma inhalers. Rapper Snoop Dogg (Calvin Broadus) makes it clear that he has asthma and openly uses his inhaler. It is essential to reinforce images like Dogg's in order for students to feel comfortable using their inhalers.

Medications used to control asthma in children fall into one of five groups: inhaled bronchodilators, anti-inflammatories leukotriene modifiers, systemic bronchodilators, and systemic corticosteroids (ALA, 2002). Inhaled bronchodilator medications are the most effective in opening the airways, which are narrowed by asthma. They have few side effects, and administration is available by both metered-dose inhaler and nebulizer. For children with mild asthma, this may be the only type of medication needed. Because this medication is so effective, it tends to get overused, which is a great danger to the child. Recent studies suggest that overuse of these medications may actually worsen the asthma and increase the possibility of death from it (ALA, 2002).

The National Heart, Lung, and Blood Institute (NHLBI) recommends daily use of anti-inflammatory medications (such as cromolyn and nedocromil) for children with asthma classified as mild intermittent, moderate, or severe (ALA, 2002), in order to control inflammation of the airways. These medications are considered to be safe, have minimal side effects, and are available for adminstration by metered-dose inhaler or nebulizer. Anti-inflammatory medications oftentimes fail because they are not taken regularly. They do not have an immediate effect and are often mistakenly discontinued (ALA, 2002). The most recent asthma medications approved by the U.S. Food and Drug Administration are the leukotriene modifiers (ALA, 2002). These medications are taken in pill form and sold under the names of Accolate, Singulair, and Zyflo. Parents should consult with their doctor to determine whether this new class of anti-inflammatory medication will benefit their child.

Theophylline is the principal systemic bronchodilator medication, used in pill or liquid form for children (ALA, 1997). This class of medication is effective but has more reported side effects in children, such as agitation and restlessness. When taking teophylline, a child's blood levels should be monitored to reduce side effects and ensure the proper dose (ALA, 2002).

Systemic corticosteroid medications are highly effective in controlling asthma and reversing episodes (ALA, 2002). However, these medications can cause serious side effects when used for long periods of time. Because of this, their use is limited to chronic severe asthma that cannot be controlled with the first three groups of medications discussed above.

With each of these medications, parents should always consult with their doctor as to the best treatment option(s) for their child. Each child has unique and special needs and the asthma treatment should address them. The medications used for asthma treatment are safe and effective when taken correctly. If not taken properly, these medications can, in some cases, cause harm.

Back to the General

If this chapter were a general informational chapter on asthma, there would be discussions for parents or caregivers about proper medical care, learning the correct treatment, and contacting the school nurse for additional support and information. The reality in urban teaching dictates that we would be wrong to assume that there are any school facilities that deal with illness, wrong to assume that there is a school nurse, wrong to assume that all parents/caregivers are aware of what asthma is, and wrong to assume that there is a basic understanding as to the dangers of urban asthma. We cannot assume that the facilities that are expected in suburban settings are even dimly duplicated in the urban setting. In a perfect world, the parent/caregiver would be able to speak to all those who come in contact with the child and expect that they would assist. In overcrowded, understaffed public urban schools, we do not have a perfect world. However, as teacher advocates, we can be aware that there are certain basic rights that students do have. Under the Americans with Disabilities Act (ADA), the school is responsible for making any necessary accommodations the child may require to be able to participate in all school activities. The school cannot discriminate based on the child's illness. Title III of the ADA requires a place of public accommodation and that the school make reasonable modifications to its policies, practices, and procedures where necessary to ensure full and equal enjoyment of its services by individuals with disabilities (*Alvarez v. Fountainhead, Inc.*). Asthma is a manageable condition and should not prevent children from participating in all learning and social activities with their classmates. Teachers have a responsibility to make sure that accommodation is made for instruction of students with medical conditions.

There are several issues that teachers and parents should address to ensure that a child stays healthy during school. One of the first is the development of an individualized health plan (IHP). This plan should be a complete written document providing specific information on the child's condition(s), warning signs, and medication treatment, along with details of administration or monitoring of therapy (i.e., whether the child requires assistance from teachers or the school nurse); contact information of the parents and doctors; and any other pertinent information regarding the child's medical issues (NewsRx.com/net, 2001). This document should be created with input from the child's doctor and reviewed at a meeting with the parents and all school staff who work with the child.

Parents and teachers should work together with their parents' doctors and the school administration to address the needs of children with asthma. It is essential that all parties have an ongoing dialogue regarding these children's condition. This ongoing communication is necessary for them to be able to manage their medical condition in school. In the case of asthma, one tool for providing communication between parties is a "Student Asthma Card" and/or "trigger sheets" which are filled out by the student's parents and doctor (SchoolAsthmaAllergy.com, 2002), which should include criteria for specific asthma triggers and warning signs for each child. These forms can be used as a quick reference for teachers, and a master can be kept with the student's asthma action plan or IHP. Parents should review the information regularly with school staff and be alerted to any changes the staff observes in their child.

Make sure that you, the teacher, are aware of any and all medical conditions that your students have, and attempt to educate (if needed) and collaborate with parents in order to secure the best health for each student.

References

(Websites accessed November 13, 2003)

AAAAI [American Academy of Allergy, Asthma, and Immunology] (2002). *Topic of the month: August 2002: Back to school with allergies and asthma.* http://www.aaaai.org/patients/topicofthemonth/0802/default.stm

ALA [American Lung Association] (1997). *Family guide to asthma and allergies.* Asthma Advisory Group. Boston: Little, Brown and Co.

—— (2002). *Asthma medications for kids: Five asthma medication groups.* http://www.lungusa.org/asthma/ascastnedgr.html

—— (2003a). *Asthma in children fact sheet.* http://www.lungusa.org/asthma/ascpedfac99.html

—— (2003b). *Pediatric asthma: A growing health threat.* http://www.lungusa.org/asthma/merck_pediatric.html

—— (2003c). *Asthma triggers in children.* http://www.lungusa.org/asthma/asctriggers.html

Alvarez v. Fountainhead, Inc., 55 F.Supp. 2d 1048, 1051 (N.D. Cal.1999). Case No. C 99–1202 MEJ.

Butler, Rachel (Ed.) (2000). Asthma news from the American Lung Association. *Asthma Magazine* July/August, 9-13.

Immunotherapy Weekly (2001). Health tips for kids coping with asthma and allergies, 27.

SchoolAsthmaAllergy.com (2002). *Teaching toolkit: Tools for teaching students with asthma/allergies and their parents.* http://www.schoolasthmaallergy.com/2002–2003/sections/toolkit/tools_students/index.html

Katia Goldfarb

CHAPTER EIGHTEEN

Who Is Included in the Urban Family?

The *ideal* family conjures up an image of a mom, a dad, and two children—preferably, one boy and one girl, in that order. As we continue conjuring, we envision a stylish home surrounded by trees and, of course, enclosed in a white picket fence. The mother has a career, but she has chosen to stay home until the children grow up. Her position will be waiting when and if she decides to go back to work. The father happily leaves for the commute to his job every morning, as part of his conscious decision; the city is not the best environment in which to raise a family.

Families who have the economic resources to entertain this decision are the only ones who can fulfill the above mythical image of family living. Urban families are either wealthy enough to offer their members the necessary experiences to compensate for the suburban context, such as private schools, periodic vacations, and modern and spacious apartments, or they are stuck with life in the city as their only viable option. In this chapter, I will describe some of the most crucial contextual issues affecting urban families with children of low socioeconomic status and limited formal education.

The Pathologization of Families from Minority Groups

One of the most important of these contextual issues involves the right-wing pathologization of urban families of minority groups. Deploying the concept of "family values," right-wing operatives have argued that there is little we can do for urban students because they come from pathological families. The urban student signified in such representations is, of course, of color. This is accompanied by a concurrent deployment of the concept of "urban troubles," used to signal the existence of gargantuan unsolvable problems in contemporary cities. The causes of these insurmountable problems involve the demographic changes of the last 40 years. As nonwhites constituted a larger percentage of urban dwellers, they began to manifest their own family pathologies. Along with these domestic people of color, a rash of non-European immigrants (so proclaim right-wing leaders) have brought family pathologies with them to American cities that "threaten the historic identity of the United States as a 'European' country, thus endangering the country's 'character' and 'value structure'" (Bennett, Dilulio, Jr., and Walters, 1996). Thus, urban institutions such as schooling were pathologized by "these people."

In this right-wing world, crime is caused by this degraded family life, not by poverty. Thus, political and educational policies in this ideological construct see no reason to address poverty or formulate attempts to alleviate it. The best thing we can do is to bring pathological family members to Christ, many conservative politicos argue. Through Him we can restore family values and begin the process of improving urban family life for poor people and especially poor people of color. Until such salvation occurs, however, right-wing analysts such as William Bennett, John Dilulio Jr., and John Walters maintain that urban areas and their schools will be victimized by ultraviolent superpredators, the worst criminals any society has ever known. As Cornel West (1993) argues, the right-wing's use of terms such as *superpredator* and *feral, presocial beings* caters to the worst types of racial prejudice found in the United States. What is wrong with African American and Latino families, these critics contend, is a manifestation of moral poverty. Moral poverty causes criminal behavior—a tautology that can be neither proved nor disproved. The only thing virtuous white people can do in this circumstance is to punish perpetrators—lock 'em up and throw away the key in "three strikes and you're out" policies or execute them. Moral poverty is an excellent twenty-first-century way to say that the bad parenting of black and Latino parents causes socially irresponsible behavior (Bennett, Dilulio, Jr., and Walters, 1996).

In this explosive context, the pathologization of the family is central to the right-wing position. Morally impoverished black and Latino superpredators have never been exposed to loving parents who can teach them good from evil, to stay away from drugs, or to resist violence. This family collapse is a single-bullet theory of urban minority poverty and school failure. Bombarded by such crypto-racism, many educators have been induced to complain: "How can we teach these children when their parents don't care about them?" Unfortunately, many white middle- and upper-middle-class Americans don't know very much about their poor nonwhite fellow countrymen and countrywomen. As an example, contemporary popular wisdom fueled by right-wing talk shows and think tanks posits that poor minority women produce huge numbers of "illegitimate" babies. Actually, birth rates among single African American women, for example, over the last three decades have fallen by 13 percent. Incidentally, during the same decades, the birth rates for single white women increased 27 percent. Such data might induce right-wing spokespeople to tone down their descriptions of black mothers living in poverty as "brood mares" and "welfare queens" (Coontz, 1992).

As the rate of financial polarization grew in the last portion of the twentieth century, of course problems emerged in poor urban neighborhoods that worry all of us. Violence is of concern to all Americans, though African American and Latino poor suffer far more than anyone else. The right-wing effort to lay the cause of such problems exclusively at the doorstep of the alleged moral poverty of urban nonwhite people with their broken families, high divorce rates, unwed pregnancies, family violence, and drug and alcohol abuse is misleading. In this context, Joe Kincheloe (1999) argues:

> The same problems confront families whose members serve as police officers or in the military, yet most Americans refrain from blaming them for their dysfunctionality. Typically, we have little trouble understanding that the context in which police officers and soldiers operate is in part responsible for such pathologies. Work stress from danger and conflict can produce devastating results. With this in mind, it is not difficult to imagine the stress that accompanies living for just one week in an inner-city war zone. Now imagine living there with no hope of getting out. (p. 243)

The right-wing view of poor urban African American and Latino families as corrupt and morally bankrupt is not the only perspective on this matter. Many educators, sociologists, and urban studies scholars argue that such families are often very resilient, hard working, and self-sufficient, are in possession of loving kinship networks, and value education for their children (Hill, 2003). Many researchers have pointed to the strength of the extended African American family, for example (Wicker, 1996; Ashworth, 1997). The power of such families often succeeds in maintaining the lives of its individual members despite overwhelming problems and travails. To not understand the ways that cousins, grandparents, great-grandparents, aunts, and uncles provide support when times are bad is to miss a profound dimension of urban black family life. Thus, there is a dialectic of strength and weakness of African American and other poor urban families from minority groups in contemporary America. It would be misguided to argue that racism, class bias, and the ravages of poverty do not tear the fabric of such families and create profound problems for them. Concurrently, it is amazing how the inner strengths of urban minority families work to help their members persevere in spite of some extremely difficult situations.

Urban Families in Historical Context

As with any other family, urban families interact with their natural and human-built environments. Their lives are affected by the available emotional and material resources. They have to interrelate with their immediate context such as extended family, workplace, school, welfare system, and health system. They have to coordinate communication between these organizations. Their lives are influenced by policy and laws often endorsed by politicians far removed from their realities. And every day, they have to fight against the negative image held by mainstream society of low-income urban families.

The creation of this particular group of families can be traced to the capitalistic industrialization of the United States following the American Civil War. The Industrial Revolution brought a reorganization of work. Different social groups had access to different jobs that held extremely different statuses and earning possibilities. The national economy moved from the traditional colonial agricultural family-based system to a wage economy. An increasing number of goods and services were produced and rendered outside the family.

Rural migrants and high numbers of European immigrants settled in cities growing around mill towns, steam- and later oil- and electricity-powered factories and sweatshops. Within this process, a middle class based on ownership of business and industry and a working class based on low-pay and low-status jobs were created. These economic and social changes were lived very differently by varied groups. Slave society developed into a distinctive African American culture, and Native Americans have had numerous structures of family living. These groups did not share the same context as that of the old and new European immigration. However, the ideal image of the family, even though its origin can be found in the patriarchal structure of the New England colonies, is still regarded as the family form to be used in judging any other form of family living.

As cities grew, families who had the economic resources started to migrate out of the urban areas in search of what was called a "better standard of living." The odors, noises, crowds, limited personal space, traffic, and what was defined as low educational standards were among the issues used as reasons to leave the cities and build more homogeneous, stable, and private communities. The new immigrants and the working poor remained.

Parallel to these economic and social changes, the roles within the family were also reorganized. A clear differentiation between the private and public worlds was created in which the private/family domain belonged to the woman and the public/work domain belonged to the man. Working-class women and children from poor families did not have the privileges these developments were offering (Chavkin, 1993; Cherlin, 1988; Redding & Thomas, 2001).

In the present times, there are additional social forces influencing families and individuals. There is a growing production of new technologies that is changing the economy to a service/information-based system. The United States is rapidly pressing for a global economy. Big corporations are merging and/or relocating and/or investing outside the country. Lastly, there is a growing trend in which corporations are shifting from manufacturing to knowledge-based institutions. Within these processes, low-income urban families with children are facing bigger and more rapid social and economic changes. Their situation is aggravated by specific issues influencing their daily lives. Some of these areas are increasing and permanent poverty, medical care, overcrowding, mobility and loss of extended family network, immigration, language, diversity in family structure, work/family influences, violence, stress, environmental problems, access to cultural life and enrichment activities, the family/school relationship, and, of course, the class and race issues previously discussed (Ruiz-de-Velasco & Fix 2000; Delgado-Gaitan, 2001).

The Wages of Poverty

The lack of economic resources greatly impacts the dynamics of urban families. There is a constant struggle for the basic necessities. Since the working adults are dependent on weekly or monthly wages, any drastic change in the economy will have immediate repercussions. These families may face fluctuating times when they will need government assistance, requiring from them the use of their time and energy to access the necessary services. By having very limited job opportunities, children and adults will have extremely low possibilities of receiving adequate and continuous medical care. Chronic illnesses as well as prompt diagnosis will be hindered. The implications of a deteriorating health status for the responsible adult(s) will create a vicious and difficult-to-break cycle in which unemployment becomes a regular part of life. As for the children, research has shown that one of the most important issues affecting readiness to learn is the nutrition and health status of the child. Families, in turn, rely on the emergency room for medical care.

Overcrowding has been a constant issue in urban settings, whether it is within the household or as part of city life. Immigrant families especially find themselves sharing small physical spaces. In the attempt to help family or members of the community, people will be willing to sacrifice their personal space on the assumption that more economic resources will open up for the family system. In situations like this, there may be growing frictions among members and increasing frustration. Outside the household, cities also feel crowded. There are fewer and smaller public spaces. There are fewer and smaller natural spaces. Buildings are tall, imposing, almost identical. The feeling as you walk through the city is that you are moving within a contingency of people.

As economic and domestic issues become increasingly problematic, family members may decide to move in search of better job opportunities. Working-class families have relied on extended-family members for child care, economic help, and emotional support. Extended family is a crucial resource for the sustainability of low-income urban families and the well-being of the children (Ruiz-de-Velasco & Fix, 2000; Trumbull, Rothstein-Fish, Greenfield, and Quiroz, 2001).

Immigration and Language in Urban Family Life

Immigration and language are becoming increasingly crucial areas in understanding urban families. Immigration is one of the most important economic and social changes. The current immigration is influencing society not only because of its numbers but also because of its diversity. As in the past, new immigrants tend to settle in established communities of people from their own national origin. This traditional trend influences issues such as access to education, availability of jobs where fluency in English is not required, and the offering of basic services (such as health care, education) in the appropriate language. The issue of immigration has been part of the antagonism between minority groups struggling for the same scarce resources. Division and hostility are also part of the problematic between immigrants and the powerful mainstream society. They challenge the exclusive ownership and access to social goods.

One hundred years ago, 90 percent of immigration to the United States was from European countries; today, 90 percent is from non-European, mainly Latin American and Asian, countries. Therefore, there are going to be drastic changes on the face of the nation. This increases the number of U.S. residents who are foreign born and also the number of their children. Currently, in major urban settings like New York, Los Angeles, and Chicago, minority groups make up the majority in numbers but not in sociopolitical power. The United States is witnessing birth rates of racial minorities increase faster than that of the majority population. In the year 2000, Latinos outnumbered African Americans. It is clear that immigration is one of the most important issues facing major metropolitan areas.

For families, immigration implies a series of social, economic, and familial adjustments. Immigrants are entering the country in a moment of economic difficulties. There are fewer jobs available, and social and economic mobility will not be as easy as it was for prior waves of immigrants. Since the current immigration is not from European countries, new arrivals will face social and institutional discrimination. Immigrants will face the options of blending in as soon as possible, rejecting the dominant culture, increasing and strengthening ethnic ties, or developing bicultural or multicultural forms of family and community living (Kincheloe & Steinberg, 1997; Dickinson & Tabors, 2001).

Different Types of Families

Currently in the United States there is an increase in the diversity of family structures. As with any other group, low-income urban families are also facing an increase in the number of family structures that do not resemble the ideal image. There are single-parent houses with different custody arrangements; homes in which the parent has remained single by choice or as the result of divorce, separation, or death; families with two cohabitating adults and children; multigenerational families; two-parent homes of same-sex couples. There may be members of the extended family or of another, unrelated family living in the house. There are families with one child and families with many children. The low-income urban family with children is not a monolith or beyond the diversity of family structure, and we find urban families from bicultural or multicultural backgrounds.

Work/family influences are also shared by any family who has at least one member in the workforce. Low-income urban families with children face the increasing need to find permanent and well-paying jobs. Some families have to resort to two jobs, which may mean leaving the children alone for longer periods of time. There are going to be increased challenges for the adults in trying to keep up with different sets of work-related expectations. The majority of the time, the jobs that adults from low-income urban families can find are not personally satisfying. They are usually labor intensive, not stimulating, and low-paying, which only aggravates an already stressful situation. The mother or father will have a stronger probability of carrying his or her frustration from one world to the other (Grigorenko & Sternberg, 2001).

Families and Violence

Violence is an endemic problem facing low-income urban families. There is violence at the institutional level. Minority groups (ethnic/racial, gender, age, sexual orientation, social class) face constant violence in our social institutions: such as the legal system, in which African Americans are disproportionately incarcerated; the schools, where children are labeled "slow learners" because they do not speak English; and government organizations whose policies exacerbate the struggles of families with small children to keep jobs and have their children in quality day care. Children are exposed to drugs, gang activity, alcohol, and homicides. These problems are not exclusive to poor neighborhoods, but when access to quality and appropriate education does not exist, when safety in these neighborhoods is not supported, and when you can make a lot more money selling drugs than going to school to get a high school diploma, the ground is fertile for the proliferation of violence.

Environmental Dimensions of Urban Family Life

As mentioned before, families are influenced by their natural environment. The access to clean water, clean air, peace and quiet, and open spaces should be a right for all human beings. As if low-income urban families with children do not have enough to contend with, their physical and natural environments add to the challenges. Usually, these families live in multistory or high-rise apartment buildings with numerous other families, with little or no recreational space. Their neighborhoods are often located close to airports, busy intersections, commercial, and/or industrial zones, or neglected areas. Their apartments are often in need of repair. Children and adults are still exposed to lead-based paint. Buildings are not fumigated. These conditions prevent healthy development.

Access to Urban Educational and Cultural Resources

Minority and low socioeconomic status also hinders access to entertainment and enrichment activities. Shows, restaurants, movies, plays, museums are often beyond the economic reach of low-income urban families, even though they may live just a few blocks from them. All the extracurricular activities that enrich the education and the cognitive, emotional, and physical development of children may be out of reach for urban families with tight budgets unless the services are provided by a community center and sponsored by local or federal funds. Children and parents from all socioeconomic backgrounds are interested in meaningful and accessible experiences offering the optimal environment for growth.

Right-Wing Subversion: Efforts to Help Urban Families Undermined by Family-Values Ideology

All of these urban family issues are colored by the right-wing ideology of family values, with its pathologization of poor families of color. Such a way of seeing maintains that all the social and educational programs in the world cannot help such families. This is the same argument made by Richard Herrnstein and Charles Murray in *The Bell Curve*—poor people of color are genetically inferior, lacking intelligence and moral fiber, and are thus beyond salvation. We do not need more money to help them, the argument goes; they need simply to acquire more family values (SOCQRL, 2003). Indeed, in the right-wing ideological universe, it is assumed that poor black and Latino parents don't want to work to provide for their families and thus don't merit help.

In addition, the conservative use of the "absence of family values" argument has served as a convenient smoke screen to obscure the public's view of the poverty caused by free-market economics over the last 25 years. Using a "politics of nostalgia," the right wing has successfully reconstructed America's view of its family history. The perspective paints a misleading picture of a past in which extended families worked together, pious mothers protected little boys and girls from exposure to adult issues, virginal newlyweds consummated their marriages after religious nuptials, and faithful husbands devoted much of their time to familial needs (Kincheloe, 1999).

The legislation that has come out of this right-wing ideology has exerted a negative effect on the efficacy of urban families of color over the last couple of decades. The welfare reform legislation of the 1990s limited aid to the poorest families to merely five years in a lifetime and required mothers to work in order to get any assistance—even mothers with babies as young as three months. Education and job training for poor mothers are discouraged in this legislation, and states have the prerogative to deny aid for a wide range of reasons. Because of these stipulations, poor women have been forced to take low-paying, dead-end jobs instead of improving their education (Stafford, Salas, Mendez, & Dews, 2003). As poor women take these jobs, they enter into a vicious circle. Child care is hard to find in poor urban communities—especially high-quality child care (Covington Cox, 2003). Mothers who choose to stay at home with their children have their benefits cut off, while those who take jobs often face the prospect of having to leave children alone at certain times. These mothers are often charged with child neglect.

Another result of the right-wing legislation has been the rise in the numbers of poor urban African American women and Latinas in prison. Right-wing drug policies have placed disproportionate numbers of poor urban African American and Latino men and women in prison—this taking place while there is no evidence of higher rates of illegal drug use by this population. In this context we are struck by statistics such as the rate of drug-related imprisonment of black and Latino males being 30 to 40 times higher than that for white males (Drucker, 2003). The effect of this mass incarceration on poor urban black and Latino families is devastating. The sponsors and supporters of the legislation responsible for these outcomes have expressed little concern for the families affected by mothers and fathers in jail. Prisoners' families must get by any way they can. Drucker (2003) concludes that the mental and physical health of families of prisoners is so damaged that the very conditions that create the tendency toward crime are exacerbated. Such legislation serves to devalue families in the name of family values. Teachers in schools in low-socioeconomic urban areas will be forced to deal with the damage caused by such social policies, as poor children of color may be the ones most victimized by such draconian measures.

Conclusion: Poor Urban Families Face Great Challenges

The above descriptions are only some of the issues that low-income urban families with children face. High levels of stress are a constant in all of these areas. Stress influences all aspects of human development. It impacts our physical and emotional health. It can serve as an impediment to self and family realization. Natural and adequate levels of stress should help us perform better. Excessive stressors tend to result in crisis, and if the appropriate material and emotional resources (existing and new) are not available, family living is disrupted.

The family/school relationship is a common experience for all families with children. In the specific case of low-income urban families, the issues presented above permeate the context of this relationship. The quantity and, most important, quality of interaction between schools and families directly influence the development of children. It has been documented that a positive communication between schools and families improves students' achievement, especially in families from minority and immigrant groups. Although there are political, ideological, theoretical, and practical differences in the ways the partnership between schools and families is carried out, this relationship is a recurrent theme in educational reform.

The issues affecting schooling, the role of the family, and the family's relation to formal education have taken many permutations. We have defined the role of the family as "the enemy," in which parents, family, and guardians are to be blamed for everything that goes wrong with the children. We have relegated their participation to fund-raising by allowing families to be involved within the schools as long as they keep their participation connected to bringing material goods. Educational and curriculum issues are viewed as the prerogative of the experts, teachers, and school administrators.

The type of family involvement is directly connected to the school's tacit and explicit policies, which are usually supported by district policies. Regardless of the rules and regulations set by the decision makers, access to information and extent of family involvement depend on the openness of the school to maintain a genuine dialogue with families for the benefit of the children. If we continue basing the need for family involvement in school on the sole concern of improving students' academic achievement, we are in danger of removing parents from helping in problems to whose solutions they can contribute the most.

Research suggests that there is nothing to lose and everything to gain from mandating and implementing school/family partnerships. It has been found that standardized test scores are higher. In terms of family outcomes, there is evidence of a more positive self-concept, acquisition of skills, and positive attitudes. Also, such a partnership affects the school and school district by showing an increase in student attendance and reductions in the rates of dropout, delinquency, and teen pregnancy. The responsibility for educating the children should be shared. None of the current social institutions can carry out alone the enormous challenge of educating the future generation. For example, if it is not demanded that businesses (particularly those offering low-paying, low-status jobs) enact flexible and family-friendly policies, society cannot blame mothers and fathers for neglecting their children. Families are not able to attend parent/teacher conferences and other school-based activities because such attendance usually involves losing a day's pay—an unacceptable outcome for poor families.

In the context of immigrant families, it has been found that language and prior experiences are the real reasons for lower levels of family involvement. The majority of our urban children are being educated by middle-class white female teachers who often do not speak the students' language(s). Such families get the hidden message that they are not important in the formal educational process of their children. A common practice in schools is to use the children as translators for their parents and in family interactions at school—by so doing, research shows, there is a potential for conflict in the role reversal between children and adults and the perception that cultural practices are not being respected by school personnel. Another barrier to immigrant families' involvement in schools is the lack of understanding of the American educational system. Immigrants are neither tutored in becoming nor expected to become active decision makers in the process of schooling their children. Another reason for the ostensible lack of involvement is that different cultural practices give to the teacher the honor of establishing communication, as the expert (Hiatt-Michael, 2001).

Most of the adult immigrants in low-income urban families were not able to go to school past the third grade. They feel that they do not have the knowledge or the language skills to engage in meaningful communication with the teachers and school administrators. It has been found that often, the school administrators and teachers view such parents' absence from the school as a lack of interest in the education of their children (Britto and Brooks-Gunn, 2001).

Educators at all levels should be trained to understand the importance of working *with* and not *on* the community and the families. Families should be seen as equal partners in the education of their children. Their voices should be heard and respected. We live in difficult times of war, economic troubles, violence, racism, class bias, and terrorism. As educators, we are not sufficiently prepared to recognize and deal with the overwhelming influence that social, cultural, and linguistic contexts have in the life of our children. We need families and communities to face the challenges of educating the next generation.

References

(Websites accessed November 18, 2003)

Ashworth, Pam (1997). POS334-L: The race and ethnicity book review discussion list. [Book review of *Tragic failure: Racial integration in America*]. http://lilt.ilstu.edu/gmklass/pos334/archive/wicker.htm

Bennett, William J., & Diluliio, Jr., John, & Walters, John. (1996) *Body count: moral poverty and how to win America's war against crime and drugs.* Simon and Schuster.

Britto, Pia Rebello, & Brooks-Gunn, Jeanne (Eds.) (2001). *The role of family literacy environments in promoting young children's emerging literacy skills.* San Francisco: Jossey-Bass.

Chavkin, Nancy F. (1993). *Families and schools in a pluralistic society.* Albany: State University of New York Press.

Cherlin, Andrew J. (Ed.) (1988). *The changing American family and public policy.* Washington, DC: Urban Institute.

Coontz, Stephanie (1992). *The way we never were: American families and the nostalgia trap.* New York: Basic Books.

Covington Cox, Kenya (2003). *The effect of childcare imbalance on the labor force participation of mothers residing in highly urban-poor counties.* http://www.nul.org/documents/all_abstracts.doc

Delgado-Gaitan, Concha (2001). *The power of community: Mobilizing for family and schooling.* Lanham, MD: Rowman and Littlefield.

Dickinson, David K., & Tabors, Patton O. (Eds.) (2001). *Beginning literacy with language: Young children learning at home and school.* Baltimore: P. H. Brookes.

Drucker, Ernest M. (2003). *The impact of mass incarceration on public health in black communities.* http://www.nul.org/documents/all_abstracts.doc

Grigorenko, Elena L., & Sternberg, Robert J. (Eds.) (2001). *Family environment and intellectual functioning: A life-space perspective.* Mahwah, NJ: Erlbaum.

Hiatt-Michael, Diana B. (Ed.) (2001). *Promising practices for family involvement in school.* Greenwich, CT: Information Age.

Hill, Robert B. (2003). The strengths of black families revisited. http://www.nul.org/documents/all_abstracts.doc

Kincheloe, Joe L. (1999). *How do we tell the workers? The socioeconomic foundations of work and vocational education.* Boulder, CO: Westview.

Kincheloe, Joe L., & Steinberg, Shirley (1997). *Changing multiculturalism.* Buckingham (UK) and Philadelphia: Open University Press.

Redding, Sam, & Thomas, Lori G. (Eds.) (2001). *The community of the school.* Lincoln, IL: Academic Development Institute.

Ruiz-de-Velasco, Jorge, & Fix, Michael (2000). *Overlooked and underserved: Immigrant students in U.S. secondary schools.* Washington, DC: Urban Institute.

SOCQRL [Sociology Quantitative Research Laboratory] (2003). *Cycle of unequal opportunity.* http://www.socqrl.niu.edu/forest/SOCI270/UequalCycle.html

Stafford, Walter; Salas, Diana; Mendez, Melissa, & Dews, Angela (2003). *Race, gender and welfare reform: The need for targeted support.* http://www.nul.org/documents/all_abstracts.doc

Trumbull, Elise; Rothstein-Fish, Carrie; Greenfield, Patricia; & Quiroz, Blanca (2001). *Bridging cultures between home and school: A guide for teachers: With a special focus on immigrant Latino families.* Mahwah, NJ: Erlbaum.

West, Cornell (1993). *Race Matters.* New York: Vintage Books.

Wicker, Tom (1996). *Tragic failure: Racial integration in America.* New York: Morrow.

Derrick Griffith, Kecia Hayes, and John Pascarella

CHAPTER NINETEEN

Why Teach in Urban Settings?

Introduction by Joe L. Kincheloe

One of the key questions that should be asked in a book of inquiries about urban education involves why one would want to teach in urban schools. If urban education is faced with a perpetual crisis, is represented in the media as a gangsta paradise, is characterized by dramatic economic disparity with deteriorating neighborhoods, and is destined to limp along without a guiding vision, then why get involved in such a concrete briar patch? The answer to such a question by many prospective teachers is a resounding "It's not for me—see you in the suburbs." But there are many, of course, who take up the challenges. Why do they do it? What do they have to teach individuals pondering a career in urban education? Derrick Griffith, Kecia Hayes, and John Pascarella represent the best of the professionals who choose a career in urban education. Like urban students and urban teachers in general, they are different from one another on many levels and in their diversity present divergent reasons for becoming urban teachers. Their responses to the above question constitute this chapter.

A key premise of this book is the belief that teacher educators should be brutally honest with those contemplating going into urban teaching. No punches should be pulled, and no harsh reality should be sugar-coated for the uninitiated. Urban teaching is hard work, with some days unavoidably running over fourteen or fifteen hours, teaching loads characterized by more than 160 students a day, and stacks of papers waiting for responses and grades. And all of this work for about $15 an hour—the salary of a manager at McDonald's. Urban teachers can't help but think about this comparison as they eye the Devil's Tower of student papers littering their dining room tables. They can't listen to the Clash's "Should I Stay or Should I Go?" with detachment. Of course, few of them go into the field for the money, but "personal fulfillment" doesn't count for much when one is unable to purchase a middle-class home on an urban teacher's salary.

As if these concerns were not enough, there's the matter of society's blatant lack of respect for teachers in general and urban teachers in particular. "Why are many urban schools so bad?" people ask. Despite having to deal with every possible problem resulting from poverty, racism, and underfunding, poor urban schools fail for one reason TV talking heads and many local politicians frequently tell us: bad teachers. This single-bullet theory of urban education doesn't play well with exhausted teachers staring at student papers at 11:45 P.M. Remembering the way teacher education students were viewed as the least talented college graduates, urban teachers can hardly imagine what it might mean to work in a respected profession. I remember in my own professional life, after leaving Penn State University to come to Brooklyn College, being surprised when Brooklyn education students asked me, "Why would you leave there to come here?" The question was asked with a sense of incredulity, as in *what kind of fool* would make such an ill-advised decision? Over and over again urban teachers tell researchers that although salaries are bad, it is the lack of respect that they loathe.

While we're depressed about this lack of respect, it's important to mention the new educational reforms of the twenty-first century that have institutionalized this degrading view of teachers. The premise supporting many of the No Child Left Behind reforms involves the belief that the curriculum must be teacher-proof. This means that since teachers are so bad, we must control their classroom practice in every way possible, leaving as little as possible to their own prerogative. Thus, many urban teachers are handed scripts to read to their students and pre-made standardized evaluation procedures with which to grade them. The idea of a brilliant professional diagnosing the needs of particular students in specific situations and constructing a curriculum tailor-made for them is old, stale news in many contemporary reforms.

The central objective of these reforms involves raising published indicators of school success. Thus, raising standardized test scores for public relations purposes becomes an obsession in many urban school systems. Of course, the benefits for students derived from rising test scores may be negligible. Indeed, in many circumstances there may be an inverse relation between rising test scores and student intellectual development. The Texas educational reforms of the last decade provide an excellent example of the ways such reforms manipulate test scores, dropout rates, and real student achievement (see Ray Horn and Joe Kincheloe's *American Standards: Quality Education in a Complex World: The Texas Case* for an expansion of these themes). In such teacher-proof, deskilled, manipulated contexts, teachers are rewarded for delivering unquestioned data to students for their memorization. Even when teachers are not given scripts to read to students, that schools involve handing out "factoids" to students for their regurgitation on the test is the instructional rule of the day.

Have we had enough reality therapy yet? No teacher should walk into an urban school in the first decade of the twenty-first century without exposure to these chilling dynamics. I'm sure that some potential teachers may read this and say that urban education is not for them. It's better that they realize that now than when they are in a classroom with students who are depending on them to contribute positively to their lives. They might rather pursue another profession now than join the 50 percent leaving the profession within the first five years. A critical and rigorous teacher education must work to perfect the recipe for advice to potential urban teachers. The reality therapy that involves understanding the hard work, the problems, the frustrations, and the failures involved with urban education must always be balanced by the possibilities, the rewards, the brilliant students and community members, the resilience, and the inspiration that comes with the job. All urban educators walk a tightrope of joy and despair, of pain and pleasure, and of fulfillment and alienation. There is no way around these polarities. And just because there are daunting obstacles doesn't mean that there is no chance for urban teachers to make a difference in schools, communities, and individual student lives.

Great urban teachers make a difference in these domains every day. Indeed, brilliant students, teacher colleagues, and tough-minded and visionary community leaders make a difference in the lives of urban teachers every day. I am humbled, amazed, and inspired by gifted urban teachers who motivate and support resilient urban students in their efforts to avoid the pitfalls of growing up in urban poverty. They are some of the most heroic figures of our era, working their magic in the most difficult of circumstances. These are the teachers represented by Derrick Griffith, Kecia Hayes, and John Pascarella, as they struggle with the multiple realities of contemporary urban education. In their responses to this chapter's question, you will see how they have dealt with these complicated issues in their own unique ways.

Derrick, Kecia, and John understand the perpetual crisis of urban education and the high teacher turnover rates that accompany it. Of course, a central question of urban education that we all must deal with is why so many teachers leave the profession so quickly. Our reality therapy helps us with this one. Maybe a more important question in this context is, why do so many stay? What about those teachers who after five years are still plugging away in urban schools? Many of those who stay are the Derricks, Kecias, and Johns of the profession—those who possess a clear understanding of what urban education entails and are not shocked by the first day of school. Such educators build networks with other teachers, community members, parents, helpful organizations, and professionals in other fields. They respect their students, work to understand what their lives are like, and accordingly struggle to figure out how they can meet their needs. Such teachers never stop researching the answer to the question: Why teach in urban settings?

Derrick

I decided to become a teacher after taking a course in college called the Sociology of Education, taught by Professor Roslyn Arlin Mickelson at the University of North Carolina, Charlotte. It was in this course that I came to reflect upon my own educational experiences as an African American male educated in the public schools of New York City. I soon learned why there were four different levels of English, math, and social studies in middle school. I learned why my middle school guidance counselor suggested that I learn a trade as opposed to attending a college prep high school. I understood why Mr. Wilson encouraged our class of senior practical nursing students to use our new vocation to pay for college instead of the latest gear and hottest fashions.

Armed with a new way of reading and seeing education and the world, I decided that I would make a contribution to my people and "give something back" to the community. I would teach to "undo" what I perceived to be educational injustice in urban communities. So at the outset I saw myself teaching diverse students in urban communities because I had survived the "system" and now knew how to make sense of it, so that education became an act and process of becoming empowered and liberated as opposed to being stifling and oppressive to so many urban youth. To answer the question posed by this chapter, I have reflected on my early educational experiences because I now know that my teachers and my experiences in school and in life undergird my decision to teach in urban schools.

My Life: Growing up in the Chelsea-Elliot Houses

From grades 1 through 8 I lived in the Chelsea-Elliot houses in the neighborhood of Chelsea in lower Manhattan, New York. The Chelsea-Elliot houses comprise seven buildings with over 1,000 units, from Twenty-third Street to Twenty-ninth Street between Ninth and Tenth Avenues, managed and operated by the New York City Housing Authority. These housing developments are "bounded" by trendy restaurants, art galleries, privately owned brownstones, and condominiums along Eighth and Tenth Avenues from Thirtieth to Fourteenth Streets. Chelsea is also home to a thriving gay community. The neighborhood is located in Community School District 2, which is nationally known because of its commitment to progressive education and alternative assessments. I attended P.S. 33, where most of my classmates were African American and Latino, many of whom lived in the adjacent housing projects.

It was at P.S. 33 that I first came to understand the power of teachers and the effect they could have on a child's life. My second-grade teacher, Ms. Fish, was this remarkably tall and relatively young white woman. I had recently moved to New York City from the South, and I had an accent and drawl that made me the butt of many jokes. I learned very quickly to keep quiet to hide my southern drawl. Instead of talking, I became an avid reader. Ms. Fish encouraged my love for reading, would always send me home with extra books to read, and would never force me to talk. Knowing that most of the class could not afford to buy books from the monthly Scholastic book sales, she set up a book club in which we could earn "points" to buy books from her special collection. Ms. Fish's class was a refuge and place for me to imagine different worlds through books—despite the fact that most of the books featured people and places very foreign to me. I took comfort in the fact that there was a world beyond my life in the projects. It was Ms. Fish who ignited in me a love of reading and a desire to imagine the possibilities outside of my immediate environment. Luckily for me and my classmates, Ms. Fish understood the importance of lifting kids out of poverty through reading and imagination. Like Ms. Fish, I teach in urban environments because I recognize the need for children and young adults to move beyond the present to imagine different futures for themselves and their families.

All too often young people become "trapped" by their current circumstances and their familial histories. If all you see in the neighborhood are those folks who have been beaten down by "the system," you begin to associate your life chances with them as those who are closest to you and around you the most. If no one in my family has attended college, then the likelihood that I might see college as an option surely decreases. Soon you begin to buy into the images of those around you, and you become more aware of the obstacles than the possibilities. My role as a teacher in urban schools is to help students understand the importance of individual action for collective progress. I want to help students learn "the system" and the ways that urban conditions create inequality, so that students do not feel constrained or limited by the circumstances of today.

In third grade I had a teacher who would not stop screaming! I cannot remember her name, but I do know that I hated going to her class. I remember her class being chaotic, disorganized, and terribly boring. When she was not screaming, she talked in a flat monotone. It was as if the only emotion she had was anger. It was in third grade that I tuned out for the year, which eventually turned out to be a bad thing—to this day I struggle with math because I refused to learn from her. In fact it was in third grade that I came to be known as a "kid with a mouth." I'd ask her all the time, "Why do you have to scream?," which would only make her yell all the more and put me in the corner, which I enjoyed because I could read a book. I realized much later that I had a problem with other people screaming at me. My mother and aunt yelled all the time, so the last thing I needed in school was another yeller!

Ms. "Yeller" taught me the importance of creating a classroom environment based on mutual respect. I bet Ms. Yeller thought that the best way for her to control the class was to yell. Little did she know, at least with me, that I just wanted her to respect my feelings and me. I was a very shy and sensitive child, and in truth all that yelling hurt my feelings. She had taught many generations of students and had come to "know" that this was the best way to "control" the class. As an urban educator, I work to create a classroom and school environment that is based on respect for self and others. In our society, adults who feel that 'children should be seen and not heard' disrespect young people all the time, then wonder why kids don't respect adults and authority.

By the time I had reached fourth grade, I had begun to dislike school, primarily because my peers began to tease me about my feminine qualities (such as reading—I liked to read as opposed to playing basketball). I was short and skinny, hated athletics, and had no interest in girls. My idea of a good time was playing manhunt and "playing" church. My adopted father figure, Father Frew, became increasingly important in my life because I believed that God would deliver me from the projects. If I prayed long and hard enough, I would escape the bullies who had found me a very easy target. At the same time that church became my refuge, Mrs. Bercovicci's classroom became my sanctuary at school. Mrs. Bercovicci was a large woman who wore bright red lipstick and whose breath *always* smelled of coffee. Mrs. Bercovicci was the most loving, caring, and easygoing teacher in the building. Whenever we misbehaved, Mrs. Bercovicci would turn the lights out and wait for the disruptive behavior to stop. Pretty soon we all came to love Mrs. Bercovicci and would do nothing to disappoint her. Mrs. Bercovicci was also the teacher who kept me out of special education.

One afternoon we were engaged in one of many individual and group projects that she assigned periodically throughout the year. As I was working in the back of the room, one of my classmates came up to me and whispered that I was "a faggot just like my mama." All of a sudden, I snapped. I picked up a chair and proceeded to move toward the student, who was much taller than me. I heard Mrs. Bercovicci scream out my name as she moved between the offending student and me. I can only tell you that I had finally had enough of being picked on because of my size, my interests, and my mother's sexual orientation. After four years of being silent and ignoring my feelings, I exploded. The next thing I remember is sitting in the principal's office with my guidance counselor, my mother, and Mrs. Bercovicci.

My mother's take on the incident was that she was glad I had finally fought back. You can imagine how unhappy the principal was to hear that. My guidance counselor felt that I should be tested for emotional and behavioral problems. Mrs. Bercovicci fought both the principal and the guidance counselor and demanded that I spend more time with her instead of being suspended. I remember her words as if she said them yesterday: Derrick is a very bright boy; he's in the fourth grade and has an eighth-grade reading level, and he's extremely sensitive. Let me work with him.

From that day forth, I became a different person. I went from shy and reserved to expressive and talkative. I loved Mrs. Bercovicci for what she had done and I worked very hard to please her by excelling in everything I did. Interestingly enough, I earned another label in the neighborhood. Kids never messed with me again because they thought I was crazy and had a really bad temper. Whatever they thought was fine with me because Mrs. Bercovicci would always tell me, "You are going to do great things and you can't let other people weigh you down." Mrs. Bercovicci was a source of strength for me, and it was in the fourth grade that I began to see a future for myself through education and schooling. At the end of the year I was ecstatic to learn that Mrs. Bercovicci would be my fifth-grade teacher. I knew that fifth grade would be a blast, and I couldn't wait to spend another year with Mrs. Bercovicci. She created a classroom environment in which all of her students were protected from abuse, bullying, and stereotypes. In this environment I felt free to learn, challenge, and question knowledge as I tried to make sense of the world around me.

Because of teachers like Mrs. Bercovicci, I teach in urban schools, because I know firsthand the importance of creating a classroom that does not reproduce inequalities and internalized oppressions common in low-income communities of color. As a teacher, I use my power to ensure that all students are treated fairly and to create a space where we interrogate the ways that we as individuals and as communities oppress and hurt one another because of stereotypes and images of what is "proper" behavior for young men and women.

Kecia

I grew up in a racially and socioeconomically isolated urban neighborhood that was plagued with crime, drugs, poverty, and all of the social ills that we tend to think about when we think about urban communities. I attended public schools, except for my elementary schooling, which was in the only Catholic school in the neighborhood. From a societal perspective, I, as an African American girl from the 'hood, was not expected to achieve much. I experienced this perspective through the commentary of some of my teachers, media reports of my neighborhood, and interactions that subjugated me when I engaged in border crossings, like when I'd go to a department store or supermarket and be followed by the staff.

In contrast to these external messages from society, my parents reinforced an oppositional perspective of what it meant to be an African American girl from the 'hood. They explicitly expected high academic success and the personal development of self that was not reflective of the statistics for African American girls. Not only did they expect this from me, they expected it of all of my friends, some of whom lived in very dire situations. From my parents' perspective, which they clearly communicated, the expectation of academic success was grounded in the history of the educational experiences of African Americans and a cultural legacy of our heritage from which I would not be exempted. While I internalized the messages that I received from my parents, I was always aware of the contradictory images of me that existed in society. For my parents, education was the means by which I could transgress society's false representations of me, to achieve personal success and fulfill my civic responsibility to our community.

Along the way, I encountered several teachers and other adults who shared my parents' beliefs and worked hard to effectively inculcate in me a love of learning. It is from these experiences that my interests in urban education emerged. My professional, graduate school, and volunteer experiences ultimately helped to shape my interests and to direct the path upon which I would embark in terms of the ways in which I would become involved in urban education. While I didn't realize it at the time, I now understand that my conceptualization of education exceeds the confines of school and is fundamentally a community endeavor.

After completing my undergraduate studies, I entered the corporate sector as a human resources professional and often counseled individuals whose limited educational achievements prevented them from effectively competing within the local, much less global, labor markets. In his book *The End of Work*, Jeremy Rifkin (1995) discusses the concept of *economic irrelevance*, which characterizes the lives of individuals who have no possibilities of contributing to society due to their lack of desirable skills or significant purchasing power. Most of those whom I counseled had economically irrelevant lives, and I wondered what had happened to them from an educational perspective. If, as my parents had strongly communicated, education could empower me to transform my life, why didn't it enable others to do the same as I (and many others from the 'hood) had done? With this realization, I began to more clearly think about the paradox of education as it exists within schools.

Rhetorically, education is the great equalizer that empowers individuals to achieve social mobility; yet, practically, it reproduces paradigms of oppression and social inequality. This paradox in the functionalism of education has always existed in the culture of American schools but is perhaps most striking in the educational experiences of children who reside in our urban centers. Despite the hard work of many individuals, there are significant numbers of poorly performing schools in our urban communities that fail to appropriately prepare children to effectively participate in our society as adults. Generations of children are experiencing a social violence of inadequate education that ultimately leads to continued cycles of economic, political, and social marginalization and dependency. Their lack of cultural capital to fully participate within society only exacerbates their alienation and disempowerment. They are economically irrelevant. Breaking the social violence cycle in which many urban children are caught is imperative in building community capacity. It is from this perspective that I finally began to understand that I really wanted to work more directly as an urban educator. But here was the question: How do I do this?

I elected what I thought was the path of least resistance and spent a full eight-hour day at 110 Livingston Street (the former headquarters of the New York City Board of Education). However, when I left the building, I knew that I didn't want to become a teacher. I was astonished that not one of the many people with whom I had spoken ever asked me about my experiences with children, whether I liked children, why I wanted to be a teacher, or what my educational philosophy was. It was clear that education within schools would not reflect the transformative power that was embedded in the messages I had received from my parents or that was necessary for the community-capacity building that I felt was critical for urban neighborhoods. With this disappointing experience, I decided that I had to choose another path, so I looked within the community.

Soon thereafter, I began working with a grassroots Harlem-based community organization focused on enhancing the social and educational opportunities of urban youth. Through this organization, children who are generally "underserved" engage in after-school educational activities to increase their technological literacy, expand their understanding of historical events and people through thematic curricula and experiential excursions, explore social issues through research and debate, and develop their civic capacity by creating their own sense of community. Additionally, the program has an outreach component to parents to help them develop the necessary skills and understandings to be effective consumers and advocates of education for their children. I had finally found the educational space that allowed me to be the type of educator that I thought would be most helpful to urban children and families. It represented a broader conceptualization of an educational system, one which acknowledges that communities are educational resources that can help schools meet the varied needs of urban youth. Additionally, it was an opportunity and space in which to create alternative educational models for urban communities.

In *What Is Indigenous Knowledge?* Ladislaus Semali (1999) notes, "In order for schools to effectively educate all youth, families and communities must become full partners in the process. But how can schools and community become full partners while schools devalue and disregard the local knowledge produced by the community?" (p. 105). Within the after-school setting, I easily became an educational partner with the communities and families from which my students came. The point of entry for many of our learning activities is the knowledges and experiences that the students bring to the space. This is critically important for me because it enables me to fully comprehend how they make sense and meaning of their worlds. It requires that I acknowledge the role of *symbolic interactionism*, which "functions on the basis of three premises: that people act toward things on the basis of the meanings that the things have for them; that the meanings of the things are derived from, or arise out of, social interactions; and that these meanings are modified through an interpretative process" (Casella, 1998). As I work to understand the students and their communities, I can more relevantly connect education to their experiences, which helps to prevent them from becoming alienated from learning.

In order to effectively engage students and their communities, I have had to become a *humble* educator, in that I had to be willing to be transformed by the knowledges and experiences of my students, just as I worked to transform them. This is not an easy task because it means that notions of self are challenged and pushed. I cannot effectively engage with my students and maintain a position that suggests that I know who they are by virtue of the fact that we share the same racial and class backgrounds. Such an assumption reflects a cultural essentialism which "is commonly understood as the belief that a set of unchanging properties (essences) delineate the construction of a particular category." Although I share the racial and class categorizations of many of my students, I cannot essentialize cultural meanings and operate from a fixed interpretation of what it means for them to be urban youth of color from working-class families. I must be vigilant about my commitment to engage my students' own conceptualizations of who they are as cultured beings because it provides a place for us to begin to interrogate similarities and differences of knowledges and experiences. In this vein, the students are empowered within the space because they begin to realize that I am not the only one who is imparting knowledge to them. We all become teachers who are helping each other to grasp new concepts and understandings. Within this framework of intergenerational and multicultural learning, I can further expand the circle of learning across different community boundaries. This significantly changes the dynamic of how students are committed to the process of learning.

In *What Is Indigenous Knowledge?* Semali (1999) writes, "Through this constructivist methodology, students can generate an interest and ownership in the subject matter, because it is relevant to the learner and because the subject matter is rooted or based on the students' prior knowledge, history, and culture. It would seem that many opportunities are lost when prior knowledge of indigenous ways of knowing things are ignored by teachers" (p. 106). Unless educators are willing to attend to these indigenous knowledges, children are going to be disconnected from learning and continue to seem disinterested in education as they resist the knowledge which seems so irrelevant to their lives. Without their internalization of the idea that learning can be transformative and empower them to effectively exercise agency, they will remain economically irrelevant, and there can be no capacity building within their communities.

This is the goal that motivates all of my educational pursuits. It is clear to me through my after-school experiences that such an educational model of transformative power and the building of the capacity of a community can be achieved. I believe it can be achieved within school settings if the educational bureaucracy loosens its stranglehold on all of the stakeholders in the school. Until that happens, it is the obligation of individual educators to create those spaces where they can engage students in transformative education.

John

In college, I got asked this question a lot. Sure, I look like your typical, clean-cut, conservative white kid, but a fortune cookie recently told me, "Judge not according to the appearance." So every time I got the 'So, what's your major?' I was sure to get, 'What are you going to do *with that?*' My major was English Literature and African American Studies. When I came home for the holiday vacation in my senior year and was preparing an application to an MA program in African American Studies, I was surprised that I got so pissed off when my mother asked me the same question, "Why do you want to help *those people,* John?"

Studying African American culture was and continues to be an impassioned journey of demystification and a multifarious discovery of a rich history, expression, art, and vindication as well as a uniquely inspired self-discovery. Understanding the colonial construction of race, the system of power and privilege built upon that foundation, and the historical context of contemporary white fear was and continues to be a path of frustration, deconstruction, and realignment. What's ironic is that white fear isn't that complicated. We have managed a social system that uses race, gender, sexuality, religion, and physicality as mediums of exchange. At the top of the peak continues to stand straight white men and with few exceptions. These exceptions many whites proclaim to be evidence of progress. I argue that these images of "other" cultures are evidence of the white system being pervasively maintained by multicultural imagery. But, being a straight white male and positing a positionality of critical multiculturalism to a group of straight white peers have tripped more than a few switches in many of my classes in a Masters teaching program at Montclair State University in northern New Jersey. I humor myself while under attack by my fellow whiteys that maybe they think I'm a rogue agent for the other.

Deciding to become a teacher wasn't easy. Staying in a program alleging to prepare me for a career in public education wasn't the most appealing bait, but arriving at my first field experience in downtown Paterson, New Jersey, I became hooked, and although I've struggled to free myself and explore other alternatives, the memories of those experiences keep reeling me back in for more.

Every time I think about teaching in the inner city, I remember that cold and damp gray December day, unable to respond to my mom and an old question I thought could not be asked in new times. I had never considered a particular mission or the likelihood that I would be helping anyone with, in, or by my academic pursuits. When asked the question before Mom had, I understood the racism, the white fear prompting those less close to me to question my motives. What I was going to be became clear that day—a cultural worker, though admittedly I didn't have a label for it then. Attending preservice teaching classes the following year at Montclair, I met others who wanted to teach in the inner city—whom I was going to save became more obvious. I would save *those kids* from whitey; but could I save them from myself?

On Friday afternoons, leaving downtown Paterson, I was proved wrong: *Those kids* didn't need saving. Reading theory, watching the praxis, and continuing this discussion with doctoral students in the City University of New York's urban education program, I learned that kids, no matter the background or school setting, need an education that will test their skills of critical inquiry and privilege what Kecia describes as transformative power rather than the reproductive powers of social control. To accomplish this within an American institution born out of a system privileging whiteness, maleness, straightness, and so forth is considered by many as radical when placed in the context of a typical classroom. But taken out of context, the objective to raise collective consciousness and capacities for critical inquiry in children is not a radical task—it is a necessary and constructive one for democratic citizenship and healthy identity construction in any given American social context. The implications of such an argument are a fantastic feat to explore and justify to preservice and working teachers, the overwhelming majority of whom happen to be white females.

When I think about what's going to make me a good teacher and what is going to keep me from getting burned out, I remember what other students in my university classes have come up with in response to the same question. Being a good teacher according to most means "being a good listener," "exercising strong morals and values," and, the most popular, "knowing your students." I'll never forget my first semester in a course entitled Educational Psychology, when a student argued with our professor about being judged unfairly on an exam for not remembering the child's name from a video case study we had observed earlier that month. Dr. Anonymous lost her cool in a way I had never seen a professor do before in four and half years in higher education. I was so moved, I remember writing what she shouted in my notes, "You mean to tell me that it doesn't matter *who* that child was, as long as *you get what her problem is?*" That night, I went home and folded up my cape. Being a hero wasn't all I thought it was going to be after all.

It takes a unique individual to be a public school teacher in a country claiming to be the most powerful but not the best educated. In 2002, the Pentagon was allocated $343 billion from the total federal budget; education was given $34 billion. In May of 2003, President George W. Bush signed into law a $350 billion "tax cut" that will affect the next ten years of federal spending. As education continues to get shafted, Bush continues to push the No Child Left Behind Act in education circles around the country—a policy that purports to rid systems of schools that are failing and reward the ones that aren't. This law "requires that schools annually test 95 percent of their students in proficiency in math and reading skills." Of course, the provision gives just enough funding for the testing but does little to make sure all schools have the resources to get a fair shot at educating their students to pass them (Jacketta, 2003). The result is that rich suburban schools get richer; poor rural and inner-city schools get shut down, and to top it off, mentally disabled students and students with special needs are held to the same standards and requirements as advanced-placement students on these proficiency exams (Jacketta, 2003).

Preparing Myself to Be an Inner-City Teacher

I realize that this is only the tour-bus version of what may soon be the political struggle of my career as an educator. To be what my professors describe as a "radical educator" and a "cultural worker" is what schools need, inner-city and suburban. But to actually be one requires being ostracized by a faculty who will scoff at your "radical pedagogy" and force you to use the "closed door" method when attempting to create transformative educative spaces for your students. As if that isn't politically discouraging enough, if you're going to attempt this work in the inner city, you're most likely going to be in a building that often fails the fire codes, is falling apart in one manner or another, and has two or three students to an outdated textbook. To "listen to my students," "exercise my strong morals and values," and really "know my students" in such an environment means being deafened by my students' silent screams of: "Don't you get it? We don't care because nobody else does! Reading and writing is for white folks with white-collar jobs who live in white neighborhoods and love being white." Sounding educated to these students' means sounding "white."

So, I hear my mom asking again, why do you want to help *those people?* Mom, *those people* have been helping themselves for more than 384 years in this "New World," the land of opportunity availed to some, deferred from others; were allowed to attend white schools only less than 50 years ago; and have managed to attend the country's most elite institutions, holding the best degrees, running some of the top American corporations, and holding some of the highest political offices. But all of this matters little because the systemic ideology of American whiteness remains intact, untouched, and maintained. Even though the faces have changed in the roles of power and privilege, the screenplay has had few revisions.

Fox-TV's hit drama series *Boston Public* depicts the white heroes of an inner-city Boston high school. The "people of color" remain on the periphery of the drama played out in each episode. Sure, *those people* get to share the limelight, but the saviors, martyrs, and liberators of urban education have homes, and we view them as they explore the intimacy of their private lives and bear witness to the images that create three-dimensional white characters and reinforce interracial and intraracial color lines dating back to antebellum times. The imagery of racism in contemporary settings often works in subliminal forms in terms of what we're *not* seeing, what image we're still being sold, and why archetypes are still archetypal in mass media representations.

Stuart Hall (1990) defines ideology as "those images, concepts and premises which provide the frameworks through which we represent, interpret, understand and 'make sense' of some aspect of social existence" (p. 8). Racial ideology is a social formation, a system of which we each partake that upholds assigned powers and privileges associated with race through ideological practices such as discourse production—how we think about, talk about, and engage in race as a social practice and image construction—how racial images are created in mass media such as commercials, news reports, and entertainment representations respectively fixing and ascribing, as Hall describes, the positionality of different social groups and impacting the racial-identity development of our children (Pascarella, 2003; Hall, 1996; Goldstein, 2003; Steinberg, 1998, 2001).

So, as a white guy and an inner-city teacher, I will have two hurdles to jump every morning before crossing the threshold into my classroom. I will have to reject notions of being a white savior. I will also have to reject the implicit obligation of being a martyr in the effort to help *those kids* as part of a paternalistic white man's burden. In this context I must realize that my whiteness is not something I leave at home, hanging in the closet before making the commute to work. Engaged in these struggles, I will have to come to terms with the reality that I will never have the same resources as white suburban schools, though I will be challenged to teach to the same standards. A serious task awaits.

References

Casella, Ronnie (1998). The theoretical foundations of cultural studies in education. *Philosophy of Education Society Yearbook.* http://www.ed.uiuc.edu/EPS/PES.Yearbook/1998/casella.html.

Goldstein, Rebecca (2003). Discourse production, normativity, and hegemony in an urban history classroom. *Taboo: The Journal of Culture and Education, 7, 1.*

Hall, S. (1990). The whites of their eyes: Racist ideology and the media. In M. Alvarado & J. Thompson (Eds.), *The media reader* (pp. 7–23). London: British Film Institute.

—— (1996). Race, articulation, and societies structured in dominance. In H. Baker, Jr., M. Diawara, & R. Lindeborg (Eds.), *Black British cultural studies: A reader* (pp. 16–60). University of Chicago Press.

Horn, R. and J. Kincheloe (2001). *American Standards: Quality Education in a Complex World-the Texas Case.* New York: Peter Lang.

Jacketta, Casey (2003). Bush leaves America's students in the dust. *U-Wire.* [Website.] From the *Daily Utah Chronicle,* February 14. http://www.uwire.com/content/topops021403002.html. Accessed November 6, 2003.

Kincheloe, Joe (1999). Trouble ahead, trouble behind: grounding the postformal critique of educational psychology." In Kincheloe, Joe, Steinberg, Shirley, & Hinchey, Patricia (Eds.), *The post-formal reader: cognition and rducation.* New York: Falmer.

Pascarella, J. (2003). The manufacture of intent. In R. Goldstein (Ed.), in press.

Rifkin, J. (1995). *The end of work: The decline of the global labor force and the dawn of the post-market era.* New York: Putnam.

Semali, L. (1999). Community as classroom: (Re)valuing indigenous literacy. In L. Semali & J. Kincheloe (Eds.), *What is indigenous knowledge? Voices from the academy.* New York: Falmer Press.

Steinberg, Shirley (1998). Kinderculture: The cultural studies of childhood. In S. Steinberg and J. Kincheloe (eds.), *Kinderculture: The Corporate Construction of Childhood.* Boulder, CO: Westview.

—— (2001). *Multi/intercultural conversations: A reader.* New York: Peter Lang.

Shirley R. Steinberg

AFTERWORD

What Didn't We Ask?
Keepin' It Real

The number 19 is my metaphor for the city. It is an arbitrary marker for urban movement. Walking down the stairs to the subway in downtown Manhattan, travelers go under the 1 and the 9…the red line, the train that runs north and south on the west side of the island. The red number 1 + 9 (19) is indelible in my mind as the label that signals the cavernous expanse traveled every day by thousands, tens of thousands. Nineteen is the hurried glimpse of straphangers, school kids in uniform, subway sleepers, musicians, and beggars. Nineteen is the urban—continually moving, dirty, smelly, dark and dank, yet energetic, strong, and unyielding. The dichotomies of the urban landscape fill our every sense. And we have 19 questions…

Can we stop at 19? Have we answered all the questions? Of course not, there are 19 and 19 more…190, 1,900 more urban questions to ask. This book only scratches the grimy surface of those questions. We wrote this book and asked these questions because we love the urban, the raw, the sophisticated, the beautiful, and beastly part of cities. We love the pulsating beats of the trains, the people, and the huge police horses. The urban scape is the culmination of the postmodern condition: aged and new, traditional and cutting edge. We are committed to the urban and to urban dwellers—most importantly, to urban children and schooling. Consequently, we must ask questions and tentatively find answers and solutions to the enigmatic conditions in which we find ourselves: teachers in a love/hate struggle with the environment of the city classroom. I hope that you were able, as you read this book, to complicate the discussion and multiply both questions and answers.

Other than using the sociological and demographic definitions of *urban*, I would pose that it is indeed difficult to define exactly what the urban is. It is easier to say what the urban is not. Urban life is not gentle, yet it is not always rough. It is not spacious, yet it is not necessarily cramped; it is energetic, yet it can be lazy. Urban life is unique—urban schools and children are unique. In the context of this book, we have addressed urban existence and urban public education in its distinctly, uniquely, North American setting. We qualify our discussion by defining urban education as schooling that includes the lower and middle classes of public school children (excluding magnet schools and test-admittance schools).

I work with New York City teachers who are finishing their masters degrees in education. Several of them mentioned to me that they believed that one of the most difficult things they have had to cope with was the fact that no one in the mayor's office or district has ever asked them what they thought about urban education. Indeed, at the beginning of the school year, they were herded into Madison Square Garden for the yearly pep talk. They remarked that they were addressed by the usual politicos, union members, and supervisors—but that the voice of teachers was mute. I want to end this book with the voices of teachers. I asked a group of 30 Brooklyn teachers to write short answers to my questions:

What does it mean to be an urban student?

- Being an urban student means that transportation is difficult, and you have to use a public bus or subway and be there to catch it at just the right time—otherwise, you miss school. Sometimes it's dangerous.
- Being an urban student means you live in a rented house and have free or reduced (price) lunches.
- Being an urban student means that parents have long days at work.
- Being an urban student means that you have little opportunity to belong to sports teams.
- Being an urban student means suffering through traffic congestion and waking to the sounds of garbage trucks and car alarms.
- Being an urban student means seeing rats crawl up the buildings on garbage cans and smelling urine.
- Being an urban student means that classrooms are overcrowded and schools are rundown.
- Being an urban student means that there is less individualized attention given to you. Suburban schools can spend more time with each child.
- Being an urban student means that classes are constantly changing, and you lose and gain classmates all the time.
- Being an urban student means that school supplies are minimal if they exist at all.

- Being an urban student means that you are neglected.
- Being an urban student means no field trips. Just because we live in a city with museums and shows doesn't mean that our students go to them. Most of my students (grade 9) have hardly ever left Brooklyn.
- Being an urban student means often not being safe in school. Shouldn't schools be safe places?
- Being an urban student means that you go to the worst schools and have the least qualified teachers. Why is that?
- Being an urban student means that the odds are stacked against you.
- Being an urban student means being a guinea pig for every new school initiative and pilot program, and those programs don't work.
- Being an urban student means that you know that there are two urban school systems—for the poor and for the rich. The rich get everything, and the poor get all the attention in the news.
- Being an urban student means always being depicted in the media as a criminal, a gangster, or a loser.
- Being an urban student means that you live in a high-rise building with small or broken elevators…so it is a walk-up.
- Being an urban student means that you know which areas of town are for the haves and which are for the have-nots. Even though the schools are public in both areas, the middle- and upper-class schools (the white schools) have more.
- Being an urban student means living in a "bad neighborhood."
- Being an urban student means being told that you are bad because you are from the inner city.
- Being an urban student means being aware of corruption in every part of the education system. Someone is always getting paid off; someone is always getting laid off.
- Being an urban student means being overlooked.
- Being an urban student means you have to think about everything: how to get to school, will you be safe? Suburban and rural students don't think about those things.

Naturally my students are defining urban schools as they see them. However, these generalized statements are also stereotypical of media depictions of urban schools and characteristic of the assumptions made by nonurban teachers and parents.

In *19 Urban Questions*, we have attempted to address some of the issues raised by these teachers. We talked about differences between urban students and nonurban students. We also talked about why we were committed to teaching in urban schools. The above statements and my tenor in this chapter are not designed to discuss urban education in a deficit model. To see it in this light is to use middle-class, white, suburban eyes. Part of understanding urban schools is to *keep it real*; the only way to enlighten and empower ourselves and our students is to tell it like it is, analyze it, understand how power works to maintain conditions—and then change it.

Because urban education means dealing with masses of children and teachers, urban politicians have a tendency to make large pronouncements, intending to solve all problems and address all issues. Instead of meeting individual needs, urban school districts are subject to quick and drastic changes. We must remember that along with large populations of students, there are large populations of voters. In their attempt to capture sizable quantities of votes, cover-up solutions are rampant. I remarked in class one day that I had noticed the large amount of scaffolding on different school buildings in town. Along with that observation, I made the comment that after several years, the scaffolding was usually still up, and I saw no apparent improvement in the buildings. A student told me that her fiancé was a vice-president of a scaffolding company. She laughed and said that the scaffold was there on a semipermanent basis. There were no plans to change or improve the building—the scaffolding was erected to make sure nothing fell from the building, and to be in constant readiness in case contract bids were sent out. The city actually spent enormous amounts of money maintaining scaffolding—not buildings.

Our school systems in urban areas are surrounded by scaffolds. These have come from different contractors: Edison Schools Inc., Success for All, No Child Left Behind. All of them have been erected, maintained, and seen by citizens, but none of the buildings have been touched.

We live in a co-op in the Lower East Side of New York City, in a building maintained by the residents, all of whom are shareholders. Our maintenance fee is used for improvements. We have a board of directors that decides on any of these changes. A couple of years ago we came into the lobby to see that all the walls were being prepped for tiling. The next day, it sported new marble tiles. Three or four days later, the tile had been torn down. I thought that the inspector must have found a problem with the grouting. Several days later, new tile was up. The next week, the tile was down a second time, new boxes of tile were piled up in the hallways. The tile went up, and one more time it was taken down. After three full rounds of tile, I was sure that either the tile contractors were incredibly stupid, or the inspectors amazingly inefficient. Weeks later I asked my neighbor about the tile. He laughed and replied with the usual 'you aren't from around here, are you?' look. I was informed that in order to fulfill obligations with different contractors and accept bids from several different companies, the inspectors are paid off to insist on multiple installations. Everyone was happy with this arrangement—inspectors were compensated, and the three tile suppliers and contractors had all been given work. That was just how things ran in the city.

Success for All (SFA) was created through a seed grant from the American government. The highly successful program was instituted in myriads of urban schools. It is found in many cities. Practicing a rote, strictly monitored, teacher-proof program, urban administrators bought the program as the final solution for urban ills. The SFA group (which is a for-profit organization) now lists yearly profits in the hundreds of millions of dollars—but urban scores have not changed, and many teachers have left due to the lack of pedagogical stimulation of the program. In 2003, New York City ceased using SFA and began a hybrid program which drew from different models in the United States and Australia. Within ten years, all five boroughs of New York City have gone through two tile contractors. Who will be the next?

Urban curriculum is often designed to cover the most with the least. Urban assessment is designed to evaluate what was learned by all and usually results in scores that reflect the successful few. Authors in this book who wrote about curriculum were attempting to whet your appetite to create uniquely urban curricula. In order to reach students and capture their talents, we believe that it must be returned to the hands of skilled teachers. Using a Vygotskian notion of cultural contextualization, we believe that curriculum must be designed with the students, their lives, and their needs in mind. Student work and teacher content must be directly and intimately connected with the lives and cultures of urban students. Evaluation and assessment must also reflect these conditions.

Our authors addressed the domestic and physical surroundings of urban students. In this short book, we are unable to discuss in detail other issues that make urban education unique. We talked about the determined creativity of urban kids and parents, yet we didn't expand on the conditions in which urban families create. Issues like transportation, security, travel distance, building safety, and work stoppages are also unique to urban settings. We didn't mention movement—the mechanical and kinesthetic actions which govern cities: movement to and from school, work, and home. Conditions of movement, cost of movement, and the often limitless time spent in merely moving from one place to another on the urban grid must be considered. Urban movement can be exhausting. One must calculate large portions of time on either end of any appointment in order to be assured of appropriate arrival. That is a cultural context that suburban and rural children are not engaged in. Urban movement depends on the mechanical, as it is guided by the human. Along with that notion, we didn't discuss labor, the difficulties of being in an urban labor force and the complexities faced by urban laboring families. Again, these are chapters for the next book.

Issues of urban health were discussed in brief. The case of urban asthma was addressed. With every word that was spent on discussing asthma, another urban disease or malady was not discussed. Helen Epstein, writing in the *New York Times Magazine* (10/12/2003) asked, is simply living in America's urban neighborhoods "Enough to Make You Sick?" Discussing epidemic heart conditions, arthritis, asthma, infant mortality, AIDS, and many other maladies, the article correlates disadvantaged neighborhoods as a geographic determinant to poor health—to a "ghetto miasma." Lead-paint poisoning, dust and fallout from debris, rat and mouse droppings, nonworking toilets, limited handicap facilities, mold, poor or no ventilation, lack of air conditioning—we didn't get to those conditions. And solutions or assistance? Without health inspectors and school nurses, these conditions will remain unchanged for years. Urban health is an essential issue, yet in most schools of education it is never even addressed, let alone investigated. When was urban health made an issue in an election campaign?

What about immigration? We discussed non-English speakers, using Spanish-speaking students and parents as our example. With the scores of different languages spoken by students in urban schools in North America, we need a discussion of the unique needs of the culture and student. When can that discussion take place? When can an IEP (individualized education plan) be designed for a student from Kiev, Jakarta, or Juarez? How are teachers to connect and communicate with caregivers who have arrived with little or no instruction in American education?

The issues continue. Like the bulging urban population, the questions bulge in our minds. Teaching in urban settings is layered with complexity and unending questions. Our authors have attempted to begin the conversation with you. We have opened the door to question the issues, the possible remedies, and most importantly, the cultural context of teaching in the urban environment. Urban teaching is not for everyone. It is for the creative, strong, committed few. I hope you are one of the few. I hope you join us.

Contributors

PHILIP M. ANDERSON is Professor of Secondary Education at Queens College, and Professor of Urban Education and Executive Officer of the Ph.D. Program in Urban Education at the City University of New York. His publications center on aesthetics, reader response, curriculum development, and cultural theory. His current research examines the inherent contradictions within cultural theory and curriculum practice in the United States.

ELEANOR ARMOUR-THOMAS, currently Chairperson of the Department of Secondary Education, is also Professor of Educational Psychology. Her research interests center around assessment of cognition and culture related to classroom learning and teaching.

ROYMIECO A. CARTER, M.F.A., is Visiting Assistant Professor in the School of Computer Science, Technology, and Information Systems at DePaul University. He is also a graphic designer and lectures on design, multimedia, web design, computer graphics and animation, and social criticism.

KOSHI DHINGRA is a science educator who currently resides in Dallas, Texas, but has lived in New York City for fourteen years. She has taught middle and high school science as well as undergraduate and graduate-level science teacher education courses in New York City. Her research interests include science learned in free-choice settings such as museums, television, and the Internet.

VANESSA DOMINE is Assistant Professor of Educational Technology at Montclair State University in New Jersey. She has worked at P-16 levels with students, teachers, parents, and administrators to explore the critical and creative uses of all forms of media and technology across curricula.

DAVID FORBES teaches school counseling in the School of Education at Brooklyn College/CUNY. He received his doctorate from the University of California at Berkeley. He is the author of *False Fixes: The Cultural Politics of Drugs, Alcohol, and Addictive Relations* and most recently, *Boyz 2 Buddhas: Counseling Urban High School Male Athletes in the Zone.*

KATIA GOLDFARB, is Associate Professor in theDepartment of Human Ecology, Family, and Child Studies Program in the College of Education and Human Services, Montclair State University. Her area of research is the interconnection between school, community, and families, more specifically, Latino immigrant families.

REBECCA A. GOLDSTEIN is an Assistant Professor in the Department of Curriculum and Teaching at Montclair State University. Her research interests include urban teacher and student identity development, urban school reform, and critical educational practices. She is the editor of *Useful Theory: Making Critical Education Practical.*

DERRICK GRIFFITH began his career in education as a social studies teacher in the Rochester Public Schools. He has been a curriculum and staff developer, adjunct instructor, and senior manager for a non-profit social services agency. He currently serves as the founding Director of an alternative high school program in New York City. Derrick is a doctoral candidate at the CUNY Graduate Center.

KECIA HAYES is a doctoral student in the Urban Education Program at the CUNY Graduate Center. She is an instructor and organizational consultant with the International Center for Cooperation & Conflict Resolution (ICCCR) at Teachers College, Columbia University, and the NYU School of Education Metropolitan Center. Her research focuses on how social policies and practices impact the educational experiences of children and parents of color in urban communities.

LEAH HENRY-BEAUCHAMP is Associate Professor at Montclair State University in the Department of Curriculum and Teaching. She has done extensive work in the areas of school restructuring and inclusive education. henrybeaul@mail.montclair.edu

JUDITH HILL, soprano, sings in many NYC chamber, choral and light opera venues. A past teaching artist for several Manhattan cultural organizations, including the NY Philharmonic and the NY Fesitval of Song, she now works full time with the Lincoln Center Institute. She is also pursuing a Ph.D. at the CUNY Graduate Center in Urban Education.

WINTHROP HOLDER is a social studies teacher at Walton High School, Bronx, N.Y. He is the author of the forthcoming *Classroom Calypso: Giving Voice to the Voiceless* (Lang, 2004). He is the advisor for the student journal, *Countercurrents*, and for the Society for Independent Thought at Walton.

HAROON KHAREM is Assistant Professor of Education at Brooklyn College. He grew up in the projects of East New York. He taught in the Federal Prison at Rockville, PA, before completing his doctoral studies at Penn State University. A scholar of African American history and studies, he is also a mentor and professor in the New York Teaching Fellows Program. His recent articles deal with images of African Americans, African Free Schools, and the Moors in Spain.

JOE L. KINCHELOE is Professor of Education at the CUNY Graduate Center in the Urban Education Ph.D. Program. He was the Belle Zeller Chair for Public Policy and Administration at Brooklyn College. Kincheloe is the author and editor of over thirty books and hundreds of articles. His areas of research involve urban education, research bricolage, critical pedagogy, cultural studies, school standards, and their relation to social justice. His recent books include; *The Sign of the Burger: McDonald's and the Culture of Power, Multiple Intelligences Reconsidered: An Expanded Vision,* and *Rigour and Complexity in Educational Research: Conceptualizing the Bricolage.*

LUIS F. MIRÓN is Professor of Educational Policy Studies and Leadership at the University of Illinois, Urbana-Champaign. He is a leading scholar in the application of postmodern theories to the study of public schooling and to the transformation of its institutional practices. Previously Professor Mirón served for five years as Chair of the Department of Education, University of California Irvine.

JOHN PASCARELLA is a graduate student in a MAT pre-service teacher/initial certification program at Montclair State University. He has published a selection of poetry "Deviance" in *Cultural Studies<>Critical Methodologies*. He is the assistant editor of *Taboo: The Journal of Culture and Education.*

ELIZABETH QUINTERO is Associate Professor of Early Childhood and Childhood Education. Her research, teaching, and service involve critical literacy in multilingual, multicultural communities; particular emphasis on families of young children, early childhood programs, and community strengths; refugee mothers' strengths and needs regarding childrearing, survival literacy, and self-advocacy; multicultural children's literature in problem-posing teaching and learning. She is co-author of *Becoming a Teacher in the New Society: Bringing Communities and Classrooms Together* (Peter Lang) and co-author of *Teachers' Reading/Teachers' Lives*

ALMA RUBAL-LOPEZ is an associate professor at Brooklyn College, where she is the Bilingual Program Head and the Undergraduate Deputy in the School of Education. She earned her Ph.D. in Bilingual Developmental Psychology with an additonal concentration in Linguistics, Sociolinguistics, Psycholinguistics and Applied Linguistics at Yeshiva University. She is the co-author of two very different books—one that addresses the global spread of postimperial English, *Status of English after colonialism*, and her more recent work, which depicts her childhood in the South Bronx, *On Becoming Nuyoricans.*

FLORENCE RUBINSON has been teaching in the School Psychologist Graduate Program since 1991 and is currently program head. She is interested in promoting the importance of psychology in schools and especially supports the need for psychologists to play a major role in school reform.

DEBORAH A. SHANLEY is Dean of the school of education at Brooklyn College. A life-long learner and educator, she was previously a special education teacher and also taught as a professor at Medgar Evers College.

TINA SIEDLER holds an MPH in health education, and is currently completing her Master's in the Art of Teaching at Montclair State University.

SHIRLEY R. STEINBERG is an Associate Professor of Education and the Program Chair of Graduate Literacy at Brooklyn College. Raised in Los Angeles, a student in Canada, and finally settling in New Jersey and New York, she claims she can only live and work in urban chaos. Her areas of research include youth literature, popular culture, queer theory, improvisational social theatre, cultural studies, and critical pedagogy. She is the author and editor of many books and articles, including *Kinderculture: The Corporate Construction of Childhood* (with Joe Kincheloe), and *Multi/Intercultural Conversations: A Reader.* Steinberg is the founding and senior editor of *Taboo: The Journal of Culture and Education.* msgramsci@aol.com

JUDITH P. SUMMERFIELD, Professor of English at Queens College/CUNY, is currently serving as the University Dean for Undergraduate Studies at the City University of New York. Her work on rhetoric and pedagogy earned her the Modern Language Association's Mina Shaughnessy Award in 1986. She is the author of numerous books and articles on literary studies, rhetoric, and pedagogy.

JOE VALENTINE is currently a facilitator serving students with disabilities in a New York City middle school in Park Slope, Brooklyn, and an adjunct instructor of special education at Brooklyn College. His decade of professional experience is established in early childhood, alternative elementary, and primarily middle school inclusion settings that serve children with developmental delays, behavioral disorders and emotional disturbances, and learning disabilities.

Index

urban education *(con't)*
> television-mediated learning, 225-27

solving problems of, 8-11
standardization and, 119-26
standards and, 21-22, 23, 60-61
statistics, 1, 30-32
students of, 41-51
> profiles of, 282-83

teacher education and, 11-14
teaching in urban settings, 267-70, 270-80
technology, 22, 209-210
> access and, 210-11
> ecological approach to, 212-15
> myth of, 211-12
> redefining technology and, 215-17

unique characteristics of, 5-8
writing process, 23-24, 173-86, 186-95, 195-206
urban school districts, 5
urban students, 41-51
> profiles of, 282-83

-V-
vocational education, 33

-W-
whole development, 69
writing process, 23-24, 173-86, 186-95, 195-206